Freedom and Belief

GALEN STRAWSON

CLARENDON PRESS · OXFORD
1986

Oxford University Press, Walton Street, Oxford OX2 6DP
London New York Toronto
Delhi Bombay Calcutta Madras Karachi
Petaling Jaya Singapore Hong Kong Tokyo
Nairobi Dar es Salaam Cape Town
Melbourne Auckland
and associated companies in
Beirut Berlin Ibadan Mexico City Nicosia

Oxford is a trade mark of Oxford University Press

Published in the United States
by Oxford University Press, New York

British Library Cataloguing in Publication Data
Strawson, Galen
Freedom and belief.
1. Liberty
I. Title
123'.5   JC585
ISBN 0-19-824938-1

Library of Congress Cataloging in Publication Data
Strawson, Galen
Freedom and belief.
Includes index.
1. Free will and determinism.   I. Title.
BJ1461.s77   1986   123'.5   86-17941
ISBN 0-19-824938-1

Text processed through the Oxford Text System
at the University Press, Oxford
Printed and bound in Great Britain by
Biddles Ltd, Guildford and King's Lynn

PREFACE

There is no such thing as free will. There is a fundamental sense of the word 'free' in which this is incontrovertibly true; and this has been known for a long time. There are plenty of senses of the word 'free' in which it is false. But the sense in which it is true seems to be the one that matters most to most people. Or rather, it seems to be the one that most people think matters most to them—rightly or wrongly.

Why is this sense of 'free' so important? (Why is it thought to be so important?) Because it is, among other things, the sense of 'free' that is in question when it is said that because people are free agents, they can properly be held to be truly responsible for their actions in such a way as to be truly deserving of praise and blame for them. It is the ordinary, strong sense of the word 'free'. Chapter 2 presents one version of the argument that such freedom is impossible.

If Chapter 2 is supposed to prove that there is no such thing as free will, what is the rest of the book about? It is partly about some of those senses of the word 'free' given which free will can be said to exist. But it is principally concerned with what one might call the 'general cognitive phenomenology' of freedom: it is concerned with our beliefs, feelings, attitudes, practices, and ways of conceiving or thinking about the world, in so far as these involve the notion of freedom. It is concerned with the experience we have of being free agents, and of being truly responsible for what we do in such a way that we can be truly deserving of praise and blame. It considers the causes, the character, and the consequences of this experience.

Why concentrate in this way on the experience of being free, rather than the thing itself? Because the best way to try to achieve a comprehensive understanding of the free will debate, and of the reason why it is interminable, is to study the thing that keeps it going— our experience of freedom. Because this experience is something real, complex, and important, even if free will itself is not real. Because it may be that the experience of freedom is really all there is, so far as free will is concerned.[1]

[1] It may then be said that free will is real after all, because the reality of free will resides precisely in the reality of the experience of being free—a view that will be considered below.

Many will find this hard to believe. It *is* hard to believe. And if this book makes it easier to believe, it is only very indirectly that it does so, because, from Part II onwards, it takes the form of an absolutely standard attempt to give an account of the necessary and sufficient conditions of freedom understood in the ordinary, strong sense.

Even if such an attempt cannot succeed, it can still provide a good framework within which to discuss the phenomenology of freedom. And even if freedom is impossible, it does not follow that we cannot meaningfully say what it is—in at least the sense in which we can say what a round square is: a rectilinear, equilateral, equiangular, quadrilateral plane figure all points on the periphery of which are equidistant from a single point within it.[2]

Many things conspire to produce the sense of freedom that most ordinary people ordinarily have, and by no means all of them are discussed in this book. Furthermore, when I speak of ordinary people I have markedly 'Western' individuals in mind. Some non-Western cultures lay a great and indeed fatalistic stress on fate, inexorable or capricious. Others entertain the idea that one's intentional actions can be magically controlled by others—by spirits, or other human beings—although one is completely unaware of this. Others again deny the reality of the self, or of persons, altogether. Clearly, beliefs of these sorts are bound to affect the experience of agency and therefore the sense of freedom of those who hold them, and they deserve careful anthropological investigation.

There are also interesting questions to be asked about what sorts of limits there may be on variation in the human experience of self, and of agency—given that human beings have humanity, no less, in common, with all its characteristic needs, wants, abilities, and basic modes of action. I shall touch on these questions, but only indirectly.

The main ideas for this book were worked out in two periods: in 1975-6, when I was writing a thesis for the Oxford B. Phil., and in 1979, when the temporary closure of *The Times* released me from my duties as an assistant editor at the *Times Literary Supplement*. It has been much revised subsequently, but the basic philosophical position has not changed—only the last chapter is of more recent origin. A great

---

[2] This is to disagree with Hobbes, who says, in *Leviathan* (Chapter V): 'if a man should talk to me of a *round quadrangle* . . . or of a *free subject* [or] . . . *free will* . . ., I should not say he were in error, but that his words were without meaning'.

deal of material has been omitted, however, partly for reasons of length, partly for reasons of argumentative order; including an extended discussion of H. Frankfurt's views; discussion of other, more conventional compatibilist views; and discussion of the philosophically notorious (but essentially unproblematic) phrase 'could have done otherwise' (this appeared unnecessary given the approach to the problem of free will proposed in Chapter 2).[3]

A version of Parts II and III was submitted as an Oxford D. Phil. thesis in 1983, and I am much indebted to those who supervised my work as a postgraduate student—principally Derek Parfit, David Pears, and Jennifer Hornsby, and, more briefly, Jonathan Glover, David Wiggins, and Christopher Peacocke. I am also grateful to my D. Phil. examiners, Sir Stuart Hampshire and (especially) John McDowell, for their comments; to my father, P. F. Strawson, for his; to Adam Hodgkin of the Oxford University Press, who read the whole typescript at a late stage and prompted many changes; and to Dr. Jessie Parfit and José Strawson, for acute proof-reading.

---

[3] One reason for curtailing the discussion of compatibilism is that it has been well defended in recent years (cf. e.g. J. Glover, *Responsibility*), and is thoroughly familiar to most philosophers. Many of the omitted points have recently been well made by D. Dennett in his book *Elbow Room*.

CONTENTS

1

Introduction

Are we free agents? It depends on what you mean by 'free'. In this book the word 'free' will be used in what I call the ordinary, strong sense of the word. According to which to be a free agent is to be capable of being *truly responsible* for one's actions.

The idea that people can be truly or completely responsible for their own actions, authors or originators of their actions in such a way that they can be responsible or answerable for them in the strongest possible sense, is a very familiar one, and it will seem perfectly clear to non-philosophers. But philosophers will want to ask a question: 'What is it to be truly responsible for one's actions in this way?'

For the moment this question can be answered simply as follows: so far as moral agents are concerned (and we naturally take ourselves to be moral agents), to be capable of being truly responsible for one's actions is to be capable of being truly deserving of praise and blame for them.[1]

The idea that people can be truly deserving of praise and blame for their actions—the idea of desert, that is—is also a very familiar one. But philosophers will want to ask another question: 'What is it to be capable of being truly deserving of praise and blame for one's actions?'

Perhaps the best answer to this question at this juncture is the one that draws the present chain of definition—of freedom in terms of true responsibility and of true responsibility in terms of desert—into a firmly closed circle: given that an agent is a moral agent, it is capable of being truly deserving of praise and blame for its choices and actions when and only when it is capable of free choice and free action. Freedom is now defined in terms of true responsibility, true responsibility in terms of desert, and desert in terms of freedom.

---

[1] In fact free and truly responsible agents need not be moral agents (3.3); and if they are not moral agents, then they are *ipso facto* never truly deserving of (moral) praise or blame. Reference to the notion of desert is therefore not strictly necessary in discussion of freedom or true responsibility. At the same time it is often extremely useful, given that one is often discussing agents (ourselves) who are assumed to be moral agents.

Circles like this are usually frowned upon; but this one seems to be just what is needed, at this early stage. The terms 'desert', 'responsibility', and 'freedom' just are related in this way given the ordinary, strong sense of the word 'freedom'. This interdefinition simply serves to make clear which notion of freedom of choice and action is presently in question. It simply provides a starting point for discussion. The detailed business of trying to state the necessary and sufficient conditions of this freedom in a *non*-circular fashion—the business of stating what sorts of properties a being would have to have in order to be a free agent in the present sense—has not yet begun.

Some philosophers may insist that they still do not really understand what kind of freedom is presently in question. But if they do, they are being (tactically) disingenuous. For the freedom presently in question is a property, real or imagined, that nearly all adult human beings—in the West, at least—believe themselves to possess. To say that one doesn't understand what it is is to claim to lack the most basic understanding of the society one lives in, and such a claim is not believable.

In what follows, then, the word 'free' will be used interchangeably with the phrase 'truly responsible'. Questions about what freedom is, and about whether or not we are or could be free, will be understood to be questions about what true responsibility is, or might be, and about whether we are or could be truly responsible or truly deserving of praise or blame. The equation of 'free' and 'truly responsible' is not a step that is entirely without substance, for many have maintained that although we are free (although the meaning—the true meaning—of the word 'free' is such that it is correct to say that we are free) we are not really truly responsible for our actions. These reject the present equation: they propose a fundamental revision of the ordinary central meaning of the word 'free', one that will not be adopted here.

The equation is useful for another reason. The notion of responsibility—not necessarily moral responsibility—is in many ways a clearer notion than the notion of freedom. It is, for one thing, a notion with a strong and obvious causal element. It helps to have it always in mind when discussing freedom.[2]

There are many other senses of the word 'free'. It is, for example, indisputable that we can be free in the sense—call it the *basic* sense— of being able to do what we choose or decide to do. But it is widely

---

[2] It should be clear when the word 'free' is being used in such a way that it is *not* interchangeable with 'truly responsible'.

believed that if we are free only in this basic sense then we are not free in what I have called the ordinary, strong sense of the word. For, it is pointed out, we may be free in the basic sense even if all our choices and decisions are entirely determined in us. And in that case, it is said, it is surely not true that we are free in the ordinary, strong, true-responsibility-involving sense.

I shall assume that this is correct—that freedom understood in the 'basic' sense does not suffice for true responsibility. Perhaps true-responsibility-entailing freedom is not only impossible but cannot even be fully described. Perhaps the main point of those who say that the 'basic' sense of the word 'free' is the correct sense is as much a negative as a positive point: perhaps their claim is not simply that this is all freedom is, but rather that this is all it could be.[3] Perhaps this last claim is true. Perhaps such 'basic' freedom is all we can really want in the way of freedom when we see things right (a doubtful view discussed in 16.1). Perhaps it is all we should want, because it is all we can have. Nevertheless, in this discussion the word 'freedom' will be understood in the ordinary, strong, true-responsibility-entailing sense. Coherent or not, it is our ordinary conception of freedom that is presently in question.

To talk of our ordinary conception of freedom is perhaps to appeal to a consensus that does not exist. Still, one thing that is agreeably clear is that we ordinarily suppose that we can be free in and responsible for our actions in a way that dogs—not to mention other actual or possible supercanine, but subhuman, unselfconscious beings—can never be. I shall treat this as quite uncontroversial, and the case of dogs will provide a useful touchstone in what follows.[4] This said, it may be remarked that some theorists have apparently sought to reduce human freedom to a freedom that can be accorded equally to dogs (or at least to other actual or possible unselfconscious, subhuman supercanines). Hume's account of freedom—according to which freedom is simply freedom to do what one chooses to do even though what one chooses

---

[3] See Hume, *Enquiry*, p. 95: "By liberty, then, we can *only mean* . . ." (my emphasis). He defines freedom as freedom in the basic sense—such freedom is sometimes called 'liberty of spontaneity'—and suggests that this is all we could possibly (or properly) mean by the word.

[4] The dogs who feature in what follows are as often as not dogs of theory, not of real life. Their main function is to represent genuinely purposive agents that are not self-conscious and are cognitively speaking more limited than we are. At various points their complex and attaching emotional characteristics are played down or ignored.

to do may be entirely determined—is arguably a case in point.[5]

I.2 'DETERMINISM'—A RULING

'Determinism' will be taken to be the thesis that every event has a cause—that every event or state of the world is brought about by something else, which is its cause. This intentionally highly inspecific definition is all that is needed for present purposes.[6]

There is a common definition of determinism which it is natural to call a 'stronger' definition, although there are ways of taking the word 'cause' given which the original definition is simply equivalent to the stronger definition. According to the stronger definition, if determinism is true then the whole future (or past) of the world is in principle predictable (or retrodictable): it suffices to have a complete description of the world at any one time and complete knowledge of the laws of nature.[7]

Some may wish to claim that the stronger definition of determinism is necessary if one is to argue that freedom is not compatible with determinism. An argument to the effect that this is not so is implicit in Chapter 2. But anyone who wishes is at liberty to understand 'determinism' in the sense of the 'stronger' definition, whenever it occurs in the text.[8] For one of the claims that will be defended below is that

[5] *Enquiry*, p. 95. It depends on whether one thinks that dogs can be said to choose. For an argument that they can, see 8.3. There are certainly accounts of 'liberty of spontaneity' given which dogs (or at least unselfconscious superdogs) can be said to have it.

[6] While the definition given here is quite general, and compatible with dualism, 'determinism' is often interpreted more restrictively to mean 'physical determinism', which might be expressed as the thesis that every physical event has a cause; or, more restrictively still, as the thesis that every physical event has a physical cause. The last formulation is implied by the conjunction of determinism with materialism. These distinctions do not matter here. There are many other questions about determinism and causation which are of no present concern. Even the following weakened form of determinism would do: all events are caused except one—the so-called 'Big Bang'.

[7] Where these may be conceived as non-linguistic principles of working or 'natural necessity'. The two definitions are equivalent if a cause properly speaking—a cause as it is characterized when all the facts are in—is held to be something which is not only (*a*) sufficient but also (*b*) necessary for its effect. There are perhaps two main ways of strengthening one's definition of 'cause'. One is to move from (*a*) or (*b*) to the conjunction of (*a*) and (*b*)—or simply to incorporate both (*a*) and (*b*) explicitly in one's hitherto inexplicit definition. The other is to move from a 'regularity' definition of 'cause' to a 'non-regularity' definition. The present definition is already a 'non-regularity' definition, in its appeal to the common-sense idea that a cause 'brings about' its effect. (In 'Realism and Causation' I argue that realism with respect to the external world requires the rejection of any mere regularity theory of causation.)

[8] For further discussion of it in the context of free will, see P. van Inwagen, *An Essay on Free·Will*, esp. pp. 58–65.

although determinism is certainly not irrelevant to discussion of freedom, reference to it is completely unnecessary. It is unnecessary in at least this sense: the problems which have been posed by reference to determinism can be made to arise with all their traditional lineaments without any assumption or rejection of determinism.

Given the above definition, this seems to be a good thing. The statement 'every event has a cause' is neither verifiable nor falsifiable, and so it is as well to be able to dispense with any assertion of it in the posing of a philosophical problem—except, of course, when considering the problem it poses itself.

I.3 DRAMATIS PERSONAE

Given a definition of 'determinism', one can define a number of other positions.

A *'hard determinist'*, in William James's phrase, is one who believes that determinism is true, and that it entails that we are not and cannot be free.[9] Such a one is an *incompatibilist*, holding that freedom (F) and determinism (D) are incompatible, the presence of either entailing the absence of the other; holding that $\neg\Diamond(D \& F)$.[10]

A *libertarian* is, like the hard determinist, an incompatibilist. But such a one believes that we are free, and so believes that D is false.

A *compatibilist* believes that we may be free even if D is true—that $\Diamond(D \& F)$.[11] Such a one may believe any of at least the following things:

(i) that D is true, that D does not imply that we are unfree, but that we are in fact unfree.

(ii) that D is true, that D does not imply that we are unfree, but that it has not been shown whether or not we are free.

(iii) that D is true, and that we are free.

(iv) that D is true, that we are free, and that our being free requires that D be true.[12]

(v) that D may or may not be true, but that we are in any case free.

(vi) that D is not true, but that we are free, and would be free even if D were true.

(vii) that D is not true, that we are not free, but that F is none the less compatible with D.

---

[9] William James's distinction between 'hard' and 'soft' determinism is formulated in the 'The Dilemma of Determinism'.

[10] i.e. 'not possibly both D and F'.   [11] i.e. 'possibly both D and F'.

[12] See R. Hobart, 'Free Will as Involving Determinism and Inconceivable without It'. See also Hume, *Enquiry*, pp. 98–9.

There are several other compatibilist possibilities (obtained by variously combining belief in and uncertainty about the truth and falsity of F and D).

Many modern compatibilists are what William James called 'soft' determinists, believing that D is true, and that we are free—believing (iii) or (iv). A good number may believe something like (vi), sensitive to evidence for subatomic indeterminacy; these may also hold determinism to be as good as true as far as our action in and on a world of macroscopic objects is concerned. Many of them will reject the equation of freedom with true responsibility adopted in 1.1.

All theorists of freedom may be ranged either in the compatibilist or in the incompatibilist camp, for all putative third parties who hold the thesis of determinism to be irrelevant to the question of freedom, believing (v), for example, or who simply do not mention determinism in their account of what freedom consists in, may be claimed by the compatibilists. For if determinism is irrelevant to freedom it is compatible with it. Even those theorists who claim to find all available statements of the thesis of determinism meaningless or incomprehensible may perhaps be claimed by the compatibilists. For such theorists cannot regard any statement of the thesis as posing a threat to a theory of freedom.

Using 't' for 'true', 'f' for 'false', and '?' for 'don't know', one can set out a table:

	1	2	3	4	5	6	7	8	9
Determinism	t	f	t	f	t	f	?	?	?
Freedom	f	t	t	f	?	?	f	t	?

Compatibilists may occupy any of these positions, and incompatibilists may occupy any of them except (5), (8), or (3), which is occupied by the 'soft determinist' compatibilists. 'Hard' determinists may only occupy position (1), and, of course, they hold not only that (D & ¬F)[13] but also that (D→¬F)),[14] opposed in their incompatibilism to the libertarians, who may only occupy position (2), and who not only hold that (F & ¬D), but also that (F→¬D)).

These occupants of positions (1), (2), and (3) are, together with the *non-rational commitment* theorist, or *commitment* theorist, for short, the principal figures in what follows, in various guises, some of which are described in 1.5 below; and they have traditionally been so in

[13] i.e. 'D and not F'.
[14] i.e. 'D entails not F'.

discussions of freedom. The commitment theorist holds that, given the nature of our experience (of other people, or of our own agency, say) we cannot but believe that we are free, whatever the facts are about determinism or anything else. The commitment theorist who will be of principal concern argues, not just for the fact of commitment, but from the fact of commitment (together with certain other premisses) to the fact of freedom, and is thus a 'determinism is irrelevant' compatibilist. The commitment theorist may be assigned position (8) (though able to occupy positions (2) or (3)), not as one who is by definition undecided about the truth or falsity of determinism, but as one who is willing and able to leave the issue of determinism on one side.

The curious personage who occupies position (4), and who has had little or no part to play in discussions of the problem of freedom, may be either a compatibilist, believing (vii) above, or an incompatibilist, believing that we are not free, that determinism is false, but that if determinism were true we would for that reason not be free even if the present reason why we are not free no longer held good—believing $(D \rightarrow \neg F)$. Someone else in position (4) might even couple a belief that $(\neg D \rightarrow \neg F)$ to the belief that $(\neg F \& \neg D)$, thus partly resembling the compatibilist who believes (iv)—that $(F \rightarrow D)$. Most actual libertarians, as well as most compatibilists who do believe we are free—and the term 'compatibilist' will henceforth be used to refer only to those compatibilists who have this belief—may judge that this book argues for the correctness of occupying position (4); or, more cautiously, position (7)—for determinism will never be proved false.

I.4 THE UNIMPORTANCE OF DETERMINISM

An argument for the dispensability of any appeal to determinism in discussion of freedom can be divided into two parts. (1) First, one may argue that determinism does not pose the central *problem* for freedom, contrary to incompatibilists. (2) Second, one may argue that freedom does not *require* the truth of a full thesis of determinism, contrary to the Hobartian (or Humean) compatibilist who believes (iv) above.

1. The first part of an argument for the dispensability of any appeal to determinism is given in Chapter 2. It forms part of an argument principally designed to establish the impossibility of stating any satisfactory libertarian theory. As an argument for dispensability it has a double goal: (1*a*) to show that no assumption of the falsity of determinism can help to *further* the statement of a positive theory of freedom,

contrary to the libertarian; (1*b*) to show, (partly) contrary to the hard determinist, that no *objection* to a theory of freedom can be raised by assuming the truth of determinism which cannot equally well be raised on other grounds. It claims that there are more basic grounds from which all consequences generally required of determinism by a hard determinist—and generally feared by a libertarian—follow. They are immediately better grounds than those provided by a theory of determinism if they have the same relevant consequential import but are not, like determinism, unverifiable.

The argument is radically independent of the issue of determinism in a way that may be brought out by contrasting it with another argument which is not thus radically independent: it does not rule the issue of determinism to be irrelevant by first arguing (with the libertarian) that $(D \rightarrow \neg F)$, and then (with the Hobartian compatibilist) that $(\neg D \rightarrow \neg F)$, in order to show that whether or not determinism is true, we are in any case not free. It claims, simply, that freedom—true responsibility—requires that something impossible be true; where the impossible thing is not $(D \& \neg D)$. ($(D \& \neg D)$ would be established as the absurd consequence of supposing that freedom existed by any successful pursuit of the double line of argument for irrelevance just described.)

Discussion of determinism can be dispensed with. But to say that it is irrelevant would be an exaggeration. For a common version of the double line of argument just mentioned does indeed constitute a powerful objection to any theory of freedom. Very briefly, it enquires, of any particular event of action, whether it was caused (determined) or 'random' (undetermined), and suggests that the agent's claim to freedom of action is fatally impugned either way.[15]

2. Argument is scarcely required to show that freedom does not *require* the truth of determinism. For even given a view according to which free actions must be determined, a few random events, or even a great many in the right (not in the wrong) places, would not do any harm to freedom to act, or freedom of will; and '$\neg D$' stands for 'not every event has a cause', not 'no event has a cause'. The discussion of action in Chapter 2 will I hope clarify the element of truth in the belief of some compatibilists that determinism is required for freedom, by showing that some sort of determination, although not the truth of determinism, is indeed required if freedom of action is to be possible.

[15] Cf. e.g. A. J. Ayer, 'Freedom and Necessity'.

I.5 THEORIES AND THEORISTS

In this section I wish to introduce a number of definitions and distinctions. These will become clearer as they are put to use later on.

1. *Positive theories.* A *positive* theory of freedom is one that concludes that freedom is indeed possible. But 'positive theory of freedom' will also be used to mean a theory that concludes, more particularly, that we ourselves, human beings, are free. We would after all be surprised by the conclusion that although free agents are possible, we ourselves are not among them.

2. *Capacity theories.* A *capacity* (or capacitational) theory of freedom is one that seeks to define free agenthood just in terms of the possession of certain capacities. It is not concerned with capacities for particular sorts of actions such as reading and walking, but with capacities much more generally conceived, including, obviously, those capacities whose possession is necessary for being a *purposive* agent—such as the capacity for movement, or at least self-change. It considers the question of what kind of thing can be a free agent, and supposes that a description of a being that restricts itself to citing certain *practical and cognitive capacities* that the being has can capture everything about the being that makes it a free agent. In specifying these capacities, a capacity theory typically seeks to specify a certain freedom-sufficient degree of *agentive enablement*; it seeks to specify a certain sufficient complexity of practical and cognitive *equipment*.

A being that is held to be a free agent given its capacities can be so circumstanced that it is in fact unable to act freely in any way at all. So it is that a capacity theory of free agenthood has a natural extension that considers the question of when an agent that is a free agent given its capacities can actually act freely. This extension defines the agent's freedom actually to act freely in terms of its capacities *and circumstances*. It says, for example, that the agent must not be *constrained* in certain ways if it is to be actually able to act freely.

One simple capacity theory goes as follows.

1. A free agent must obviously be an agent; it must be capable of *purposive action.*
2. Possession of the capacity for purposive action is dependent upon the possession of certain other capacities: roughly, the capacity to form and have desires and beliefs, the capacity to reason practically in some sense, and the capacity for self-movement or at least self-change.

3. A free and truly responsible agent must also be self-conscious; it must be capable of self-conscious thought. (This is argued for in Chapter 9.)

On this view, a free agent must be a self-conscious, rational agent. To adopt this capacity theory as an adequate theory of free agenthood is to hold that being a self-conscious, rational agent is not only necessary but also sufficient for being a free agent. Many compatibilists have held such a theory, explicitly or (usually) implicitly; and whether or not these capacities are held to be sufficient for free agenthood, they are likely to form the basis at least of any capacity account of free agenthood.

Other capacity conditions may be, and have been, proposed. H. Frankfurt, for example, has argued that a capacity to form second-order desires is necessary for free agenthood. Gary Watson has claimed that 'to be free is to have the capacity to affect, by unimpaired practical thought, the determinants of one's actions'. Kant sometimes seems to suggest that what is necessary for freedom is a capacity to 'determine oneself to action' by reason alone (or by the 'moral law'), independently of the influence of one's desires or natural instincts.[16] But whatever particular account one favours, it is certainly very natural to think that any worthwhile theory of free agenthood will take the form of a capacity theory. It is natural to think this whether one is a compatibilist or a libertarian. Most actually proposed theories of free agenthood take the form of a capacity theory, or can at least be cast in this form.[17]

3. *Attitudinal theories.* What is more, it seems initially plausible to suppose that a capacity theory will be able to capture the conditions of free agenthood (if any theory can) even though it places no explicit conditions on what an agent's *experience* or general view of the world (including itself) must be like if it is to be, specifically, a free agent.

It is not at all clear that this is right, however; and it will be argued that it is not. It will be argued that it matters a great deal what an agent's general experience or conception of things is like, when its freedom is in question, and that all mere capacity theories of freedom are inadequate: there are other conditions of freedom that are not

[16] Frankfurt in 'Freedom of the Will and the Concept of a Person', and in 'Three Concepts of Free Action'; Watson in his introduction to *Free Will*; Kant in *The Fundamental Principles of the Metaphysic of Morals*.

[17] *Elbow Room*, by D. Dennett, is a clear example of a purely capacitational approach to the problem of freedom.

practical-and-cognitive-equipment-specifying capacity conditions.

These conditions do not form a neat class, but they typically require that one experience or view things in a certain way; they require that one have certain *attitudes*, whether cognitive or non-cognitive, to the way things are—to the world, or to oneself. They do not merely require a cognitive or experiential capacity. They require that one *actually* take or conceive things in some particular way among others. Thus they may require that one have a certain particular and explicit *belief* —a belief that affects the nature of one's experience of agency, for example.[18] In general, they are concerned with how one sees things, with the experiential or attitudinal side of things, and I will call them attitudinal conditions.

To introduce the notion of attitudinal conditions is not to introduce anything fundamentally new into the discussion of free will, even though most theories of free will have been capacity theories. It is, rather, a way of trying to spell out, and to question, certain things that have usually been taken for granted.

Attitudinal conditions attribute attitudinal or experiential properties—such as the property (discussed in Chapter 12) of having a certain 'identificatory' attitude to one's desires, or the property (discussed *passim*) of believing that one is (or of experiencing oneself as) a free and truly responsible agent. Theories of freedom that incorporate attitudinal conditions will accordingly be called attitudinal theories. Such theories do not exclude capacity conditions; they merely claim that they do not suffice, and add attitudinal conditions.

It may be objected that this distinction between capacity theories and attitudinal theories is not hard and fast, for some capacity properties may be of such a kind that their possession entails (i.e. necessarily involves) possession of certain attitudinal properties. For example: it may be said that if a being possesses all those capacities that are necessary for being a self-conscious rational agent, then it will be bound to conceive of or experience itself as a free agent in the ordinary strong sense. Kant, for one, held that a self-conscious rational agent, just as such, cannot but "act under the Idea of" its own freedom. (It is true

---

[18] To say this is not to say that to have a particular belief is to have any particular experience. It is to say that having a certain belief may entail having a certain general attitude to things, or way of experiencing things, and, equally, that the best way to characterize what someone's having a certain attitude to or way of experiencing things consists in may be to say that that person has a certain belief.

that he gave a special sense to the word 'rational', but this does not matter here.)

If this is so—if capacity conditions can entail attitudinal conditions—then capacity theorists can reasonably count such entailed attitudinal conditions among the conditions of freedom. In which case both capacity theories and attitudinal theories can contain both capacity conditions and attitudinal conditions, and there is no clear distinction between them.

And yet the distinction appears to have some intuitive force. For there are, on the one hand, theories that hold that possession of the property of free agenthood is, ultimately, simply a matter of the possession of some set of cognitive and practical capacities: capacities which can, merely by consideration of their nature as capacities, be seen to be such that a being who possesses them is *ipso facto* free in and truly responsible for its actions. On the other hand, there are theories that require in addition that one see things in a certain particular way or light. They require that one have certain (possibly belief-based) attitudes that are not necessarily involved in or presupposed by possession of any of the very general cognitive and practical capacities that are thought to be necessary for freedom.

In order to maintain the capacity theory/attitudinal theory distinction, I shall adopt a relativized version of it: I shall say that a theory of freedom A counts as an *Attitudinal* theory *relative to* some capacity theory C if and only if A places attitudinal conditions on free agenthood which are *not* entailed by any of the capacity conditions that make up C. The proposed attitudinal conditions of freedom will be said to be *Attitudinal* conditions relative to C.

For example. Suppose that it is said that believing you are a free agent is indeed a necessary condition of being a free agent; and suppose that the Kantian or quasi-Kantian view mentioned above—that having all the capacities necessary for being a self-conscious rational agent necessitates believing you are a free agent—is shown to be incorrect. Then a theory of freedom that says that believing one is a free agent is necessary for actually being a free agent is an Attitudinal theory relative to a capacity theory that says that being a self-conscious rational agent is sufficient for being a free agent.

Consider another example. In Chapter 9 it will be suggested that having a conception of oneself as a single thing that is somehow single just *qua* mental is a necessary condition of free agenthood—an attitudinal condition. But it will also be suggested that fulfilment of this attitudinal condition *is* necessarily involved in possession of the capacity for self-conscious thought. In which case the attitudinal condition is not an Attitudinal condition relative to any capacity theory of freedom that includes the capacity for self-conscious thought among the conditions of free agenthood.

Strictly speaking, then, what conditions count as Attitudinal conditions will always be relative to a particular capacity theory. But once a particular set of capacity conditions has been settled on for purposes of discussion (this is done in 7.3) this detail can be ignored. In Part III it will be argued that all the attitudinal conditions that come up for discussion there are Attitudinal conditions relative to any (plausible) capacity theory of freedom. (None of them, that is, attributes an attitudinal property, say A, of such a kind that there is a capacity property which is both (a) necessary for freedom just *qua* practical/cognitive capacity property and (b) such that it entails A.) From now on, therefore, I shall use the expression 'Attitudinal theory' (or 'Attitudinal condition') in an unqualified manner to mean 'Attitudinal theory (or condition) relative to any plausible capacity theory', without always specifying some particular capacity theory in relation to which the theory (or condition) in question is an Attitudinal theory (or condition).[19]

4. *Subjectivists and Objectivists, subjectivists and objectivists.* All capacity theorists and some Attitudinal theorists are *objectivists* about freedom. That is, they hold that if the property of freedom is ever correctly attributable, then it is a straightforwardly objective property. But the word 'objective' is vague, and it will be useful to define a narrower position, that of the *Objectivists*—whose position is in turn best defined, at first, by reference to their opponents, the *Subjectivists*.

The general characterization of a Subjectivist theory of a thing X is simply this: reference to belief in the existence of X enters essentially into the full account of that in which the existence of X consists, so far as X exists at all. The Subjectivists who will be of principal concern in what follows hold the following view about freedom: they hold—

---

[19] There is a further deep problem about the relation between experience and freedom which I shall not consider here. It is a variant of a problem that haunts many areas of philosophy, and it arises particularly clearly in connection with the capacity theory approach to freedom. It does not concern the present suggestion that an adequate theory of freedom may have to place certain conditions on the *particular character* of the experience of any being that can be a free agent. Instead it gives rise to the (seemingly absurd) question why the having of experience should be thought to be necessary *at all* for free agenthood. See Appendix A for a brief outline of this problem.

apparently paradoxically, it is true—that believing one is a free agent
is a necessary and indeed constitutive condition of actually being a free
agent.

The Objectivists who will be of principal concern, therefore, are those
who deny just this.

It seems likely that Subjectivists about freedom will be Attitudinal
theorists. For they claim that the specific attitudinal property of believing one is or thinking of oneself as a free agent is a necessary
condition of actually being a free agent. And it seems unlikely that
having such a specific belief or way of thinking about oneself will turn
out to be a necessary consequence of possessing any of those very
general capacity properties that can plausibly be held to be necessary
for freedom by capacity theorists (this will have to be argued for at
some length, however).

Commitment theorists of freedom (1.3) are also likely to be Subjectivists. They are likely to hold not only that it is a very important
natural fact about us that we cannot but believe we are free agents, but
also, with the Subjectivists, that if we are indeed free agents we are so
essentially partly in virtue of the fact that we believe we are. It will be
assumed henceforth that commitment theorists make this claim.

Not all Subjectivists need be commitment theorists, however. For
Subjectivists may hold that believing one is free is a necessary condition
of being free independently of having any views on whether or not we
can help believing ourselves to be (or experiencing ourselves as) free.

To say that we are free agents only if we believe we are is ambiguous.
It can mean (1) that each one of us is a free agent only if he, or she,
believes of himself, or herself, that he, or she, is a free agent. That is
the claim of the Subjectivists as stated above. Or it can be asserted at
community level, and mean something rather vaguer than (1), i.e., (2),
that if we-plural (we human beings, we in the community) are properly
called free agents, then this is essentially partly because we as a plurality
believe we are. Commitment theorists may hold either (1) or (2), and it
will be useful for the moment to continue to use the word 'Subjectivist'
in a way that preserves the ambiguity. Where necessary, however, one
may distinguish Subjectivists-(1) and Subjectivists-(2), who hold (1) and
(2) respectively. After Chapter 6, concern will be almost exclusively
with Subjectivists-(1).

A positive *objectivist* theory of a thing X simply asserts that X does
really, objectively exist. A *subjectivist* theory of X denies just this,
holding that there is an important—ultimately paramount—sense in

which X does not exist at all. Such subjectivism usually involves a rejection of the common unreflective view about X. It grants that we ordinarily believe that X exists, but denies that it does in fact, and offers an explanation of the existence of our belief in X that does not involve any assertion of the existence of X itself. Or—something slightly more complex, which amounts, in effect, to Subjectivism-(2)—subjectivists may hold that to the extent that there is indeed *a* sense in which X does exist, the general belief that it does must be granted to be an essential, necessary part of what actually constitutes its existence.

Consider, briefly, the example of morality. Moral subjectivists characteristically hold that while the true account of why we believe that moral judgements are or can be true or false leads back to all sorts of things, both to feelings and attitudes and other, non-mental things in the world, it does not lead back to moral facts (nor to non-moral facts that are held to amount to moral facts, given some variety of naturalism). So that *if* there is any sense in which morality generally considered is a real phenomenon in the everyday world, this is essentially partly because we believe that this is so. Subjectivists-(2) may propose a similar argument about freedom: Chapter 5 considers a theory that has this general form. Chapter 3 considers a Subjectivist-(1) theory of freedom.

After Chapter 6 concern will, as remarked, be almost exclusively with Subjectivism-(1). A crucial question will be whether Subjectivism-(l) entails subjectivism about freedom. Or, in other words, whether to hold (i) that no being can be a free agent without believing it is one is to be committed to the view (ii) that there is a vital—ultimately paramount— sense in which no being can be a free agent at all. It does not seem obvious that to hold (i) is to be committed to (ii), though (i) is certainly problematic in certain respects; and perhaps the best available theory of freedom will turn out to be a *Subjectivist objectivist* theory.

5. *The principle of independence*. The Subjectivist claim (i) above directly contravenes what I shall call the *principle of independence*: the prima facie very plausible principle according to which if one has a certain belief, B, and if B is true, then the obtaining of the state of affairs in virtue of whose obtaining B is true cannot be in any way dependent on the obtaining of the state of affairs of one's having B: one's having a belief cannot be a condition of that same belief's truth. Respect for the principle of independence may be taken to be positively definitive of the position of the Objectivists.

While there are apparently exceptions to this principle, it is extremely natural to think, with the Objectivists, that the case of freedom cannot be one of them. What the Objectivists claim is simply that an agent's belief that it is a free agent is true only if it has certain properties, not including the property of believing it is a free agent, that are sufficient for free agenthood and, hence, sufficient for the truth of its belief that it is free.

The Objectivists' and Subjectivists' disagreement about this issue is the subject of Part III. As already remarked, one major question is this: must any theory of freedom that can plausibly be called 'objectivist' in the wider, ordinary sense grant to the Objectivists that the principle of independence must be respected in the case of freedom? That is, does objectivism entail Objectivism, in the case of freedom? The question whether Subjectivism entails subjectivism is the same question.

(Note that the belief in freedom that will be of concern in what follows will only be an agent's (standing) belief that it is a free *agent*, considered independently of particular circumstances, its belief that it is a thing of a kind that is able to act freely; not any belief that it may have, at some particular time, that it is then free to *act* in some particular way. An agent in an unlocked room can correctly be said to be free (to go) although it does not believe that it is, and believes, indeed, that it is not free (to go), believing that the door is bolted. But the fact that it can be natural to say that one can be free to *act* in some particular way when one does not believe that one is constitutes no objection to the claim that one is a free *agent* only if one believes one is.)

To summarize. One can distinguish four main ways of classifying theories of freedom—as capacity theories, Objectivist theories, Attitudinal theories, and Subjectivist theories—by reference to two types of condition—capacity conditions and Attitudinal conditions. Capacity theories require and permit only capacity conditions. Objectivist theories permit both capacity conditions and Attitudinal conditions. Attitudinal theories permit capacity conditions and require Attitudinal conditions. Subjectivist theories permit both capacity conditions and Attitudinal conditions, and—if the condition of believing one is a free agent is indeed an Attitudinal condition of free agenthood (relative to any plausible capacity theory)—require Attitudinal conditions.

Summarized in this way, these distinctions may be hard to grasp, but they will become familiar with use.

I.6 A SKETCH OF THE ARGUMENT

This book does not present a single, linear argument, but it does have a certain developmental unity, which I shall now try to illustrate.

For the purposes of Part I it is assumed that Objectivist or as one might say *conventional* compatibilism cannot give an adequate account of our ordinary, strong notion of freedom. (Part II returns to the question.) It is simply assumed—but it is obvious that any conventional compatibilist theory of freedom has to give up an absolutely crucial part of what most people think matters most about freedom. Compatibilism can undoubtedly satisfy many of the demands of our ordinary notion of freedom. This is not in dispute. But it cannot satisfy the presently crucial demand. For it is unable to give an adequate grounding to the notions of true responsibility and desert. This is all that is being claimed, and no clear-headed compatibilist has ever denied it. To think that compatibilism is not being taken seriously enough in Part I is to miss the point.[20]

What, then, of Objectivist libertarianism? It is the main subject of Chapter 2. A constraint is placed on libertarian theories (2.2): they must give some positive, detailed account of how indeterminism contributes to freedom of action in every particular case of action, and not simply assume, negatively and unspecifically, that indeterminism is a necessary condition of free action. Libertarian theories must also pursue a certain goal—they must try to give an account of *self-determination*. It is argued that they cannot satisfy the constraint in any plausible fashion; and that they cannot attain the required goal (it is in fact a goal plausibly required of all theories of freedom) because true or ultimate self-determination is provably impossible.

If conventional, Objectivist compatibilism and libertarianism are ruled out, what next? It is unclear, because (*a*) libertarianism and compatibilism are by definition exhaustive of the field of positive theories of freedom, and (*b*) it is extremely natural to think that only an Objectivist theory can give us what we want. As for (*b*): it is natural to be dissatisfied with the Subjectivist alternative on general principle, because it appears to say something like this: that we are free, if we are, essentially partly because we feel or believe we are. Instead of saying that we are right to feel or believe we are free for reasons that are independent of the fact that we feel or believe we are. As if the belief

---

[20] The defining reference to desert in 1.1 immediately suffices to differentiate the present notion of '*true*' responsibility from all genuinely compatibilist accounts of responsibility. Most compatibilists see clearly that they have to give up the ordinary strong notion of desert, and the function of the qualifiers 'true' and 'truly' is simply to keep this point clear: whatever it may be, compatibilist responsibility is not true responsibility in the present sense.

could help to make the state of affairs believed to obtain actually obtain, rather than the state of affairs' obtaining making the belief true.

Whether or not Subjectivism is defensible in any form, it is worth while to examine our apparently very powerful, and perhaps practically speaking unrenounceable commitment to the belief that we are free and truly responsible agents. For it may be that this commitment derives from certain rather specific features of our experience, and it would obviously be of value to acquire a clearer idea of what these features are, whether one sees enquiry into their nature as necessary in order to perfect the anatomy of an illusion, or whether one sees it as possibly providing a basis for a new kind of theory of freedom—a Subjectivist, commitment theory.

As far as the second of these alternatives is concerned: if one can show that we have and cannot give up such a commitment, then perhaps one can argue somewhat as follows.

(1) Whatever the world is supposed to be like considered *in-dependently* of those features of our experience mentioned in the last paragraph, freedom of will and action remain lived, experiential facts of life.

(2) It is only these experiential facts of life that are ever really—or properly—under discussion in discussion of freedom.

(3) If it is true that they are lived facts of life—and it is—then it is true that we are free; so we are free, and 'there's an end on't', as Samuel Johnson said.

In the rest of Part I the prospects for Subjectivist and commitment theories are examined, in piecemeal fashion, from a number of different points of view; some phenomenological reflections on the nature of our sense of freedom are also introduced. In Chapter 3 it is suggested that although Kant is mainly concerned to provide an Objectivist account of how it is that we can possibly be free, he can also be seen as proposing a Subjectivist (Subjectivist-(1)) commitment theory of freedom. A case is made for this view, and a general statement of the characteristic structure of commitment theories is offered (3.2). It is also argued that free agents need not be moral agents (3.3), and a description of the principal source of our commitment to belief in freedom is given (3.6). There follow, in Chapter 4, some intentionally indeterminate specu-lations on the general prospects for commitment theories as positive theories of freedom.

In Chapter 5, P. F. Strawson's article on 'Freedom and Resentment' is discussed. It is interpreted as putting forward a (Subjectivist-(2)) commitment theory of freedom, a 'non-rational commitment' theory. It is argued that such a theory cannot entirely avoid or undercut the objections it naturally provokes, and which it seeks to disarm as being simply beside the point. The discussion leads on to some more general reflections on the (cognitive) phenomenology of freedom in Chapter 6. In particular, it is pointed out that we are in some respects *natural compatibilists* in our thought about freedom, and that we are in other respects *natural incompatibilists*: appreciation of this fact is a necessary part of understanding the philosophical problem of free will.

The naturalness and power of Objectivist objections to Subjectivist and commitment theories prompts a return in Part II to the attempt to state an Objectivist and indeed compatibilist theory of freedom. In Chapter 7 a new *analysandum* is proposed (7.2): the question is not 'What are the necessary and sufficient conditions of freedom?' but 'What are the necessary and sufficient conditions of *potential free agenthood*?' Only the term is new, however: a potential free agent is defined simply as a being that is *capable* of free action in certain circumstances. We consider we are potential free agents, whereas dogs, say, are not—we consider that they can never act freely in the way in which we think we can.

What are these circumstances in which *potential* free agents can *actually* act freely? In answering this question, the theory takes up a basic compatibilist idea: potential free agents act freely whenever they act without being *constrained* or forced into doing what they do.[21] The theory's fundamental question, 'What is it, exactly, to be a potential free agent?' is then usefully changed. It becomes 'What must a being be like if it is to be such that it can act freely when it acts free from constraint?'

First of all, a simple *capacity* theory (1.5.2) of potential free agenthood is attempted: it seeks to establish possession of some set of capacities as sufficient for an agent to be such that it acts freely when it acts free from constraint. Clearly not all purposive agents act freely when they act free from constraint. Dogs do not. And it also seems that *Nemo*—who is hereby defined as being just like a human being in all respects in which it is possible to be like a human being without

---

[21] In fact there is nothing intrinsically compatibilist about this idea. Most libertarians can accept it (though they may disagree with compatibilists about what constitutes constraint); and they can also agree with compatibilists about the task it sets—that of saying what a being has to be like, exactly, in order to be able to act freely when free from constraint (i.e. that of saying what a free agent is).

being self-conscious—is not capable of acting freely, simply because he is not self-conscious. Other cases are examined. The general question is this: if human beings are indeed free agents, then which, precisely, of their features suffice to distinguish them from purposive agents like dogs or Nemo in respect of freedom? It is not at all clear what these features could be. But to try to find them is a good way of examining our thought about freedom.

In Part II, then, certain basic Objectivist capacity conditions of free agenthood are proposed and briefly commented on. A definition of ability to choose is given in Chapter 8, and reasons why we think that self-consciousness is necessary for freedom are considered in Chapter 9.

In Part III the debate between Objectivists and Subjectivists is reopened. The latter claim that believing one is a free agent is a necessary constitutive condition of being one. The former claim that this cannot possibly be so. In Chapter 10 the terms of debate are established. In Chapter 11 some other cases in which one's believing one has a property is apparently a condition of one's having it are considered. In Chapters 12 to 14 various arguments are offered against the broadly speaking Kantian claim that a self-conscious rational agent, just as such, cannot but believe it is a free agent. The upshot of these chapters is, first, that a further Objectivist condition of free agenthood is proposed—an attitudinal condition of a sort that capacity theories cannot admit;[22] and, second, that the principal Subjectivist claim that believing one is free is a necessary condition of being free is endorsed. The consequences of this are examined in Chapter 15.

There are at least two good reasons for proposing a short cut through this book. On the one hand a fair amount of the ground covered is familiar in its general features. On the other hand some discussions of particular issues diverge from the main line of argument in pursuit of (relatively speaking) inessential detail. The main attempt to introduce a new perspective on the problem of free will takes place in Part III, where the debate between Objectivists and Subjectivists is staged, and those who wish to concentrate on this can skip most of Part I. They need only read 2.1, the last paragraph of 2.11 (which gives a definition), 3.3 (which introduces the notion of non-moral freedom), and 3.6 (which describes one central source of our belief in freedom), before moving on to Part II. In Part II they can omit Chapter 9, in Part III 10.12 and

[22] It is, therefore, an Attitudinal condition.

11.4–11.8. Those in a hurry could perhaps also omit Chapter 8. Those in less of a hurry might consider taking in Chapter 6 on their way through Part I.

The general method of the book is very conventional; it attempts to establish strong conclusions of the form 'X is a necessary condition of Y'—in the knowledge that failure may be as revealing as success.

I

METAPHYSICS AND COMMITMENT

2

Libertarianism, Action, and Self-determination

2.1 INTRODUCTION; THE ARGUMENT SUMMARIZED

'Objectivist' theories of freedom suppose, naturally enough, that the task of showing that we are free involves showing that we have certain properties, *not* including the property of believing we are free, that are necessary and sufficient for freedom. Such theories usually take the question of whether determinism is true or false to be important when one is trying to answer the question whether we are free. And they regularly come up against the sceptical objection that, whether determinism is true or false, we cannot possibly be free either way.

It is a compelling objection. Surely we cannot be free agents, in the ordinary, strong, true-responsibility-entailing sense, if determinism is true and we and our actions are ultimately wholly determined by "causes anterior to [our] personal existence"?[1] And surely we can no more be free if determinism is false and it is, ultimately, either wholly or partly a matter of chance or random outcome that we and our actions are as they are?

So far as Objectivist theories go (and nearly all theories are Objectivist theories), the sceptical objection seems fundamentally correct. Neither of the two options, *determined* and *random*, seems able to give us or allow us what we want. But together they exhaust the field of options. It is true that an action may be the result of a complex cause, some of whose components themselves have causes that can be traced back indefinitely far, while others are either themselves genuinely undetermined events, or can be traced back causally to undetermined events. But it seems clear that a mixture of determined and undeter-

---

[1] H. Sidgwick, *The Methods of Ethics*, p. 66. This familiar objection to the claim that we can be truly responsible agents is of course disputed (and indeed scorned) by compatibilists, but it is entirely sufficient for establishing the structure of the present discussion. Those who do not find it compelling should recall the description given in 1.1 of the kind of freedom it is meant to be an objection to. Those who still do not find it compelling should recall that reference to determinism has in any case no essential part to play in the argument against freedom—a fact that will emerge shortly. Cf. also *An Essay on Free Will*, by P. van Inwagen.

mined antecedents cannot help to make an action free, whatever the proportion of the mixture.

If neither determinedness nor randomness (nor any mixture of the two) can either permit or provide for what we want in the way of freedom, in the ordinary, strong sense (this qualification will be taken for granted henceforth), then there is no more to say—so far as Objectivist theories of freedom are concerned. But what exactly do we want?

One can partially describe the state of affairs that would give us what we want in terms of the notion of self-determination: for if one is to be truly *responsible* for one's actions, then, clearly, one must be truly *self-determining* or truly *self-determined* in one's actions. True responsibility presupposes true self-determination.[2]

Is this any help? It may be said that to talk of self-determination in this context is to do little more than re-express our ordinary, strong notion of freedom or true responsibility in one more way. But it is nevertheless worth asking what such self-determination might be.

The first thing to note is that the notion of self-determination is ambiguous. If one is going to employ it at all, one has to eliminate the ambiguity. It can be understood in a compatibilistic sense, as follows: (1) one is self-determined, or self-determining, in any particular case of action, just so long as what one does is indeed a result of one's own choices, decisions, and deliberations. In this sense, one can be self-determining in one's (physical) *actions* even if one is not self-determining with respect to one's *choices* or *decisions*—one can be self-determining in one's actions even if one's choices, decisions, and deliberations are entirely determined phenomena, and are phenomena for whose occurrence and nature one is not truly responsible. Such self-determination is clearly compatible with determinism (it corresponds to freedom understood in the 'basic' sense discussed in 1.1).

Here, however, 'self-determination' will be used in a different way: according to which (2) one is truly *self-determining*, in one's actions, only if one is truly *self-determined*, and one is truly self-determined if and only if one has somehow or other *determined how one is in such a way that one is truly responsible for how one is*.[3] Such self-determination may seem evidently impossible. But it can also seem to be clearly

[2] One could equally well express this requirement as the requirement that one must be a true *originator* of one's actions, but I shall stick to the formulation in terms of self-determination.

[3] Just as the qualifier 'true' is used to mark off the ordinary, strong conception of responsibility from any standard compatibilist conception of responsibility (ch. 1 n. 20),

necessary if one is indeed to be truly responsible for one's actions and, hence, free in the present sense. The argument for this will be given shortly.

There is another natural picture of self-determination according to which (3) one can somehow or other be truly self-determining in one's decisions or choices, and hence in one's actions, even if one is not truly responsible for how one is (in respect of character, etc.). I shall not discuss this picture directly until 2.9 and 2.10, where it will be argued that the objections to it are at bottom exactly the same as the objections to self-determination understood in sense (2).

It is clear, I think, that the truth of determinism excludes self-determination understood in sense (2). One cannot have determined how one is, in such a way that one is truly and ultimately responsible for how one is, and hence for how one acts, if how one is is ultimately wholly determined by 'causes anterior to one's personal existence'. I shall assume that this is so. To make this assumption is not to ignore the claims of compatibilism, for nearly all compatibilists agree with it. They agree that true responsibility and true self-determination are impossible if determinism is true. That is why they standardly attempt to define freedom in such a way that it does not involve true responsibility (or true self-determination): for they want to reach the conclusion that we are indeed free.

It is true that some compatibilists claim that one can in some manner take over true responsibility for one's actions despite determinism.[4] Others are tempted by the idea that mere possession of the ability to engage in fully self-conscious deliberation is sufficient for true responsibility understood in the strongest possible sense, irrespective of whether or not determinism is true, and irrespective of whether or not we can be self-determining in way (2). Such claims will not be considered until later, however.

so too it will be used to mark off the strong conception of (true-responsibility-underlying) self-determination from any compatibilist conception of self-determination (e.g. (1) above). (In fact 'self-determination' will be understood only in this strong sense in what follows, and so it will be possible to bracket or omit the word 'true' without risk of ambiguity.)

[4] Frankfurt's theory of freedom, as expounded in 'Freedom of the Will and the Concept of a Person' and 'Three Concepts of Free Action', is (among other things) an interesting attempt to characterize a notion of self-determination which shows it to be compatible with determinism. As an attempt to define a notion of true-responsibility-entailing freedom, however, it is open to fundamental objections of the sort discussed in this chapter.

Given that (true) self-determination is impossible if determinism is true, the only remaining question is whether it is possible if determinism is false. Many will think it obvious that indeterminism cannot help with self-determination. But it will merely for the sake of discussion be supposed that it is not obvious. Indeed it will be supposed that what any serious libertarian has to try to do is to give some account of how self-determination is possible given the falsity of determinism. What follows will therefore be a discussion of libertarianism. Detailed reasons, stated in the terms of a particular theoretical frame, will be offered as to why self-determination is not possible. But the general argument for the impossibility of self-determination is very simple, and does not depend essentially on the particular theoretical frame; it should be restatable to fit any preferred picture of the nature of mind and action. It goes as follows.

(1) Interested in free action, we are particularly, even if not exclusively, interested in rational actions (i.e. actions performed for reasons), and wish to show that such actions are or can be free actions.

(2) How one acts when one acts rationally (i.e. for a reason)[5] is, necessarily, a function of, or determined by, how one is, mentally speaking. (One does not at present need to be more precise than this; one could add 'at the time of action' after 'mentally speaking'.)

(3) If, therefore, one is to be truly responsible for how one acts, one must be truly responsible for how one is, mentally speaking—in certain respects, at least.

(4) But to be truly responsible for how one is, mentally speaking, in certain respects, one must have chosen to be the way one is, mentally speaking, in certain respects. (It is not merely that one must have caused oneself to be the way one is, mentally speaking; that is not sufficient for true responsibility. One must have consciously and explicitly chosen to be the way one is, mentally speaking, in certain respects, at least, and one must have succeeded in bringing it about that one is that way.)[6]

---

[5] This is the *only* sense of 'rational' that is of present concern. In this sense one may perform a rational action even if one's reasons for that action are highly irrational from some ordinary point of view.

[6] It is true, (*a*), that someone can correctly be said to have made a choice without there having been any process of conscious deliberation, or silent 'let it be so'; and it is perhaps true, (*b*), that there are choices which are in a sense not made for any reason. But the choice mentioned in (4) as required for true responsibility cannot be of kind (*b*); nor can it be of kind (*a*), I think—though this matters less. In so far as the agent's true responsibility depends on the choice, it must be a conscious, explicit choice.

(5) But one cannot really be said to choose, in a conscious, reasoned fashion, to be the way one is, mentally speaking, in any respect at all, unless one already exists, mentally speaking, already equipped with some principles of choice, 'P_1'—with preferences, values, pro-attitudes, ideals, whatever—in the light of which one chooses how to be.

(6) But then to be truly responsible on account of having chosen to be the way one is, mentally speaking, in certain respects, one must be truly responsible for one's having *these* principles of choice P_1.

(7) But for this to be so one must have chosen them, in a reasoned, conscious fashion.

(8) But for this, i.e. (7), to be so one must already have had some principles of choice, P_2, in the light of which one chose P_1.

(9) And so on. True self-determination is logically impossible because it requires the actual completion of an infinite regress of choices of principles of choice.

That's really all there is to the argument, although another model of self-determination, which one might call the Leibnizian model, will also be considered and rejected below.

It is (3), perhaps, that is most likely to be resisted. It may be objected that one does not have to be at least partly truly responsible for how one is, mentally speaking, but only for how one decides; and that one can make a fully rational decision and be truly responsible for it even if one's character, say, is entirely determined (or entirely not self-determined). But it will be argued that this is, in a crucial sense, simply not so.

(4) may also be objected to—in particular the idea that one must have *chosen* to be the way one is. Of course this seems, in a way, an absurdly artificial condition to place on true self-determination. But one should ask oneself what else being at least partly truly responsible for how one is, mentally speaking, could possibly consist in. (4) can be put in a slightly different way: 'one must oneself have consciously and intentionally brought it about that one is the way one is, in certain respects, at least'. But then the rest of the argument goes through as before, with only minor alterations.

In fact essentially the same argument can be given in a much less artificial and extremely familiar form. (1) It is undeniable that one is the way one is as a result of one's heredity and experience. (2) One cannot somehow accede to true responsibility for oneself by trying to change the way one is as a result of heredity and experience. For (3) both the particular way in which one is moved to try to change oneself, and the degree of one's success in the attempt at change, will be determined by how one already is as a result of heredity and experience. (And any further changes that one can successfully bring about only after certain initial changes have been brought about will in turn be determined, via the initial changes, by heredity and experience.)

It may be objected that the kind of freedom this argument shows to be impossible is so obviously impossible that it is not even worth considering. To this the reply is simple: the kind of freedom that it is an argument against is just the kind of freedom that most people ordinarily and unreflectively suppose themselves to possess. The idea that we possess such freedom is central to our lives. It is therefore worth examining the argument in detail. In particular, it is worth seeing how it fares in the context of certain other assumptions about rational agency.

The aim of the present chapter is not merely to show that this particular argument against self-determination is valid, however. If this were its only aim, it would be much too long. The objections to libertarianism that it contains are routine; I don't suppose any of its main contentions are original (any that are are probably not true). It is, however, also intended as a contribution to the 'cognitive phenomenology' of freedom—as an examination and dramatization of certain more or less definite, more or less dubious aspects of our general, unreflective, implicit, non-philosophical conception of ourselves as free agents in the ordinary strong sense. Many of the untenable positions presented in what follows are worth noticing principally or only because they form part of, or underlie, this general conception (going through these positions will be more useful to those who are relatively unfamiliar with the free will debate than to the experienced).

Curiously, it seems that we have this general conception of ourselves as free in the strong sense although our most ordinary notions of decision, choice, and action already contain within themselves everything that is necessary in order to demonstrate the impossibility of such freedom—as in the argument just set out.[7] Our apparently unrenounceable commitment to this general conception coexists with our

---

[7] Given these notions, the argument proceeds completely a priori. The issue of the truth or falsity of determinism is not even raised. Furthermore, no view about the nature or 'substantial realization' of the mind is presupposed; the debate about the nature of mind that goes on between identity theorists, dualists, and so on is entirely irrelevant to the basic problem of free will.

everyday employment of notions that can quickly furnish a clear proof that such freedom is not possible. It appears that we tolerate some very deep inconsistencies in this area, and that our general conception of ourselves as free has many highly diverse and indeed incompatible aspects. (In Chapter 6, for example, it is suggested that we are simultaneously naturally incompatibilist and naturally compatibilist in our thought about freedom.) In the discussion that follows, the argument against self-determination is restated with calculated laboriousness within a certain theoretical frame. The crucial libertarian question, 'Can indeterminism help in the search for true self-determination or freedom?' is answered in the negative—for familiar reasons. Parts of the discussion are rather slow, because it is written in the presence of a great host of imaginary objectors. If there were no libertarians left, it would be largely superfluous. But there are still libertarians. They appear to be on the increase.[8] This is surprising in a way, because the prospects for a detailed libertarian theory seem magnificently hopeless. But it is quite unsurprising in another way, because the time-honoured incompatibilist intuition is, fundamentally, sound.

2.2 LIBERTARIANISM; A CONSTRAINT

Incompatibilism is the view that the falsity of determinism is a necessary condition of freedom. In itself, it involves no view about whether determinism is true or false, or about whether or not we are free. 'Libertarianism', by contrast, is the name of a positive incompatibilistic theory of freedom, one that purports to show that we are free and so assumes (or argues) that determinism is false.

This is agreed on all sides. But I shall also take it that no theory can be properly counted as a libertarian theory unless it gives an account of action-production which shows in detail how and why some sort of actual indeterministic occurrence is a necessary feature of the production of any and every free action (i.e. is among the antecedents of any and every free action). A libertarian theory that simply assumes, incompatibilistically, that the falsity of determinism is a necessary condition of free action, while failing to integrate this negative necessary condition into the positive, detailed account it gives of how free action

---

[8] Four out of five of the most recent books on freedom that I have seen are either libertarian or at least incompatibilist—*Free Will: A Defence against Neurophysiological Determinism*, by J. Thorp, *Time, Action and Necessity: A Proof of Free Will*, by N. Denyer, *An Essay on Free Will*, by P. van Inwagen, and *Free Will and Responsibility*, by J. Trusted. (*Elbow Room*, by D. Dennett, is the exception.)

actually comes about, makes no serious claim on our attention as a libertarian theory.

This should be obvious. But here is an argument. Consider any description D given by libertarians of the antecedents of an action A that they claim to be a free action, which allegedly makes it clear *why* A is a free action, and from which it does *not* follow that A's antecedents are partly indeterministic in nature. Given such a description one may say this: (1) let us suppose that these antecedents have determinedly come to be the way they are; for D does not rule this out. (2) But D is meant to show why A is free. (3) So to say that if these antecedents have determinedly come to be the way they are then the action is not after all a free one, as these libertarians must, is to admit that D has not after all made clear why A is a free action. (4) It follows that any adequate libertarian account of free action which purports to show how and why actions can be free must point to actual indeterministic elements among their antecedents, and must in addition explain how the indeterministic elements contribute to the actions' freedom.[9]

Not all libertarians will agree with this. And they will say that their reasons for claiming that the falsity of determinism is a necessary condition of freedom are quite independent of any positive detailed account of free action that may be given. This is true; but it does not affect the above argument. Libertarians are notoriously bad at giving any positive account of freedom at all. But they must do so if they are to merit being taken seriously. A libertarianism that gives no role to indeterminism in its detailed account of free action is little more than a covert compatibilism with an idle incompatibilist premiss danglingly subjoined.

It is recognition of this requirement on libertarianism that motivates the present approach. One could put the main point as follows: freedom, reason, and indeterminism—free action, rational action, and indeterminism—are a hard trio to unite. And since the first two at least must be united, the third must be united with them both.

Clearly the first two must be united: we must be able to include rational actions among free actions, if our definition of 'free action' is to be acceptable. Even if there can be genuine actions that are not rational actions (i.e. not performed for reasons), and even if not all free actions are rational actions, still some rational actions must qualify as

[9] It is no good appealing to quantum physics or the Big Bang to support the (unverifiable) claim that there are absolutely undetermined events without offering any positive account of how such events might be supposed to contribute to freedom.

free actions. (In fact, the vast majority must.) Otherwise, even if we are free, and morally responsible, it is not as rational agents that we are so—an absurd consequence. (Mystical views about freedom that might accept this consequence are not of present concern.)

So the question is this: where can the assumption of the truth of indeterminism be put to work, in a detailed, positive libertarian account of the nature of action-production that shows actions to be free because not determined? In trying to answer this question on behalf of the libertarians we may suppose that they have metaphysical *carte blanche*—liberty to assume, for the purposes of argument, whatever kind or quantity of indeterminism that they think may help. But before any answer is attempted, it is worth saying something about the notion of action.

I shall propose a view of action that is controversial in some respects. Doubts about its controversial aspects should not affect the argument about freedom, however. For as far as the question of freedom is concerned, the claim about action that matters is just that actions that have true rational explanations (true explanations in terms of reasons) can be free actions, if any actions can; and this claim is not controversial at all. (Parts of the next section are rather involved, and it may be omitted by those who have no special interest in the notion of action.)

2.3 RATIONAL EXPLANATIONS OF ACTIONS

2.3.1. I assume that rational explanations of actions can be simply true, and that when they are simply true they really do state why the actions they explain were performed.[10] This assumption looks trivial, but some of its consequences are worth examining. I shall do so briefly, and, accordingly, rather bluntly.

Consider an agent, a man, *a*, who is a free agent if any of us ever is. Assume that *a* acts rationally; that is, that he acts for reasons. What are these reasons? I take it that there is a clear sense in which they are real things, as real as roses.[11] In fact this must be so, if rational explanations of actions can be simply true—as will shortly emerge.

If the reasons for which *a* actually acts are real things, what kind of

[10] Is this ever doubted? I am not sure that it is not incompatible with certain versions at least of a widely accepted view of action explanation that stresses the essentially 'holistic' nature of the attribution of beliefs and desires in interpretation and explanation of action (or behaviour).

[11] This claim is part of a general position of realism about the mental; realism about the *intentional* (and cognitive) mental, in particular (as opposed to the sensational-

thing are they? I take it that there is no harm in calling them mental states. For when it is simply true (as it often is) to say that a person like *a* had a certain reason, R, for performing an action, A, his having reason R can clearly be said to be his being in a certain *state*—a certain 'reason-state'.

If reasons are mental states,[12] which mental states are they? Well, because it is all that is necessary for the purposes of the present discussion, I shall adopt the widely accepted simple model of reasons for action according to which *a*'s reasons or reason-states are standardly compounded of beliefs (or belief-states) and desires (or desire-states); and I shall interpret the word 'desire' very broadly, in a familiar way, as a word interchangeable with 'want' that covers any non-cognitive state that can be cited non-redundantly in a true reason-giving explanation.[13]

So much for *a*'s reasons; they are real things, desires and beliefs, things that he actually has. Or, in an alternative idiom, they are real states of *a*, desire- and belief-states, states that he is actually 'in'. He 'has' desires and beliefs, or is 'in' desire and belief-states, just in so far as statements of the form '*a* believes that *p*' and '*a* desires *x* (or desires that *p*)' can be simply true.

The next question is this. How are *a*'s reasons related to his actions? Clearly, *a*'s desires and beliefs (or *a*'s being or coming to be in a certain desire-and-belief state, or events in *a* characterizable as events of desiring and believing) must, in most ordinary cases in which he acts,

mental). Such realism is not committed to asserting the existence of conscious or occurrent mental goings-on that do not in fact go on. It insists, though, that desires and beliefs are not simply a matter of what it is appropriate to ascribe. They are things we really have, and rational explanations of actions that ascribe reasons to agents are, truistically, true only if the agents have those reasons. No amount of epistemological delicacy about the 'holistic' nature of mutually interdependent desire and belief ascriptions, or about what we can know for certain, can threaten this realism.

[12] Here I am concerned with reasons *only* in this sense; I am not concerned with the sense of 'reason' in which one may be said to have a (good) reason to do something although one has no idea that this is so.

[13] Or: any non-cognitive state other than a mood or emotional state—one may suppose that whenever a mood or emotional state can be correctly cited in a true rational explanation of an action, a corresponding desire or want (one that is caused or otherwise occasioned by or somehow integral to the mood or emotional state) can also be cited in a true rational explanation of that action. Nothing essential hangs on this supposition, and all the claims made about rational explanation in this section should be restatable to fit more complex accounts of the motives of action. The present ruling is made for the sake of ease of expression and introduces no fundamental distortion into discussion of freedom. (G. Watson might disagree—see his paper 'Free Agency'.) Notice that the view that an agent's reason for action may consist only of beliefs has not been ruled out.

be supposed to cause, or at any rate to play a crucial role in whatever process it is that finally determines the nature of, his action. Why? Simply because there will in the ordinary case of action be a *true, full* rational explanation of the action. And a rational explanation citing reasons, such as '*a* wanted W and believed B', cannot be a true and— *qua* explanation citing mental antecedents—full explanation of why *a* performed action A unless there is *some* sort of real relation between his having the desires and beliefs he does have, on the one hand, and his performing the action he does perform, on the other hand, which is such that the former somehow or other decisively shapes the nature of the latter. Obviously. The linguistic explanation-statement links two things, *a*'s having the reasons (those real things) he does have, and *a*'s action (that real thing). If it is true, then, necessarily, it is true because of some real *non*-linguistic relation between the former and the latter, which is such that the former somehow or other gives rise to the latter.

Here it becomes clear why reasons must be supposed to be real things if rational explanations of actions can be simply true: there must be some robust sense in which reasons are as real as actions (those physical occurrences) if it is indeed to be true that the former can stand in some relation to the latter which is such that they somehow or other give rise to, and have a decisive influence on the nature of, the latter.[14]

2.3.2. This is certainly so. But it makes the following digression necessary. For it may be said that giving rational explanations of actions is essentially a matter of making actions intelligible; and that rational explanations can mention reasons (desires and beliefs) that *a* does *not* have, as well as reasons that he does have, in making his action intelligible. If, for example, *a* lacks a very widespread belief, his action may not, when explained just in terms of the desires and beliefs he actually has, be rendered intelligible to those who simply assume he has the widespread belief. Generally, different explanations of the same action may be appropriate for different contexts and different audiences.

This is true. And it is true that some of the things that rational explanations can legitimately cite, in explaining *a*'s actions, are not reasons at all in the present sense, mental states, real things. They are

---

[14] This is so whether or not reason-states (or events characterizable as events of desiring or believing) are such that there is some sense in which it is true that they have full descriptions in purely physical terms—even immaterialism grants that mental states are as real as we think roses are.

not *a*'s reasons nor anyone else's. Nevertheless, given a rational action, there must always be *some* true rational explanation of it that cites only real reasons in the present sense—reasons that the agent does actually have; and I will call rational explanations of this kind 'rational*' explanations, in order to distinguish them from other explanations that are properly called rational explanations and that may (for example) make reference to desires and beliefs that the agent does not actually have.

It is clear that there are many very ordinary cases in which a true rational* explanation of *a*'s action is a *full* explanation of it, in the sense that it gives, while citing only *a*'s actual reasons, a full account of what it was about *a*, mentally speaking, that made it the case that he performed the action he did perform. Such ordinary cases are of central importance. They form, after all, the great majority of those cases of action that we want to show to be free.

More generally, one may say that at the core of any true, compendious rational explanation of an action there must lie the rational* explanation of that action. Why? Because—this is a quite general truth—any true and fully spelt out explanation of the occurrence of any event has to represent, in some descriptive vocabulary or other, what it was that was (1) actually there and (2) such that the event in question came about as a result of it. Now rational explanations of action are couched in mental vocabulary. It follows that any true and fully spelt out rational explanation of an event of action has to state what it was that was actually there mentally which was such that the event of action came about.[15]

In the present terms, then, a true, *full*, rational explanation of an action is not a true rational explanation that renders the action fully intelligible; for what suffices to render an action intelligible is always relative to an audience.[16] It is, rather, a true rational explanation that either is, or contains as a part, the true, full rational* explanation of the action. I will say that a true rational explanation is a full rational

[15] Here a sense of labouring the obvious is offset by an equally strong sense that some will think that even this claim involves an unacceptable degree of realism with respect to the mental—the intentional-mental.

[16] Sometimes it suffices to mention just a desire, sometimes just a belief, sometimes it is necessary to mention a desire or a belief that the agent has *not* got. (In fact a false rational explanation can render an action fully intelligible to us—even when the action is identified, for purposes of explanation, by means of a description that is also appropriate to the description of the agent's intention in performing it.)

explanation just in case it cites all those of the agent's desires and beliefs that were actually involved in the action's coming about, whatever else it also cites.[17] True full rational explanations differ from true full rational* explanations simply in this: they may cite desires and beliefs that the agent has not got, as well as those it has got. (True full rational* explanations are thus a subclass of true full rational explanations.) But any action must have a true full rational* explanation, if it is indeed a rational action (i.e. an action of which it is correct to say *sans phrase* that it was performed for a certain reason); whether or not we can work out what that rational* explanation is.[18]

This may seem crude. But it seems to be part of what one is obliged to say if one takes seriously the supposition that rational explanations of actions can be simply true. (Nothing is implied about what—if anything—must be occurrently present to the agent's mind.) And we undoubtedly do suppose both that rational explanations can be and very often are true and full explanations in the present sense and, crucially, in the present context, that actions which have true and full rational explanations can be free actions (if any actions can be).

2.3.3. In 2.3.1 the cautious phrase 'to play a crucial role in whatever process it is that finally determines the nature of' was offered as an alternative to 'to cause'. This was for the sake of those who are unhappy about the fact that reasons can truly be said to cause actions. Consider now the less cautious expression 'fully determine' ('fully determinative of'), which, as applying to the relation between reasons and actions, may be defined as follows: *a*'s reasons R fully determine (are fully determinative of) his action A just in case the rational* explanation of A that cites R and R only is a true and full rational explanation of A.

Here the notion of full determination is simply *defined* in terms of true full explanation.[19] So those who doubt the causal theory of action

[17] This may be thought to be very simplistic. But the facts of the matter are often very simple when we act, and the simple cases are very important. It is not being claimed that we can always know what the full rational explanation of an action is, however. Cf. D. F. Pears, 'Sketch for a Causal Theory of Wanting and Doing', pp. 128 f.

[18] Here it is supposed that the truth of the matter can be independent of what we can find out, contrary to those, influenced perhaps by Donald Davidson, who appear to believe that the language of desires and beliefs is little or nothing more than a theoretical scheme we impose for the purposes of explaining behaviour, a scheme that involves no reference to a mental reality that exists independently of our natural explanatory needs and habits.

[19] There is no present need to give any independent account of what such determination might actually involve or consist in.

cannot object to the use of the notion of full determination on the grounds that it presupposes the truth of the causal theory. It does not. One does not have to accept the causal theory in order to accept the centrally important fact that rational explanations which cite only reasons (desires and beliefs) that *a* actually has can be true and full explanations of his actions. In general, the following discussion does not presuppose the truth of the causal theory of action.

In speaking of 'fully determinative' I have simply the following sort of connections in mind: *a* turns on the light, because he hears something moving in the room, wants to see what it is, and believes that the way to satisfy this want is to turn on the light—and *that's all there is to it*. *a*'s having the desire and belief fully explains his action so far as it is a turning on of the light, and is to the same extent fully determinative of it. (We may suppose that *a* has no other desires at the time of the action, given present concern to establish a simple paradigm; but the case in which *a* acts to satisfy one rather than another of two conflicting desires is equally a case in which the desire and belief which together form the reason for which he actually acts can correctly be said to be fully determinative of the action.) This is true even though it would of course be ridiculous to try to establish explanation-relations between statements about the desire and belief as such and statements about particular features of the trajectory of *a*'s hand in groping for the light switch.

It may again be objected that the simple model of action-production, according to which desires and beliefs or reasons (reason-states) can determine and indeed fully determine actions, is too crude. It may be said that its crudity permits one simply to beg the question against libertarianism. But this is not so. It is of course true that our thought about action and its antecedents is conducted in vaguer and more various terms than the simple model allows. (Perhaps one reason why this is so is that it protects us from seeing the ultimate indefensibility of our ordinary notion of freedom.) But the simple model is, although crude, neither fundamentally inaccurate in itself, nor such as to lead inevitably to inaccuracies when employed in discussion of freedom.[20]

[20] This is very widely acknowledged—and even if the simple model is not adequate for all cases, cases for which it is clearly adequate bulk large among those which any satisfactory theory of freedom has to be able to show to be free. (One thing that is not excluded by the simple model is the possible propriety of saying that an agent's reason for its action consisted only of beliefs. One might want to say that the reason for which *a* performed action A in situation S was simply that he believed that a situation of type

One objection to the simple model may be that it leaves out the agent, *a*, and sets up a picture of action-production that represents him as separate from and determined by his desire-and-belief-states, when he performs an action A because he believes B and desires D. But this objection is misconceived. The whole description can easily be recast in terms of the agent and his states. It is of course *a* who performs A. What remains true is that he performs A *because* his desire-and-belief-state, or reason-state, is what it is. Desire-and-belief-states retain their position as explanatorily vital in this recasting. For if we choose to characterize the agent as the cause or determiner of A, the next question is then this: *why* did *a* perform A (at time *t*)? By reference to which of his many features, mental and physical, may we give a correct explanation of why he performed A? In particular—given that we want a rational explanation—by reference to which of his mental features?[21] And the answer is, of course, by reference to his desire-and-belief-states. To claim that *a*'s having belief(s) B and desire(s) D was fully determinative of his performing action A is in no way to set up the desire-and-belief-state as some sort of *rival* to *a*, as the source or determiner of A. It can be true both (i) that *a* and only *a* performed A, and (ii) that to cite *a*'s reasons is to give a true and full explanation of A—although (ii) entails (iii) that *a*'s reasons were fully determinative of A in the present sense. For (iii) is entirely compatible with (i). To discern a tension between (i) and (iii) is to adopt a view of the nature of the agent/reasons relation that is completely untenable, whatever its initial attractions. (It is discussed in 2.9 and 2.10.)

2.3.4. As already remarked, we ordinarily suppose that actions that have true, full rational explanations can be free actions. In other words (given the definition of 'fully determinative'), we ordinarily suppose that *a*'s actions can be free actions when *a*'s reasons are fully determinative of them. 'Because he desired D and believed B' can be the whole truth, in mental terms, about why *a* performed action A, and A be none the less free for all that. So says common sense. For when *a*'s reasons R are said to be fully determinative of the occurrence of his action A, all that is meant is that the rational explanation of A by reference to R is a true and (*qua* explanation citing (conscious) mental antecedents) full explanation—it is entirely on account of the fact that

S obtained and believed that it was right to perform actions of kind A in situations of type S. See, e.g., J. L. Mackie, *Hume's Moral Theory*, p. 55.)

[21] Mental features mentalistically described—should there be non-mentalistic descriptions of mental features.

a has R that he performs A. Now this is a very common occurrence, and if there are any actions that are properly called free, actions that are fully determined by reasons in this sense must certainly be among them.[22]

It may be objected that when we are explaining an action we sometimes feel the need to mention some sort of fiat, or *nihil obstat*, some sort of permitting the reasons to go ahead and move to action, on the part of the agent, in addition to mentioning its desires and beliefs. The theory of freedom to which this feeling corresponds is considered in 2.9 and 2.10 along with the 'Leibnizian' picture of the relations between reasons and actions, according to which the former incline the agent towards the performance of the latter, but cannot be said to 'fully determine' the latter in any strong sense. For the moment, though, attention will be restricted to the simple model of action already adopted—principally because, properly understood, the picture just mentioned collapses back into the simple model. (In fact there are several attractive pictures of the process of action-production, and each has its advantages, depending on its emphases. It should appear, from the generality of the requirements placed on free action in what follows, that it is not necessary to frame discussion of free action in any other terms than the present ones. At least one of the other pictures will be considered, however, in order to show that its different terms do not permit a different conclusion.)

The situation is then this. We cannot give up the belief that rational explanations can be true; and it is principally (if not entirely) actions performed for reasons, actions which have true rational explanations, that we suppose to be free; actions, moreover, which are such that true rational explanations of them are *full* explanations of them (in mental terms). So even if some free actions are *not* actions which have true and full rational explanations, we still have to show that actions which are of this kind can be free.

For suppose we simply accept that reasons can stand in relations of

---

[22] 'Why did he cross the road?' 'Because he wanted an ice-cream, and believed he could get one in the shop across the road ($\pm$ and there was nothing else he wanted to do more at that moment, $\pm$ he did not believe that crossing the road was an offence punishable by death, $\pm$ etc.'—these optional negative clauses may help to render the action intelligible to someone, but they do not cite reasons that the agent has). That's all. Simple cases like this are the deep anchor of the claim just made in the text. They form the great majority of those actions we must suppose to be free, if we suppose we are free. (Morally significant actions can be equally simple.)

more or less complete determination to actions, ranging from cases in which it is correct to say that reasons are fully determinative, to cases in which this is not so. It is not as if this gives us any grounds for thinking that the cases in which the reasons *are* fully determinative of the action are *less* likely to be cases of free action than the cases in which the reasons are *not* fully determinative of the action. We do not suppose that the freedom of an action diminishes in proportion as the action is more fully determined in its occurrence by reasons; that is, we do not suppose its freedom to diminish in proportion as the true rational* explanation of it comes closer to being a full explanation of its occurrence. In fact we are more likely to suppose the contrary.

This being so, libertarians have to give an account of how an indeterministic antecedent can make an action free in a case in which reasons are fully determinative of it in the present sense; and they have to do this even if there are importantly different cases of free action in which the reasons are not fully determinative of the action.[23] This is sufficient justification for restricting attention, here, to cases where there is a true rational explanation of the action which is a full explanation of it. These are in any case the cases that matter most to us.

2.4 LIBERTARIANISM: THE CONSTRAINT APPLIED

Libertarians have to locate an indeterministic occurrence among the antecedents of any free action—and they have to show how its presence helps to make the action free.

Given the present restriction of attention to those cases of action that have true, full rational explanations, the question of where the indeterministic input is to enter in is usefully simplified. Consider a particular action A performed by *a*. *Ex hypothesi*, A is truly and fully rationally explicable by reference to a reason-state R made up of desire(s) D and belief(s) B (or by reference to events characterizable in terms of desire and belief), while it also has an indeterministic input X among its antecedents. So where can X be? Clearly

(1) X cannot somehow intervene between R and A. For then an explanation of A by reference to R alone will not after all be a true full explanation of A. The explanation 'A occurred (*a* performed A) because *a* believed B and desired D' will not be

---

[23] In fact, of course, such cases of free action will not be importantly different—and certainly not in the sense that there are different reasons why they are free actions.

true. To make it true, the words 'and X occurred', at least, will have to be added. In this case there is, contrary to hypothesis, no true, full rational explanation of A.

It is also clear

(2) that X cannot be supposed to feature among the antecedents of A in such a way that it is (*a*) simultaneous with R at that stage, S, at which R comes to be such that it is determinative of A,[24] and (*b*) unconnected with R. For if X is unconnected with R and yet has a determining effect on A, then, once again, the explanation of A in terms of R will not be a true, full rational explanation of A, contrary to hypothesis.

It seems, then, that

(3) X can only come in by occurring prior to S. But once again X cannot be unconnected with R, for reasons just given.

So

(4) X must come in prior to S in such a way that it has some effect on R's being the way it is. Only in this case can an explanation of A in terms of R be a true, full rational explanation of A while it is also true that X is a determinant of A. How the occurrence of X can in this case help to make A free is no doubt completely mysterious. That is the libertarians' problem. The present point is just that this is their only option for locating indeterministic inputs among the antecedents of action, at least in all those extremely common and for that reason centrally important cases where actions have true, full rational explanations.

This argument could be refined, but I think the idea is clear. The same point can be made much more generally, however, without specific reference to actions that have true, full rational explanations, and without reliance on the account of rational explanation of action adopted in 2.3: for it is, crucially, *sub specie rationalitatis* that we seek to show our actions to be free; it is specifically *qua* reasons-reflecting, reasons-determined things that actions must be shown to be free. If so, the indeterministic input allegedly necessary for free action cannot possibly be supposed to contribute to freedom either by interfering with or

---

[24] i.e. comes to be such that, because of how it then is, the subsequent rational explanation of A in terms of R is a true explanation. (This way of putting it designedly avoids unnecessary enquiry into what exactly this most common sort of occurrence involves.)

interrupting the determination of actions by reasons,[25] or because it is a contributory determining factor that is wholly independent of reasons for actions. So it can play a part only by playing a part in shaping or determining what the agent's reasons for actions are. Libertarianism cannot plausibly locate the indeterministic influence anywhere else.

Will it help to locate an indeterministic influence here? Well, clearly one thing indeterminism can always be invoked to substantiate is the claim that the agent's reasons or reason-states (desires and beliefs) need not have been as they were in fact, in any particular case of action. It seems unclear, however, how this in itself could make a difference to the agent's freedom of action. How could it, in itself? We must ask what more may be thought to be needed.

2.5 LOCATING INDETERMINISM

It has been argued that the only way in which libertarians can plausibly give indeterminism a positive, freedom-creating role in the process of action-production is by holding that indeterminism must affect the agent's reasons or reason-states, and play a part in their being as they are. Libertarians have nowhere else to locate the indeterminism that they must show to enter into the process of action-production in such a way as to make actions free. But how can indeterminism do what is expected of it, given that reasons are compounded of beliefs and desires?

That *beliefs* are regularly determined in us by the way the world is is easy to accept, difficult to reject. Their primary business is just to match the way the world is as well as possible. There are other ways in which beliefs are determined in us—by wishful thinking, for example. But we are on the whole concerned simply that our beliefs be true. We do not wish to be undetermined by anything, so far as the formation of our beliefs (and therefore their content) is concerned; nor do we wish to be self-determining with regard to the content of our beliefs; nor do we think we are. (We may of course choose to acquire a lot of beliefs about this or that, but once we are in pursuit of such beliefs we do not wish to be able to choose what their content will be, we just want them to be true.) Rather, we think (and hope) that what we believe is determined by, and as a result reflects, how things are.[26] The topic of the deter-

---

[25] Remember that this notion of determination is defined in terms of the notion of true explanation.

[26] There are some minor qualification to this claim that are of no present importance— see the lepidopterist in n. 29. On the general topic of determination of belief, see D. Wiggins, 'Freedom, Knowledge, Belief and Causality'.

mination of belief is a large one, but no one is likely to want to claim that the freedom of an action stems from the agent's being either (*a*) determined by nothing or (*b*) self-determined with respect to the content of its beliefs, and, in particular, with respect to the content of those of its beliefs that form part of the reasons for which it acts.[27]

That *desires* are determined in us is also easy to accept, in certain contexts of discussion, at least. But if libertarians are to connect indeterminism with free action at all, then it seems that they must show that indeterminism plays some part in the agent's having the desires that it does have. For since we ask no more of beliefs than that they be determined in us by the way the world is, according to some reliable process which is such that they generally come out true, it would appear to be far more promising for libertarians to postulate indeterminism in the acquisition or having of desires than in the acquisition or having of beliefs. Prima facie, at least, the Faculty of Desire is a far more promising place to look than the Faculty of Belief when one is seeking a point of entry into the action-producing process for some element which, by being undetermined, can help to introduce freedom into that process.

Apparently, then, a cogent libertarian theory must seek to make its case by rejecting the determination of desires; or at least of some desire or desires implicated in the determination of the occurrence of any particular free action. . . .

2.6 CAN INDETERMINISM HELP?

The pursuit of the discussion in these terms is already highly artificial. For it seems obvious that what is required for true responsibility, and hence for freedom, is not merely that the agent be *un*determined in its nature in some respect, but that it be *self*-determined in some respect, and, therefore, undetermined by anything else in that respect. It appears that libertarianism must establish not only that some at least of our desires are undetermined, in their occurrence or presence in us, by anything that is external to us, but also that we are able to determine what some at least of them are. Given the undeniability of reasons/

---

[27] It is possible that those who hold the view that reasons for actions can consist only of beliefs (see n. 20) may want to claim this, with respect to certain beliefs, at least. But if they are libertarians, and are looking for some account of self-determination, this view may only create extra difficulties for them (see n. 29).

actions determination,[28] we need agent/reasons determination. More particularly, we need self-determination as to desire—since we cannot usefully ask this for beliefs.[29] Such self-determination as to desire may presumably be only partial, and not cover things like desire for food or drink at particular times. But it would seem that some desire with respect to which the agent is self-determined must be operative in the coming to occur of every free action. The question, then, is how *in*determinism can possibly help to establish any such kind of *self*-determination.

2.7 EVASION: THE NOTION OF CHOICE

This whole approach may now seem beside the point, for in fact we think of nearly every action as free, even actions which are primarily motivated by desires with respect to which we do not suppose ourselves to be in any way self-determining—like the hunger-derived desire for food. Here we are likely to locate our freedom in our possession of a power to choose whether or not to eat which we have quite independently of having the non-self-determined desire to eat. Obviously enough. What we are likely to say is that the fact that we have the desire to eat is not a sufficient explanation of why we do eat, given that we act freely in so doing, because what must also be mentioned is the fact that we *chose* to eat.

But will this do? *a* is hungry. He wants to eat. He decides or chooses to eat. Why does he so decide? 'Because I'm hungry, and I want to eat.' 'But does that want *determine* your action?' 'No; I could, if I had so chosen, not have eaten.' 'Why, then, do you choose to eat?' 'Well, I'm hungry, I want to eat, I've no reason not to—no wants that conflict with my want to eat.' This banal exchange illustrates the difficulty. For presumably, if *a* had chosen not to eat, it would have been because he had *reason* not to despite his hunger and desire to eat. But then we may ask where and how self-determination and true responsibility are

[28] As noted at the end of 2.3.3, the fact that it is natural to say that agents, not their reasons, determine actions provides no grounds for an objection to this way of putting the matter.

[29] Libertarians who are trying to show that indeterminism could be a foundation for true self-determination may get into special trouble if they think that reasons for action can consist only of beliefs. For if one cannot plausibly see oneself as self-determining with respect to what one believes (except in the presently irrelevant sense that one can, as an aspiring lepidopterist, set oneself to acquire a great many beliefs about butterflies), then if one acts as one does just because of what beliefs one has, when one acts morally, it would seem that one cannot be self-determining or, therefore, truly responsible or free in so acting.

supposed to enter the picture, unless *a* is somehow responsible for his reasons. It seems clear that what *a* does when he acts intentionally is, ultimately, always and necessarily just some more or less complex function of his reasons; and that he cannot therefore be truly self-determining unless he can somehow be self-determining with respect to his reasons and, hence (2.5), with respect to his desires. So the question, once again, is how indeterminism can help with this.

This may yet be said: 'I just decided to do X, but not because of any reason I had. It was just me, it was just up to me, I just freely decided to. That's the fundamental fact behind freedom.' The main reply to this line of thought is given in 2.9. A brief reply is this: it may be that there are intentional actions that are almost entirely undeliberated in their performance, and that are therefore not performed for a reason, where 'performed for a reason' is taken to entail some explicit pre-meditation. Perhaps there may even be supposed to be actions that are not performed for a reason in a stronger sense, according to which there just is no reason at all which can correctly be given for them (though this is an obscure idea). Such cases are however of little interest, where freedom is in question, because it is above all, even if not ex-clusively, our most premeditated and fully rationally explicable actions that we hope to show to be free. The 'I just decided to' line cannot possibly be supposed to provide a general foundation for the claim that we are free.

Suppose that the introduction of the notion of choice into the simple model of action is now recommended as suitable for the description of *all* free action, and not only for the description of those actions, like eating when hungry, which are such that we cannot even begin to suppose that the primarily motivating desire either is or could be self-determiningly chosen.

Well, such a manner of description is undoubtedly very natural. But it merely shifts the difficulty sideways. We may grant that our having the non-self-determined desire to eat does not of itself determine that we do eat, and that whether or not we do also depends on our decision or choice; but then the decision or choice must itself be shown to be free if the ensuing action is to be. It is for the libertarian *ex hypothesi* not free if determined. But it is no good if it is merely undetermined, or a chance occurrence. The fundamental libertarian thought is (or ought to be) that it must, if it is to be our free choice, issue from us in such a way that we are truly self-determining in making it. But, surely, for this to be the case it must also be the case that we choose to eat because, all things considered, we want (or judge it best or right) so to choose. But then this want (this judging right or best) must enter into the true rational explanation of why we choose as we do, as the crucial determinant of the choice. But then questions arise about this determinant, the same questions as before. Is it determined or undetermined? More importantly, are we, the agents, self-determined with respect to it? If not, then, once again, how can we be said to be truly self-determining, and hence free, in our choice and in our ensuing action?

All this is obvious enough—not to say tiresome. The demand for true self-determination, which is presently being taken to be the fundamental libertarian demand, begins to look slightly (or completely) crackpot in the context of such a mundane example as this, of hunger and eating (the example is useful partly for that reason).[30] And yet it still seems to be, somehow, the right demand, especially when it is from the notion of moral responsibility that one sets out in pursuit of that in which freedom could possibly consist.

It may now be suggested that the reason we are truly self-determining free agents is simply that the process of deliberation (however perfunctory or inexplicit) that leads us to make whatever choice we do finally make is truly *our* deliberation, our doing, ours in such a way that we are truly responsible for whatever we do as a result of it. This is of course an attractive idea.[31] It corresponds closely to our natural, pre-philosophical, unreflective picture of the basis of freedom-founding self-determination. But it is heir to all the difficulties already discussed. For, briefly, in the end such deliberation comes down to a process of (practical) reasoning that necessarily takes one's desires (values, etc.) and beliefs as starting points. And, given that one does not want to be self-determining either with respect to (simple, factual) belief or with respect to one's canons of reasoning, but simply wants truth in beliefs

[30] It is precisely in the heat of the pursuit of the notion of radical, determinism-incompatible true responsibility that one naturally takes up elements of the contrary compatibilist idea that liberty of spontaneity—which is, basically, simply freedom to do what you want or choose to do, and which is, as such, entirely compatible with determinism and non-self-determination—is all we could ever really want in the way of freedom. The conflict of intuition that produces this reversal or oscillation of views (the psychological explanation of which is a crucial part of a full account of the problem of freedom) is like a perpetual-motion machine. It promises to provide a source of energy that will keep the free will debate going for as long as human beings can think.

[31] For an example of a theory of freedom according to which *a*'s responsibility for his actions consists simply in their being determined by his deliberations, the deliberations themselves not having been determined by anything, see *Time, Action and Necessity*, by N. Denyer (esp. §§ 45, 73, 76).

and validity in reasoning, once again the question arises as to how this process of deliberation can possibly give rise to true self-determination in action. And once again it seems that self-determination with respect to desires is the only possible foundation for true self-determination in action. No doubt it is folly to seek such a foundation. (To force libertarians to think their position through in this way is to provide powerful negative support for compatibilism.) But let us consider the question directly.

2.8 THE IMPOSSIBILITY OF SELF-DETERMINATION AS TO DESIRE

We may presume it to be a fundamental postulate of the libertarian theory presently under consideration that we have at least some of the desires that we do have undeterminedly—desires 1-*n*, say; and that it is in this manner that the assumption of the truth of indeterminism is introduced into the detailed account of the nature of action-production, in the way held to be necessary in 2.2: reference to indeterminism features in the account of action-production because it features in the account of the provenance of action-determining desires. This, then, is given as a factual assumption.

But clearly this indeterminism is not in itself enough for true self-determination or freedom. What must also be true, it seems, is that we ourselves are able to govern how we become (in respect of desire) in such a way that we can correctly be said to be truly responsible for how we become (in respect of desire). Just to be as we are undeterminedly from the point of view of physics is obviously not enough; nor is it enough if some of our desires rate as completely undetermined on any true psychological theory about what determines our becoming the way we are—one, for example, that refers to heredity and environment. What must also be true, it seems, is that we have *chosen* to have desires 1-*n*; that we have, at least partly, chosen to be the way we are.

This leads to the principal difficulty: so to choose, we must have reasons for our choice, prior principles, prior preferences, according to which we choose. Even if we allow that there may be choices made at random, made for no reason, they are of no use here. Even if one could intelligibly be supposed to have made a completely random selection of what desires to have, a choice that was undetermined by anything on all true psychological and physical theories, its mere undeterminedness would do absolutely nothing to make it one's own free choice, whereby one became truly responsible for (certain at least of) one's desires, and, therefore, for one's actions. If one is to be truly responsible for one's actions because one has chosen the desires (values, etc.) which lead one to act as one does, then one must clearly be truly responsible for this choice of desires in turn. And one can be truly responsible for this choice of desires only if one makes it in a reasoned, conscious, intentional fashion. But one cannot do this unless one chooses according to values and preferences one already has in the matter of what desires to have.

But then what about these values and preferences, these principles of choice according to which one chooses? One may be determined by nothing in one's possession of them; but this will not make one the captain of one's soul. For one will need to have chosen these principles as well, in order to be truly responsible for the character-shaping choice of desires which they govern, and which is meant to be such that it makes one truly responsible for one's actions.

This, of course, is a regress we cannot stop. We cannot possibly choose our root principles of choice, our conative base-structure, in the required way. So, if we are truly self-determining as agents, this cannot be because we are truly or ultimately self-determining, self-instituting, self-made, with respect to our desires or values or general character. No amount of postulation of logically possible indeterminism can help with this difficulty, because what is required for its solution is that an infinite regress of choices of principles of choice have a beginning and an end, and that is impossible. No appeal to subatomic indeterminacy can help to provide some sort of way in for the free will, because the impossibility of ultimate self-determination as to desire is a simple conceptual truth. Immaterialists and dualists are as powerless against it as physicalists or materialists.[32]

Russell made the essential point, perhaps, when he said that even if you can act as you please, you can't please as you please.[33] But true self-determination seems a clearly necessary condition of freedom, as freedom is ordinarily conceived. And many thinkers—those who have not either simply avoided the question, or decided that we are not really

---

[32] We can, of course, cultivate tastes, traits, and dispositions, and in that sense we can be said to change, and be responsible for, how we are. But this is not the sense that matters for true responsibility. If we undertake such self-change at all, we do so for reasons we already have, as remarked in 2.1, and which we are not responsible for having. A man who sets out to change—reform—his own character, and is judged to have been successful in doing so, is no more truly responsible for how he is and what he subsequently does than anyone else.

[33] Perhaps he was echoing Locke, *Essay*, II. xxi. 25—the point is an old one.

free at all—have supposed it to be fulfilled. Kant wrote of "man's character, which he himself creates"; Sartre, of "le choix que tout homme fait de sa personnalité"; E. H. Carr asserts that "normal adult human beings are morally responsible for their own personality". It is fairly clear that Aristotle believed both that we are or at least can be responsible for our own characters, and that such responsibility is necessary for freedom.³⁴ Where this idea is not already explicit in the common moral-metaphysical consciousness, it can easily enough be elicited from its non-explicit regions by judicious (and non-coercive) Socratic questioning.³⁵

Even Hume, having in the *Enquiry* given his classic compatibilist account of 'hypothetical liberty' in line with Hobbes and Locke, goes on to state, indirectly, the real problem about freedom—which he leaves unanswered. (It is curious that he does not in the case of freedom explicitly adopt his characteristic double position: that of inevitable philosophical scepticism about true responsibility on the one hand, and equally inevitable commitment to natural belief in true responsibility on the other hand. It is especially curious because the case for scepticism about true responsibility is essentially stronger than the case for scepticism about, say, the existence of the external world. For in the latter case what philosophy establishes is only that we cannot know that the external world does exist, not that we can know that it does not exist. Whereas in the case of responsibility the stronger conclusion does seem available. The reason Hume does not explicitly adopt the double position in this case is perhaps one of caution—although it is at least as much a desire to indulge in some heavy irony at the expense of theists: for he states the deeper objection to belief in true responsibility in indirect, theological terms, when he could equally well have stated it in terms of godless determinism.)³⁶

---

³⁴ The quotation from Kant is from *Critique of Practical Reason*, trans. L. W. Beck, p. 101 (*Ak.* V. 98). Cf. also *Religion within the Limits of Reason Alone*, trans. T. M. Greene and H. H. Hudson, p. 40 (*Ak.* VI. 44): "Man *himself* must make or have made himself into whatever, in a moral sense, whether good or evil, he is to become. Either condition must be an effect of his free choice [*Willkür*]; for otherwise he could not be held responsible for it and could therefore be *morally* neither good nor evil." The quotation from E. H. Carr is from *What is History?*, p. 89; it is discussed by I. Berlin, in *Four Essays on Liberty*, pp. xvii ff. Aristotle's views on the subject are in Bk. III, ch. V of the *Nicomachean Ethics* (but perhaps he did not really have what I call true responsibility in mind). For an early version of the opposing view, see Plato, *Timaeus* § 45.

³⁵ Which is not to say that its direct opposite cannot also be elicited, for reasons discussed in ch. 6.

³⁶ Cf. *Enquiry*, pp. 99–103. It could be argued that although Hume does not explicitly adopt his double position, it is there in essentials, connected to his moral subjectivism. Hume was surely aware of the sense in which true responsibility is impossible, God or

2.9 RELOCATING INDETERMINISM

The plan was to give an account of what conceivable factual conditions could justify a belief in freedom of action understood in the ordinary, strong, desert-entailing sense—and to do this before asking whether these conditions either were or could be actually satisfied. It had to be a consequence of the resulting theory of freedom that we are free when we act rationally and deliberately in such a way that our actions have true full rational explanations (2.3.1). Self-determination as to desire seemed to be necessary—but turned out to be impossible.

It is the indissoluble connection of the notion of freedom with that of reasons for action that forces one to reject any libertarian theory that proposes a different possible point of entry for an undetermined and *ipso facto* freedom-creating element into the process of action-production. Consider now the suggestion that human freedom is based upon some special power to intervene between one's reason-determined decisions to act[37] and one's initiations of action: one's freedom lies in the possibility of one's making a special interventionary choice or decision to do other than what one has in fact decided to do given one's actual desires and beliefs, a choice that is somehow disengaged from one's necessarily not-self-determined belief-desire (or reason) complex, and is, in particular, undetermined by it, and is for that reason free.

What of this? We are stipulated to be free because capable of these belief-and-desire disengaged choices: it is in so far as they flow from such choices that our actions are free. But then it follows that whenever we are able to give a true full rational explanation of an action, that action, at least, is not free. And this consequence deprives the stipulation of any interest; it does not give us what we want. Even if this supposed independent power to choose to do or not to do something standardly just ratifies (as it were) the decisions put out by one's belief-

no God. And he was, surely, aware of our deep commitment to belief in true responsibility, for it is built in to our natural disposition to praise and blame and to distinguish vice and virtue in actions, and these distinctions are "founded in the natural sentiments of the human mind, [which are] not to be controuled by any philosophical theory or speculation whatsoever" (p. 103). He would have certainly have agreed that we cannot give up belief in true responsibility, even if true responsibility is impossible, and not (like the existence of the material objects) just unprovable: "it is a point, which we must take for granted in all our [practical] reasonings"—to adapt what he says about belief in material objects (*Treatise*, I. iv. 2, p. 187).

[37] Recall that 'determined', in its present use, is defined in terms of true explanation (2.3.3).

desire complex, still, so long as one's choice of action is in any way genuinely independent of, and is indeed not a direct result of, one's having the reasons one has, one's resulting 'free' action cannot be a fully rational action, truly explicable just by reference to reasons (so far as mental antecedents are concerned). For now a necessary condition of its being free is that one has made a desire-and-belief-independent choice to perform it. So it is not a rational action at all. The rational explanation we give of it will fit, and will look valid, but it will in fact be false, vitiated by the crucial hiatus introduced by the reason-independent power of choice (or 'choice').

This suggestion, proposing a different possible point of entry for something that could make it true that we are truly self-determining, certainly answers to something that has an important place in the phenomenology of people's experience of the absolute 'could-have-done-otherwiseness' of action; but it cannot supply us with what we want, given that free action must in general be rational action. It seems that one may well, if suitably cautious, postulate a post-decision event (a neural event, whatever else it is) of volitional ignition of motor activity.[38] But this, if held to constitute a separate stage in the process of action-production, must clearly be conceived to be itself reason-determined and not an intervention on the part of the putative free agent that is radically independent of that agent's state of desire and belief. Otherwise the link between freedom and reason—between free action and action done for a reason—is once again broken, and one's theory is once again condemned to fatuity.

2.10 A 'LEIBNIZIAN' VIEW

And yet the phenomenological self-evidence of our power to do otherwise, in a way that makes us free in the strongest sense, remains untouched. Can nothing be done to give belief in such a power a respectable factual or metaphysical grounding? Well, it may now be suggested that the picture of the wholly reasons-independent power of choice proposed in 2.9 is too crude; and that the real reason why one can both be truly free and act rationally, despite the fact that one is necessarily not self-determined with respect to one's reasons, is that one's (necessarily not self-determined) reasons can genuinely *affect* one's decisions about action without its being the case that one is as a

[38] Cf. D. F. Pears, 'The Appropriate Causation of Intentional Basic Action', pp. 64–7.

rational agent *wholly* determined in one's decisions by the way one's reasons are.

Consider the agent in its mental aspect—the 'agent-self', as it were. The agent's freedom of action is now held to reside in the fact that, although it cannot be ultimately self-determining with respect to its reasons for action, it has an at least partially reasons-independent power of decision as to action. The necessary link between free action and rational action is maintained, because the agent's decision is, in any particular case of action, affected by, but not wholly determined by, its reasons.

The basic picture may be said to be Leibnizian in character: reasons for action affect agents' decisions, but in so doing only incline them towards, and do not necessitate them in, particular decisions to perform particular actions. But the following question now arises: upon what, exactly, are the agent's decisions about actions now supposed to be based, other than upon its reasons? The agent-self is represented as sitting in detached judgement upon its reasons (desires and beliefs) as they develop and combine in such a way as to become reasons for action. It then decides on an action *in the light of* these reasons for action. And although it cannot be truly self-determining with respect to these reasons for action (2.8), it is still truly self-determining in action because it is not fully determined in action by these (non-self-determined) reasons for action, but rather decides in the light of them, and so acts both rationally and truly freely.

The trouble with the picture is familiar. If the agent is to be truly self-determining in action this cannot be because it has any *further* desires or principles of choice governing the decisions about how to act that it makes in the light of its *initial* desires or principles of choice. For it could not be truly self-determining with respect to these further desires or principles of choice either, any more than it could be self-determining with respect to its initial desires or principles of choice. But if it does not have any such further desires or principles of choice, then the claim that it exercises some special power of decision or choice becomes useless in the attempt to establish its freedom. For if it has no such desires or principles of choice governing what decisions it makes in the light of its initial reasons for action, then the decisions it makes are rationally speaking random: they are made by an agent-self that is, in its role as decision-maker, entirely non-rational in the present vital sense of 'rational': it is reasonless, lacking any principles of choice or decision. The agent-self with its putative, freedom-creating power of *partially* reason-independent decision becomes some entirely non-rational (reasons-independent) flip-flop of the soul. And so this theory collapses into fatuity in exactly the same way as the theory discussed in 2.9, which proposed a power of *wholly* reason-independent decision: according to it no free action is a fully rational action, an action truly and fully explicable by reference to reasons.

The only alternative is to suppose that the agent-self is after all equipped with some extra set of desires or principles of choice. But then the freedom-founding event of decision becomes nothing more than the moment of contact between two distinct but equally non-self-determined[39] reason clusters, and the supposedly crucial power of partially reason-independent decision disappears. The picture is now this: the (putatively only inclining and not necessitating) reasons for action, R_1, having achieved summation in provisional decision, come before the agent-self which, given its own further set of reasons for action, R_2, decides in the light of these whether to let the first and as it were only prima facie action-prompting reasons R_1 actually motivate its action. The actions are now once again performed for, and are truly explicable just by reference to, reasons. But, by the same token, the original objection regarding the fact that the agent cannot be self-determined with respect to these reasons applies once again with full force.

The fruitlessness of these devices is plain, and it may be objected that the whole current frame of discussion is very unnatural in holding that some type or other of radical self-determination is necessary for freedom. It may be said that there are other intuitively attractive conceptions of free agency that make no such claim.

This may be so. It is certainly true that the claim that such self-determination is vital for freedom can look very odd. But it is also an extremely natural claim. It is at least as natural as it is odd. The views considered in 2.9 and 2.10 are not included merely as philosophical decoration—as unrealistic and obviously hopeless proposals. For they represent, albeit in an unusually and designedly vulnerable idiom, two versions of exactly the kind of thing that ordinary people are likely to say when challenged to defend their conviction that true responsibility for

---

[39] It is not meant by this that the reasons are not themselves self-determined, of course, only that the agent whose reasons they are is not self-determined with respect to them.

actions is possible even if it is true that one cannot be truly self-determining with respect to one's desires or reasons.[40] However implausible or uninteresting these suggestions may look to professional philosophers, they represent natural attempts to substantiate a fundamental view about freedom, according to which one's decisions can be truly free even if one's motives are determined (not self-determined).[41] They are not merely examples of what P. F. Strawson calls the "panicky metaphysics" of theoretical philosophical libertarianism.[42] For they are also centrally representative of those vague, ill-formed theories that have a crucial role in structuring our attitude to the notion of freedom. This alone is sufficient reason to set them down. They are important to anyone concerned with the cognitive phenomenology of freedom, and anyone seriously concerned with the philosophical problem of freedom must be concerned with the cognitive phenomenology of freedom.[43]

Optimists may be undeterred by these difficulties. They may say that it is obvious that self-determination as to desire is impossible, and deny that it is needed for freedom. They may be sure that there is still room for some freedom-founding power of ultimate choice, in any particular case of action, which is untouched as a foundation for freedom by the argument for the impossibility of self-determination as to desire. They may gesture at the phenomenological self-evidence of the could-have-done-otherwiseness of choice, decision, and action. Or again, they may appeal to the phenomenon of 'identification' with one's desires, holding that one can by some mysterious (regress-stopping) act of identification with one's desires take over true responsibility for them, and that one can do so even though one cannot be ultimately self-determining with respect to them.[44]

[40] They may well express their grasp of the fact that such self-determination is impossible in terms of the familiar idea that one is the way one is as a result of one's heredity and environment.

[41] This natural view is discussed further in 3.1 and 3.6 below.

[42] 'Freedom and Resentment', p. 25.

[43] See Appendix B, for another philosophically natural but untenable view. Note that the views discussed here make uncritical use of a notion of the self (or 'agent-self') that is itself open to well-known philosophical objections of a sort recently discussed by D. Parfit in *Reasons and Persons*—objections that gain purchase independently of problems that arise when one tries to give an account of how such an 'agent-self' might be free.

[44] As does Frankfurt—see n. 2. From the present perspective his theory is most usefully seen as a vivid dramatization of certain aspects of the 'cognitive phenomenology' of freedom, for it is inadequate as an account of true responsibility.

The detailed arguments against the acceptability of this last suggestion are just variants on the arguments already given in 2.8-2.10, and will not be set out here. These arguments may look unimportant because they are arguments against positions that few are likely to admit to holding. Their point becomes fully apparent only when one begins to see (*a*) the extent to which they underlie our common pre-philosophical thought about freedom, and (*b*) how many philosophical (libertarian) views of freedom can be forced back into the positions against which these arguments are directed. I suggest that no genuinely libertarian theory of freedom (one that meets the constraint described in 2.2) can deliver any substantive account of freedom or true responsibility without becoming vulnerable to these arguments; and in becoming vulnerable to these arguments it ceases to be plausible.

As for appeals to the experience of freedom or true responsibility— well, we certainly do have such experience; and possession of a disposition to have such experience may even be a necessary condition of true responsibility, as the Subjectivists (1.5.4) suggest. But even if this is so, it does not follow that there are any sufficient conditions of true responsibility. And the fact that we have and perhaps cannot help having such experience does not enable us to avoid the question as to whether it is actually veridical. Here it has been argued that it cannot be shown to be veridical, either by appeal to indeterminism or indeed in any other way, because true self-determination is both necessary for freedom and logically impossible.

2.11 RESTATEMENT AND CONCLUSION

Libertarians have to give indeterminism a place in their detailed account of the nature of action-production; and they also have to show how the indeterminism they postulate makes actions free. Two different possible points of entry for indeterminism into the process of action-production have been considered (in 2.8, and in 2.9-2.10). Neither would do; neither could provide for self-determination. And it does not look as if there are any others that can escape the sorts of problems that these two encountered. It seems clear that we cannot be truly self-determining in the way that still seems essential for true responsibility, even if determinism is false. Consider, finally, a general restatement of the argument.

1. If there is such a thing as human freedom, it is on account of our

action that we may be called free. It is not a property that we can display in some purely spiritual manner. Nor is it a property, like physical beauty, that we can ascribe without reference to (mental or physical) actions. It is a property that must manifest itself in or through our actions, if at all. A creature incapable of self-change, mental or physical, is in no sense free in the present sense, even though it be a free spirit enjoying civil liberties.

2. It is clear that our psychical states (or events in our psyches) may properly be said to determine—to be the producing condition of—what we do, in any case in which we act advisedly and in which there is a true rational explanation of what we do.[45] If, then, we are free, truly responsible agents, we must, whatever our nature, stand in such relation to these psychical states (or events or processes) that we have at least some partial control over, and responsibility for, them. Whatever this relation is (even if it is the relation of identity, or of whole to part), it must be such that we ourselves are on account of it responsible for some part at least of the actual cause, determinant, or producing condition of any action that is rightly called free. At some point in the account of the production of the action, the free agent must figure either as truly responsible for (at least) part of the producing condition of the action, or as itself part of the producing condition.

3. What, then, is the relation between the agent, *a*, and the psychical states that must be granted to determine his actions, which is such that he and his actions are free? This is the question we get when we choose to describe action-production in this particular way, denominating psychical states as the determinants or producing conditions of actions, in order to articulate the matter. (If we denominate *a* himself as the determiner or producing condition of actions, it comes to the same thing in the end. For then we have to ask what his relation is to those of his features which are such that he performs the actions he does perform in virtue of his possession of them.) Having first in-compatibilistically assumed that *a*'s psychical states cannot be wholly

---

[45] Recall that to say this is in no way to suggest that the psychical states are in some way independent of, or in potential opposition to, the agent whose states they are, or that they determine the agent's action independently of the agent himself (cf. 2.3.3). Nor is it to presuppose the causal theory of action, except in so far as the theory is trivially true; it is just barest common sense. Nor is it to deny that actions done on the spur of the moment, without conscious aforethought, or in a purely habitual manner, can be counted as free actions. Nor is it to deny that materialism may be true.

determined, we consider what sort of true-responsibility-creating relation *a* may be supposed to have to his psychical states if *indeterminism*
is true. But it soon appears that indeterminism cannot help at all. For
the requisite relation must be such that *a* is radically *self*-determining
with respect to certain at least of his psychical states. And this is
impossible even if indeterminism is true. The attempt to characterize
some such self-determination leads to infinite regress.[46] One cannot
ultimately choose one's psychical condition; we cannot describe this.
It's not simply that we don't know how to, but that we know we cannot.
Not even God could be truly self-determining as to his motives for
action; nor therefore could he be truly responsible for what he did in
any ultimate way.[47]

It may now be suggested that people are properly held responsible
simply because we may in effect *identify* them, *qua* rational agents
considered in their mental aspect, with their desires or motives. This
suggestion is perfectly reasonable, and may be developed in several
ways, but it cannot escape the problem of the impossibility of self-
determination. To be truly responsible for his actions, *a* will still have
to be truly responsible for himself in the impossible way, in certain
respects, at least.

Another suggestion may be that *a* is truly responsible for his actions
just because the reasons that determine his actions are indeed *his* and
nobody else's in the normal case, when he is not subject to any sort of
psychical constraint. But although *a* is in this case master of his *fate*,
proprietor of what is fated for him so far as character and motivation
are concerned, he is not truly the *master* of his fate, conatively autogen-

---

[46] Suppose one could choose a new character and have it installed by a hypnotist.
Would this be a route to freedom? It would not be, if freedom involves true self-
determination, because one would not be self-determining with respect to the principles
of choice that moved one to choose the new character one did choose (cf. n. 32). One
might feel that this would not matter—our feelings about the conditions of freedom
are changeable and inconsistent, and only some of them support the demand for true
self-determination. One might think: one big choice of character, and after that one is
on one's own, truly responsible for what one does. But the reasons for being dissatisfied
with this idea will always return in the end. And it cannot of course be any part of an
explanation of how we as we actually are here and now are truly responsible.

[47] While Spinoza holds that God is the "free cause" of the world (cf. *Ethics*, Pt. 1,
Prop. XVII, Coroll. II), he also states that "God . . . cannot be said . . . to act from
freedom of the will" (Pt. 1, Prop. XXXII, Corolls. I and II). And it seems that he holds
God to be a 'free' cause simply in the sense of not being caused or determined by
anything else. No sort of true responsibility follows from this.

ous, *causa sui* with respect to character and motivation. This is the essential (and obvious) impossibility, this, too, the thing that it still seems (obviously) right (and yet foolish) to require for desert-entailing freedom.

I conclude that (Objectivist) libertarians can give no satisfactory positive answer to the question 'In what quality of an agent, choice, action, or will does its being a free agent, choice, action, or will consist?'—given that it is our ordinary, strong notion of true-responsibility-entailing freedom that is in question. The general conclusions of this chapter are not essentially dependent on the particular view of the nature of reasons and rational explanation adopted in 2.3.

It should be clear that (Objectivist) compatibilists can do no better, so far as providing an account of true-responsibility-entailing freedom is concerned. Nearly all compatibilists would agree that this is so, as remarked in 2.1. Compatibilists can however benefit from the above argument against libertarianism. For if it helps to show that assuming the falsity of determinism can never be of any positive use in the attempt to describe how it is that we are free, it must simultaneously help to make it clear that whatever kind of freedom we can reasonably hope to establish, it must be compatible with determinism—or, in other words, that if it is right to say that we are free then compatibilism must be true.

And yet it seems that it must be reasonable to hope to be able to establish the reality of something we are convinced we have: true-responsibility-entailing freedom of the kind compatibilists must reject as impossible. And so it goes on—the oscillation of intuition (cf. note 30). Much of what follows can be seen as an illustration of this oscillation, rather than a direct commentary upon it. But there are also passages of direct commentary upon it (in 4, 5.3, 6.4–6.5, and 14.6–14.8, for example).

So far, then, it seems that (upper-case) Objectivism cannot deliver any satisfactory positive theory of freedom. Although it may seem obvious that Subjectivism is inherently unsatisfactory, and can do no better, I turn now to consideration of Subjectivist theories of freedom.

It will be convenient to have a name for those who believe *both* that self-determination is necessary for freedom *and* that it is impossible. The name is not ideal, but I will call them the 'non-self-determinationists'.

3

Kant and Commitment

3.1 COMMITMENT THEORIES: THEIR STRUCTURE

The next four chapters do not develop a connected argument. Instead they respond to the argument of Chapter 2 by considering the prospects for Subjectivist theories in a piecemeal way, and by accumulating a number of points about the nature and causes of our experience of freedom. This chapter offers a general statement of the characteristic aims of commitment theorists, and then suggests that Kant attempted to put forward some sort of Subjectivist, commitment theory of freedom—a theory to the effect that we are free partly in virtue of the fact that we cannot but believe that we are.[1] *En passant*, it argues that non-moral agents can be free agents, if any agents can be (3.3), and makes a suggestion about the deepest source of our commitment to belief in freedom (3.6).

A commitment theory of freedom might have three main parts. It might first seek to show

(1) why belief in freedom is inevitable given certain forms of experience—the forms of experience being specified without reference to the fact that they give rise to belief in freedom.

Belief in freedom might for example be argued to be inevitable for a being that experiences itself as something possessed of a will, or power of choice, that is in some manner independent of, i.e. not merely a determinate if complex function of, its particular pro-attitudes or motives generally considered. Belief in freedom might be argued to be inevitable for a being that experiences itself, considered as decider and deliberator, as something which is in some way essentially over and above all its particular motives, and which is therefore capable of

[1] Although he often takes himself to be attempting the merely negative task of showing that freedom is not a contradictory concept given deterministic causality in the phenomenal or empirical realm. Cf., e.g., *Fundamental Principles of the Metaphysic of Morals*, *Ak.* IV. 456–9 (trans. H. J. Paton, pp. 124–7, Harper and Row edn., trans. T. K. Abbott, pp. 73–7, Bobbs–Merrill edn.); *Critique of Practical Reason, Ak.* V. 46 (trans. T. K. Abbott, p. 135, trans. L. W. Beck, p. 47); *Critique of Pure Reason*, B585–6.

making decisions independently of, and in the light of, those motives. Such a picture of the self may not be a true picture of anything that could actually exist.[2] But it may still be a true picture of how a being can *seem* to itself to be. After all, most human beings see themselves in this way, more or less consciously. And the fact that this is so is crucial to the human phenomenology of freedom.

Secondly, a commitment theory might seek to show

(2) that we, human beings, do standardly have some such form of experience as is described in (1).

From (1) and (2) a commitment theory can deduce that we must believe that we are free.

Thus far it is merely a theory about commitment to belief in freedom; it is a theory about the nature of causes of such commitment. It becomes a commitment theory *of freedom* in moving on to claim

(3) that we are free, and are so essentially partly because we not only do believe we are free, but also cannot help believing we are.[3]

It does not, of course, claim that belief in freedom is by itself sufficient for freedom, but only that it is sufficient given the fulfilment of certain other conditions (see (iv) below).

A fourth part of a full commitment theory might seek to show in detail

(4) why we have, and perhaps must have,[4] a form of experience of the kind specified in (1).

(4) might lead back into the theory of evolution, and into genetic psychology.

A commitment-theoretic argument might thus have the following general structure:

(i) Every being that has X-type experience of self believes that it is a free agent (cf. (1)).

(ii) a has X-type experience of self (cf.(2)).

Therefore

(iii) a believes that he is a free agent.

[2] See 2.9–2.10 above, and 9.4 and Appendix E below.

[3] I take it that all commitment theories claim that if we are free we are so essentially partly in virtue of believing we are, and that they are therefore Subjectivist theories.

[4] At no point need it be claimed that all human beings must have a form of experience which is such that they must believe they are free. The claim need only be that, having such and such a form of experience, people must believe they are free; and that they do in fact have such a form of experience.

(iv) *a* is *Y* (*Y* being a specification of a set of further properties necessary but not sufficient for being a free agent, such as the properties of being a purposive agent, and being self-conscious).

(v) Every being that believes it is free, and is *Y*, is indeed free (cf.(3)).

Therefore

(vi) *a* is a free agent.

A commitment-theoretic rider might be added:

(vii) Every being that is of kind *Z* has, or comes to have, *X*-type experience of self (cf.(4)).

This may not look very promising; (3), and so (v), are fundamentally paradoxical. But then—I submit—nor does anything else. Questions about (3) and (v) are considered in more detail in Part III. Here it is worth observing that commitment theorists are not 'as if' theorists, whose position is quite distinct. 'As if' theorists may make a variety of claims. They may claim that whatever the case may be with regard to conventional (Objectivist) theories, or commitment theories, we would do well to live our lives *as if* we were free. Or their claim may be the Kantian-sounding one that to live our lives as if we were free is a practical or moral necessity—a necessary supposition of pure moral-practical (as opposed to purely theoretico-speculative) reason. But the 'as if' clause suggests the possibility of exercising *choice* about the adoption of belief in freedom as a regulative principle for one's conduct; and the Subjectivist commitment theorists, whose greatest regret may be that they have not been able to find a satisfactory Objectivist theory, are likely not only to deny that there can be any such question of choice, but also to react with Sidgwickian contempt to the (to them) facile compromising of the 'as if' theorists:

I cannot fall back on the resource of thinking of myself under a moral necessity to regard all my duties *as if they were* commandments of God, although not entitled to hold speculatively that any such Supreme Being exists. I am so far from feeling bound to believe for purposes of practice what I see no ground for holding as a speculative truth, that I cannot even conceive the state of mind which these words seem to describe, except as a momentary half-wilful irrationality, committed in a violent access of philosophic despair.[5]

---

[5] H. Sidgwick, *The Methods of Ethics* (seventh edition), p. 507.

3.2 'NEUTRAL' AND 'RATIONAL' FREEDOM

"Freedom is a mere *idea*, the objective reality of which can in no way be shown according to laws of nature."[6] One who says this gives us reason to suppose that any positive theory of freedom that he may put forward will be of a special character.[7] As is well known, Kant sought to ground the possibility of freedom of the will in the unknowable noumenal self, in a way that showed freedom to be compatible with the holding of (deterministic) laws of nature in the 'empirically real' world. Here I wish to suggest that Kant also tries to establish our freedom in another way, a way connected to but distinguishable from his argument to freedom from consciousness of the moral law. In particular, I wish to suggest that he advances a kind of commitment theory of freedom, holding not only that we really are free in the ordinary strong sense, but also that this is partly because we cannot help regarding ourselves as free, given that we are rational (and self-conscious) beings.

Such a suggestion is not only paradoxical, it is also directly in conflict with some of Kant's (dauntingly complex) views. Certain caveats and restrictions are called for, therefore. The first is this: that I will not go into the question of what exactly 'we' really are, on Kant's view—noumenal selves, or whatever. I shall take it that we are what we think we are, human beings with real physical bodies. Secondly, I will be concerned with Kant's theory of freedom only in so far as it is simply a theory of freedom to choose, a theory of 'liberty of indifference', a theory according to which *a choice of the morally worse of two options may be a truly free choice*.[8] I will not be concerned with Kant's other conception of freedom, according to which a rational agent's action is truly free only if it is in accordance with reason, or Reason, or the Moral Law; for according to this second conception, a truly free choice is always a morally correct choice. Kant tried to combine these two lines of thought, but they are for the most part pretty clearly distinguishable. In Sidgwick's terms, present concern is with Kant's theory

---

[6] *Fundamental Principles*, *Ak*. IV. 459 (Paton 127, Abbott 76).

[7] Especially when he says such things, close to the incompatibilist's heart, as "what we wish to understand, and will never understand, is how *predeterminism*, according to which voluntary [*willkürliche*] actions, as events, have their determining grounds *in antecedent time*, can be consistent with freedom" (*Religion within the Limits of Reason Alone*, *Ak*. VI. 49–50 (trans. T. M. Greene and H. H. Hudson, p. 45 n.)).

[8] A theory of liberty of spontaneity, standardly opposed to a theory of liberty of indifference, could also, of course, hold that a choice of the morally worse of two options was a free choice. For the distinction, see J. Thorp, *Free Will*, pp. 5–7.

of "Neutral" (or "Moral") freedom of choice, rather than with his theory of "Good" or "Rational" freedom.[9]

3.3 NON-MORAL FREEDOM

Kant's claim that we necessarily think of ourselves as free, or 'have the Idea of' (our own) freedom, is closely bound up with his claim that having the Idea of one's own freedom is (or presupposes) being aware of the self-given moral law: 'the moral law is the only condition under which freedom can be known'.[10] But, taken in one very natural way, this last claim seems false: it seems that a being that is a rational agent in all ordinary senses of this phrase can acquire the idea of its own freedom (and can have a form of experience which is such that it cannot but form the idea of its own freedom) without having any sort of specifically moral sense at all. Its circumstances may be such that it has acquired no sort of moral habit of thought, but has vivid and repeated experience of being able to do two incompatible desirable things, and of deliberating as to which to do—experience of precisely the kind that can give rise to the characteristic absolute sense of being able to choose freely. If one considers the matter independently of Kant's theory for a moment, it seems obvious that a grasp of moral notions is not necessary for having the idea of oneself as free, even if it is sufficient.[11]

Nor is a grasp of moral notions necessary for freedom itself. We certainly do not think that our non-moral choices or actions are in some way less free than our morally weighted choices or actions; if we are free at all, we are as free in the former as we are in the latter. But it seems clear that a being with no grasp of moral notions at all could be at least as free in its (uniformly) non-moral actions as we are in our non-moral actions—we may suppose that it has a vivid and fully self-conscious sense of facing choices, and so on. And it follows that it

---

[9] Sidgwick, op. cit., pp. 511–16.

[10] *Critique of Practical Reason, Ak.* V. 4 (Abbott 88 n., Beck 4 n.). Kant claims that consciousness of the moral law is not only necessary for knowledge of freedom, but also sufficient, for "if there were no freedom, the moral law would never have been encountered in us". Hence it is the *ratio cognoscendi* of freedom, the means by which we know we are free.

[11] One cannot plausibly argue, against this, that language, and, hence, membership of a community, is necessary for freedom because necessary for self-consciousness, and that membership of a community of self-conscious agents is in turn sufficient for acquisition of a grasp of moral notions; so that freedom does after all indirectly entail a grasp of moral notions. For, first, a solitary, self-conscious, linguistically endowed rational agent could logically possibly be created by divine fiat, or occur by chance; second, it seems that there could possibly be a community of self-conscious, rational agents with no grasp of moral notions (cf. 6.5 below).

could be as free as we are *tout court*. Generally, if an agent's choice (or action) is free, then, intuitively, this is simply a matter of the choice's (or action's) being *genuinely up to the agent*, in such a way that the agent is truly responsible for it.[12] And whether or not the choice or action is morally weighted is entirely irrelevant to whether or not it is genuinely up to the agent in this way. It is not irrelevant on Kant's theory (or on parts of it, at least). But, given the avowedly Procrustean nature of the present discussion of Kant, it is profitable to try to diminish the role that he gives to the moral law in his theory of freedom to as great an extent as possible, and to see what remains.

In *Religion within the Limits of Reason Alone* Kant explicitly rejects the suggestion that experience of radical freedom to choose is independent of experience of specifically moral obligation.[13] He states quite specifically that "the concept of the freedom of the will [of *Willkür*, 'neutral' freedom of choice] does not precede the consciousness of the moral law in us but is deduced [i.e. derived by us] from [our experience of] the determinability of our will [*Willkür*] by this law as an unconditional command."[14] But his argument for this is rather shaky, and does not undercut the present suggestion that an entirely non-moral being could have "consciousness of the freedom of the will" in essentially just the same way as we do, experiencing things as being entirely up to it in such a way that it is truly responsible for what it does.

3.4 'WILL' AND 'DESIRE'

Before stating Kant's commitment theory, it is worth commenting briefly on his use of the words 'will' and 'desire'.

1. *Will*. When Kant says that, as a rational agent, one believes that one possesses a "will, that is, . . . a faculty distinct from desire",[15] he means, as often as not, that one believes that one is able to 'determine oneself to action' (purely) in accordance with Reason, and, in particular, in accordance with the self-imposed moral law. But to say that one believes oneself to possess a will distinct from desire may also be to say

---

[12] Whatever exactly this involves.

[13] Independent not only in that one can have the former without the latter *in a particular case* (even if the converse is not true), but also in that there is no *general* genetic (ontogenetic) dependence of the former on the latter.

[14] *Religion*, *Ak*. VI. 49 (Greene and Hudson, 45 n.). Cf. also *Critique of Pure Reason*, Bxxxii–xxxiii, and *Critique of Practical Reason*, *Ak*. V. 30 (Abbott 119, Beck 30).

[15] *Fundamental Principles*, *Ak*. IV. 459 (Paton 127, Abbott 76).

something simpler and more plausible than this. It may be to say simply that one believes oneself conscious of having a will or power of choice that is distinct from all particular given motives *of whatever sort*, moral or non-moral; one believes oneself to possess a power of determining oneself to action that operates independently of any and all of one's particular given motives or reasons for action;[16] a power of deciding how to act which is such that one's choices are not necessarily some possibly complex but nevertheless inevitably determinate function of one's particular motives, but are 'up to one' in a way that is incompatible with their being some such determinate function.

Certainly we do normally and more or less unreflectively believe ourselves to have such a will, and such a power—as remarked in 3.1.[17] These terms just provide one way among others of describing the characteristic form of our experience of ourselves as free agents. One might say, in Kantian phrase, that we believe ourselves to have a will that is autonomous (or a 'law to itself') just in so far as it fits the description of the will just given, and not because of any sense that we have of ourselves specifically as moral beings.[18] The common experience of being autonomous in this sense seems to be quite independent of any experience that might be said to involve recognition of the moral law in Kant's sense.[19]

2. *Desire*. I suggest that we do no violence to Kant's essential intent in taking the word 'desire', in his use, to stand quite generally for 'determined motive'; that is, motive with respect to the having of which one is determined by something other than oneself, or 'heteronomously determined'.

3.5 KANT'S COMMITMENT THEORY

The elements of Kant's (or 'Kant's') commitment theory are as follows. Having first said that freedom is a 'mere idea', Kant goes on to say

[16] Among motives we may include beliefs that actions are right, and motives that have the character of being apprehensions of duty.

[17] Cf. Hume, *Treatise*, p. 408: "We feel that our actions are subject to our will on most occasions, and imagine we feel that the will itself is subject to nothing. . . ."

[18.] This can be so even if we cannot show that such a will could actually exist, and even if we can show that such a will could not exist—cf. 2.9 and 2.10.

[19] To phrase things in terms of *the will* is to give a quasi-impersonal account of this fundamental feature of our experience of agency. In a way this is unnatural, and it may be better to say that the central phenomenological fact is rather that one is a law to *oneself* in being *oneself* a thing that is somehow over and above all one's particular motives. After all, the will does not feature as a separate mental thing in one's experience, separate from oneself. The basic belief is simply that *I* am, as a choosing and acting being, somehow autonomous whatever my given desires and motives in any particular case.

that this idea of freedom

(I) "holds good only as a *necessary hypothesis of reason* in a being that *believes* itself conscious of a will, that is, of a faculty distinct from mere desire".[20]

That is, for any being *x*, if

(*a*) *x* believes itself "conscious of a will . . . distinct from . . . desire"

then

(*b*) *x* necessarily believes that it is free.

(This corresponds to step (i) in the commitment-theoretic argument set out in 3.1 above: a certain form of experience X, i.e. that which is involved in believing that one has a will distinct from desire, gives rise inevitably to a belief in freedom.)

Kant also says

(II) that "every being that cannot act except *under the idea of* freedom [i.e., in the terms of (I), every being for whom the idea of freedom is a necessary hypothesis of reason] is *just for that reason* from a practical point of view really free".[21]

That is, for any being *x*, if

(*b*) *x* is such that it necessarily believes that it is free

then

(*c*) *x* really is free (from a practical point of view).

(This corresponds to step (v) in the commitment-theoretic argument set out in 3.2: the conditions *Y* mentioned in (v) are, for Kant, the conditions of being a self-conscious rational agent; as such, they are identical to the conditions *Z* mentioned in (vii).)

Notice that Kant does not here say that the idea of freedom is a necessary hypothesis of reason in a being that *has* a faculty of will distinct from desire, but only that it is a necessary hypothesis of reason in a being that *believes* itself conscious of such a faculty. Thus it is not as if the actual possession of some mysterious faculty is being required; only belief that one possesses some such faculty is being required. And no reference has been made to the moral law.

In fact, though, Kant does connect the notion of the will distinct

---

[20] *Ak.* IV. 459 (Paton 127, Abbott 76); my emphasis.

[21] *Ak.* IV. 448 (Paton 115, Abbott 64); second emphasis mine. (There is indefinite scope for quotation and counter-quotation, in support of different interpretations; my concern is to pick out one strand of Kant's thought.)

from desire with the moral law. For he goes on to say that a faculty of will distinct from desire is a "faculty of determining oneself to action . . . by laws of reason independently of natural instincts". And by laws of reason he means, in effect, the moral law (or the maxims derived from it). Still, it was suggested in 3.4 that one can plausibly understand the notion of a will distinct from desire in such a way that belief that one has such a will does not necessarily involve any sort of moral awareness, or consciousness of the moral law. And we may adopt this suggestion here. This duly yields a 'naturalized' version of (I) in which the phrase 'will distinct from desire' is understood to involve no reference to the moral law.

What, then, of (I)—(I) naturalized—and (II)? Together they entail that any being that believes itself conscious of a will distinct from desire is (from a practical point of view) really free: for (*a*) believing oneself conscious of having such a will entails (*b*) believing one is free, and being unable not to believe this, and (*b*) entails (*c*) really being free—so far as acting is concerned. ("So far as acting is concerned" corresponds to Kant's "from a practical point of view".) But—it might be said—we are when concerned with freedom principally concerned with actions. And if we are really free with respect to our actions then we are indeed really free; and if not, not. One cannot escape the consequences of asserting that we are free agents by adding 'from a practical point of view'. To say that we are really free from a practical point of view is to go further than saying merely that we cannot help thinking we are free, when we act. It is to say that we really are free when we act. It looks, then, as if Kant has proposed a straightforward positive theory of freedom.

3.6 THE INESCAPABILITY OF BELIEF IN FREEDOM

(II) is the crucial step in Kant's argument, and it is worth trying to bring out something of the immense plausibility—from one perspective, at least—of the suggestion that belief in one's freedom is sufficient for actual freedom, given that one is an ordinary (unhypnotized)[22] self-conscious rational agent. (Its immense implausibility from other perspectives will not be considered here.)

Consider the following simple case of a man, *a*, an ordinary self-

---

[22] A man might be subject to post-hypnotic command, or something like it, in such a way that he believed himself free to choose either X or Y, but was in fact unable not to choose ('choose') X.

conscious rational agent. *a* has a general conception of himself as a free agent. He faces a button. The good and bad consequences of pressing it or not pressing it, in the next twenty minutes, are finely balanced and momentously different. Nothing constrains him. It is (it seems) quite clear to him that he is able to choose freely. But then surely he *is ipso facto* able to choose freely? He may be familiar with determinism, and believe it is true. But, he reflects, although he will, as soon as the twenty minutes are up, be able to say truly that what he did was determined, that in no way changes the fact that he now knows that he is able, now, to choose completely freely. It is (it seems) an inescapable fact, for him, that this is so. Suppose that the choice is a very difficult and painful one. What may oppress him most is precisely his (seeming) knowledge that he cannot escape the choice or his absolute freedom with regard to it: it is his to make and he must make it.

This is the heart of freedom as an 'experiential fact'. It is the central fact of the phenomenology of freedom. It is above all the (frequent) occurrence in our everyday lives of situations essentially like this one that makes it seem so impossible that we should ever cease to believe that we are free.[23] And the notion of moral responsibility doesn't have to be mentioned at all. Difficult choices, one could say, are the fundamental experiential guarantors of the belief in freedom. (Note that this reflection belongs to part (1) of the commitment theory sketched in 3.1.)

Now imagine *a*'s situation to be identical, except for the fact that he does *not* have any general conception of himself as a free or truly responsible agent. (Kant, of course, holds that this is impossible, given that *a* is a self-conscious rational agent.) Suppose that he has no conception at all of what it is to be a free agent. Well, then, it seems that he cannot *be* free: it seems that an agent cannot be held to be free in the performance of, or truly responsible for, an action, in the normal strong sense, if, when acting, it has no sort of conception of itself as so free or responsible. If this is so, then *a*'s possession of the idea of freedom is certainly *necessary* for his freedom, whether or not it is also sufficient, given his other properties, as Kant's (or 'Kant's') commitment theory of freedom suggests. And if so, no theory of freedom can be correct unless it is a Subjectivist theory. (This claim is discussed at length in Part III.)

---

[23] But see 14.8, where this is questioned.

3.7 ANOTHER APPROACH

At one point Kant ties the commitment-theoretic approach in with his metaphysics of the noumenon. But he does so in a way that suggests that he may have conceived the commitment-theoretic line to be in some way more fundamental than the noumenal-metaphysical line. For he asserts that "the idea of freedom [which is a necessary hypothesis for me] *makes me* a member of an intelligible [or noumenal] world".[24] He seems strongly attracted by the idea that it is simply having the idea of one's own freedom that really matters for freedom—given, of course, that one is a rational agent. And he seems to be reasoning in the following slightly peculiar way: since true freedom is evidently impossible for a merely empirical being, given determinism, and possible only for an unconditioned, intelligible, or noumenal being, and since belief in freedom is sufficient for freedom, in a rational being, it must be the case that belief in freedom actually *makes* me a member of the intelligible or noumenal world. Kant also says that a rational being is "involuntarily forced [to] . . . transfer . . . [itself] to the point of view of a member of the intelligible world . . . by the idea of freedom": it is forced to do this simply because it believes it is a free agent.[25] Significantly, it seems, Kant moves in successive paragraphs from the claim that "a rational being must *regard* [itself] . . . as belonging . . . *qua* intelligence . . . to the intelligible world" to the claim that man, "as a rational being . . . consequently *belong*[s] to the intelligible world"; as if thinking it is so can actually suffice to make it so (from a practical point of view).[26]

It may be unjust to attribute the reasoning set out above to Kant. But there is clearly some havering going on. It may be suggested that his views on freedom had by the time he wrote the *Grundlegung* evolved, in certain respects, beyond the point at which appeal to the noumenal had much part to play in them. On the other hand, he would doubtless

---

[24] *Ak*. IV. 454 (Paton 122, Abbott 71); my emphasis.

[25] *Ak*. IV. 455 (Paton 122, Abbott 72).

[26] *Ak*. IV. 452 (Paton 120, Abbott 69); my emphasis. Against this should be set the fact that Kant later (458, 126, 75) remarks that the concept of the intelligible or noumenal world is "only a *point of view* which reason finds itself constrained to take up outside the appearances *in order to conceive itself as practical*". But elsewhere (e.g. 453, 121, 70–1) the intelligible world is presented as something much more solid, metaphysically speaking (thinkable and in some sense real, even if not knowable in the way that the world of sense is); as something which "*contains the ground of the sensible world*". And it is in the paragraph after the paragraph containing these words that Kant says, *sans phrase*, that (my possession of) "the Idea of freedom makes me a member of the intelligible world".

have been quite unprepared to tolerate the metaphysical insubstantiality, so to speak, of the purely commitment-theoretic approach, and would thus have wished to retain the noumenal metaphysics as serving, in some avowedly incomprehensible way, to ground and substantiate our freedom.

3.8 A SUBJECTIVIST CONCLUSION

The line of thought sketched above leads to the conclusion that we are free, and are so—this is the specifically Subjectivist claim—essentially partly because we believe we are. Commitment theorists go one step further in claiming that we are free essentially partly because we cannot but believe we are, not merely because we just do happen to believe it. Kant appears to be attracted by this step. It is clearly important to him that we cannot but believe it, that it is a *necessary* hypothesis of reason for us. It gives a kind of objectivity to freedom, where firm metaphysical grounding is not to be had.

Subjectivists (and *a fortiori* commitment theorists) are committed to the claim that to cease to believe one is free is *eo ipso* to cease to *be* free—if one is free at all, that is.[27] Thus suppose there is a being that can truly be said to be a free agent: if it then becomes a *genuine* incompatibilist determinist,[28] or non-self-determinationist, it will thereby cease to be free—in ceasing to believe it is free. This corollary is not necessarily unpalatable to the Subjectivists, however. For they may have good independent arguments to support it (these were touched on at the end of 3.6, and are discussed in Part III below). And they are aware, in any case, that radical measures are required if our freedom is to be demonstrated. It is clear to them that no conventional, Objectivist, compatibilist or libertarian theory can establish that we are free in the ordinary sense of the word, the sense according to which if we are free then we can be truly responsible for our actions.

The principal difficulty with the attempt to prove that all such Objectivist theories must fail is the great number of different descriptive frames within which the problem can be discussed, the many senses of the word 'free', and the correspondingly multifarious and inconsistent

---

[27] Subjectivists may claim that belief in freedom is necessary for freedom while denying that anything is actually sufficient.

[28] As opposed to a merely *theoretical* incompatibilist determinist, who holds this view merely as a philosopher. I take it that there are not many genuine incompatibilist determinists about—if any. Cf. 6.2.

hintings of intuition.[29] But if conventional Objectivist compatibilism and libertarianism cannot give us what we think or find we want—two millennia of debate give considerable support to the view that they cannot—then it seems worth while examining the prospects for Subjectivist theories, hopeless as they may seem. It may be that such examination will only turn up some other necessary conditions of freedom, and will fail to provide a set of necessary and sufficient conditions. This question will be considered in Part III.

Another particular commitment theory will be considered in Chapter 5. First, though, some very general reflections on Subjectivist and commitment theories, and on what they make of the notion of truth.

[29] Though it can seem obvious to any first-year student that they must fail.

4
Commitment, Illusion, and Truth

4.1 DOUBLE STANDARDS

It seems that human beings cannot help believing they are free agents, in the ordinary, strong, true-responsibility-entailing sense of the word. Commitment theorists are rightly impressed by this fact, and treat it as a possible foundation for a positive theory of freedom. At the most general level, they think like this: even if freedom has no demonstrable 'objective reality', as Kant held, it may be seriously inadequate simply to dismiss it as a mere illusion, if it is really an inescapable illusion, given our nature and the form that our experience has given our nature. It is true that the arguments that it can have no objective reality look very strong. But perhaps the whole conception of objectivity and truth that these arguments presuppose needs to be questioned.

The idea that a certain view may be inescapable and therefore somehow permissible or even correct, despite the fact that we are apparently able to get into a position in which we can see it to be false—or so we think—is very problematic.[1] Surely "irresistibility does not entail truth"—even species-wide irresistibility?[2] It is easy, furthermore, to be dissatisfied with a simple 'two standpoints' view, according to which we really are free *from the point of view* of practice and action, but are really not free from the point of view of theory and science (such a view is sometimes attributed to Kant, and has been endorsed in various

[1] Compatibilists who think that they have simply avoided this problem should think again. It is true that they nearly all hold that true-responsibility-entailing freedom is impossible; but they nearly all continue to behave in everyday life as if they firmly believed in it.

[2] Bernard Williams, *Descartes*, p. 187; we can make sense of the idea that a whole species should be so constituted that its members cannot but believe that *p* although it is not the case that *p*. Another suggestion about irresistibility is the Kantian-sounding suggestion that belief in freedom may be irresistible for all rational agents. For a non-Kantian version of this view, see 3.6. For an attempt to challenge it, see chs. 12–14. For a modern version of it, see N. Denyer, *Time, Action and Necessity*, pp. 63–6 and 93–6. Denyer goes so far as to argue that because rational agents have to assume that determinism is false when deliberating about what to do, it must therefore actually be false (accepting, in effect, that irresistibility can entail truth). But he omits, crucially, to offer an account of how indeterminism can help to make us free.

forms by others). Commitment theorists may not explicitly adopt such a view, but it is not clear that they do not implicitly make use of some dubious two-standpoints double standard.

Is there any way of making the problem less acute? Clearly the notion of freedom has complex conceptual linkages. In an attempt to assess the best response to this complexity it may help to shift discussion on to a more tentative level for a time.

One might first suggest that attributions of the predicates 'free' and 'unfree' are answerable to two different sorts of things. They are answerable both to what might (very roughly) be called experience-independent or non-experiential facts about the world—such as facts about agents' capacities and circumstances and facts about the impossibility of true self-determination—and to what one might call 'experiential facts': 'facts' which are facts only in the sense that they are integral parts of unrenounceable "forms of life" (in Wittgenstein's phrase) or are objects of inescapable "natural beliefs" (in Hume's sense) about the world—beliefs, in particular, about actions, decisions, choices, deliberations, and intentions.

To suggest this is not to suggest that all facts of the first kind lead us to conclude that no beings are free, while only 'facts' of the second kind can support belief in freedom; that is patently untrue. But it is nevertheless by appealing to 'facts' of the second kind that one may attempt to resist an extremely powerful argument (of which Chapter 2 gives one version) against freedom that makes use only of facts of the first kind.

This may look like just one more 'two standpoints' approach. But the fact that we appear to have a genuine antinomy of thought or reason to face makes it seem worth continuing a little way. For many—perhaps all—of those who say they are incompatibilist determinists, or conventional Objectivist compatibilists, silently contradict themselves daily in their dealings with other people. And they do so even more in their dealings with themselves: for they naturally hold themselves to be truly responsible for what they do (recall the button described in 3.6). To this extent they are *unable* simply to dismiss the idea of freedom (or true responsibility) as mere illusion.

4.2 EXPERIENTIAL FACTS

One could characterize an 'experiential fact' as follows. Suppose I unequivocally believe, or feel, or *experience* that I am free. Then the experiential fact is what follows the 'that', i.e. 'I am free '. In such a case it is a non-experiential fact that I feel/experience that I am free, and the claim is that the fact that it is an experiential fact (for me) that I am free must at least be taken into account in deciding whether or not I am free.

Is this at all plausible? If I am deluded by a mirage of an oasis, then it is an experiential fact for me that there is an oasis there. But we do not take such an experiential fact to provide any sort of justification for the claim that there is an oasis there. The case of freedom is different in at least one crucial respect, however, if commitment theorists are right that no ordinary (human) self-conscious rational agent can fail to believe that he, or she, is free, whatever his, or her, particular perceptual relation to the world. Deluded by the mirage, one has only to move or shut one's eyes in order for the experiential fact that there is an oasis there to dissolve. But one cannot do anything similar in the case of one's belief in freedom. One cannot simply shift one's attitude at will in such a way that one immediately achieves a full and unwavering realization of the fact that freedom (in the sense of true responsibility) is an illusion.

It is true that freedom may appear impossible—obviously impossible—from a certain theoretical position. But even when one occupies that theoretical position freedom goes on being an experiential fact for one in everyday life. One may acquire knowledge of facts that explain why one has, and perhaps must have, the conviction that one is free.[3] But such knowledge need not undermine the force of one's conviction in any way: knowing why something attracts one need not diminish the feeling of attraction; nor need knowing what caused one to come to have a certain belief bring one to doubt the truth of the belief.

One might propose the following parallel between the account given of the feeling or concept of freedom, and the scientific realists' account of colour. In both cases we can, given knowledge of the nature of our constitution, discern causes of our experience (of colour and of freedom) and give reasons why we cannot possibly not experience things this way; and at the same time—though here the two cases may be thought to diverge—we can admit a sense in which the two concepts have no proper application to things as they are in themselves.

Someone might conclude from this, that just as we are *in no way*

---

[3] Some of them are discussed in 3.6 above, and 6.5 below.

wrong to see or experience—to treat—things as coloured, even though there is a sense in which things as they are in themselves are not coloured, so too we are *in no way* wrong to see or experience ourselves as free in the way that we ordinarily do. And if it is true that we are in no way wrong to see or experience ourselves as free, then it cannot be the case that belief in freedom is simply false.[4] In which case any general conception of truth or objectivity that rules otherwise must be misguided; and arguments of the sort presented in Chapter 2 must also be misguided.

4.3 APPEARANCES AND THEIR REALITY

Perhaps the last suggestion is of little help. A different analogy is furnished by Frazer's spiral—a series of concentric circles (or rather, short discontinuous black and white lines of a certain curvature arranged together in concentric circles) which, presented on a background of a certain kind, appear to form a single continuous spiral.

Looking at Frazer's spiral, one may be fully intellectually aware that it is a series of concentric circles and, picking out a particular one, one may be able to trace it round and thereby see it as a circle. But this visual aspect quickly escapes one, and one cannot in any case see the picture as a whole as a series of concentric circles, only as a spiral. One could say that it is an experiential fact (for all human beings) that it is a spiral, not a series of concentric circles. Perhaps we cannot but believe we are free in just the way in which we cannot but see Frazer's spiral as a spiral.

But what follows from this? The following development may suggest itself. Appearances may be appearances of some reality that is distinct from them, but they have their own reality, just *qua* appearances. And perhaps their reality as appearances may in some cases be as important as those other real things that they are presumed to be appearances of, when it comes to saying what is really there (i.e., perhaps our usual criteria for distinguishing what is really real and what is mere appearance relative to what is really real, need revision, in some cases). So,

---

[4] It may be questioned, however, whether this attempt to establish a sense in which we are in no way wrong to see ourselves as free permits any direct move to the claim that we are in no way wrong to treat people as truly deserving of praise and blame, reward and punishment.

for example, it is not clearly right to say that since circles are what are actually there, in Frazer's spiral, the picture is really a picture of circles. How it inescapably appears seems more important than how it is (really is, in some sense).

Suppose it is a picture whose function it is to represent something. It indubitably succeeds in representing—in being a picture of (in the non-relational sense of 'is a picture of')—a spiral. Given that one is talking about a picture, it seems that one may move directly from a

statement about how it appears to a statement about how it is: how it appears is how it is.

So too, one might in the case of experience of freedom ('experience of' corresponding to 'picture of') say that it is not clearly right to say that our experience of ourselves as free is experience of beings who are (given the non-experiential facts about determinism or non-self-determinability) not really free. Consider the parallel. What is depicted? A spiral. This really is a picture of a spiral. What is experienced? Freedom. This really is experience of freedom. It is not just experience *as of* freedom. For freedom is what is experienced.

Somewhat similarly, it might be said that a sustained hallucinatory experience as of hearing sounds qualitatively identical to some performance of Richard Strauss's *Metamorphosen* is not only just as good as really hearing *Metamorphosen*, it really is hearing it, in one clear sense—a sense which does not of course require any causal connection between Strauss and one's hallucination. So too (it might be said) having an inescapable but from one point of view apparently delusory experience of freedom is not only as good as experiencing freedom, it *is* experiencing freedom.

This is fairly flimsy stuff; if it proves anything, it may prove too much. There are some familiar ambiguities here, and many complications. Ignoring most of them one could say this: a picture may be a picture of a spiral without being a picture *of* anything in the sense in which a portrait is necessarily a picture of something that exists independently of it. Even if (even though) Frazer's spiral cannot *possibly* be an accurate picture (relationally) of a spiral that exists independently of it, it can still be true to say *sans phrase* that it, a really existing thing, is indeed a picture of a spiral. Similarly, even if experience of free agenthood cannot possibly be veridical experience of a property, free agenthood, that exists independently of it, it can still be true *sans phrase* to say that it, a really existing thing, is indeed experience of free agenthood.[5]

Problems and disanalogies remain. In the case of circles and spirals a picture-independent account can be given in geometrical terms of what it is for a figure to be objectively spiral or circular. But in the case

---

[5] One variation of this line of thought considers a three-dimensional object, rather than a picture, that produces an inescapable visual illusion. In this case, analogies between 'picture of' and 'experience of' are no longer in question. There is just a real thing of which one has an inescapably incorrect view.

of free agenthood it seems that we can give no parallel, experience-independent account of what free agenthood (i.e. true responsibility) might objectively consist in. That is precisely the present problem. But the present suggestion braves this fact. It amounts to the claim that even if there is no experience-independent objective property of freedom, to say that it cannot exist thus independently is not to say that it cannot really exist, objectively, at all: *a*'s exemplification (unrenounceably) of the objective property of experiencing himself as a free agent just is sufficient for *a*'s exemplification of the thereby really existing property of free agenthood.

Later on it will be argued that such experience is *necessary* for free agenthood. Here the suggestion that it is also sufficient is being considered. One natural objection to this is that one must also be a self-conscious rational agent—that this, at least, is also necessary for free agenthood. The present suggestion can accept this; for it can claim, plausibly, that one could not have the required experience of oneself as a free agent if one were not also and already a self-conscious rational agent.

The impossibility of self-determination remains untouched by all this, however. And it seems to be as much of a problem as before.

4.4 REALITY AND ITS APPEARANCES

It is hard to stop the movement of proposal and objection registered here; it can shift terms indefinitely. But the general objection to the present line of thought will never go away. Expressed in terms of appearance and reality, it is this: that *whatever* our experience is like, we have to grant that what appears experientially to be the case may be only appearance, in the sense in which appearance is contrasted with reality.

Against this, the present line of thought insists that it may in certain cases be permissible or indeed correct to give special weight to the appearance (especially when the appearance is inevitable and perhaps demonstrably inevitable) when the question of what is objectively or really the case is raised, even if everything that is believed about what is really the case *independently* of the appearance suggests that the appearance is not objectively speaking veridical.

The distinction between appearance and reality has been expressed in more cumbersome terms, here—in terms of 'experiential facts', and so on. This is simply because such terms seem to fit better a case in which the divergence between (*a*) the irresistibility and (*b*) the apparent indefensibility of a belief (in freedom of action) does not arise on account of anything characterizable either as an abnormal malfunction in, or as a possibly normal inadequacy of, our normal means of receiving or deducing information about the world—as is arguably the case both for the oasis and the spiral. It arises, rather, on account of the character of a primordially important "form of life": on account of the way in which we experience our agency; on account of *the* form of life of self-conscious rational agents like ourselves. Naturally seeing spirals where there are circles, or oases where there are none, are oddities that stand out clearly against the background of the massive reliability of sight as a guide to how the world is. But if naturally believing in freedom is an error, then it is an error about an entire dimension of experience. For if it is an error, then there is no free/unfree distinction to be drawn at all. We are not just wrong about some actions, we are wrong about them all.

It may still be felt that these manoeuvres get nowhere. It may be thought that the point about unrenounceable commitment has little force, in the end, even if it is true. The argument to the impossibility of self-determination given in Chapter 2 may still appear effortlessly fatal to the idea that the notions of true responsibility and desert can have application.

But to register this argument, to agree with it, and then to continue to lead a normal life, continuing to think of oneself and others as truly responsible, is to deny the force of the point about commitment while proving it in one's life and conduct. Proving it with especial force, indeed: for one is showing it to be so strong that rational people can deny that freedom is possible while continuing to behave exactly as if it were a reality.

Many will still hold that the theoretical argument for the impossibility of self-determination must in the end be given greater weight than any appeal to unrenounceable commitment. They will be impatient with the attempt to establish 'experiential facts' as a possible special source of justification of beliefs in special circumstances. But perhaps this impatience reveals that they have a further commitment—a very deep commitment to a certain view of the nature of reality which is such that they cannot even conceive of the possibility that a true account of reality (of what is really there) could defensibly invoke experiential facts in the suggested way, in claiming that we really are truly responsible agents at least partly because we believe (and perhaps cannot but believe) that we are.

This further commitment is assuredly a very natural one. Our most basic understanding of what objective truth is is closely bound up with it.[6] But can we be sure that this basic understanding is sound? It is worth noting what Sidgwick was led to say in *The Methods of Ethics* when faced with the conclusion that duty and self-interest are ultimately irreconcilable. Replacing "duty" and "self-interest" by 'true responsibility' and 'the impossibility of self-determination' in the last paragraph of his book yields the following:

> If . . . the reconciliation of true responsibility and the impossibility of self-determination is to be regarded as a hypothesis logically necessary to avoid a fundamental contradiction in . . . our thought, it remains to ask how far this necessity *constitutes* a sufficient reason for accepting this hypothesis. This, however, is a profoundly difficult and controverted question . . .: it could not be answered without a *general examination of the criteria of true and false beliefs'*.[7]

Sidgwick does not think that it is just obvious that our ordinary criteria of truth and falsity are correct. And it does seem reasonable to say that we should be prepared to undertake a serious re-examination of our ordinary criteria of truth and falsity (and of all the metaphysical assumptions that underpin them) if they lead us as philosophers to say that something of which we are ordinarily convinced (in everyday life) is in fact false.[8] I cannot at present see any future in such a project; but I think it is true to say that any discussion of freedom that dismisses close study of the phenomenon of our commitment to belief in freedom and true responsibility as simply irrelevant to the real problem must

---

[6] Though see Denyer, op. cit., pp. 95–6: "There might still linger the sceptical thought: of course everyone must *think* that everyone has free will, but might this not be because we are all constrained to be under a massive and permanent delusion. I do not understand the conception of truth that this doubt presupposes."

[7] *The Methods of Ethics*, pp. 508–9; my emphasis.

[8] Recall that there is a respect in which the case of freedom is quite unlike the case of belief in material objects, or in an external world (cf. 2.8). For in the latter case the philosophical conclusion is just that we don't know (can't prove) that the external world of material objects exists. It is a merely sceptical conclusion, and there is no incompatibility or contradiction between the philosophical unprovability of the existence of material objects and our natural and inevitable belief in them. But in the case of freedom the philosophical conclusion is apparently that we can know that freedom does *not* exist. And this conclusion simply contradicts our natural and arguably inevitable belief. And so the case of freedom is far more problematic than the case of material objects.

remain superficial—however sophisticated it may be in other respects.[9]

This chapter simply gestures at a few possibilities; it identifies a general position without examining it in any detail. The next chapter considers an approach to freedom that attempts to subvert the whole traditional framework that makes a certain way of trying to establish that we are free seem to be both necessary and bound to fail. This approach arguably constitutes a particular development of the general position just sketched.[10]

---

[9] Ch. 16 returns to the question.

[10] On the general topic of this chapter, see T. Nagel, 'The Limits of Objectivity', especially Part I, §§ 1–5. He argues that "we have to think of objectivity as something general enough to admit of different interpretations for different subjects of enquiry". See also *Skepticism and Naturalism*, by P. F. Strawson, in which he argues that we must acknowledge an irreducible relativity in our judgements about what is really the case.

5

Non-rational Commitment: A View of Freedom

5.1 INTRODUCTION

Both compatibilism and libertarianism have been rejected as viable theories of freedom, in their Objectivist versions; and doubt has been cast on the prospects for any Subjectivist commitment theory. But I wish now to consider another commitment theory of freedom, one which stresses our commitment to certain *attitudes* and *practices* which appear to presuppose belief in true responsibility, rather than directly stressing our commitment to belief in true responsibility.[1] I will suggest that it cannot by appealing to the notion of commitment show the worries of incompatibilist determinists to be wholly misconceived or groundless; and in Chapter 6 I will suggest that it may mislocate the true centre of our commitment in our interpersonal rather than in our self-regarding attitudes.

In so far as it holds the truth or falsity of determinism to be irrelevant to the question of whether or not we can correctly be said to be free, Strawson's view counts as a variety of compatibilism (of kind (v)—see 1.3), and one may therefore avail oneself of the assumption that determinism is true in putting it to the test. However, the determinism-independent argument for the impossibility of self-determination given in Chapter 2 poses exactly the same problem for freedom as determinism does. And so although this chapter speaks in a traditional fashion of determinism and the problems that it poses, it could equally well (if more laboriously) speak of the problems posed by the impossibility of self-determination. The basic question is this: can a commitment theory of freedom really avoid the problems that seem to be posed by determinism (or non-self-determinability)?

5.2 FEELINGS, ATTITUDES, PRACTICES, CONCEPTS, AND BELIEFS

Consider a man who becomes a determinist. He is often pictured as being faced first and foremost with the problem of what he is to make

[1] Propounded by P. F. Strawson in 'Freedom and Resentment'.

of other people, given his new belief. But of course his judgement of determinedness extends also, and far more immediately, to himself. He cannot see himself as an ordinary (and ordinarily responsible) man in an otherwise determined world. Or if he does—as he may, if the self-regarding aspects of commitment to belief in freedom are indeed less easy to renounce than the interpersonal ones—he should not. His first problem is himself.

But still, what should he make of other people? It seems that most people would find abandonment of the ordinary, strong notion of responsibility intolerable, not to say practically speaking impossible, from a social point of view. It would undermine the foundations of their conception of what human life is. For it is not as if one can excise one's inclination to praise and blame people while leaving all one's other attitudes to them untouched. If determinism is called upon to justify any such excision, one whole central range of what Strawson calls 'personal-reactive' or 'reactive' feelings and attitudes is thereby put at risk: attitudes and feelings, both moral and non-moral, to and about oneself and others; feelings, more or less considered and complicated, of condemnation and approbation, of gratitude and resentment, of despite and scorn; certain feelings of admiration for people's achievements and creations; certain aspects of feelings of hatred, anger, love, affection, and so on; feelings of guilt and remorse, pride and shame with regard to oneself and one's doings.

Such feelings and attitudes, and associated practices like praising and blaming, are all similarly threatened to the extent that their propriety depends in some way on our supposing that people are truly responsible for what they do.[2] The connection of dependence seems very clear in the majority of cases even if, irrational and anthropomorphistic, some of our feelings for and attitudes to non-human and even inanimate entities go by the same name. It is also clear that we are deeply committed to the belief that people can be truly responsible for what they do. Just as it is clear that determinism (or non-self-determinability) raises a major prima-facie doubt about the validity of this belief.

Can appeal to the undeniable fact of our commitment to these personal-reactive attitudes and practices show this doubt to be unwarranted? One argument that it can might go as follows: there is indeed a clear connection between (*a*) the personal-reactive attitudes and practices and (*b*) belief in true responsibility. Indeed one can argue

---

[2] In 'Self-Creation' Jonathan Glover calls these attitudes the 'desert-based' attitudes.

from the fact of our practically speaking unrenounceable commitment to these (at least partly) non-epistemic things, these feelings, attitudes, and practices, *to* the conclusion that no claim that the belief in true responsibility is false needs to be taken seriously. For if the truth of the belief in true responsibility is indeed *in some sense* a necessary condition of the justifiability of these attitudes and practices, the justifiability of these attitudes and practices is by the same token a sufficient condition of the truth of the belief. So if these attitudes and practices are independently justifiable, in some sense of 'justifiable'—if they are justifiable without appeal to the belief in responsibility (perhaps just by appeal to the fact that it is an absolutely fundamental natural fact about us that we are deeply and perhaps unrenounceably committed to them)—then they can plausibly be taken to uphold the belief in responsibility, when pressure is put upon it. Instead of being supported by it, they can support it, being supported in turn by the ground-floor fact of our unrenounceable commitment.

Strawson does not offer precisely this argument. But he does claim, in a comparable way, that we are *non-rationally* committed to the personal-reactive attitudes and practices—and, hence, presumably, to belief in the applicability of the concepts of responsibility and freedom—in such a way that it cannot be right to suppose that to give them up would be the correct or rational thing to do if determinism were shown to be true. In fact, he suggests, we are in any case incapable of giving them up, practically speaking. We could not at will adopt a completely 'objective' attitude to people (including ourselves), never praising or blaming them, never, in short, treating them as if they were properly responsible agents.

Feelings, attitudes, practices, concepts, and beliefs are all different things, and Strawson is mainly concerned with certain of the personal-reactive *feelings*, *attitudes*, and *practices*—those which have in common that they involve reacting to people as if they were genuinely self-determining and truly responsible agents. He has less to say about the more problematic-seeming questions that arise about the applicability of the related *concepts* of responsibility and freedom, and about the truth or falsity of *beliefs* in responsibility and freedom. But, considering the concept of moral responsibility in § 6, he does link attitudes and practices to concepts and beliefs. He suggests that the "pessimist" (or incompatibilist) about freedom is wrong to think that one cannot by appealing to the personal-reactive attitudes and practices "fill the gap" in the "optimist's" (or conventional compatibilist's) account of the concept of responsibility.

I take this suggestion to involve the claim (*a*) that the concepts of, and belief in, moral responsibility and freedom are *in some sense* shown to have application, and to be justified, respectively, by the mere fact of the existence of our commitment to the personal-reactive attitudes and practices; and (*b*) that the concepts of responsibility and freedom that are in this way shown to have application are in *some* way essentially stronger or richer concepts than those that can be admitted by conventional compatibilists. For they 'fill the gap' in the conventional compatibilist account.

It may be, though, that Strawson's argument is best understood simply as an attempt to draw attention to, and connect up, the two following things: the viability of (1) the conventional compatibilist account as far as it goes, and (2) the natural fact of our commitment to personal-reactive attitudes, emotions, and practices. They connect up in that reference to the latter fills the gap that the pessimists discern in the former. But, on this view, reference to (2) does not fill the gap in (1) in the sense that it supports and straightforwardly justifies belief in the proper applicability of a notion of responsibility that is essentially *stronger* than that allowed for in (1). It fills the gap in (1) only in the sense that it supplements (1) with an account of the primordially important role in human thought and action of a belief in a kind of responsibility that (1) can never show to be justified: it fits this belief into, and illuminates it in its proper place in, the general human 'form of life'. And, once placed in its true (and, essentially, partly non-rational) context, the belief can be seen to be immune, in some vital respect, to attack by any argument from determinism (or non-self-determinability). One could put this in a Humean way: belief in responsibility is "more properly an act of the sensitive, than of the cogitative part of our natures".[3] So the products of the pessimists' excogitations, although properly called beliefs, simply fail to connect with our *non*-cogitatively natural belief in responsibility in such a way that they and it can be assessed (with negative result) for mutual consistency.

This is an attractive reconciliation. One thing that someone who adopts such a position may simply underestimate, however, is the equal naturalness of the pessimists' position, when they insist that determinism is incompatible with freedom. Secure in theoretical in-

[3] Hume, *Treatise*, I. iv. 1, p. 183.

defeasibility, the reconciler may tend to mistake for a failure of subtlety in his opponent what is in fact a proper sensitivity to the power of the basic incompatibilist intuition that determinism is incompatible with freedom. The fact that the incompatibilist intuition has such power for us is as much a natural fact about cogitative beings like ourselves as is the fact of our quite unreflective commitment to the reactive attitudes. What is more, the roots of the incompatibilist intuition lie deep in the very reactive attitudes that are invoked in order to undercut it. The reactive attitudes enshrine the incompatibilist intuition. The notion of true responsibility comes easily to the non-philosophizing mind, and is not found only in (or behind) what Strawson calls the 'panicky metaphysics' of philosopher libertarians.

On balance, then, it is not clear that Strawson's appeal to commitment can undercut the pessimists' demand for an account, incompatible with determinism, of what it is that actually makes us truly responsible. Nor can it clearly assuage the pessimism of those who think that no such account can possibly be given (whether for reasons given in Chapter 2, or for other reasons).

5.3 COMMITMENT AND RATIONALITY

Strawson suggests that a question (1) "about what it would be *rational* to do if determinism were true, a question about the rational justification of ordinary inter-personal attitudes in general", could (2) seem "real only to one who had failed to grasp the purport" of the point about "our natural human commitment to ordinary inter-personal attitudes. This commitment is part of the general framework of human life, not something that can come up for review . . . within this general framework."[4] It is, (3), "*useless* to ask whether it would not be rational for us to do what it is not in our nature to (be able to) do".[5] If (4) "we could imagine what we cannot have, viz. a choice in this matter [a choice in the matter of our commitment to the ordinary interpersonal attitudes], then we could choose rationally only in the light of the gains and losses to human life, its enrichment or impoverishment; and the truth of falsity of a general thesis of determinism could not bear on the rationality of *this* choice."[6]

He concludes, (5), that "the question . . . of the connection between

---

[4] 'Freedom and Resentment', p. 13.
[5] Ibid., p. 18.
[6] Ibid., p. 13.

rationality and the adoption of the objective attitude to others is mis-
posed when it is made to seem dependent on the issue of determinism";
and, (6), that "it would not necessarily be rational to choose to be more
purely rational than we are . . . if such a choice were possible".[7]

With regard to the first three quotations: one might again object,
that while we have a deep and perhaps inderacinable commitment to
the reactive attitudes and practices, it is also in our nature to take
determinism to pose a serious problem for our notions of responsibility
and freedom. (This is so even if we grant that indeterminism cannot
help.) Our commitments are complex, and conflict. Although our
thoughts about determinism appear in actual fact quite impotent to
disturb our natural and unconsidered reactive attitudes and feelings
(this reveals one commitment), it also seems very difficult for us not to
acknowledge that the truth of determinism or of non-
self-determinability brings the propriety of the reactive attitudes seriously into doubt (this reveals the other commitment). Defenders of the
reactive attitudes may be unwise to seek to strengthen their position by
appealing to the fact that commitment to the reactive attitudes is, unlike
the opposed commitment, *practically* basic. For the incompatibilist
'pessimists' may then reply that, while the commitment they are concerned to stress is of an essentially more theoretical character, it appears
to represent the simple *truth*. There is a very real conflict of
commitment.

At one point in his characterization of the nature of our commitment
to the reactive feelings and attitudes, Strawson compares it to our
commitment to belief in the validity of inductive procedures. This commitment to inductive belief-formation is "original, natural, non-
rational (not *ir*rational), in no way something we choose or could give
up".[8] It cannot be supposed to be purely rational, as Hume showed.
Yet it can plausibly be said to be a commitment we are not wrong to
have—it is quite implausible to say that it is simply irrational. It is very
hard, furthermore, to see how we could give it up. And it seems absurd
to suppose that it might be rational to do so, or more rational to do so
than not to do so.

The claim implicit in the comparison appears to be this: that our
commitment to the reactive attitudes and, derivatively, to belief in

---

[7] Ibid., p. 13 n. For a more recent statement of his position, see *Skepticism and Naturalism*, pp. 31–8.

[8] 'Freedom and Resentment', p. 23 n.

responsibility, is similarly non-rational in such a way that it is something that we are not wrong to have in the face of determinism (or
non-self-determinability). But there appears to be an important difference. The correct sceptical objection to commitment to the validity
of inductive belief-formation is not that it involves a demonstrably false
belief, but only that it involves a belief that cannot be shown to be true,
and in that sense cannot be justified, although it may in fact be true (it
may in fact be true that there is a real material world governed by
certain fundamental forces that are intrinsic to the very constitution of
matter, a world in which everything takes place in accordance with
what one may perfectly well call 'natural necessity'). The sceptical
objection to belief in true responsibility, however, is that it is a belief
that is apparently demonstrably false. This objection is then extended
into a criticism of the reactive attitudes as demonstrably inappropriate
given their essential dependence on a belief that is demonstrably false.

Even if the two commitments are of the same depth and strength just
qua commitments, then, there is a respect in which they are different in
nature. But are they in fact of the same depth and strength? They may
resemble each other in this, that it would no more be right or rational
to (try to) give up the reactive attitudes than it would be to (try to) give
up reliance on inductive belief-formation. But merely placing them side
by side does not show that this is so; and it does not seem so inconceivable that we should weaken in our commitment to the reactive
attitudes as it does that we should weaken in our commitment to
inductive belief-formation. (One possibility not allowed for by this
all-or-nothing view of our commitment to the reactive attitudes is that
of local erosions, within the general framework of human life, of certain
facets of this commitment.)

On balance, it does not seem that the question about what it would
be rational to do if determinism were true can yet be rejected as an
unreal one. It is in our nature to be deeply committed to the reactive
attitudes. But it is also in our nature to take determinism (non-
self-determinability) to pose a serious problem for the notions of freedom and responsibility.

Quotations (4)–(6) have roughly the same import, but they merit separate comment. Consider a man who is an incompatibilist, and who
comes to believe that determinism is true. He has a great love of truth,
or, rather, a great desire to be correct in all things, to have justified
attitudes. Surely he can act rationally in choosing to (try to) adopt the

objective attitude to people, in the light of this desire and belief in determinism? The quotations suggest that the truth or falsity of determinism is never relevant to such a choice, and that the nature of human commitment to the reactive attitudes is such that one can legislate quite generally about what constitute gains and losses to human life, without considering the widely differing aims and preferences of individuals. But even if most people agree that the truth of determinism does not give them good reason to try to adopt the objective attitude, given other considerations about gains and losses to human life, the egregious lover of truth just mentioned, who now believes in determinism and so feels that his reactive attitudes are not justified, can reasonably claim that it is rational for him to try to adopt more objective attitudes. It is true that belief in determinism cannot *by itself* make it rational to adopt the objective attitude. But this is merely because no non-evaluative belief of this kind can ever provide a reason for action by itself.

In general, it simply is not clear that the fact of commitment makes it a mistake to suppose that the truth of determinism renders one's personal-reactive attitudes unjustified in some way.[9] Nor is it clear that the fact of commitment makes it impossible for us as we are to adopt universally objective attitudes to people.[10] And it surely cannot make it impossible for us to *try* to adopt the objective attitude (though in 6.3 I will suggest that newly fledged incompatibilist determinists may find themselves unable to adopt any rational plan of action at all, given their belief in determinism).

In the other case imagined by Strawson, that of choosing between our actual world and a world in which everyone adopts the objective attitude, we would, certainly, make our choice "in the light of the gains and losses to human life". But again this is not to say that there is a single rational choice. For it depends on what the chooser wants or thinks best, and there is a crucial sense in which desires and values are simply not comparable in respect of rationality.[11] Most would opt for

[9] This may be so even if assuming the falsity of determinism is of no help in an attempt to demonstrate their appropriateness—as ch. 2 suggests. (Those who agree that indeterminism is no better than determinism, so far as the prospects for freedom are concerned, can replace '(the truth of) determinism' by 'the way things are' throughout this chapter.)

[10] It is conceivable that one could have a choice in the matter—it could be a simple matter of wiring up one's brain and pushing a button.

[11] If I desire something impossible—to grow parsley on the moon—I am not *in any way* irrational, only unlucky; and I am not irrational, only subject to conflict of desire, if I desire to achieve something achievement of which is incompatible with achievement of my other desires. One's fear of (English) spiders may be said to be irrational because

the actual world. But a utilitarian who believed that personal-reactive-attitude-involving human relations cause more suffering than happiness overall would think it right or rational for us to choose to be more purely rational than we are, given the choice, in order to cancel the balance of suffering.[12]

In conclusion: it does not follow, from the fact that the truth of determinism cannot by itself make it rational to try to adopt the objective attitude, or from the fact that there is no single rational choice to be made in this case, that the correctness of the objective attitude does not in some sense follow from the truth of determinism. It does seem to be true that praising, blaming or resenting what other people do is in some sense completely inappropriate, given the truth of determinism, even if it is odd to talk of 'correct' attitudes. (For if determinism is true, then to pass moral judgements on people, and to say that they acted morally rightly or wrongly, is, in a crucial respect, exactly like saying they are beautiful, or ugly—something for which they are not responsible.) And it seems that this is so whatever one's desires are, and whatever one thinks one should do. Finally, while there may indeed be no single right answer to the question of what it would be rational to do if determinism were shown to be true, the question has not been shown to be unreal. It will be considered further in the next chapter, in conjunction with some more strictly phenomenological themes.

it is only rational to fear what one believes to be harmful; and such irrationality may be supposed to infect one's corresponding desire not to come into contact with spiders. But even if one's desire is wholly derived from a fear that can properly be called irrational, it is not in itself irrational; one can have the same desire without the fear. (Derek Parfit has argued convincingly that certain patterns of preference may be intrinsically irrational; see *Reasons and Persons*, § 46. But his unusual cases do not affect the present point.)

[12] A man might rate more highly than anything else a diminution in the rate of *crimes passionnels*; he might find this kind of killing far more terrible than any other kind. Confident that this would diminish drastically upon universal adoption of the objective attitude, he might regard all the other effects of its adoption as a price well worth paying.

6

Phenomenology, Commitment, and What Might Happen

6.1 FEELINGS AND THE CAUSALITY OF REASON; DOINGS AND HAPPENINGS

Many of our ordinary 'personal-reactive' attitudes and feelings seem to be somehow inappropriate or incorrect, given the truth of determinism (or non-self-determinability).[1] It is true that feelings and attitudes are correct or incorrect, if at all, only in some derivative sense— only in so far as they are tied to beliefs. Nevertheless, it seems reasonable to say that if determinism is true (or since true self-determination is impossible), the attitudes and feelings presently in question can be shown to be appropriate only by appeal to beliefs which are in fact incorrect; it seems that they stand in a sufficiently close relation to certain beliefs to depend for their correctness or appropriateness on the correctness of those beliefs. Accordingly, there appears to be room for the exercise of reason in thinking through the consequences of one's beliefs for one's attitudes and feelings. It does not seem that the bare fact of one's commitment to these attitudes and feelings renders any such exercise of reason simply pointless.

How might such reasoning go? Well, just as believing 'if p then q' and coming to believe 'p' is likely to *cause* one to come to believe that q, according to what one could call the 'natural causality of reason', so, similarly, if one genuinely believes that the propriety of certain of one's feelings presupposes the correctness of certain beliefs, and if one then comes to think that these beliefs are false, then this may understandably cause one to cease to have these feelings; it may cause them to change or weaken, at least. On the other hand, if the feelings are linked to inherently non-rational emotions and desires, the natural 'causality of reason' will be impeded. Clearly it will vary in its operation with the individual case.

But does this have any consequences for the question of what one

[1] If the argument of ch. 2 is valid then the falsity of determinism is no help.

should *do*? If a change in one's feelings and attitudes were produced in this way by one's coming to believe in determinism, this would be something that happened to one, not something one did.[2] And the difficulties that attend Strawson's question about what it might be rational to do if one came to believe, say, that both incompatibilism and determinism were true are not diminished by the fact that there is a real and unproblematic question about what might *happen* to one in such a case.

So: what should one do—if anything? What might one do, in any case?

One can hardly decide to take no notice of what one now believes— that people, including oneself, are, in some unequivocal sense, in no way responsible for their actions. But if one's reaching this theoretical conclusion (many have) has not in fact caused one's reactive attitudes to change in any way (this has often been the case), is one then bound to *try* to stop treating people as proper objects of gratitude and resentment, praise and blame, and to undertake some course of action to that end? Say one doesn't want to. Isn't that a sufficient reason not to?

It is not clear that it is; or rather, it is not clear that these questions really arise. For it is of course true that if one believes that there are okapi in San Diego zoo, but has not been to check, there is no reason why one should check if one doesn't want to. But the present case is different. One has formed a belief, and there is in a clear sense nothing hidden from view that remains to be actively checked. To claim that one need not try to take into account the apparent fact that people are not proper objects of reactive attitudes if one doesn't want to seems rather like claiming that one need not believe something one believes if one doesn't want to. But one doesn't have such a choice; belief is not subject to the will in this way.[3]

All this may be true; and yet it is also true that the theoretical incompatibilist determinists' reactive attitudes are very unlikely to have been much perturbed by their theoretical views. But can they reasonably tolerate this? Shouldn't they do something about it? It seems that we have to ask once again whether the fact of non-rational commitment

---

[2] This is part of a general point about reasoning. One does not really act at all, in reasoning. Rather one 'sees'—one realizes—that this follows from that. Reasoning is more like sensation (or perception) than action: the action in reasoning is at most the getting of the premises together, and the bringing of the mind to bear on them, if it is anything. It is not the reasoning as such; that is what happens when you do these other things. The same goes for thinking in general.

[3] Although one could hire a hypnotist to wipe out one's belief.

can somehow justify, as well as explain, their imperturbability; or whether, alternatively, it can somehow pre-empt the need for any such justification.

The problem is important, because it is not just a problem for incompatibilist determinists. The fact of the impossibility of true self-determination threatens to propel us all into this difficulty—whatever we believe about determinism. People do not make themselves to be the way they are. And this gives rise to a vital sense in which they are not ultimately responsible for what they do. But they go on thinking of themselves as if they were thus responsible.

It is no good saying 'I am determined to go on having these feelings and attitudes'. To suppose that this dissolves the problem is to make the mistake of fatalism (the mistake of thinking that nothing one can do can change what will happen). It may be true that one is so determined that one does make this mistake. But it is also true—even if everyone is determined to believe everything that he, or she, believes—that it is a mistake, and that people who think clearly will not make it.[4] And if such people are not convinced that appeal to the fact of non-rational commitment can justify as well as explain our reactive feelings and attitudes, or decisively pre-empt the demand for justification, then they cannot really avoid the problem of what now to think, what now to do.[5]

6.2 DETERMINISM, ACTION, AND THE SELF; A THOUGHT-EXPERIMENT

Reflections such as these can start up odd intellectual fatigues, veering sleights of mind, or a deep and almost contemptuous rejection of the apparently manifest demands of reason. One's commitment to the reactive attitudes is instrumental in this; largely, I suggest, because one's deepest commitment is not to belief in the appropriateness of the interpersonal reactive attitudes, but to belief in the appropriateness of

[4] Here I am assuming the invalidity of the argument that one cannot believe in determinism because this belief undercuts one's right to appeal to the notions of truth and falsity altogether (cf. J. R. Lucas, *The Freedom of the Will*, § 21; cf. also 2.5, and the reference there to D. Wiggins). Materials for one kind of answer to this argument may be derived from the theory of evolution, and its account of how true-belief-forming creatures may evolve in a deterministic world (and cf. n.2 above). It may also be noted that even if belief in determinism did pose a problem of this sort, the supposition of indeterminism would (as usual) contribute nothing to its solution.

[5] "Carelessness and in-attention alone can afford us any remedy. For this reason", Hume says, "I rely entirely upon them" (*Treatise*, I. iv. 2, p. 218).

certain self-concerned reactive attitudes. One's deepest commitment is to the view of oneself as truly responsible, both in general and in particular cases of action. The sleights of mind begin because the biggest problems raised by the apparent demands of reason concern oneself. Trying to think through the consequences of these demands, it seems that one risks thinking oneself out of existence, as a *mental someone*. ('A mental someone' is a good description of one absolutely central way in which we think of ourselves. Here as elsewhere I am concerned only with this fact of 'cognitive phenomenology', and not at all with the question of what if anything a 'mental someone' could possibly be, factually or metaphysically speaking.)

Why does one risk thinking oneself out of existence as a mental someone? Because what one naturally takes oneself to be, *qua* mental someone, is a truly self-determining agent of the impossible kind.[6] One takes it (however unreflectively) that this is an *essential* aspect of what one is, mentally considered: given the way I am, mentally considered, I could not continue to exist and lack this property. So the risk is not merely that a process of tenacious concentration on the thought of determinism (or non-self-determinability) might force me to cease to believe that I had a certain property—true responsibility—whose possession meant a lot to me. It is rather that there might remain nothing that was recognizable as me at all; nothing recognizable as me, the 'agent-self', but only a bare consciousness-function, a zombie.

Perhaps the best way to see the force of this suggestion is by means of the following thought-experiment; for it may seem rather vague and far-fetched. It is not particularly vague, in fact. What may be true, though, is that one really does have to stop and think about it for oneself with concentration and imagination.

The thought-experiment consists simply in the rigorous application of the belief in determinism to the present course of one's life: one does one's best to think rapidly of every smallest action one performs or movement one makes—or indeed everything whatsoever that happens, so far as one is oneself concerned—as determined; as not, ultimately, determined by oneself; this for a minute or two, say.

*

This should have the effect of erasing any sense of the presence of a freely deciding and acting 'I' in one's thoughts; for—so it seems—there

---

[6] The fact that one also takes oneself to be an embodied agent capable of physical action is not presently relevant.

is simply no role for such an 'I' to play. It may even be strangely, faintly depressing; or it may give rise to a curious, floating feeling of detached acquiescence in the passing show of one's own psychophysical being; a feeling, not of impotence, but of radical uninvolvement. Or alternatively the feeling may be: I am not really a person; there isn't really anyone there at all.[7]

I take this effect to indicate that one's sense of self is of a profoundly libertarian cast; and to indicate that one naturally and unreflectively conceives of oneself, *qua* the mental planner of action, as standing in some special—impossible—relation of true-responsibility-creating origination to one's choices and actions. One disappears in the thought-experiment because it reveals that one is not possible, so conceived.

At the same time, of course, one does not—cannot—disappear just like that. One's thought naturally and inevitably occurs for one in terms of 'I',[8] and one's conception of this 'I' remains a conception of a truly responsible self-determining someone. So while one's attempts to grasp the consequences of determinism fully may succeed in bursts, they will in the longer term always break up on one's rock-hard commitment to a self-conception which is wholly incompatible with fully fledged, continually applied belief in determinism.[9]

When this happens, one may continue to have, and to try to apply, the thought that everything about one is determined; but it will not be striking with its full force. And when it is striking with less than its full force the thought of one's total determinedness will probably not make it seem that one does not really exist at all (as a mental someone), but, rather, that although one does somehow or other exist (as a mental someone), and although one does continue to act in various ways, still one cannot truly be said to do anything oneself, because determinism gobbles up everything, revealing everything one does to be not really *one's own doing*. (Remember that this is a claim about how things will appear to someone who takes the problem of free will seriously and

[7] The thought-experiment might make a good meditation exercise for certain schools of Buddhists—see further 6.6.

[8] This is why Lichtenberg's famous objection to Descartes—that he should not have affirmed the certainty of 'I think' but only of 'It thinks' or 'It's thinking' (on the analogy of 'It's raining')—is wrongly put. The correct point is simply that when one makes Descartes's move one should not suppose that any conclusion about one's substantial nature follows from the certainty of 'I think'. See also 9.3 below, and Appendix E.

[9] Hardened conventional compatibilists are likely to have the most trouble with the thought-experiment, for they are most likely to confuse their theoretical opinions (or prejudices) with their real everyday attitudes to themselves and their actions—in a way that makes it difficult to see the problem.

pursues the thought-experiment; as such it is not a rejection of theoretical compatibilism.)

I suggest, therefore, that there are two principal poles around which one's thought is likely to oscillate when one is trying to apply the thought that one is totally determined. At one pole, the freely deciding and acting 'mental someone' somehow goes out of existence altogether. At the other pole, the mental someone continues to exist, but one can no longer see oneself as a freely deciding and acting being in any way. One's thought is likely to oscillate around this second pole when the thought-experiment has not been engaged with full force, and is not having its full effect of strangely dissolving the (sense of) self.[10]

This is not likely to convince anyone who does not seriously attempt the thought-experiment; and such an appeal to thought-experiment is likely to encounter scepticism. But I do not think that the point can be made adequately in words.

It may be claimed that the thought-experiment is not practicable: the 'I' as it occurs in thought[11] can never fully attain the thought that it is itself just part of the determined world, because it can never quite catch up with itself: any judgement of determinedness on its part necessarily involves its taking an external view of the object of the judgement, which it cannot have of itself *qua* the thinking subject presently making the judgement. But this is no real problem. Even if one were to become aware of this point,[12] it would not check the *general* effect that would be produced in one by thinking of everything one is and does as totally determined—the effect of seeming to erase the 'I' as ordinarily conceived. Suppose one did think about one's thinking in particular as a completely determined phenomenon. Then whatever thought one had, one would, pursuing the thought-experiment, think of that thought too as determined. And, this being so, no thought would ever be able to emerge as the true product of the familiar 'I', the putative true originator of thoughts, decisions, and actions that is not a merely determined phenomenon: this 'I' would perpetually evanesce, however far one pursued the possible regress of thoughts about thoughts about

---

[10] It is at the second pole that we encounter what Thomas Nagel calls "the . . . erosion of what we do by the subtraction of what happens". See his 'Moral Luck', esp. pp. 37–8. Cf. also Bernard Williams's paper on 'Moral Luck', to which Nagel's paper was a response.

[11] Here again I am concerned only with the *character* of our thought, not with the idea that there could be some special mental entity called the 'I' or the 'self'.

[12] Discussed by Ryle in 'The Systematic Elusiveness of "I" ', *The Concept of Mind*, ch. 6, § 7.

thoughts. (This is just one way among others in which the thought-experiment could develop.)

In fact the idea that one cannot be supposed to be a truly responsible originator of one's thoughts or ideas can acquire experiential (as opposed to merely theoretical) impact without recourse to the tricky rigours of this thought-experiment. The point is a familiar one (already touched on in note 2). Thoughts simply 'occur' to one; one just 'has' ideas, they simply 'come to one'—whether they are philosophical, mathematical, or scientific (in which case the occurrence of one's thoughts and ideas is somehow controlled by one's wish to arrive at the truth) or whether they are musical, fictional, or poetical (in which case their occurrence may be controlled by many things). There is a commonly felt sense in which one has no real responsibility for any of them.[13] I think it is helpful to dwell on this (it is is part of doing philosophy). And it is worth reflecting on Hume's famous observation, that when one earnestly inspects one's own mind for the 'I', the self, one never finds anything there.[14]

Serious incompatibilist determinists (or non-self-determinationists, 2.11) should try the thought-experiment; for them, after all, undertaking it involves nothing more than dwelling with special concentration on something they already believe to be true. Those who learn to maintain the state of mind induced by the thought-experiment will be well on the way to a truly thoroughgoing, truly lived, or as I shall say *genuine* belief in determinism or non-self-determinability. (They may be well on the way to nirvana.) But it is important to be clear what this involves. A person may *theoretically* fully accept that he, or she, is wholly a product of his or her heredity and environment—many of us do—and yet have *no* such self-conception as is here required of the genuine incompatibilist determinist (non-self-determinationist). In fact such a self-conception seems scarcely possible for human beings. It seems to require the dissolution of any recognizable human sense of

---

[13] It is worth quoting Rimbaud's well-known remarks in full: "C'est faux de dire: Je pense: on devrait dire on me pense. . . . JE est un autre. Tant pis pour le bois qui se trouve violon" (letter to Georges Izambard, 13 May 1871); and again "Les romantiques . . . prouvent si bien que la chanson est si peu souvent l'œuvre, c'est à dire la pensée . . . *comprise* du chanteur. . . . Car Je est un autre. Si le cuivre s'éveille clairon, il n'y a rien de sa faute. Cela m'est évident: J'assiste à l'éclosion de ma pensée [I am a spectator at the unfolding of my thought]: je la regarde, je l'écoute. . . ." (Letter to Paul Demeny, 15 May 1871.)

[14] D. Hume, *Treatise*, I. iv. 6, p. 252.

self. Certainly one cannot adopt such a radically 'objective' attitude to oneself at will.

Perhaps this is not very clearly expressed. But I think the general idea will become clear to most of those who concentrate on the problem, or undertake the thought-experiment. Those who disdain the thought-experiment, or claim that it does not work, may fail to grasp the general idea. It does work; and this is a very important fact about us.

6.3 WHAT MIGHT HAPPEN

These considerations suggest that there may after all be a sense in which the question (considered in 5.3) about what it would be rational to do if determinism were true is an 'unreal' question. For it may be an unreal question for anyone who has become a *genuine* incompatibilist determinist (non-self-determinationist) in the present sense—for anyone who has gone beyond merely theoretical acceptance of determinism (or non-self-determinability).

Consider a man who is an incompatibilist and who has just come to believe that determinism is true, and who is struggling to attain a true perspective on his situation. How is he to think of himself as he sits back, rubs his eye, looks for a book in the bookshelves, debates whether to give more money to famine relief, thinking perhaps, of each of his thoughts and movements that it is determined, and thinking that his thinking this is determined in turn, and so on?

We may suppose that he does not make the fatalist mistake—the mistake (for example) of ceasing to try to get what he wants because he thinks it is already determined whether he will get it or not, in such a way that he can do nothing about it. He knows perfectly well that his own planning and action are real and effective parts of the continuing deterministic process. It is rather that when he does something intentionally which he feels to be reprehensible (say), he may then think to himself: that was determined to happen, and yet if I had not done it that too would have been determined to happen. This is a very ordinary thought in philosophy. But what is it like to take it seriously in life, trying to apprehend every detail of one's life as determined?

He may find that he feels that *he* (i.e. he the truly responsible agent, he as he automatically conceives of himself in his natural, unreconstructed thought about himself) can do nothing at all. Here he is at the second of the two main poles of serious self-applied determinism: he feels he exists, but that he cannot really *act* at all. This is how he puts it, at least. Or rather, this is how he would put it, were it not for the fact that, relaxing his application of the thought of determinism to himself, and being an as yet unreconstructed incompatibilist determinist, he still feels completely responsible for what he has done. He feels he simply knows that he knew at the time of action that he could have done otherwise. He is unable to accept that he is exempt from responsibility or blame, or indeed from praise, because it was determined to happen as it did. (Perhaps he faces the button described in 3.6, and can either press it or not press it.) Yet he also now believes that the way he is, and his decision, are things for which he is ultimately in no way responsible. And when, see-sawing back, he concentrates again on this thought, he finds, again, that he can no longer make sense of the idea of his performing an action that is truly *his* action. For the sense of self he naturally has (and which is expressed here by the italicization of 'he' and 'his') is irremediably incompatible with any deep acceptance of the idea that all he is and does is determined.[15]

He may think as follows: that to choose to (try to) abandon his personal-reactive attitudes is not really possible, because only a free agent, which he does not now consider himself to be, can really have a reason for action which is really its own reason. There may be a train of practical deliberation going on in his head, but he feels that it is not really *his* thought at all (although it feels just like it, as soon as he stops concentrating on his determinedness), but (because) a determined process. He thinks that he cannot reason or deliberate in a way that culminates in a decision which is truly his, and which is such that the ensuing action is something for which he is truly responsible; or indeed something that *he* really did. For he knows that what he thinks of as his choice is determined, however much he may hesitate or contrasuggestibly change his mind. And so, stuck with his unreconstructed sense of self, he cannot think of it as really *his* choice. To talk of freedom here, as compatibilists do, is, he thinks, to talk of the freedom of the turnspit, or of the self-sealing tank.[16] It is the "wretched subterfuge" of compatibilism, a "petty word-jugglery".[17] It is "so much gobbledegook".[18] It is not really to talk of freedom at all.

So the whole picture of the thoughtful incompatibilist determinist

[15] With suitable minor adjustments, the same story can be told of a non-self-determinationist.

[16] Cf. Kant in the *Critique of Practical Reason*, p. 191 (*Ak.*V. 97); and D. Davidson in 'Freedom to Act', p. 141.

[17] Kant, op. cit., pp. 189–90 (*Ak.* V. 96).

[18] G. E. M. Anscombe, 'Causality and Determination', p. 146.

coming to believe in determinism, and then raising the question of what to do about it, may be ill-conceived. The question may be completely unreal for him, so long as he concentratedly applies the thought of determinism to himself. For he may then feel that he cannot really choose to do, or do, anything, in the way he thought. This rejection of the possibility of real choice or action is, certainly, a piece of reasoning on his part. But it too cannot be thought to have any practical consequences, or to rationalize any decision—such as a decision not to choose or decide anything on the grounds that it is strictly speaking impossible to do so. One cannot decide not to decide anything on the grounds that one cannot decide anything.

But nor can he decide to abandon himself to his determinedness, for that too would be something determined, hence not something he really did, in the vital sense. He cannot think 'I find that these reasons to do X occur to me, and *since* X now appears to me (determinedly, I know) to be the best thing to do, I will do X', as if he thus had access to a further reason to do X—the knowledge that reasons to do X have determinedly outweighed reasons to do anything else (or, worse, as if ability to take account of what was determinedly the case, so far as his reason-state was concerned, somehow gave him access to a secret, undetermined fulcrum point of free decision). These would be simple mistakes. Correcting himself, and foreseeing the paralytic regresses that threaten, he may tell himself not to think about the nature of his practical reasoning any more than he used to. But this too will involve a decision—a decision to try to think nothing. So it will not really be his decision, in his view.

This is a strange drama, an enactment of the deep problem of free will. In the end only the exigencies of everyday life will carry him forward. The continual tendency of his unreconstructed thought will be to reinsert him, conceived as a truly self-determining mental someone, into his thought and deliberation. And continually he will correct this tendency. For nothing, he realizes, can be done by him, so conceived. Nothing can be done by him in the sense that matters to him; things can only happen. Whatever he starts to plan and do, it is whipped away from him, only to appear as not really his own, by the thought that it is entirely determined.

It seems, then, that a genuine belief in determinism or non-self-determinationism, uneasily coupled with an unreconstructed conception of self, may produce a *total paralysis* of all purposive thought as it is ordinarily conceived and experienced. To experience things in this way is not to make the mistake of fatalism. It is simply to experience the clash between determinism (non-self-determinationism) and our ordinary conception of freedom in a particularly vivid manner. (It is useful to think of morally weighted choices here.)

There are certainly other more compatibilistic ways of thinking and theorizing about deliberation and action, some of which will be discussed in the next section, and which are of such a kind that when we employ them, we may find that we are quite untroubled by the thought of determinism. But it does not follow that the present story is not accurate as a story of what might happen to a newly fledged, thoughtful incompatibilist determinist (non-self-determinationist). What may follow is that we are deeply inconsistent in our characteristically very vague thought about freedom, action, deliberation, and ourselves. (Seasoned philosophical compatibilists are likely to find it much harder than most to appreciate the force of these points. Perhaps they should imagine facing the following choice: if you agree to submit to twenty years of torture—torture of a kind that leaves no time for moral self-congratulation—you will save ten others from the same fate. (Perhaps they should agree to be hypnotized into believing that they really are facing such a choice—hypnotized in such a way that, afterwards, they remember exactly what it felt like.))

This story is not just a curiosity, for if the argument of Chapter 2 is correct, we ought all to be non-self-determinationists. It is worth considering some other suggestions about what might happen to a new incompatibilist determinist or non-self-determinationist. One possibility is this. One might simply cease to believe that the specifically moral reactive attitudes and practices of praise and blame were justified or appropriate, and losing this belief might cause one to cease to be moved to praise and blame. Generally, believing determinism to be true and just being generally speaking very rational*istic* might cause a man to come to have more objective attitudes, without his trying to *do* anything. And this might occur despite the fact that he felt that the quality of his life suffered greatly as a result. On the other hand, his moral and non-moral reactive attitudes might be quite unaffected by his new theoretical belief, given the strength of his commitment to them. (This is what usually happens.) We are all effortlessly capable of the magnificent inconsistency of beliefs and attitudes that this appears to involve. And this, of course, is something that gives extremely powerful support to the commitment theorists' claim about the unrenounceability of the commitment.

Perhaps one may picture the reactive feelings and attitudes as composing a spectrum. At one end—this is very rough—there are the most basic feelings and sentiments of pleasure and 'unpleasure', aggression, animal attraction, fear, anger, and so on—the 'true' passions, those most clearly undergone or suffered. At the other end there are the most purely moral sentiments and feelings of approval and disapproval, praise and blame. Resentment and gratitude may be seen as lying somewhere near the centre of the spectrum, distanced from the basic passions by their appearing to involve a considerable degree of mental sophistication, but distanced also from the most purely moral feelings and sentiments—for resentment and gratitude could survive recognition of inappropriateness where tendencies to praise and blame succumbed: 'I realize it's absurd to blame him (the lunatic), but I can't help feeling resentful'; 'I know it's only an android robot, but I can't help feeling grateful.'

There are different ways of categorizing emotions and feelings, but this ranking according to basicness seems to match closely the ordering which may be derived by comparing their dependence for appropriateness upon certain beliefs, such as belief in true responsibility, and the relative likelihood of their alteration given change in these beliefs. Dependence upon beliefs varies inversely with basicness. For example: a tendency to get angry with people is less likely to diminish in response to belief in determinism than a tendency to blame them (inanimate objects can make one angry, and it does not seem that this is irrational, whereas blaming them is).

Any individual's case will be far more complicated than this schema suggests, however. In a particular case there will doubtless be special non-rational dependencies, formed as a result of traumatic experiences, for example, or a religious upbringing. And then, some people are naturally far more quick to anger—and to forgive—than others. One man's anger at people might turn to anger at the whole of creation by his acquiring a belief in determinism—this would be a case of a 'basic' feeling responding to a change in belief. Alternatively, he might hold that a natural and ultimate feature of creation was a rigid code of punishment, and thus retain his practice of moral judgement even after coming to believe in determinism: 'It is perhaps a terrible fault in creation, but you have done wrong and are to blame.' This would be a case of a more purely moral sentiment failing to respond to change in belief. Calvinists do not hold (earthly) punishment to have a purely pragmatic justification.

What would happen generally is unpredictable. But it does seem conceivable that a highly rationalistic and generally un-neurotic man, low on non-rational dependencies, might lose (not actively abandon) only those attitudes which were in his view justifiable only by his discarded belief in true responsibility; being one in whom, as one might say, the causality of reason was strong, and non-rational commitment to belief in true responsibility weak. But he could not simply lose them by choice. Nor does calling him 'rationalistic' carry any implication that others would be rational to set about trying to abandon these attitudes. Nor do I think that we can fully imagine what it would be like to be him, if he did lose all the attitudes in question.[19]

6.4 NATURAL COMPATIBILISM

Our sense of self and of freedom is in many respects profoundly libertarian in character. But it is also naturally and unhesitatingly compatibilistic in many other respects. And since this *natural compatibilism* is part of what underlies our commitment to belief in freedom, it deserves some consideration at this point. (A full treatment of it would be a lengthy matter; but Hume made some of the relevant points in the *Enquiry*, and many others have been made by compatibilists since.)[20]

The principal idea is this: so far as many aspects of our general sense of ourselves as free agents are concerned, we are not inclined to think that they are put in question *in any way* by the truth of determinism or non-self-determinability. Sometimes this is a reasonable attitude on our part, sometimes it is not. It depends on what aspect of our sense of freedom is in question. But in either case it is a natural compatibilist attitude, in the present sense of the phrase.

1. Thus—for example—many people are naturally (prephilosophically) inclined to accept accounts of how they came to be as

[19] The quite remarkable readiness with which human beings slip into adopting apparently true-responsibility-presupposing attitudes (like blame, resentment, and gratitude) to many classes of objects—animals, stones, cars, aeroplanes, computers, the world in general—that they would not in their cooler moments dream of classifying as free agents can be interpreted in more than one way. It can be seen simply as further evidence of how profoundly we are committed to true-responsibility-presupposing feelings and attitudes. Or (less usefully) it can be seen as casting doubt on the extent to which these attitudes are essentially true-responsibility-presupposing. The truth is that they are true-responsibility-presupposing; it is just that we are even more irrational than we think.

[20] D. Dennett's *Elbow Room* is among other things a contribution to the description of the extent of our natural compatibilism.

they are that simply rule out any kind of true self-determination; and they can in addition easily be brought to see that true self-determination is not really possible. (To say this may seem inconsistent with the account of our natural sense of self given above; but the inconsistency is in our view of ourselves, not in the account given of our view of ourselves.) Many people accept that they are, ultimately, entirely determined in all aspects of their character by their heredity and environment. But it follows from this that, whether the heredity-and-environment process that has shaped them is deterministic or not, they cannot themselves be truly or ultimately self-determining in any way. And yet they do not feel that their freedom is put in question by this—even though they naturally conceive of themselves as free in the ordinary, strong, true-responsibility-involving sense. To this extent they are natural compatibilists. This is a very common position.

Those who occupy this position cannot have thought about the matter very hard, you may say. That may be so. But very many thoughtful and intelligent people occupy exactly this position. Even those who are, as philosophers, revisionary compatibilists who hold that our ordinary strong notion of freedom is indefensible, reveal unmistakably, in the everyday conduct of their lives, that they too occupy it.

2. To this one may add the fact, noted in Chapter 2, that we are neither inclined to suppose that we can be self-determining with respect to (the particular content of) our beliefs (for we simply desire that what we believe should be determined in a reliable, truth-inducing manner by the way things are), nor inclined to suppose that we can be radically self-determined with respect to our desires—or, generally, with respect to all those things other than beliefs that motivate our actions. It is true, as remarked, that we can cultivate tastes and traits; but we readily recognize that, if we do so, we do so because we are motivated to do so by certain desires and attitudes that we already have; or by certain beliefs about what is true or right that we already have, beliefs with respect to which we have our normal attitude: that of supposing that they are true, and, briefly, that we have in coming to hold them been determined to do so simply by the way things are. That is, in our ordinary thought we recognize, more or less explicitly, that true self-determination is impossible—even independently of acknowledging the truth of physical determinism or heredity-and-environment determinism. But we also feel that the fact that it is impossible poses no threat at all to our freedom. And in this we are again natural compatibilists.

It is true that one reason why we feel that this impossibility poses no threat to freedom is that we naturally credit ourselves with an *in*compatibilistically conceived power of free decision that we see as rendering us somehow independent of our ultimately non-self-determined beliefs, desires, and so on (2.9, 3.4). But we also naturally accept that explanations in terms of ultimately non-self-determined beliefs and desires can be *full* explanations of our actions, without our freedom being threatened; and it is this that makes it reasonable to see the present point about beliefs and desires as illustrating part of our natural compatibilism.

3. The above description of natural compatibilism involves reference to determinism, and in particular to heredity-and-environment determinism, and it may be questioned to what extent it can be said to articulate a *natural* (unreflective, pre-philosophical) compatibilistic outlook. The claim that it is natural can be defended by appeal to the idea that even if people do not ordinarily think at all about heredity and environment, or about how or why they are free, still there are certain things that they—we—would naturally be led to say if asked certain questions about freedom. Presented with objections to their initial responses (questioned further in a genially aporetic manner) there are certain further moves that they would also be naturally inclined to make. All these can be supposed to form part of natural compatibilism as presently understood.

As remarked, a full discussion of natural compatibilism would be a lengthy business. Here, by way of example, I propose to consider just one natural compatibilist aspect of the general phenomenology of freedom: a point about our attitude to our desires or non-epistemic motives generally considered. (Note that the phenomenology of freedom is not restricted to description—to saying what our sense of freedom is like. It can also offer explanations—explanations of why we have the sort of sense of freedom we do have.)

4. For any desire with which we are concerned at some particular time, we are not usually in the least concerned to be able to say that we are, somehow, the originators of the desire—whatever sense can be made of this. Our unreflective attitude to it is that it is simply there, in the way that a chair, a feature of the world, is simply there. I don't and I can't choose my desires. And I don't have to choose them for them to be mine (or to be free when they move me to act). They are just a part of me. This is how I am. One's desires are not of course publicly observable in the way that chairs are. The point of the analogy is rather one's desires are or can be as much a fact about the world that one

confronts as the fact of a chair's being there. I like loganberries, the chair is there in front of me. A desire can be importunate, I can bump into a chair. There are of course important differences in the 'being-there' of desire and chair—in the experience one has, with respect to both desire and chair, of being passive with respect to the fact of their existence or presence. But there are also important similarities.[21]

One might say that some desires are more like the fact of having a body of a particular sort than they are like chairs in particular places, in that they are part of oneself, and are more permanently 'just there', and are unthinkingly taken into account in one's thought and action (as is one's body both by proprioceptive and kinaesthetic sense, and by one's less immediate sensory and cognitive awareness of it). This point does not displace the point about chair-like objectivity of some desires, however, it only complicates it. For it remains true that many desires are in an important sense apprehended by us as just being there; as being in a sense external to the mental self that confronts them. And it remains true that their just-thereness is not seen as posing any sort of threat to freedom. And this fact forms part of the explanation of part of our natural compatibilism. It forms part of the explanation of why we may be naturally quite unworried when confronted by philosophers with the thought that our desires can be said to be determined in us in the sense of not having been freely adopted during some process of self-determination: we never really thought they were the result of self-determination anyway, or that they had to be if we were to befree.[22]

But it also forms part of the explanation of our natural *in*compatibilism. (This is a typical complication in the phenomenology of freedom.) For it also forms part of the explanation of the strength of our tendency to conceive of ourselves as possessed of a self separate from, and somehow irreducibly over and above, all its particular desires, pro-attitudes, and so on. And in this respect it turns out to be central to the naturally occurring libertarian notion of the truly self-determining 'agent-self' that is in its choice of action potentially completely independent of any of its particular (determined or not self-determined) desires, pro-attitudes, and so on. This is just one more instance in which naturally compatibilist and naturally incompatibilist (and indeed lib-

[21] Moral beliefs also characteristically have this sort of just-thereness; one confronts the chair, one confronts one's belief that one ought to do X.

[22] It is *also* arguable, however, that there is a (rather slippery) sense in which we conceive our relation to our desires, pro-attitudes and so on as if they were things we were somehow or in some degree responsible for. See the next section. Both arguments may be correct.

ertarian) elements in our thought about freedom share common roots.

5. The principal idea behind the suggestion that there is a sense in which we are naturally compatibilist in our thought about freedom is, as remarked, simply this: there are a great many aspects of our experience of ourselves as free agents which, *either for good or for bad reasons*, we do not feel to be threatened in any way by the truth of determinism or non-self-determinability. Most presentations of natural compatibilism have been undertaken by philosophers who are themselves compatibilists, and who wish to show that compatibilism is true. They are therefore only interested in the good reasons. But uncommitted phenomenology of freedom takes the bad reasons with the good, and finds them of equal interest in giving an account of the ways in which we are naturally compatibilist.

In conclusion, let me mention something which has intentionally been ignored until now, and which not only provides one of the strongest arguments in favour of compatibilism considered as a philosophical theory, but is also one of the principal features of natural compatibilism. It is this. Behind the whole compatibilist enterprise lies the valid and important insight that, from one centrally important point of view, freedom is nothing more than a matter of being able to do what one wants or chooses or decides or thinks right or best to do, *given* one's character, desires, values, beliefs (moral or otherwise), circumstances, and so on. Generally speaking, we have this freedom. For determinism does not affect it at all, and it has nothing whatever to do with any supposed sort of ultimate self-determination, or any particular power to determine what one's character, desires, and so on will be. It is true that the fact that we generally have this freedom provides no support for the idea that we are or can be 'truly' self-determining in the way that still appears to be necessary for true responsibility. But we can indeed be self-determining in the compatibilist sense[23] of being able by our own action, and in the light of our necessarily non-self-determined characters and desires, to determine to a very considerable extent what happens to us.

Compatibilists who stress this point have a powerful question to ask: 'What else could one possibly suppose, or reflectively require, that freedom could or should be, other than this?' But the old incompatibilist answer remains. This account of freedom does nothing to establish that we are truly responsible for our actions, nor, in particular, to establish that we are or can be truly *morally* responsible for our actions, in the ordinary, strong, desert-entailing sense. Nor, correspondingly, does it provide any reason for thinking that people either are or can be free or

[23] Cf. 2.1.

truly responsible in a way that could render the 'personal-reactive' attitudes discussed in Chapter 5 truly appropriate. It seems that nothing can do this. But this still seems to be what we want.

So much for natural compatibilism; it can be developed much further. I wish now to say something more about our natural incompatibilism, and in so doing to return to the question of the nature of our commitment to belief in freedom.

6.5 THE TRUE CENTRE OF COMMITMENT

If our commitment to belief in freedom and responsibility were entirely (or even only primarily) grounded in our experience of other people, then I think we would lack a truly satisfactory explanation of its strength. Such an explanation is swiftly forthcoming when it is realized that it is grounded primarily in our experience of our own agency, and only secondarily in our experience of other people as proper objects of the reactive attitudes. The true centre of one's commitment to the notion of human freedom lies in one's attitude to and experience of oneself. The notion is integral to one's deepest sense of oneself as a self-determining planner and performer of action, someone who can create things, make a sacrifice, do a misdeed.

To say that the true centre of one's commitment lies in one's attitude to and experience of oneself is not to deny that one's attitude to and experience of oneself is deeply determined by one's interaction with others, and, in particular, by the kind of interaction necessary for acquisition of language (though it will be argued later that a solitary being could have an ordinarily strong sense of self as truly responsible). So far as human beings are concerned, it is simply to consider two things that develop in us in the course of our necessarily social development—our sense of ourselves as truly responsible and our sense of others as truly responsible; to claim that the nature and causes of these two things can profitably be distinguished, in certain respects at least; and to claim that the former is more important than the latter, so far as our general commitment to belief in true-responsibility-creating self-determination is concerned.

A naturalistic explanation of this sense of self-determination would connect it tightly with our sense, massively and incessantly confirmed since earliest infancy, of our ability to do what we want to do in order to (try to) get what we want, by performing a vast variety of actions, great and small, walking where we want, making ourselves understood, picking up this and putting down that. We pass our days in more or less continual and almost entirely successful self-directing intentional activity, and we know it.[24] Even if we don't always achieve our aims, when we act, we almost always perform a movement of the kind we intended to perform, and in that vital sense (vital for the sense of self-determining self-control) we are almost entirely successful in our action.

This gives rise to a sense of freedom to act, of complete self-control, of responsibility in self-directedness, that is in itself compatibilistically unexceptionable, and is quite untouched by arguments against true responsibility based on the impossibility of self-determination. But it is precisely this compatibilistically speaking unexceptionable sense of freedom and efficacy that is one of the fundamental bases of the growth in us of the compatibilistically speaking *im*permissible sense of true responsibility. To observe a child of two fully in control of its limbs, doing what it wants to do with them, and to this extent fully free to act in the compatibilist sense of the phrase, and to realize that it is precisely such unremitting experience of self-control that is the deepest foundation of our naturally *in*compatibilistic sense of true-responsibility-entailing self-determination, is to understand one of the most important facts about the genesis and power of our ordinary strong sense of freedom.

One reason why we advance from the permissible to the impermissible sense of freedom is perhaps a merely negative one, remarked on by Spinoza: ignorant of the causes of our desires, we do not normally experience our character, desires, or pro-attitudes as determined in us in any way at all; let alone in any objectionable way. We don't think back behind ourselves as we now find ourselves. It can happen that we do so, of course. But even if it does happen—even if some particular desire is experienced, in its importunacy, as somehow foreign, imposing itself from outside the self, as it were—this probably only serves, by providing a contrast, to strengthen our general sense that our desires and pro-attitudes are not determined in us. For if a desire is experienced as importunate, as imposing itself on one, as unwanted, then there must be present some other desire or pro-attitude in the light of which the first one is experienced as unwanted or as imposing itself. And the second desire or pro-attitude will presumably

[24] Most of these actions are routine or trivial, more or less thoughtlessly performed. But this in no way diminishes the importance of the experience of their performance as a source of the sense of self-determinability that we ordinarily have.

not also be experienced as an imposition, as alien. It will presumably be a pro-attitude which one 'identifies' with, and apprehends as part of oneself, and acquiesces in.

A great deal is locked up in this acquiescence. (It is here that our naturally incompatibilist thought appears to run directly counter to our naturally compatibilist acceptance of the 'just-thereness' of desires discussed in the last section.) For although it is unlikely to involve any explicit sense that one has been in any way actively self-determining as to character, it does nevertheless seem to involve an implicit sense that one is, generally, somehow in control of and answerable for how one is; even, perhaps, for those aspects of one's character that one doesn't particularly like.[25] As for those pro-attitudes and aspects of one's character that are welcome to one, it is as if the following ghostly subjunctive conditional lurks in one's attitude to them: if *per impossibile* I were to be (had been) able to choose my character, then these are the features I would choose (would have chosen).[26] This, I suggest, contributes importantly to the impermissible sense of true responsibility for themselves that most people have, more or less obscurely, more or less constantly.[27]

But it is not the principal reason for which we have the impermissible sense of true responsibility. The principal reason, I think, concerns the nature of our experience of choice, discussed in 3.6. It is simply that we are, in the most ordinary situations of choice, unable not to think that we will be truly or absolutely responsible for our choice, whatever we choose. Our natural thought may be expressed as follows: even if my character is indeed just something given (a product of heredity and environment, or whatever), I am still able to choose (and hence act) completely freely and truly responsibly, given how I now am and what I now know; this is so whatever else is the case—determinism or no determinism.

This thought is reinforced by the point just considered: according to which something that is in itself negative—the absence of any general

[25] Consider the sense of sin. People who see themselves as sinners do not only feel guilty about giving in to bad aspects of their character; they also feel guilty about (responsible for having) these bad features in the first place.

[26] It is hardly surprising that the subjunctive conditional as it were confirms the central, acceptable *status quo*; for the 'I' that features in the conditional is in a sense actually constituted, as something with pro-attitudes that imagines choosing its pro-attitudes, by the very pro-attitudes that it imagines choosing.

[27] To say this is not to say that people cannot occasionally—or even chronically—be disgusted by themselves. There are many complications here. Some of them are illustrated by H. Frankfurt in the papers cited in ch. 2 n. 4.

sense that our desires, pro-attitudes, character, and so on are *not* ultimately self-determined—is implicitly taken as equivalent to some sort of positive self-determination. Certainly we do not ordinarily suppose that we have gone through some sort of active process of self-determination at some particular past time; but it seems accurate to say that we do unreflectively experience ourselves rather as we would experience ourselves if we did believe that we had engaged in some such activity of self-determination.

There are many complexities here. But the main causes of the development of our sense of true responsibility out of our unremitting and compatibilistically speaking unexceptionable sense of complete self-control may perhaps be summarized as follows.

1. We tend to think that we have a will (a power of decision) distinct from all our particular motives (cf. 3.4).
2. In all ordinary situations of choice, we think that we are absolutely free to choose *whatever* else is the case (even if determinism is true, for example), and are so just because of the fact of our full appreciation of our situation (cf. 3.6). (Our experience of freedom is of course particularly vivid in cases of morally significant decisions.)
3. In some vague and unexamined fashion, we tend to think of ourselves as in some manner responsible for—answerable for—how we are (cf. the above, and, e.g., the quotations from Kant, Sartre, and Carr in 2.8).

All these aspects of the sense of true responsibility directly concern only one's experience of oneself and one's own agency.[28]

[28] There are a number of other familiar things that prevent us from experiencing ourselves and the world as determined in a way that might undermine our sense of freedom. For example: there is the fact that a person's own future choices and decisions are 'unpredictable in principle' for that person (cf. e.g. D. M. MacKay, 'On the Logical Indeterminacy of a Free Choice', and D. F. Pears, 'Predicting and Deciding'). There is the experiential quality of uncertainty and dithering indecision: it seems that things could so easily go either way (cf. Hume, *Treatise*, p. 408): it seems absurd to say that it is entirely determined which way they do go. There is the fact that even if determinism is true, what happens in the world in general does not produce any sense in us that it is deterministic in character (though we may be convinced materialists and believe firmly in the existence of deterministic laws of nature). For there are so many things that 'could so easily have happened' that did not happen in fact (or vice versa). One might so easily not have met one's lover, husband, or wife. Glancing at a newspaper left on the underground train, one may pick it up and read an announcement that changes one's life. Most lives contain many events of this sort. What happens seems to us to have an essentially fluid and open character. Perhaps we are not sufficiently reflective, but it is hard for us, in such circumstances, to be very *impressed* by the thought that our choices and actions may be entirely determined phenomena.

Various other ways of bringing out the independence of the sense of oneself as truly responsible from the sense of other people as so responsible suggest themselves. For example: surely one could come to be a sceptic about other minds and still continue to believe as strongly as ever in one's own freedom?

To this it may be objected that belief in the existence of other minds is at least a genetic condition of acquisition of commitment to belief in freedom. But the objection can be met as follows: (*a*), belief in other minds, may perhaps be a genetic condition of—or at least an invariable concomitant of—(*b*), the acquisition of a sense of self, and of (*c*), language-acquisition (and indeed of (*d*), acquisition of the intellectual complexity necessary for conceiving explicitly of, and then doubting the existence of, other minds). And (*b*) and even perhaps (*c*) may be conditions of the possibility of (*e*), the acquisition of a sense of oneself as truly responsible. But a genetic-condition claim of this sort is simply not a claim of the right kind to provide grounds for an objection to the view that one could come to doubt the existence of other minds without this affecting one's conviction as to one's own freedom in any way; and there does not seem to be any special, independent connection between (*a*) and (*e*), such as might be shown to hold if it could be shown that possession of other-reactive attitudes were actually essential for possession of the notion of true responsibility.[29]

More simply: it seems possible that a being might develop a strong sense of freedom (a sense of freedom that was in all essentials the same as ours) in a world in which there were no other creatures like itself, and no creatures which were such as to cause it to come to suppose that they were free—although there were, we may suppose, creatures which were such as to cause it to form the belief that they had experiences and pursued goals. The solitary being's sense of freedom might derive from its having to make difficult choices, life-determining choices, perhaps, about which of several equally attractive but very different and not co-attainable ends to pursue. It would not have to have any sense of moral good and bad (cf. 3.3). It might simply have a

[29] Furthermore: although unreflective belief in the existence of other minds is doubtless an invariable concomitant of language-learning here on earth, and as things are, it seems quite possible that a child might learn a language from other people (or even from actually experienceless robots) a constant theme of whose everyday conversation (or 'conversation') was that there was nothing it was like to be them. Although this might not at first make much sense to the child, and although it might at first suppose them to be like itself, it could presumably grow up into the firm (and possibly true) belief that there was nothing it was like to be any of its interlocutors. Growing up in this way, it could acquire a normally powerful sense of its actions being up to it in some absolute fashion.

powerful sense that it was entirely up to it what it did. (This said, it must be granted that a sense of moral right and wrong acts powerfully in fostering a sense of true responsibility, as Kant saw.)[30]

It may be objected that the solitary being would have to be linguistically endowed, and self-conscious, in order to be free—that these may be necessary conditions of free agenthood (cf. 7.3). If so, it might be said, it would need company, in order to acquire a language. However, logical possibility provides for the idea that it may just be created self-conscious and already possessed of a language, or at least of the capacity for language-like thought.[31] Alternatively, it may be brought up by other members of its own species to a point at which it is fully possessed of language, and then left to fend for itself after all memory of the existence of other sentient beings has been wiped from its mind. Surviving and flourishing, making difficult choices, it may develop or retain a strong sense of freedom of choice without any thought of others at all.

Suppose that this solitary being is persistently but by no means always hindered by constraining circumstances in the execution of its intentions. This being so, it may acquire a sense of freedom of *action*— that which it feels when unhindered—which is importantly different from the sense of freedom of *choice* just mentioned.[32] Neither of these senses of freedom depends essentially on interaction with other people,

[30] Here there is a complication worth noting. It is true that the general experience of difficult choice contributes vitally to the 'impermissible' sense of true responsibility, in the ordinary case. But the phenomenology of making a difficult (and let us say non-moral) choice in which one believes that there is a *right* and a *wrong* decision, if only one could work out which was which, need involve nothing at all that conflicts with a wholly compatibilistic view of things. In this case one considers and reconsiders the pros and the cons, and what one wants is simply that it should become clear which is the right choice. One wants to come to see which is best; and there is nothing in this experience that either involves or gives rise to any sense of true responsibility—any more than there is in considering which of a number of melons is ripest, or in wanting to be able to read the words on a sign that is just too far away. In cases like this the phenomenology of difficult choice is essentially that of wanting to form a true belief (cf. 2.5), and, so far at least, need involve nothing of the sense of radical freedom that may be produced by facing a dramatic conflict of duty and desire, or an important, life-determining choice between two very different morally neutral options which are in one's opinion equally attractive all things considered (between which there is 'nothing to choose').

[31] Possessed, that is, of at least the following: a disposition to have just the same sorts of experience, qualitatively speaking, that a solitary Robinson Crusoe who had forgotten that other people existed might have, so far as those of his experiences that he himself would be inclined to classify as experiences of thinking or speaking in language were concerned.

[32] See ch. 13 below, where both these senses of freedom are considered, and where it is suggested that one can have either without the other.

or upon preparedness to attribute freedom to others, but only on the private experience of deliberation and action. One's belief that others are free has the power it has because it is, first and foremost, a belief that they are like one finds oneself to be. We attribute to others the same sort of consciousness of responsibility for, and hence freedom of choice and action that we cannot but attribute to ourselves. It is not as if adversion either to the circumstances of our learning the word 'free' as members of a linguistic community, or to the dubiety of the 'argument from analogy', can undercut this point. On the contrary: the availability of this point, and others like it, illustrates the risk of exaggerating both the consequences of Wittgenstein's 'private language' argument, and the error allegedly involved in putting forward the argument from analogy in answer to certain sceptical puzzles.

Certainly our acquisition of an understanding of the words 'free' and 'truly responsible' proceeds in such a way that we are, ordinarily, as prepared to apply these words to others as we are to ourselves. And certainly we are in being committed to the reactive attitudes to other people committed to the belief that they are truly responsible agents. This is not denied. The claim is merely that the deepest point of attachment of one's commitment to belief in true responsibility lies in the experience one comes to have, *as* a social, linguistic being, of one's own agency. Even if it were true that a being could not develop in such a way as to come to attribute true responsibility to itself without having been participant in a social and linguistic community, this fact would provide no basis for an objection to the above claim, which is merely a claim about the deepest foundation of our present commitment to belief in true responsibility, not about the conditions of our past acquisition of such a belief.

It is not the 'general framework' of social life, then, that is presently in question. It is the agent's private experience of agency. It is one's commitment to belief in one's own efficacy, control, self-determination and total responsibility (in normally unconstrained circumstances) rather than one's commitment to holding others responsible and treating them as proper objects of reactive attitudes, that is primarily unrenounceable.

It only remains to say that, to the extent that it is primarily in one's attitudes to and conception of oneself that the roots of one's commitment to belief in responsibility lie, the problems which deter minism (and non-self-determinability) raises for that belief are particularly acute in one's own case. What on earth is one to think that one is, or is doing, if one thinks that one cannot really be responsible at all for what one does? Those who have fully understood what the application of the thought of determinism to themselves involves should be bewildered by this question (recall the thought-experiment in 6.2).

But it is likely to leave them undisturbed. And it is this equanimity in the face of the problem, this equanimity with which we continue to discuss the problem of freedom and determinism, that is perhaps the best indication of the strength of our commitment to belief in freedom.

6.6 SATKĀYADṚṢṬI

The suggestion that one's commitment to belief in freedom and the reactive attitudes may be of such a kind that its abandonment is practically speaking impossible has not so far been challenged. But it has been suggested that one might be able to engineer (or might simply undergo) partial but not total erosions of this commitment; and that it is perhaps not equally unrenounceable in all areas. For example: one's commitment to belief in one's own responsibility for action seems to be more deeply founded than one's commitment to belief in the responsibility of others, even if this difference is not revealed in a difference of surface strength in everyday life; and so it seems correspondingly more likely that one might cease to be moved to blame others, on account of belief in determinism or non-self-determinability, than that one might cease to feel guilty about what one took to be one's own miscreance.

But perhaps one can raise a more general doubt about arguments for unrenounceable commitments to attitudes or beliefs that appear to be false from some natural point of view. Consider certain Buddhist philosophers who argue, on a variety of metaphysical grounds, that our natural notion of the persisting individual self is a delusion. Having reached this conclusion, they set themselves a task: that of overcoming the delusion.

There are several routes to the doctrine of *satkāyadṛṣṭi*, the 'false view of individuality'.[33] Which one is taken is of no present importance.

---

[33] *An-ātman*, or 'no-soul', denotes the corresponding positive doctrine that there is no soul or self; and the experiential or phenomenological correlate of the factual or metaphysical error involved in *satkāyadṛṣṭi* is called *asmimāna*, or the " 'I am' idea". See *Selfless Persons*, by S. Collins, pp. 94–5, 100–3.

The Buddhists presently in question hold that (*a*), the false sense or conception of self, leads to (*b*), suffering, because it is essentially bound in with, as a necessary condition of, (*c*), the having of desires and aversions, which is itself a condition of the possibility of suffering.[34] To realize that there is no such thing as the individual self, to undermine the false view of individuality in oneself, is to cease to be bound by desires, cravings, and aversions, and hence to achieve liberation from suffering. It is, ultimately, to achieve the 'blowing out' of self in nirvana, and thereby to cease to suffer and to fear old age, sickness, and death.

These Buddhists not only have theoretical reasons for believing that their natural sense or conception of self is delusory; they also have powerful practical reasons for trying to improve their grasp on the fact of its delusoriness. They recognize, however, that one cannot simply abolish one's sense of individuality, by some sort of effortless, rationally motivated, self-directed intellectual fiat. Delusions delude, after all; and the ordinary, strong sense of self (and hence of self-determination) is a particularly powerful delusion. They therefore recommend the adoption of a certain practice—that of meditation—the eventual effect of which, they claim, is to cause the delusion to dislimn.[35]

Now a decision to adopt such a practice of meditation is presumably motivated by some desire. It can be simply a desire for an undeluded view of things—a love of truth or of correct attitude. In the Buddha's case, the originally predominant motive was his desire to overcome his horror of old age, sickness, and death: suffering, decrepitude and death are fearful only to a man who has desires and aversions of such a kind that he confronts himself as an object to worry about, and who has a sense of himself as a continuing entity, a person.[36]

What is curious about this general project is that if one attains nirvana, or at least a state of desirelessness, then one's desire for truth or correctness of attitude, or one's wish to escape from one's fear of mortal ills, lapses with all other desires, so that it is no longer there to be finally fulfilled by the course of action that it set in motion. Thus a

[34] (*b*) requires (*c*) and (*c*) requires (*a*). So to eliminate (*a*) is to eliminate (*b*). Obviously the unselfconscious—dogs, bats, and so on—can also suffer. The point is made in this particular way because it is the basis of a practical recommendation for human beings.

[35] Perhaps we may suppose that their goal is to achieve some kind of affectively speaking selfless but cognitively speaking fully self-conscious state of mind. See however Appendix E, § III.

[36] If there is, in a sense, no 'I', then there is nothing to fear in death and dissolution and there is no one there to feel fear in any case. For it is precisely the 'I' 's dissolution that is feared, and it is precisely the 'I' that does the fearing.

man who attains nirvana, or a state of desirelessness, can never give any current reason—if this involves adducing a present desire presently satisfied—for being the way he is. Nevertheless, given his love of truth or of correctness of attitude, or his fear of old age and death, his adoption of the practice of meditation *was* rational, even if he is now (practically speaking) non-rational, and is so as a result of that practice.

The foregoing enables one kind of person, at least, to answer the question of what it would be rational to do given belief in determinism and incompatibilism (or in non-self-determinability): someone who had such a belief, and wished to lose any sense of self as free or truly self-determining in any way, in order to achieve a more correct attitude to the world, would do well to adopt the allegedly self-dissolving practice of meditation. A sense of self is not only a necessary condition of fear for one's future; it is also, obviously, a necessary condition of possession of the allegedly illegitimate sense of oneself as a truly self-determining planner and performer of action.

A more general point is this. There appear to be powerful lines of reasoning available, within what Strawson calls our 'general framework' of attitudes and ideas, which question the correctness of the framework—or of paramount aspects of it—from within. There are, to say the least, some major tensions in it. No doubt a decision to adopt the 'objective' attitude to oneself and others cannot be implemented overnight, given the nature and strength of the framework and our commitment to it. But there is no such difficulty with a decision to initiate some practice which may more gradually undermine or alter the supposedly inflexible constraints of the framework. And, if we admit the possibility of partial alterations in attitudes or habits of thought to which we are as things are deeply committed, then this points to the possibility of a progressive abandonment of these attitudes or habits of thought which, gradually achieved, amounts to a total abandonment relative to the original position. It is not implausible to suppose that Buddhist monks and other mystics have succeeded in altering quite profoundly their experience of themselves (and others) as acting, thinking, and feeling beings.

And—finally—it is not implausible to say that they have in so doing achieved what is in certain respects a more correct view of the world, precisely to the extent that they have ceased to regard themselves and others as truly self-determining sources of actions, and have thereby come to adopt the objective attitude.[37] Having done so, they are certainly inhuman, in some way. And, as remarked, I do not think that we can really imagine what it might be like to be them. But there is no reason to think that they need be inhuman in any pejorative sense; and whatever nirvana is supposed to be like, it is clear that adoption of the objective attitude is in no way incompatible with compassion.

[37] It is arguable that philosophers who believe that true responsibility is impossible, and who see themselves as committed to the pursuit of truth, ought to undertake some practice of meditation. For it may enable them to come to appreciate the truth of their theoretical conclusion in a way which they are presently incapable of.

II

THE OBJECTIVIST BASIS

7

Objectivism: Preliminaries

Our commitment to belief in freedom (true responsibility) is as deeply rooted as it is widely ramified. It may be that it is practically speaking unrenounceable, both in thought and in action. But one may well be unimpressed by this fact, as a theorist: so far as beliefs are concerned, it seems natural to suppose that their unrenounceability or irresistibility can never entail their truth; and that an adequate account of free agenthood must show why our belief in free agenthood is true without appealing to the fact that we have the belief and are committed to it. Surely a demonstration that a belief is true cannot appeal to the fact that we believe it is (or are committed to it) without flouting the *principle of independence* (1.5.5)—the principle that the truth of a given belief cannot be dependent on anyone's having that same belief?

This is a natural train of thought. It puts the *Objectivist* point of view. (Respect for the principle of independence is the defining characteristic of the Objectivist approach to the problem of freedom, just as preparedness to reject the principle of independence defines the *Subjectivist* approach.) But in Part I both compatibilism and libertarianism were rejected as Objectivist theories of freedom. And since all positive theories of freedom are necessarily either compatibilist or libertarian (1.2), to reject both, in their Objectivist versions, is to conclude that no satisfactory Objectivist account of freedom can be given at all.

Faced with this conclusion, Part I went on to consider the prospects for Subjectivism, with particular reference to two arguably Subjectivist and indeed commitment theories, attributed to Kant and Strawson respectively. The first of these concentrated on the individual's experience of agency, the second on our commitment as social beings to a whole network of freedom-and-responsibility-presupposing 'personal-reactive' attitudes. The first appeared to involve the claim that we really are free, in the ordinary strong sense of the word. The second made no such simple claim, seeking rather to undercut the usual terms of debate altogether.

But it did not seem that either of these theories could provide adequate grounds for rejecting the natural Objectivist objection to Subjectivism just mentioned; and so I shall now return to the attempt to state an Objectivist theory of freedom or true responsibility—if only to try to show in more detail why such an attempt must fail. (It is not that the argument of Chapter 2 is inadequate to show this. It is rather that taking a different line provides a framework for considering some further issues in the 'general cognitive phenomenology' of freedom.)

The Objectivist theory that will be sketched is a compatibilist theory. But those libertarians who think (contrary to 2.2) that including a condition requiring the falsity of determinism in a theory that seeks to state the conditions of freedom is sufficient to turn the theory into a libertarian theory can add such a condition to the other necessary conditions of freedom that will be proposed in what follows, and can treat the resulting whole as a libertarian theory.

In fact, none of the necessary conditions of freedom that will be proposed in what follows are of such a kind to recommend themselves more to compatibilists than to libertarians: both groups are equally likely to agree that they are *necessary* conditions of freedom. Generally, libertarians are usually quite ready to accept the necessary conditions of freedom that compatibilists propose. They simply insist that any set of conditions that compatibilists propose as both necessary and *sufficient* for freedom must be incomplete, and can never be complete so long as it does not include a condition requiring the falsity of determinism.

The following, then, is concerned with questions about necessary conditions of free agenthood that arise *before* determinism becomes an issue—questions that arise before compatibilists and libertarians begin to disagree. It will be argued that all Objectivist theories of freedom run into insuperable difficulties before traditional problems relating to determinism (or non-self-determinability) have been raised at all, and that Subjectivism is not only of interest for negative reasons (as the only available alternative once conventional Objectivist compatibilism and libertarianism have been rejected): there are positive arguments in favour of its basic tenet that belief in freedom is a necessary condition of freedom. Objectivists have to try to meet these arguments *before* they turn to face the problems posed for freedom by determinism (or non-self-determinability). The threat they face is that their approach to the problem of free agenthood will not only prove inadequate, but will prove inadequate before the age-old question of determinism has even been raised.

To make it absolutely clear that the question of determinism is not now at issue, it will henceforth be assumed, simply for the purposes of argument, that compatibilism is a viable enterprise, and that compatibilists are right to suppose that the truth of determinism (or the impossibility of true self-determination) raises no insuperable problem for the claim that we are free. This assumption is no doubt false. It is made here simply in order to keep problems about determinism and self-determination right out of the way. In due course it will dropped.[1]

Some may think that questions about determinism, or rather self-determinability, are so obviously central, when one is trying to give an account of what true responsibility might be, that they cannot simply be bracketed out in this way. And indeed they are central. Nevertheless many other important aspects of the general structure of our thought about freedom can be discussed without raising questions about determinism and self-determinability. (If the aim of the present discussion were just to establish whether freedom in the sense of true responsibility were possible, it could have stopped at Chapter 2.)

What, then, is the Objectivist approach? How should Objectivists define free agenthood? This chapter and the next discuss this question at a very basic level, and move rather slowly. First of all the Objectivists give a more precise account of their *definiendum*. In what follows they do not ask 'What are the necessary and sufficient conditions of freedom, or free action, or free agency, or of the truth of "*a* is a free agent"?' but 'What are the necessary and sufficient conditions of the truth of "*a* is a *potential free agent*"?'

7.2 POTENTIAL FREE AGENTS

Many of those who have written about freedom have concentrated on seeking a distinction between free and unfree action. Their analyses have tended towards an account according to which actions are free if[2] those who perform them are, when they perform them, neither physi-

---

[1] A further reason for having no qualms about the possibly limiting effect of operating within a compatibilist framework is provided by the conclusion, reached in 2.11, that assuming the falsity of determinism can never be of any positive help in trying to state a detailed theory of freedom.

[2] Or at least only if—libertarians would add conditions, e.g. one that asserts the falsity of determinism, to a compatibilist account.

cally nor psychically constrained in any of a variety of more or less precisely specified fashions.

Such analyses take people as their subject, of course. For dogs are purposive agents, and may act when not constrained in either of the two ways mentioned, and yet we do not wish to say that they then act freely. We may perhaps grant that there is a sense in which they do then act freely; but we still do not think that they are or can be free in every sense in which we are or can be, or that they are or can be free in the vital sense which is of present concern.

We therefore require an account of just what it is that makes us different from dogs in respect of freedom. It must be an account that makes no use of the notion of constraint in distinguishing what is free from what is unfree, since dogs and people can be identical in respect of lack of constraint and yet differ in respect of freedom.

The main task, then, is not to distinguish between free and unfree *actions*, but between free and unfree *agents*; to distinguish, that is, between those who *can* be free and those who can never be; to give a description of those features of a *purposive* agent in virtue of the possession of which it can be a *free* agent. Here one is not concerned with the conditions of actual freedom to act in a particular case—which characteristically include conditions relating to the absence of circumstances held to constitute physical or psychical constraint. One is concerned only with the conditions that an agent must fulfil if it is to be such that it *can* be free to act in given unconstrained circumstances; one is concerned with what I shall call *potential free agenthood*.

'Potential free agent' is a semi-technical term. But the adjective 'potentially free' is only intended to capture that current and familiar sense of the word 'free' according to which we conceive of freedom as a permanent, generic, non-act-relative property of some agents—normal adult human beings, for example; as when we say 'human beings are free agents'. We hold that people (unlike dogs) are *actually* able to *act* freely, in the ordinary, strong sense, just so long as they are ordinarily unconstrained. And this is because we hold that they are free *agents—potential* free agents, in the present sense—even at times when they are constrained and are for that reason not actually able to act freely.

Because 'potential(ly)' simply makes explicit a feature that the word 'free' already possesses when used in a generic and non-act-relative way to designate a presumedly permanent property of agents, it will regularly be bracketed or omitted in what follows. The fundamental idea is simply this: if people can act freely and truly responsibly at all—if, unlike dogs, they are on account of their general nature or constitution objects of a kind that can act freely—then they must presumably have some persisting intrinsic property or properties that dogs (and Nemo)[3] do not have; they must have some persisting property or properties in virtue of which they are actually able to act freely when unconstrained, and which they still possess when constrained and unable to act freely.

An agent is a potential free agent, then, if and only if it is an agent of such a kind that it acts freely whenever it acts and is unconstrained.[4] But there is no need to consider whether or not it is ever actually free or unconstrained, when concerned with potential free agenthood. Nor need one consider in detail what actually constitutes freedom-limiting-or-eliminating constraint—what those constraints are whose absence is a necessary condition of actual freedom to act. A discussion of freedom that treats of potential free agenthood (treats, that is, of one central sense of the word 'free') can be carried on entirely independently of discussion of the notion of constraint. For it is concerned only with kinds of agents, and with differences in their nature as agents, and not at all with their surrounding circumstances.[5]

Discussion of constraint and its varieties is therefore complementary to, and essentially secondary to, discussion of potential free agenthood. If there really is a distinction to be had between agents who can act freely (truly responsibly) and agents who can never do so (a distinction between potential free agents and all others), then it is a distinction that would exist even if no actual agents were ever subject to any kind of constraint. If we lived in a world in which there were no constraints of the kind that are standardly counted as limiting or eliminating freedom, we might well still want to say that we were free and truly responsible agents while dogs were not. So it is not the case, as many have claimed, that the meaning of the word 'free' is to be elucidated wholly (or even primarily) by reference to the contrasting notion of constraint. If we are indeed free, and in a way that dogs can never be,

[3] Nemo was introduced in 1.6. He is as similar to an ordinary human being as it is possible to be without being self-conscious.

[4] It is arguable that there is a crucial sense of the word 'free' in which a potential free agent must be said to act freely whenever it acts at all. That is, it is arguable that it cannot be constrained in such a way that it can both act and yet not be able to act freely. If this is right, the words 'and is unconstrained' in the text are superfluous. (I argue for this in 'On the Inevitability of Freedom (from a Compatibilist Point of View)'.)

[5] I take 'surrounding circumstances' to include not only those external physical circumstances that can constitute constraints on the agent, but also those internal mental circumstances that can count as psychical constraints—hypnotic commands, obsessional neuroses, kleptomaniac impulses, and so on.

then there is another theoretically prior contrast; the contrast between potential free agents and all others.

Infants are not potential free agents, but become so, if we are. But if they are truly agents before they are free agents, as they surely are, then their case suggests that the distinction between free agents and unfree agents may not be an absolute or all-or-nothing one. For children may come gradually into this state; in which case it admits of degrees. (Similarly, those who go, or cease to be, insane, may be thought to lose and regain potential free agenthood by unclear degrees—unless we suppose that true insanity is simply a form of psychical constraint that is as such compatible with potential free agenthood.) But even if one allows that there may be unclear degrees of free agenthood, it still seems to be true that one is, as an ordinary adult person, wholly a free agent, if one is a free agent at all. A normal adult dog is never a free agent (we suppose), while a normal adult person's free agenthood is complete and unchanging, ascribed simply on account of his or her mental and physical nature. To this extent the distinction between free agents and unfree agents is an absolute distinction, despite children and lunatics.

Since the following discussion of freedom will at various points be conducted in terms of the question of what it is to be able *to choose* freely, it is worth introducing the notion of being potentially able to choose freely (or, equivalently, being a potential free chooser) at this point. A being is a potential free chooser if and only if there are possible circumstances—unconstrained circumstances—in which it can actually choose freely (i.e. in such a way that it is truly responsible for its choice). Substituting 'chooser' and 'chooses' for 'agent' and 'acts' in the last paragraph but two gives an alternative definition of freedom in an obvious way: an agent is free if and only if it is an agent of such a kind that it chooses freely whenever it chooses and is unconstrained (in its choice).

Talk of action and talk of choice introduce different emphases.[6] But if a being is free or truly responsible in the ordinary, strong sense of the word, then it must be, equally, a potential free agent and a potential free chooser. It is to be presumed that these two forms of words do not describe significantly different conditions, or have different applicability-conditions deep down, even if it is natural to characterize them differently on the surface. (Here as elsewhere one is up against the extraordinary slipperiness of the crucial terms of the free will debate.)

[6] Though choices can be actions, and actions, therefore, choices.

Given this statement of the *definiendum*, we may now turn to the Objectivists' definition.

7.3 A PROVISIONAL DEFINITION

What account does an Objectivist give of potential free agenthood? This is a large question, but a large part of the answer is obvious. As remarked in 1.5, most actual theories of free agenthood take the form of *capacity* theories; and capacity-citing conditions are bound to form the basis at least of any theory of free agenthood.

An initial capacity-citing definition might go as follows: a being is a potential free agent (a potential free chooser) if and only if it is
(1) capable of entertaining desires,
(2) capable of forming beliefs about its circumstances,[7]
(3) practical-rational, that is, capable of practical reasoning,
(4) capable of self-movement (or self-change),[8]
(5) capable of self-conscious thought.

These basic Objectivist conditions will be called the 'S conditions', for a reason that will emerge shortly.

Another way to present one's initial definition is as an account of when a *purposive* agent is a *free* agent; after all, we are concerned only with beings who are capable of purposive action, and with the question of what more has to be true of them if they are to be capable of free action. If one does this, the first four S conditions—or whatever version of them is finally preferred—may be taken to be definitive of the phrase 'purposive agent'. The fifth condition relating to self-consciousness then emerges as of paramount importance, and, indeed, as that which makes the difference between purposive agents in respect of freedom. It will be argued, however, that it cannot be supposed to do this on its own.

Books may be and have been written about what exactly is involved in satisfaction of the first four S conditions. Here a general understanding of what they involve will be taken for granted. This will be supplemented by the account of ability to choose in Chapter 8; but a few comments about them are worth making now. The fifth S condition, relating to self-consciousness, will be discussed in Chapter 9.

---

[7] With all that this presupposes in the way of possession of 'standing' beliefs, possession of concepts, and so on.

[8] The bracketed formulation takes account of the fact that there may be mental actions, and leaves open the alleged possibility that there may be immaterial minds.

As regards (1), first, a being need only be capable of entertaining desires, potentially desire-entertaining, because a purposive agent doesn't always have to have some desire or other in order to be a free agent. Second, some may be inclined to assimilate being desire-entertaining to being desire-satisfaction-seeking. They may thus think that (1) implies (4), being capable of self-change, as well as (3), being practical-rational. But a being could possibly be desire-entertaining, and yet not be disposed to link up its desires to action at all.[9] Or it could be desire-satisfaction-seeking, in the sense of being disposed to seek to satisfy certain desires, while being in fact wholly incapable of satisfying them—ever.[10] And this inability might not be the consequence of any constraint to which it was subject, but permanent and constitutional.

It is therefore clearer and simpler to include a separate condition of kind (4) that presents self-changeability as a basic requirement for a purposive agent. Condition (3) may be seen as similarly non-redundant in placing a certain condition on its desire-entertaining and belief-forming capacities: it requires that these capacities connect up in a certain way—in such a way that its desires and beliefs (or, generally, motives from whatever source) are susceptible of being combined, or of combining, in some sort of action-oriented, conscious or non-conscious mental process possibly productive of further beliefs or further desires, as well as actual actions.

Analysis of what is involved in (3), practical rationality, is a very complicated matter. Perhaps (3) must be allowed to involve (4), capability for self-change, both because practical reasoning is itself plausibly seen as an *activity*, in certain cases at least, and because it is not uncommon to include under the heading of practical reasoning not just

[9] Not all our desires are of the right sort to link up with action, given that we believe what we do believe; consider the desire that it rain tomorrow (unless you believe in the efficacy of rain dances). There could be a race of beings—the Weather Watchers—that had many desires about the weather, but were incapable of forming potentially action-prompting desires, and were not purposive agents at all. (Surprisingly, this claim is thought to be contentious by some philosophers, who think that one can't make sense of the notion of desire independently of the notion of action.) A purposive agent must be capable of having desires which are such that it can come to believe that there is something it could do about satisfying them, given what else it believes. This is a condition on its beliefs and desires that requires no particular beliefs and desires. It only requires that, whatever desires an agent is capable of forming, it must be capable of forming a certain belief about at least some of them—to wit, that they are possibly satisfiable by action on its part. (Note that a being may be a free agent even if it never does anything, either because it wants to do nothing, or simply because there is nothing it wants to do. Cf. the case of Mark Tietjens in *Last Post*, by Ford Madox Ford.)

[10] There being nothing at all, perhaps, that, for it, constituted even *trying* to do so.

the reasoning about what to do, but also the actual doing of what gets decided upon.

It would be necessary, in a full acount of these things, to define a rather weak notion of practical rationality, because it is being allowed that dogs can act. And it might become questionable to what extent mental practical reasoning is an activity, in the sense of something intentionally directed, given the notion of practical rationality that would emerge. But these details simply do not matter to the present attempt to state sufficient conditions of freedom. Given the present approach, it just doesn't matter if the S conditions are too rich, as purportedly minimally necessary and sufficient conditions of self-conscious purposive agenthood. For it will be argued that even if they are too rich in this sense, they are still not sufficient for free agenthood. The problems that are of principal concern lie ahead, and have to do with the question of whether Attitudinal conditions (1.5.3) must be added to whatever set of capacity conditions are finally proposed by Objectivists.

The term 'capacity condition' is not an ideal one, in fact, because it forces the statement of the basic S conditions into explicitly capacity-citing terms. But one can easily restate these conditions as follows: a being is a potential free agent (if and) only if it is a (3) practical-rational (5) self-conscious being that has (1) desires and (2) beliefs and is (4) capable of self-change. I shall adopt this restatement.

Since not all the basic S conditions explicitly cite capacities, given this restatement, it will be better not to call them capacity conditions. I will call them the '*Structural*' conditions ('S' stands for 'Structural'); for they clearly constitute the basic structural framework—purposive agenthood plus self-consciousness—of anything that could be worthy of the name of potential free agenthood. Those who claim that the analysis of the conditions of freedom can be fully stated in these terms will accordingly be called the 'Structural theorists'.

They are in effect the capacity theorists under a new name; and they inherit the capacity theorists' refusal to admit Attitudinal conditions into the set of conditions of freedom. They think that to be free is just to have a certain sort of *agentive and cognitive structure* that can be described in very general, purely functional terms, as in (1)-(5) above. (The word 'Structural' is admittedly vague. But that is part of the reason for adopting it, as a convenient name for a natural class of conditions that has no natural name.)

The *Attitudinal* theorists may be redefined accordingly, as those who hold that there are, among the conditions of free agenthood, conditions requiring the possession by the agent of attitudinal or experiential properties whose possession is not entailed by any of the general Structural properties that get proposed by Structural theorists.

8

Choice

The basic Structural conditions of free agenthood have now been stated. They are unremarkable. They lay down that any free agent must be a fully self-conscious rational agent.

Self-consciousness is the subject of the next chapter. In this chapter I wish to give an account of the notion of ability to choose—simply because it is natural to discuss the problem of freedom not only in the light of the question 'What makes a purposive agent a free agent?' but also in the light of the question 'What makes an agent that is able to choose not only *able* to choose but able to choose *freely*?' These two questions sometimes seem to prompt rather different lines of approach to the problem of free will. But, as noted at the end of 7.2, they both aim at the same thing, and, unsurprisingly, trying to answer the second can enter into trying to answer the first.

Ability to choose will be characterized in such a way that it is certainly true that we are able to choose. It will be characterized in such a way that we are able to choose even if determinism is true, and whether or not we are able to choose freely. For it is the notion of free choice, not that of choice, that is presently problematic.

Of course one way of putting the determinist case is to say that we are never really able to choose at all (and *a fortiori* never able to choose freely), and that this is so simply because we are determined. But it is much better to put the determinist case by saying that although we are certainly able to make choices, we never really choose *freely*, i.e. in such a way that we are truly responsible for our choices and for what we subsequently do. For it is obvious that we are often able to choose— able to choose *what to do*, that is. People make such choices all the time; and they could hardly make such choices and not be able to choose.

The discussion that follows is narrowly focused, and rather involved in places, and may be skipped by those with no particular interest in the notion of choice. Those who skip should take note of the definition of 'is aware* that' on p. 135, however, and of the description of the sense in which Fido the dog is able to choose, which is given in the first and third paragraphs of 8.3.

8.2 ABILITY TO CHOOSE

We are concerned, then, with ability to choose what to do—ability to choose among courses of action. For purposes of exposition it is best to take the simplest case, that of choosing between just two options: between performing an action of kind X (an X-action) and performing an action of kind Y (a Y-action).[1] The account in terms of two options can be expanded in an obvious way to fit choice between any number of options, and is in this way quite general.[2] It goes as follows. A purposive agent, b, is actually able to choose between performing an X-action and performing a Y-action, at time t, so long as

> (1) it thinks, or believes explicitly, at t, that it is now (given its capacities and circumstances) able to perform either an X-action or a Y-action,

and

> (2) it is not psychically constrained,[3] either (i) in such a way that (unknown to it) it cannot help determining on an X-action, or (ii) in such a way that it cannot determine either on performing an X-action or on performing a Y-action.

In case (i), it may well look as if b has made an ordinary choice, and b will think it has done so. But it will be wrong.

That's all there is to it (the use of the word 'explicitly' will be discussed below). We regularly fulfil these two conditions. The kinds of things

---

[1] In the simplest case, Y-ing may be just not X-ing—it may, for example, be a question of pushing, or not pushing, a problematic button.

[2] I take it to be obvious that choices and decisions can be actions—though nothing in what follows depends on this. Doubtless there are cases where one may have reason to say that a choice or decision has occurred while having reason to doubt whether any event clearly identifiable as an action has occurred (and there are also cases of physical action where there seems to be no good reason to say that any sort of preceding choice or decision has occurred). But this fact raises no real difficulties for the view that certain choices and decisions, including the clearest cases of pondered, premeditated, and consciously rehearsed choices and decisions, are actions.

[3] By, for example, a post-hypnotic command, a terrifying threat, or a compulsion deriving from an obsessional neurosis. (Only psychical constraints need be mentioned here, because it is only the psychical action, process, or event of choice that is presently in question.)

that count as constraints are familiar from compatibilist theory.[4] Notice that the account is an account of being *actually* able to choose (between X and Y) at a given time. A being is *potentially* able to choose (is, that is, a being of a sort that can make choices) just in case it is such that it can in given particular circumstances be actually able to choose, where this is defined as above.

It may be objected that agents that cannot be said to have beliefs or thoughts (in the way that we do) can be said to choose, and, *a fortiori*, to be able to choose, and that the above definition does not allow for this. This objection will be considered below; it will be suggested that dogs can properly be said to be able to choose.

In ordinary use the expression '*b* is able to choose between X and Y' is ambiguous. It can imply (*a*) that *b* is able to put its choice into effect. But it can mean simply (*b*) that *b* is able to make a choice between the options just in the sense of being able to decide mentally for one or the other, and in this case nothing is implied about *b*'s ability to put its choice into effect.

It is only (*b*), the second, less common, but more fundamental sense which is of concern here. Given this sense of 'able to choose', a being can correctly be said to be able to choose—i.e., to go through the conscious or non-conscious mental process of, or perform the mental action of, choice—whether or not it does, or can, actually put the choice into effect in any way.

I shall now consider the two conditions of ability to choose in more detail.

To begin with—the word 'explicitly', qualifying 'believes' in (1), is notoriously vague. One can limit although not eliminate this vagueness by giving the word a special restricted sense. This will be marked with a cross—'explicitly[+]'—and characterized by reference to another neologism: 'is aware* that'.

'Is aware* that' stands in exactly the same relation to 'is aware that' as 'believes that' stands to 'believes truly that'. Thus one can be aware* of something that is not in fact the case, while one cannot be aware of something that is not the case. (That is, '*x* is aware that *p*' entails '*p*' whereas '*x* is aware* that *p*' does not.) The star superscript simply cancels the 'factive' or 'success verb' implication of 'is aware that', allowing one to retain the word 'aware' as usefully if vaguely descriptive of a certain general kind of cognitive state. Later on I shall introduce

[4] See, for example, *Responsibility*, by J. Glover.

other such terms—'is conscious* that', 'grasps* that', 'realizes* that'
and so on—these too being taken to stand in exactly the same relation
to the 'success' verbs 'is conscious that', 'grasps that', and 'realize
that' respectively as 'believes that' stands to 'believes truly that'. The
somewhat barbarous form 'experiences* that', to be understood on the
same lines, may also be added to this list.

I will say that a belief p—that is, a belief that p—is *occurrent* in
thought when one is occurrently thinking that p. Sometimes, for brevity
I shall simply say that the belief p is occurrent. Occurrent beliefs o
thoughts are actual episodes of conscious entertaining of thoughts o
beliefs that p or that q.[5]

'Explicit+' may now be defined as follows: a being b explicitly+ believes
that p if and only if b is *presently aware** that p. Given this definition
an explicit+ belief may very well be occurrent; but it need not be, for
given our natural use of the word 'aware', one does not have to be
thinking occurrently that the door is open for it to be true that one is
presently aware* (and, doubtless, aware)[6] that the door is open. But i
the explicit+ belief is not occurrent then it must be—here the ineliminable
vagueness—'near at hand' in the mind, present to mind in some way in
which a belief or thought can be present to mind without actually being
occurrent. Thus, for example, if you are reviewing two kinds of courses
of action, X and Y, which you believe to be the best (or only) one
open to you, and if, having assessed the pros and cons of X in conscious
occurrent thought, you then pass to the assessment of Y in the same
way, your belief that you can perform an action of kind X may well be
explicit+ in the present sense, although not occurrent. It need not be the
case, though, for a belief to be explicit+, that it should previously and
recently have been the direct object of conscious attention. It can be
just there, present to mind in the sense sketched, not consciously entertained.[7]

---

[5] It may be protested that there are no occurrent beliefs—that beliefs, unlike thoughts,
are simply not items of the sort that can be said to *occur* in the course of conscious
experience. This must be granted. 'Occurrent belief' is a (semi-)technical term. But it
refers to something quite unmysterious: for to entertain or have an occurrent belief that
p is simply to think, occurrently, the thought that p. The belief, one might say, is the
content of the thought, and to that extent is occurrent when the thought is thought.
(Given this ruling, 'thought' and 'belief' will often be interchangeable.)

[6] The star superscript can be dropped whenever the awareness is veridical.

[7] Some may think this attempt to define a type of cognitive state has a false (and
absurd) air of exactitude about it; it is true that the notion of belief is irredeemably
vague. But although there are no sharp divisions to be found in this area of reality, there
are none the less real differences, and, therefore, distinctions, and they can reasonably

Given this account of explicit+ belief, we can consider condition (1) of the account of ability to choose.

In order to be able to choose (at *t*) between performing an X-action and a Y-action, one need not actually be able to put one's choice into effect, according to condition (1). But one must (at *t*) at least think or believe explicitly+ both that one can now perform an X-action and that one can perform a Y-action: possession of such a thought or belief is essential to these two courses of action being truly objects of choice for one, now. For if one has no such belief, or thinks that one cannot in fact perform either an X-action or a Y-action, then one cannot mentally determine on either, deciding 'I will perform an X-action (or Y-action)'. One cannot make a choice between them at all. (One cannot, after all, intend to perform an action of either kind.)

If one's belief that one cannot perform such actions is false, then there is admittedly a sense in which one can now choose between them: for one can now perform them and, in that sense, one can choose between performing them—did one but know it. But the qualification 'did one but know it' is crucial. There remains a fundamental sense in which one cannot now choose between them: if there are 'in fact' three courses of action open to me but I am (wrongly) sure that one of them is not open to me at all, then I can only choose between the two I do believe to be open to me. That is, only these two are possible objects of reasoned choice for me now, given my belief. I can't intend to pursue, now, the third course of action. Believing you can do something (now) is not a necessary condition of being able to do it (now), but it is a necessary condition of being able to choose or decide to do it (now), in the present sense of 'able to choose'.[8]

be marked in such indefinite terms as the present ones. (One does not have to worry about all possible details or cases—about whether or not a whole quantity of explicit+ beliefs have to be attributed to one when one is preoccupied and drives fifteen miles without noticing, for example.)

[8] It is true that *not* believing that one can perform an X-action is not the same as believing one cannot perform such an action. But it seems that one cannot choose to perform an X-action even if it is not the case that one believes that one cannot perform it, but only that one does not believe that one can perform it. For if one does not believe one can perform an X-action, then either (*a*) one believes that one cannot perform an X-action, or (*b*) one has no belief about performing X-actions at all, or (*c*) one is aware of the course of action X, as in (*a*), but one has no belief either way about whether one can perform such an action; or one thinks one cannot, but is simply not sure. Case (*a*) has been dealt with. In case (*b*) one clearly cannot choose to perform an X-action: if there are 'in fact' three courses of action open to me, but one of them has not even occurred to me, then I can only choose between the other two—only those two are open to me in actual fact. As for case (*c*), one cannot choose to do something one has no

It may be objected that condition (1) is not sufficient as a belief condition. For the following may be proposed as a possibility: that one should now explicitly+ believe that one is able to perform actions of kinds X, Y, and Z, while simply failing to add Z in with the other courses of action that are being considered *with a view to choosing between them*—even though Z is clearly an option worth considering in the circumstances. In this case, it may be said, one may after the event think oneself idiotic not to have thought of Z—not to have thought of it as *up for choice*, that is—but one's not thinking of it as up for choice did effectively rule it out from among one's real options at that time.

If this case is accepted, it prompts the suggestion that in addition to the original condition (1), which requires that one believe explicitly+ at *t* that one is now *able to perform* actions of kinds X and Y (and Z), one must add a further condition requiring that one also think explicitly+ of X and Y (and Z) as *up for choice*. Call the original condition (1A). The present suggestion is that one must add a new condition, (1B), requiring that one believe explicitly+, at *t*, that one is now *able to choose* between X and Y (and Z).

This suggestion has some force. To say, as in (1B), that one can now choose between performing an X-action and performing a Y-action only if one believes one can looks paradoxical, because it appears to contravene the principle of independence (1.5.5). But it can also look obviously true, given the present approach. For it can seem very natural to say that the objects of one's choice are partly constituted as such precisely by one's taking or believing them to be such. It seems that nothing can be in your actual range of choices, now as you wonder what to do, unless it is now taken by you to be in your range of choices.

The best way to accommodate this suggestion, and the apparent problem that it raises, is I think as follows: it seems plausible to say that if one now thinks or believes explicitly+ (1A) that one is now able to perform actions of kinds X, Y, and Z, then there is a sufficient sense in which one *ipso facto* thinks or believes explicitly+ (1B) that one is now

belief that one can do, or about which one is completely unsure whether or not one can do it, one can only choose to have a go at it, or to take steps towards becoming such that one can do it. And the action of having a go at it (or of taking such steps) will be an action that one does believe one can perform. Quite generally, it is no objection to the claim that one can choose to do only what one believes one can do to say that one can choose to have a go at doing what one does not believe one can do (e.g. perform an X-action), or believes one cannot do, or believes one has only a very small chance in succeeding in doing; because in this case too one is in fact choosing to do something one believes one can do—i.e., to have a go at performing an X-action.

able to choose between them. To think *explicitly*⁺ of them as actions one is now able to perform just is to think of them as open to one, as options, as *eligibilia*. For they are, now, 'near at hand in the mind', now as one considers what to do.

But is this right? Martin Luther may be introduced by those who wish to deny that (1A) entails or in a sufficient sense implicitly contains (1B), in the way proposed in the last paragraph. For Luther, confronted with a choice, made his choice and said 'I can do no other.'

Is this grounds for an objection? Not really. For when Luther said this, he clearly believed (knew) that he was strictly speaking able to do other than he did do. Let us call what he did do 'X'. He knew, in fact, that he was both able to do X and able not to do X; he knew that he was also able to do Y or Z, say. All he meant by 'I can do no other' was, in effect (for he was not deranged), 'There are indeed these different possibilities of action, X, Y, and Z, but my commitment to my principles is such that there is only one I can possibly opt for.'

Suppose this is accepted. It may nevertheless be claimed that although Luther had the (explicit⁺) (1A)-belief that he was able to perform actions of kinds X, Y, and Z, he simply did not have the (1B)-belief at all: he simply did not really consider Y and Z as up for choice. So (1A) and (1B) can come apart after all. But the reply to this is simple: attribution of the (1B)-belief, in the sense that is presently of concern, does not really go beyond what is already contained in the (1A)-belief. To the extent that Luther has the (1A)-belief he *ipso facto* has, in the required way, the (1B)-belief that all of X, Y, and Z are objects of choice for him, things that he can possibly choose between, and in fact has to choose between.

The possibility proposed above—the possibility that one may at *t* believe explicitly⁺ that one is now able to perform actions of kinds X, Y, and Z and yet somehow not *ipso facto* think of Z as at least in principle up for choice—may thus be rejected. No doubt to do this is simply to propose to understand the word 'explicitly' in a certain way— to give it a certain force. But it seems a plausible view in any case.

What follows? Well, to put things in this way is to say that (1A) implicitly contains and hence entails (1B).[9] But in this case (1B) is automatically a necessary condition of ability to choose, in so far as it is entailed by (1A)—even if all one actually needs to mention, in giving the conditions of ability to choose, is (1A); in which case the principle

---

[9] Obviously (1B) entails (1A)—one can't have the former belief without having the latter.

of independence is contravened. What is more, something like the concept of choice must be attributed to any creature that is said to be able to choose.

These things will be considered later. In the meantime the original account will be left as it is—though condition (1) will continue to be called (1A)—in order for a certain further point to be made. This is the important point, already mentioned, that even if it turns out that one cannot in fact perform any of the kinds of actions one believes one can perform, and proceeds to choose between, in a particular case (because of some instantaneously descending attack of paralysis, say, or simply because of error about what kinds of actions one is able to perform), still one's choice can be a fully genuine choice, just *qua* mental decision. It can, after all, be a morally assessable choice, if one is a moral agent. A moral agent can be morally praised and condemned for its choices or decisions even if it is completely unable to put any of them into effect—ever. It must of course believe that it is able to put them into effect, both for the moral judgements to obtain purchase and, as condition (1A) points out, for it to be said to have made a choice at all. But its (1A)-belief can be false while its choice is a genuine choice. One can be wrong in thinking that one can perform either an X-action or a Y-action, and nevertheless face a genuine and possibly tormenting choice between them, given that one now believes that one can now perform them; and one's subsequent choice can be morally praiseworthy or condemnable (and hence free), if one is indeed a moral (and hence free) agent, even though no further action results.[10]

So much for (1A), the belief condition of ability to choose. If one fulfils the belief condition, then it suffices, for one to be able to choose, simply that one also fulfil the lack-of-constraint condition, condition (2). This is clearly a further condition. For even if one fulfils the belief condition, believing that one is now able to perform either an X-action or a Y-action, one can still be psychically compelled or constrained—by post-hypnotic command, or by some other unconscious compulsion—

[10] According to the fundamental sense of 'able to choose' which is presently of concern, then, a being constitutionally incapable of any sort of physical action, but continually deluded about this, believing itself to be capable of performing a wide range of physical actions (or, more generally, actions, including mental actions, which are not actions of choice), can make genuine choices. And, given that choices can be actions, it follows that if there are free agents at all, then they can act freely in making choices even if they are unable to perform any other sorts of actions at all. (This point is crucial when one considers what the minimal case of free agenthood might be. See also Appendix C.)

in such a way that one can in fact only 'choose' one thing; in such a way, that is, that one is not really able to choose at all, although one believes one is. So it is not enough that one believe that one is able to choose. Obviously, the belief must also be true, and it doesn't guarantee its own truth, which depends essentially on such things as (2)—on whether or not one is subject to some sort of psychical compulsion.

To summarize. There are two main conditions on ability to choose: (1A), a belief condition, and (2), a lack-of-constraint condition. I take them to be sufficient conditions of ability to choose in the following sense: if a being actually makes an apparent choice, and fulfils these two conditions, then that apparent choice is a real choice.

8.3 FIDO'S CHOICE

Given the present account, there is a clear sense in which dogs like Fido (and *a fortiori* Nemo—and Nemo even if not Fido) can be able to choose. Consider the following case. Fido is an affectionate dog, trained for life-saving. He stands at the end of an island, facing the point of bifurcation of a river, watching his master and mistress being carried away equidistantly down the two channels of the river. He looks from side to side, agitated, hesitating, then plunges after—one of them. Here it seems clear that Fido is able to choose. For although he is not a fully self-conscious being, it seems clear that he is, as he hesitates, in some straightforward sense now (1A) (explicitly+) aware of being able to perform either an X-action (save his mistress) or a Y-action (save his master).[11] And it seems clear too that he is, in some sense, *ipso facto* (1B) aware of being able to choose between them. There is, then, a crucial respect in which dogs (not to mention superdogs, and Nemo, and other possible unselfconscious beings) and human beings are similar as agents, however different they are in other respects: they are similar in being able to choose in the present sense.

---

[11] 'Explicitly+' is bracketed because the word 'aware' already suggests the required sort of explicitness—a fact exploited by the characterization of 'explicitly+' in 8.2. It is perhaps slightly more natural to talk of awareness than of belief in the case of dogs, and this may be because the phrase 'is aware*', as a phrase attributing cognitive attitudes, is thought to be usefully weaker than 'believes'. Here, however, 'belief' and 'awareness' are understood to be interchangeable in the way proposed in the characterization of 'explicit+' in 8.2. Obviously, what follows 'is (explicitly+) aware', by way of specification of the content of the awareness state, cannot in the case of Fido be supposed to be something he can think, occurrently and linguistically, in the way that we can do.

Fido is not merely aware* that he can now do two different thing
without any thought of choosing between them. He is also aware*, i
some sense, that he can—and must—choose between them.[12] His hea
turns from side to side. He exhibits signs of distress recognizable a
such from other contexts. He hesitates visibly, half starting one way
half the other, the muscles playing in his legs. Given his state of aware
ness, he *faces a choice*. And, this being so, he is able to choose so lon
as he is not psychically determined with respect to the choice in a wa
that counts as a constraint. And he is not so determined, in the presen
case. He has two goals of his own, reinforced by training, indeed, bu
both non-compulsive features of his general 'goal-structure'.

Fido, then, is capable of states of awareness of such a kind that it i
true to say of him, when he is in them, that, subjectively, he faces
choice; and in such cases he really does face a choice, given that he i
not psychically constrained. He really is in a position in which he i
able to choose. But although Fido and *a fortiori* Nemo are able t
choose, on the above account, we do not think they are able to choos
freely, i.e. in such a way that they may be truly responsible for thei
choices, in the way in which we think we can be. We do not think the
are potential free agents.

But why not, exactly? We need to know more about what exactly i
is that makes an agent a potential free agent. For even when we gran
that we are in essentials just like Fido and Nemo so far as basic abilit
to choose is concerned, we still think that we, unlike them, are not onl
able to choose, but are also able to choose freely. So we need an accoun
of what it is about us that makes the difference.

A natural suggestion is that self-consciousness makes all the dif
ference: human beings are able to choose freely simply because the
can know fully self-consciously *that* they are able to choose. This sor
of idea will be taken up below in 9.4, and questioned in Part III.

The problem of the apparent contravention of the principle of in
dependence remains. There is a fundamental sense in which the object

---

[12] Here the words 'choose' and 'choice' appear in specifications of the contents o
Fido's states of awareness. This seems an entirely natural way of describing things, an
the question of whether Fido can properly be said to possess the *concept* of choice seem
unimportant. In a strong sense of 'concept', perhaps, he does not. But in another sens
he clearly does, apprehending the scene and the dilemma in the way that he does. If it i
insisted that possession of the concept of choice is necessary for ability to choose, then i
will be reasonable to insist, to a corresponding extent, on the sense in which Fido doe
possess it. (The idea that possession of the concept of choice in a strong and Fido
excluding sense is necessary for 'true' ability to choose will be considered in 14.10.)

of one's choice are partly constituted as such precisely by one's believing them to be objects of choice for one: a sense in which two types of course of action, X and Y, say, are options *for a* only if *a* believes that X and Y are options for himself.

But this suggests that one must have a fully articulated self-conscious belief in order to be able to choose; and Fido's case seems to show that this isn't true; for he is not properly speaking self-conscious. He thinks of X and Y as options, but not expressly as options *for himself*. So if Fido is able to choose, there is no outright contravention of the principle of independence after all: it is not a necessary condition of X and Y having the property of being options for *a* that they are believed (by *a*) to have that very property of being believed to be options *for a*. Of course for Fido to think of X and Y as options at all just is for him to think 'implicitly' of them as options for him. This is what creates the sense of a problem. But here the stress falls strongly on 'implicit'. It is a vague word, as vague as 'explicit'. But it can still serve a purpose. Here it can serve to support the view that there is no outright contravention of the principle of independence in the present case despite the crucial sense in which something is not an option for one unless one has thought of it in such a way that it is placed before one as an option.[13]

8.4 CONCLUSION

It should be stressed that to adopt the present account of ability to choose is not to beg any questions about freedom. What it says is this. There is something, call it 'Q', that we and Fido and Nemo have in common. One can call this 'ability to choose', and reasons for doing so have been given. But if one has reservations about doing so, it doesn't matter; one can just call it 'Q' instead. The question is then this. What more is needed to turn Q, or 'ability to choose', or whatever one wishes to call it, into ability to choose freely? Is self-consciousness enough, for example? (It will be argued that it is not, even when the problem posed by determinism is waived.)

One further point does need to be made now. Obviously, ability to choose is a condition of ability to choose freely, and, hence, of free agenthood generally considered; and so the question arises as to its

[13] This is not completely satisfactory, and the problem of contravention is returned to in ch. 10.

relations with those conditions of free agenthood that have already
been proposed, the Structural S conditions (7.3). Is the ability to choose
condition entailed by the S conditions, or, rather, by the first four of
them, the defining conditions of purposive agenthood, which Fido and
Nemo are understood to fulfil? Or is it an extra condition that needs to
be added on?

I shall suppose that it is entailed by the first four S conditions as
already stated. This is really a matter of expository decision, rather
than something that has to be argued for. In effect, it amounts to taking
the third S condition concerning practical rationality in a certain way
taking it to include the capacity to be able to choose in at least the
sense in which Fido can be able to choose—the capacity to be aware of
facing options, and to choose and act in the light of that awareness.

This seems a natural and economical way of disposing things for
purposes of discussion. It may be objected that a being can be a pur
posive agent without being able to choose in the present sense. But the
reply to this is simply that the phrase 'purposive agent' is presently
being understood in such a way that to be a purposive agent capable
of practical reasoning *just is* to be able to choose in the present sense
If saying this involves taking the phrase 'purposive agent' in a restricted
and relatively strong sense, so be it; those who think that it does, and
wish to mark this fact, can simply add the ability-to-choose condition
into the set of S conditions as an extra condition—number (6).

Finally, it may be objected that the conditions of ability to choose
proposed in 8.2 are not sufficient but only necessary conditions. It may
be said that if one fulfils them, in a particular case, then one is indeed
fully in a *position* to choose, but that actually choosing involves exercise
of some further capacity which one must also possess if one is really to
be *able* to choose. Just what further condition might be proposed is
very unclear. It does not seem that it could be further described in any
non-circular fashion: for it is just the ability, when in a position to
choose as defined by conditions (1A) and (2), actually to choose.

This objection need not detain us. As far as ability to choose is
concerned, it suffices for present purposes to claim as before that *if* a
being makes an apparent choice, then, if it fulfils (1A) and (2), its
apparent choice is a real choice. (This leaves open the possibility that
there might be some further condition of ability to choose—possession
of the capacity to do whatever is involved in actually making the
choice.)

I turn now to self-consciousness, the last thing that needs to be

iscussed before considering the Subjectivist challenge to the
bjectivists.

9

Self-consciousness

Let 'mental reflexivity' be defined as follows: a being *b* has the property of mental reflexivity if and only if it is capable of being aware of its own mental goings-on—capable of having beliefs, thoughts, desires, or generally, *mentations* about its own mental goings-on.

It seems clear enough that a being could possess this property, and be able to be aware of its own mental goings-on, even though it had no grasp of the idea that they were its own, nor any sense of self. Suppose that *b* is thinking that *p*. *b* may then display mental reflexivity in having the further thought 'There is the thought that *p*', or 'It is thought that *p*', while having no thought *that* the thought that *p* is its own thought, nor any sense of self.

If this is mental reflexivity, what is self-consciousness? I shall be concerned with what we normally mean by 'self-consciousness' and its cognates. We clearly mean more than the least we might plausibly mean. We do not mean consciousness of self just in the sense of consciousness of something that is in fact oneself. For if we did, then mere mental reflexivity would be sufficient for self-consciousness. Indeed a dog's observing its paw or a kitten's chasing its tail would be self-conscious activities. But they are not. One might say that what is in question, in such cases, is that a being is conscious of itself relationally speaking, but not notionally speaking.[1] That is, the being is conscious of something that is in fact itself, but is not conscious *that* that thing is itself. It is itself the *object* of its consciousness, but that it is the object of its consciousness is no part of the *content* of its consciousness. Apprehending itself in some way, it does not in any way apprehend that it apprehends itself. And some such apprehension as this seems crucial to, and perhaps constitutive of, what we ordinarily take self-consciousness to be, however mysterious it may seem.

In what follows I will be concerned with what one might call '*full*

---

[1] For the distinction, see W. V. Quine, 'Quantifiers and Propositional Attitudes'.

self-consciousness—self-consciousness such as ordinary adult human beings ordinarily have. The word 'full' is introduced simply to preclude debate about degrees of self-consciousness: debate, for example, about whether there is a sense in which dogs and cats can and indeed must be said to be self-conscious, although our ordinary use of the word does not allow this, and coincides with what is here called full self-consciousness.[2] Concern with freedom justifies this approach. For it seems clear (*a*) that we are self-conscious in some important sense in which dogs and cats are not, and (*b*) that whatever this difference in respect of self-consciousness is, it is likely to be important when it is claimed that we, unlike them, are free agents. And so it seems best simply to define us as fully self-conscious, and then to ask what this involves.

'Unself-conscious' will accordingly be understood throughout to mean 'not fully self-conscious'; and 'fully' will sometimes be taken as understood, and omitted. I will at times use the word 'thought(s)' in the broad and familiar Cartesian sense to cover propositional attitudes in general, perceptions, and so on.

Nemo is the official representative of our intuition that an un-selfconscious agent cannot possibly be a free agent. Nemo is like a person in all respects in which it is possible to be like a person without being fully self-conscious. He may be imagined to be able to have thoughts (in the general Cartesian sense) of a Lichtenbergian kind, thoughts about his mental states, as well as thoughts about his non-mental or physical states,[3] without being self-conscious in anything like the way we are; without grasping himself *as himself*, or his thoughts as *his own*; without having any sense of self at all. There is, we may suppose, something very varied and complex that it is like, experientially, to be Nemo. But we still feel that, simply because he is not fully self-conscious, he is not and cannot be a free agent truly responsible for his actions—in the way in which we think we are.[4]

[2] Consider, for example, the patently jealous or 'what about me?' behaviour of a favoured cat, when a new cat takes its place in its owner's lap. See n. 15.

[3] Or parts. This qualification will be taken for granted henceforth.

[4] It is extremely natural to think that self-consciousness could never be correctly attributed to the entirely experienceless, and I shall proceed on the assumption that this is so. Against this, however, one must set two facts: (*a*) that it is plausible to suppose that self-consciousness is, minimally, just an ability to have certain kinds of thoughts (in the ordinary, non-Cartesian, sensory-experience-excluding sense of 'thought'); (*b*) that it is widely agreed that thinking need have no experiential correlate at all, and often has none in our own case. For some further discussion, see Appendix A.

But why? What does self-consciousness, in the intended strong sense, involve? For present purposes, it seems sufficient to give just two defining or elucidating conditions as follows. (In fact the second encompasses the first.) A fully self-conscious being, *b*, is

(1) able to survey or be aware of itself; it is able to survey or be aware of (certain at least of) its own properties—i.e. its mental states or thoughts, and/or (certain at least of) its non-mental states if any.[5]

(1) may be called the basic reflexivity condition.[6]

(2) *b* is able to be aware of or conceive of (certain at least of) its properties—its mental states or thoughts or non-mental states (if any)—*as its own*; whatever exactly this involves.[7]

In effect, (2) simply states that a fully self-conscious being must be capable of thoughts about itself that are not only relationally but also notionally about itself. It appears to entail that a fully self-conscious being must be capable of thoughts that contain some referring expression—represented here by the 'it' of 'as its own'—that the being takes to refer to itself. It must be able to entertain thoughts given whose content it is true to say that it can conceive of itself, *grasped or conceived of as itself*, as being ϕ, or ψ.[8]

It may be objected that (1) and (2) are simply obviously—tautologously—conditions of full self-consciousness, and that they fail to provide any real elucidation of it. It may be said that the crucial phrases

[5] Its physical states, for example (the possibility that fully self-conscious beings may have non-physical substantial 'realizations' need not be considered here). "If any" allows for the entirely obscure possibility that there may be unembodied (and indeed substantially unrealized) minds.

[6] Nemo may as remarked fulfil the basic reflexivity condition with respect to his mental states. A tail-chasing kitten fulfils it with respect to its physical states or parts. There is a sense in which even a machine can be said to fulfil it, both with respect to its physical parts and with respect to its internal informational states: for it can be designed to survey its own informational states, and, indeed its own surveyings of its own informational states—since these surveyings themselves consist in its being in informational states.

[7] One could put this even more simply, in Locke's way: a self-conscious being is one that "can consider it self *as it self*" (*Essay*, II.xxvii.9; my emphasis). But it seems helpful to articulate this a little further.

[8] It is not being claimed that something like the phrase 'my own' has to occur as a part of any adequate representation in English of the notional content of those thoughts or experiences which count as fully self-conscious. It can equally be on account of the being's having, explicitly, such ordinary thoughts as 'I want X' or 'My hand hurts' or 'I am soaking wet' that apprehension of its want (or hand or body) *as its own* is correctly attributable to it. (In fact a fully self-conscious being might always use a proper name to refer to itself in thought and speech.)

in the account—'can conceive of its states *as its own*', and 'can conceive of itself, *conceived of as itself*—are themselves in need of analysis and elucidation, and that self-consciousness remains as mysterious as ever.

Any true definition is ultimately a tautology, and moving from a noun phrase like 'full self-consciousness' to a couple of clauses like (1) and (2) may be worth while whether or not (1) and (2) are further analysed. But this is perhaps not a very helpful thing to say, and in the next section I will try, by reference to the theory of evolution, to make the abilities referred to in the crucial phrases seem less puzzling. Then, in 9.3, I will attempt some further analysis of condition (2)—of what is necessarily involved in fulfilling (2). This analysis will be pursued in a way that is dictated by an overriding concern with the question of what makes self-consciousness seem important for freedom, however, and no attempt will be made at direct elucidation of phrases like 'as its own' or 'conceives of itself as itself'. (In fact, it is not clear that much more of philosophical interest can be said about them.)[9]

Note that the present characterization of full self-consciousness is intentionally framed in such a way as to avoid a mentalistic emphasis—an emphasis that treats awareness of one's mental states as one's own as somehow more important than (more properly a manifestation of truly self-conscious thought than) awareness of one's non-mental states as one's own. It may be said that it is precisely this that gives force to the suggestion that there is a sense in which dogs must be said to be self-conscious. For it may be said that even if a dog cannot in any sense be aware of its mental states as its own, it can be aware, in some sense, of its paw (say) as its own—suppose it withdraws it, after due observation, and in a seemingly deliberate, non-reflex manner, from the path of an oncoming projectile.

But this is not grounds for an objection to the definition. It is clearly right (*a*) to avoid the mentalistic emphasis, while (*b*) continuing to deny that dogs are fully self-conscious.[10] As for (*a*), it is clear that thinking

---

[9] An alternative to giving priority to such phrases in characterizing what is peculiar to self-conscious thought is to talk of 'I-thoughts'. But this useful expression can also have a strangely thought-stopping quality.

[10] Note that to oppose the mentalistic emphasis is not to rule out the possibility that there could be an unembodied being that was fully self-conscious. Nor, more importantly, is it to rule out the possibility that there could be a fully self-conscious being that was physically (or non-mentally) embodied (or realized), but had no awareness of this fact. Such a being might spend all its time thinking about higher mathematics; it might (*a*)

that one is bald is not in any way inferior, as an example of fully self-conscious thought, to thinking that one believes that p. As for (*b*), it seems that one can, in attempting to express why dogs cannot be supposed to qualify for full self-consciousness, say something like this: if a being is fully self-conscious, then its awareness of its mental or non-mental states as its own must be capable of being *explicit*,[11] in a sense in which a dog's conception or consciousness of itself is (we suppose) never explicit, even if it can be in some sense aware of its paw as its own.

The word 'explicit' is vague, as already observed; but it is not hopelessly vague. It may well be that our only viable model for the required sort of explicitness necessarily involves reference to language; but it may be that this model will do perfectly well for present purposes. We can say this: if a being is fully self-conscious, then it must be capable of awareness of its mental or non-mental states as its own that is explicit in something very like the way in which the awareness that a being has of its mental or non-mental states is or can be explicit when that being expresses or is able to express the thought that they are its own to itself in a consciously entertained, occurrent, linguistic form of thought. Full self-consciousness may not require linguistic capability as we know it, but it seems that it must involve language-*like* thought, at least. For there must be a medium of thought which, as a representational medium, permits thoughts correctly characterizable as involving a conception of something as myself, or as my own (this being a characterization of their notional content). And this conceiving of something *as* oneself, or *as* one's own, seems to involve representation that is abstract, in a clear sense. (It cannot be literally pictured, it cannot be represented in some merely sensory mode.) It is abstract in such a way that linguistically articulated thought is our only model of what it might be like. And dogs, we suppose, are incapable of such (possibly conscious) abstract thought.[12]

once have known that it was embodied, and have forgotten this, or it might (*b*) never have known it. Some philosophers might accept (*a*) and deny (*b*). But it is natural to suppose that the first possibility simply entails the second, since, if a being can be fully self-conscious and forget that it is embodied, then it is logically possible that a second being whose mental goings-on are exactly like the first being after it has forgotten, and who has never known that it was embodied, could be created immediately—or just occur.

[11] Not explicit+ in the sense of 8.2, but explicit in the (or at least an) ordinary sense of the word.

[12] Though they can of course perform the complex but entirely non-conscious calculations necessary for catching a ball, or closing in smoothly on a quarry moving across their line of approach.

9.2 AN ATTEMPT AT DEMYSTIFICATION

Self-consciousness can seem very hard to understand.[13] Yet the basic facts are apparently simple. On earth, processes of evolution have given rise to beings that are cognitively and sensorily very well equipped, beings that are prone to latch on to the local facts, whatever they may be. Naturally, any such being is aware (at least relationally) of itself, for it is itself an important object in its local environment.

Now if it is (relationally) aware of itself in this way it need not be fully self-conscious, but if it is also fully self-conscious then this is not something that is particularly puzzling. For it is, as just remarked, (*a*) naturally relationally aware of itself, aware that it has certain properties; and, being generally prone to latch on to local facts, it may very well also become aware of this fact (*a*)—for (*a*) is indeed just that, a straightforward objective fact about something in its immediate environment. That is, it may become aware that it is itself the something that is aware that it has certain properties; and so, in effect, achieve full self-consciousness. There will be nothing very surprising in this, given its general level of cognitive and sensory equipment—its naturally evolved capacity to receive information both about its external environment and about its own informational or mental states. It is no great leap. Think, after all, of how it happens to any human child (assuming there is no major mental disorder).

It seems, then, that there may really be nothing very hard to understand either in the nature of self-consciousness or in the fact that it has arisen on earth. But it may yet be objected that while a being's capacity to receive information about the external environment, including its own body, is easily explicable in evolutionary terms, a capacity to receive information about one's own *internal* mental or informational states—an introspective capacity, for short—needs a separate evolutionary explanation: for what is the 'survival value' of such a capacity?

One answer can be derived from a suggestion of Nicholas Humphrey's.[14] It is, in the present terms, a proposal specifically about full self-consciousness, and does not concern unselfconscious forms of introspective capacity.

Somewhat simplified, it is this: self-consciousness may first arise by chance in an individual member of an already fairly sophisticated spe-

---

[13] The mentalistic emphasis just rejected, which is shared by many approaches to the problem of self-consciousness, has undoubtedly contributed largely to the sense of puzzlement. Gareth Evans provides a wealth of reasons for opposing the mentalistic emphasis in ch. 7 of *The Varieties of Reference*.

[14] In *Consciousness Regained*, chs. 1–5.

cies of animals that live in internally competitive social groups (perhaps they already possess some primitive naming practices, or other (proto-) linguistic habits). If it does, it will tend to spread, because it will bestow a significant advantage on whoever possesses it. It has 'survival value', because it enables (and disposes) one to survey and consider what it is that motivates one to act, and so enables (and disposes) one to predict, by employing the 'argument from analogy' in a highly natural fashion, what others will do. It enables one to predict what others will do more successfully than they are able to predict what one will do oneself, given that they are not self-conscious, and so are not thinking in this way. Self-conscious individuals, therefore, can outsmart their un-selfconscious fellows, rise in the dominance hierarchy, and reproduce more successfully, transmitting their (gene-carried) capacity for self-consciousness to descendants who prosper in turn. And so self-consciousness will spread through the community as the generations succeed one another.[15]

Another answer is as follows. Self-consciousness may have survival value for something like the reasons that Humphrey gives. But a more gradualist account of its evolution is required. Considered in isolation from other capacities, self-consciousness may have no such direct evolutionary explanation as is proposed above (and it may have no specific genetic basis that it can call its own). But the emergence of our various (introspective) capacities to receive information about and think about our own internal mental or informational states does have some such direct evolutionary explanation. And the emergence of our capacity for specifically self-conscious thought may have an indirect evolutionary explanation just in so far as it is plausible to see it as first arising naturally from the progressive development of these other capacities— being at first a kind of natural 'spin-off' from them, as it were (one that catches on more and more widely on account of the operation of some

---

[15] There are a number of problems with this story. E.g.: (1) Why couldn't there be an entirely non-conscious analogue of conscious self-conscious thought that was functionally equivalent to it and so equivalent in survival value? This question raises again the 'deep' problem about consciousness and experience discussed in Appendix A. See also n.4 above. (2) It may be said that a being B does not have to be fully self-conscious to benefit from the way of thinking described. It may just think something like this: 'This creature [in fact itself] is inclined to do X in this situation. Those other creatures are like this creature. So they are probably inclined to do X too. But, this being so, this creature would do better if it did Y instead of X.' If B then does Y directly as a result of this reasoning, one may be inclined to say that B just is self-conscious, practically speaking. And yet one may well intuitively feel that it hasn't properly 'realized that it's someone', and so isn't yet fully self-conscious after all. This intuition is discussed further in 9.4.

mechanism of cultural transmission rather than as the result of the spreading of some specific gene).[16]

The gradualist story goes something like this. As we evolve, our thought is, increasingly, less immediately and inevitably directed on to the external environment. (1) It allows more and more for the internal rehearsal of present and future possibilities in imagination. (Note the at least implicit awareness *of* introspection that this implies: for we do not take these rehearsed possibilities as realities but in some sense grasp them as mere mental rehearsals.) (2) We become more and more able to consider, in a cool fashion, which of two incompatible desirable courses of action to pursue. (3) We become more and more able to consult memory and, perhaps, grasp its deliverances *as* information about the past; and so on. (4) More generally, thought begins to contain awareness of itself as one of the things that is going on in the immediate locality. Notice that none of (1)-(4) involves anything like full self-consciousness, taken by itself; but they are clearly all useful abilities to have, and their evolution is to that extent explicable by reference to their survival value.

Any idealized story of this sort is bound to be fairly vague. The point of this one is simply that it offers, however sketchily, an evolutionary explanation of our developing introspective capacities as opposed to our capacities for receiving information about the external environment: these introspective capacities, which, in themselves, do not involve full self-consciousness, can clearly help to make one a more successful agent. And, as a general ability for introspective awareness develops, the ground is prepared for the beginnings of full self-consciousness. Certain facts come together in the simple but crucial way described at the beginning of this section: one is relationally aware of oneself as an extremely important object in the local environment and as having certain properties; and one is, given one's introspective capacities, aware of this awareness. And, putting one and one together, one becomes aware that (somehow it dawns on one that) one is oneself the thing that is aware that it has certain properties. This is by now an extremely natural further step.[17] (Think again of children, each of whom recapitulates the process.) A large part of the present point is

---

[16] There is no doubt that the evolution of linguistic practices plays some vital role in this.

[17] The fact that one's own well-being is the principal object of one's overall emotional and conative concern is also important.

that unselfconscious beings can evolve to the point at which it is in itself a very small step, though its consequences may be great.

On this view, then, self-consciousness does not arise as a result of some specific physiological random mutation. Rather, selective pressures produce a general increase in sensory and intellectual capacity (after a certain stage, this is largely the result of selective pressures created by competition within—and between—social groups). And this reaches a point at which many increasingly introspective but not yet fully self-conscious individuals may be as it were teetering on, and then over, the edge of full self-consciousness: given their other capacities, and the genetic basis that those capacities have, all the necessary conditions of the possibility of self-consciousness are fulfilled in them. And, after a certain time, the possibility of explicitly self-conscious thought becomes an actuality, at first sporadically, and later invariably—and no doubt the language-based processes of acculturation that form such an important part of our normal development play a vital part in this.

As remarked, self-consciousness can seem very hard to understand. But the idea that there is something mysterious about it may be an illusion—the way in which children acquire it so readily is perhaps the best indication that this is so. Evolutionary stories of the sort just considered can help with the difficulty if, by offering an account of how self-consciousness may have arisen, they succeed in making its intrinsic nature seem less mysterious. Nothing in what follows depends on accepting either of them, however; and, whatever their value, they do not appear to have much bearing on one of the great sources of mystification—on the way self-consciousness characteristically gives rise to a sense of a 'mental self'. I turn now to this question, and, in so doing to consideration of what else may be necessarily involved in fulfilment of the conditions of full self-consciousness proposed in 9.1.

9.3 THE IDEA OF MENTAL SINGLENESS

It is arguable that if a being is not only

    (1) capable of being aware of itself,

but also

    (2) capable of being explicitly aware of its states or thoughts as it own

then this necessarily involves

    (3) its having some sort of conception or general experience of itsel

as a thing which is, somehow, *single just qua mental*; as a thing which has some sort of singleness considered purely in its mental aspect—even if it *also* has, and believes itself to have, singleness considered in its physical or overall psychophysical aspect.

This is not to claim that it must necessarily have some explicit conception of itself as a *diachronically* single mental thing, as a mental thing that is single *qua* something persisting through time—although it will almost certainly have some such conception, more or less explicitly. It is to claim only that when it thinks fully self-consciously it must then have the idea of itself as something that is somehow single simply *qua* mental; it must be true to say of it that it conceives of itself as single just *qua* mental at given particular times, to the extent that it has fully self-conscious thoughts at those times.[18] So that if it is generally speaking given to fully self-conscious thought, then it must be generally speaking true to say of it that it has some sort of conception of itself as something that is in some way single just *qua* mental.

This claim may be thought surprising; though we certainly all have some such conception of ourselves, more or less consciously, both when we consider ourselves at particular times, and when when we think of ourselves as things extended through time.[19] But it will be argued that a fully self-conscious being must have some such conception of itself as single just *qua* mental even if it is in fact an indissolubly psychophysical thing, and even if it also conceives of itself as such; and even if it is never expressly concerned with its own mental features in self-conscious thought or speech, but only with its physical (or non-mental) features.[20]

[18] One could say that this is a point that has to do with Kant's second rather than his third Paralogism; or that it has to do with Hume's problem of personal identity rather than Locke's, having to do with the identity of the self at a given time rather than through time.

[19] It may also be thought trivial. The search for counter-examples may lead one to ask whether Buddhists who attain nirvana (i.e. 'nirvana-in-life', or 'nirvana-with-substrate'—see S. Collins, *Selfless Persons*, pp.83 and 206) can intelligibly be supposed to divest themselves of any such conception. If the argument of this section is correct, they cannot do so while remaining fully self-conscious. See further Appendix E, § III.

[20] The point here is emphatically not that we or anyone might always be able to individuate collections or series of mental states, events, or features simply on the basis of their mental characteristics—in such a way as to be able to distinguish them from one another without reference to physical embodiment or location (or at least to some sort of 'substantial realization'). It seems clear that this could not always be done. (Suppose two series of thoughts were, as such, qualitatively identical.) The present idea is simply that, *given* a single collection or series of thoughts or mental goings-on, *given* that it is a single collection, the question can arise as to whether it has a certain property considered

The first point to make, perhaps, is that it is very doubtful whether a being that never ascribed anything but non-mental states or features to itself could in fact be counted as a free agent. And if this is so, then, given a primary concern with freedom, it may be that one need only consider beings that do ascribe mental states to themselves, in order to ask whether they must necessarily have a conception of themselves as somehow single just *qua* mental. In this way, one might be able to establish that (3) was a necessary condition of free agenthood whether or not it was also a necessary condition of (2), and, hence, of full self-consciousness.

The way seems to be open to a much more general argument, however—an argument for two connected conclusions:

(A) that any fully self-conscious being must have a conception of itself as a mentally endowed or aspected thing,

and

(B) that it must also have a conception of itself as somehow single just *qua* mental.

Consider three claims.

(I) I take it to be evident that if a being is capable of fully self-conscious self-ascription of mental states, then it has some sort of conception of itself as mentally aspected or endowed. (A child could clearly be said to possess such a conception even though it had not yet mastered any word like 'mental'.)

But,

(II) it does indeed seem to be possible that a being's fully self-conscious thoughts or utterances might without exception be concerned only with ascription of *non*-mental states or features to itself.

Still,

(III) it does also seem to be true that no being could be capable of fully self-conscious self-ascription of non-mental states and not also be *capable*, at least, of fully self-conscious self-ascription of mental states (though this has yet to be shown).

If so, the truth of (II) does not suffice to show that (A) is false. And

purely in its mental aspect—the property of being such that we can truly say that the being whose series of thoughts it is conceives of itself as a thing which is somehow single just *qua* mental. And the question can arise as to whether having this property is necessary for full self-consciousness.

defending (III) brings out the reasons for asserting both (A) and (B), given the truth of (I).

What, then, of (III)? It appears that it is an essential part or pre-condition of one's engaging in any specifically fully self-conscious con-ceiving of a state or part of oneself, mental or otherwise, *as* a state or part of oneself, that one have some conception of oneself (conceived of *as* oneself, in the way characteristic of full self-consciousness) as a mental thing, or at least as a thing with mental attributes. It appears that even a being's apprehending its hand (or other prehensile extremity) *as its own* presupposes its having some grasp of itself (grasped as itself) as mental, and indeed, as already remarked, as somehow *single* just *qua* mental. And it seems that this is so even if it also has a conception of itself as essentially and indissolubly psychophysically single.

Why? Well, what is it, exactly, for it to apprehend its hand *as its own*? It seems that it is, necessarily, even if only implicitly, for it to apprehend its hand as the hand of the thing that is doing the ap-prehending. 'Implicitly': this thought of itself as the thing that is doing the apprehending need not be part of the content of the apprehension as it occurs (say) in occurrent, subvocalized thought. The content may simply be something like 'My hand is hot'. It is, rather, part of what we have to talk about when we try to say what such a thought of something's being one's own involves.

This is, perhaps, not very satisfactory. Avoiding such talk of what is implicit, it may be better to say this: involved, in some sense, in any fully self-conscious self-ascription of a physical state ϕ is some sort of conception of oneself (conceived as oneself) as the thing which does the ascribing. Even more cautiously: one must at least possess or have access to such a conception, or be capable of such a thought of oneself, in order to be truly said to have ascribed ϕ *to oneself*, even if it is better not to say that such a conception is 'involved, in some sense' in such a self-ascription. Perhaps it is not true *sans phrase* to say that to ap-prehend any property in a fully self-conscious manner as a property that one has just *is* (at least in part) to apprehend it as a property of the thing that is doing the apprehending—to apprehend it, that is, as a property of the thing, oneself (conceived as oneself), that also has the mental property of being the thing that is doing the apprehending. But it seems clear that possession of the *ability* to ascribe mental properties to oneself is already (and necessarily) involved in possession of the ability to ascribe *any* property to oneself in a fully self-conscious manner.

For how can we make sense of the idea that the apprehending being does indeed apprehend the property as its own—*as its own*—if we suppose that it may not even be capable of any thought of itself as possessed of mental properties, such as the property of being the apprehender of the property in question? Given that the phrase 'my own' is or can be part of the (notional) content of thoughts that it has, or at least part of a correct description of what those thoughts can be said to involve, what account can we give of its understanding of the 'my' or the 'my own' (the 'I', the 'my', the 'mine', or whatever) if we suppose that it may have no conception or experience whatever of itself as mentally aspected or endowed?

Indeed, it seems that one may return from the weaker claim that it must be *capable* of thought (or experience) of itself as mentally aspected or endowed to the stronger claim that some such thought (or experience) of itself is actually involved, in some way, in its having any fully self-conscious thought about itself as having some property. For, surely, if it is indeed true that it has the thought that it has the property ϕ, then the reference to 'it', which is part of the content of the thought,[21] must be supposed by us to be understood by it as somehow or other involving reference to itself considered as the thinker or haver of the thought (whether or not it is also understood by it as involving reference to itself considered as the psychophysical or physical thing that it also is).

So much for (A).

As for (B): it seems that it is not merely grasp of oneself as mentally aspected that is in question. What also appears to be necessarily involved in possession of the ability to ascribe properties to oneself in a fully self-conscious manner is possession of some sort of conception of oneself as *a* mental being—that is, precisely, *the* thinker or apprehender—and, hence, as something that is somehow *single* just *qua* mental (even if it is also single in other respects). For, as has been said, either an *actual* reference to oneself as a (the) thinker or apprehender is implicitly (or explicitly) involved in any fully self-conscious ascription of properties; or at the very least possession of the *ability* to have thoughts involving reference to oneself conceived as the mentally single apprehender is a necessary condition of possession of the ability to ascribe properties to oneself in a fully self-conscious manner.

The idea is a very simple one, but it is perhaps not always taken

---

[21] Occurring as 'I' or 'my' or some expression or thought-element (possibly a proper name) that it takes as referring to itself (conceived of *as* itself).

sufficiently into account. To have a fully self-conscious thought is to attribute some property to oneself conceived as oneself; it is (as it were) to present it to oneself as one's own. And if one can do this, then, however unreflective one is, one cannot but have some sort of conception of (one cannot but be capable of some thought of) oneself as *an* (as *the*) attributer, thinker, presenter, ascriber, apprehender, experiencer, or whatever, that is apprehending something as its own. But a view of oneself as singular, and as singular just *qua* mental, singular in respect of one's mental nature or activity (of attribution, apprehension, or whatever) is, quite simply, an indispensable part of such a conception.

'I am falling.' 'I am here.' 'I am six feet tall.' Who is? I. Who is this I? It is this psychophysical I. But it is also this I that is *I who am thinking that* I am falling, or here, or six feet tall. This must be a thought that one can have, if one is truly fully self-conscious. The view or conception of oneself as having singularity just *qua* something mentally aspected, just *qua* the thinker or subject of consciousness, is thus a necessary part or aspect of full self-consciousness—even (to repeat) if one also conceives of oneself as psychophysically single.[22] Of course self-ascription of a physical state, as in 'I am soaked', is in fact ascription of a property to a psychophysical thing. But that is compatible with its being the case that the ascription is ascription by a thing which cannot but have a conception of itself as, somehow or other, single just *qua* mental.

We as we ordinarily are all ordinarily have some such conception of ourselves as single in this way, as 'mental someones', as it were—however unexamined and elusive this conception may be. The question here is simply whether such a conception is actually inevitable for a fully self-conscious being. It does seem to be so; even a completely emotionless being, a mere or pure thinker, must have some such self-conception if it is indeed capable of fully self-conscious thought. For it cannot truly be said to apprehend properties as its own and not have

---

[22] It follows that no fully self-conscious being pursuing the first positive stage of the Cartesian project can honestly conclude only that 'There is thinking going on', as Lichtenberg recommended, rather than that 'I think' (here I take 'I think' to stand for any expression involving the thought of oneself as single just *qua* mental). What is true, though, is that no conclusion asserting the existence of a single mental *substance* follows from the inevitability (for the fully self-conscious) of the conception of oneself as mentally single. (Compare one interpretation of the argument of the First and Second Paralogisms in Kant's *Critique of Pure Reason*, according to which Kant's main point is that no conclusion asserting the existence of a single mental substance follows from the fact that a certain unity of mind—which he calls 'transcendental unity of consciousness'—is a demonstrably necessary condition of the possibility of experience.)

it. If so, then, even if 'the self' is an illusion, it is, for the fully self-conscious, a necessary illusion.[23]

Having reached this conclusion, it is important to stress that it has only been claimed that any fully self-conscious being must have some *idea* or *experience* of itself as something that is single *qua* mental. Questions about the ultimate metaphysical or ontological propriety of the idea of the single mental self are questions of a different order, which have not been considered here.[24] In fact, if being fully self-conscious does indeed necessarily involve (3), conceiving of oneself (conceived of as oneself) as somehow single just *qua* mental, then it may indeed be that it necessarily involves having some sort of illusory conception: whether one merely considers oneself as mentally single at given particular times, or whether one has a definite conception of oneself as a temporally extended single mental thing.

This may be true, in particular, if (3) in turn necessarily involves (4), having some conception or sense of oneself as a mental self more or less traditionally conceived—a sense of oneself as a single diaphanous-but-definite mental something, with a certain specific character or 'content'.

A further question also arises: does (4) in turn necessarily involve (5), having a conception of oneself as something that is, mentally considered, somehow separate from, irreducible to, over and above, or as one might say *transcendent* with respect to, all one's particular thoughts and mental states generally? And does (3) entail (5) even if it does not entail (4)?[25]

Such questions will not be considered here.[26] Instead two points will suffice. First, that it is not an objection to the definition of full self-consciousness just as such that it makes the having of some strictly speaking illusory form of experience a necessary condition of full self-consciousness, if that is indeed what it does do. Second, as far as the

---

[23] This would explain why Hume found himself unable to maintain his belief in the conclusion he reached in I.iv.6 of his *Treatise*.

[24] The present discussion is simply an attempt to characterize, without any metaphysical commitment or implication, the purely 'informational', and indeed intrinsic, structure of self-consciousness considered just as a form or manner of thought.

[25] Part of the problem with this sort of conception of the self is not peculiar to debates about the self. It is like one of the traditional problems of substance: the problem which arises when we are led to think of the substantial 'substratum' of an object as an in itself propertyless bearer of all properties of the object. (For a development of the parallel, see C. McGinn, *The Character of Mind*, pp. 54–6.)

[26] For some further discussion, see Appendix E.

connection between self-consciousness and freedom in particular is concerned: even if it were to prove to be the case that full self-consciousness as above defined ((1) and (2)) must be held to involve some kind of putatively illusory experience or conception of self (i.e. (3) and/or (4) and/or (5)), this would in no way cast into doubt a claim that self-consciousness so defined was a necessary condition of free agenthood, as ordinarily conceived. We, after all, paradigm candidates for free agenthood, all ordinarily have experience not only of kind (3), but also of kind (5), and this surely does not count against our claim to free agenthood. Indeed if it turned out that a definition of full self-consciousness were available according to which it did not necessarily involve having the conception or experience of oneself as mentally single described in (3), then we might be led to require that any potential free agent must not only be fully self-conscious, but must also have the form of experience described in (3): this now being an Attitudinal condition (1.5) on free agenthood which earned its place among the conditions of free agenthood not because it was integral to full self-consciousness,[27] but on its own merits.

9.4 SELF-CONSCIOUSNESS, SOMEONEHOOD, AND FREEDOM

Why might one wish to claim that (3), a sense of oneself as single just *qua* mental, is a condition of free agenthood even if it is not necessarily involved in full self-consciousness? The essentials of an answer to this question begin to emerge if one tries to give some simple direct statement of the connection between self-consciousness and freedom, and of why we see the former as so important to the latter.

It seems oddly difficult to do so. Perhaps this is because it is too obvious to see clearly. Bordering continuously on triviality, one may seem not to have said anything at all. But one thing seems clear. In some very strong and straightforward sense, we intuitively require that there be a *mental subject* in the case of any free agent, a mental subject that is in some way or other properly distinguishable from all its particular thoughts (beliefs, desires, etc.); a mental subject that is moreover present to itself as such in some way. Whether or not there can correctly be said to *be* such a thing, we require at the very least that any free agent's thought or experience be such that it is overwhelmingly natural

---

[27] Nor because it was entailed by any of the other Structural conditions of free agenthood.

for us (and for it) to talk in terms of such a subject, when characterizing its thought or experience.

It may well be that we require that it be simply correct to talk of such a mental subject, in the case of any free agent. But for present purposes we may restrict ourselves to the claim that it must at least be overwhelmingly natural to talk in terms of such a subject: in terms of something which is in *some* manner correctly characterizable as a single thing when purely mentally considered; or at least in terms of something that is, mentally considered, somehow or other essentially more than a mere bundle of beliefs, desires, attitudes, and so on, tied to a single body (in a way, this is all that Fido and Nemo are, by comparison with ourselves—or so we are likely to think). Considering the agent in its mental aspect, we require something that can be seen as a single rational planner of action that is present 'in there', and that can as such be held to be fully responsible for its actions. It seems that self-consciousness is at least necessary for this. And this alone makes self-consciousness necessary for free agenthood, as ordinarily conceived.

On this view there is no free agent without self-consciousness because there is no agent there at all, in the required sense. There is no agent because there is no one there at all, in the required way; no single 'mental someone', no single mental planner of action. It is not enough that there should be a psychophysically single purposive agent like Fido or Nemo, a haver of beliefs and desires, a pursuer and attainer of goals with a certain character. In their case the—very definite—feeling is that there is simply no one there who can be held responsible for his actions in the way in which we think we can legitimately hold each other responsible. That is our intuition.

Intuitions are only intuitions, but it is hard to imagine that any satisfactory account of free agenthood could undercut or ignore this one. We think that there is in the unselfconscious case nothing more than a psychophysical agent-system containing action-motivating contents (such as desires and beliefs). There are true rational explanations to be given of Fido's and Nemo's actions, but the single mental desirer, planner, and intender of action is, crucially, absent. Fido is of course a single agent, but one has to consider him as a psycho*physical* whole in order to get the required sense of single-agentness. One might say that it is a process, not an agent, that produces plans of action in the canine case. There is a primordial sense in which the desires, beliefs, etc. alone, and not an agent, can be said to be determining action, at the mental stage. There is no agent there at all, in the required mental sense—

although it is perfectly natural to say that a dog has fixed preferences, or a marked character, or a sweet disposition.[28]

We think we are deeply different (unless we are Reductionists about selves or persons). Somehow, we suppose, self-consciousness gives rise to, or at least indicates the presence of, a single mental thing, the planner and intender of action. And yet there are strong philosophical arguments to the effect that self-consciousness cannot be supposed to make a difference of this kind, and that what it makes possible (or consists in) is simply the occurrence of a certain further kind of thought (in the broad Cartesian sense): it makes possible thoughts whose content is correctly represented by sentences of the form 'I am F', 'My G is H', 'I think that p', 'I desire that q', and so on; and that is all: it neither gives rise to nor indicates the presence of some further mental thing—the self, or a 'mental someone'.

Our feeling that there must be some such 'mental someone' is un-diminished, however. There must be a 'mental someone' if there is to be a free agent, because it is the mental someone that is the true subject and object of our attitudes, ascriptions, and practices of approval and disapproval, responsibility and desert, and praise and blame—the true subject, most generally, of our *interest*, in so far as we are interested in what we take to be a truly responsible agent. Of course it is also natural to say that the whole psychophysical agent is the subject and object of these things. But in an ineliminable sense it is the conception of the person as essentially single just *qua* mental, as the source of actions *qua* the mental intender and hatcher of them, that is crucial. It follows that if there is indeed an unavoidable sense in which it is impermissible to think of people like ourselves in this way, as Parfit, for example, has suggested, then free will may be impossible for that reason alone.[29]

[28] A being may display *consistency* in its beliefs (possessing an ability to adjust them in the direction of greater consistency), a certain *coherence* among its desires or pro-attitudes, and a certain *constancy* of general character, without being self-conscious (and without there being any sort of 'mental someone' of the sort that full self-consciousness is supposed to yield). Here I disagree with Colin McGinn, op. cit., p. 21, and Sydney Shoemaker in *Personal Identity*, p. 102: a minded being (or even a machine) may be so constituted that its beliefs (or 'beliefs') get compared for consistency without its grasping them as its own, or grasping itself as itself—without its being self-conscious; unless self-consciousness is taken to be mere mental reflexivity.

[29] See D. Parfit, *Reasons and Persons*, Part III. A 'Reductionist' may put the problem by saying that there is a vital sense in which the descriptions of Fido and Nemo, which were supposed to show what they lacked in the way of freedom-necessary mental unity, are also correct when applied to human beings. (Lacanian psychoanalysts may agree; so may structuralist advocates of the 'disappearance of the subject' who see people as ultimately centreless collections of separate agencies, mentally considered. So may cognitive psychologists who stress the 'modularity' of mind.)

The connection between the notion of the self and that of free will (understood in the ordinary strong sense) is an obvious one, but its closeness can be underestimated. Curiously, it seems that some philosophers are prepared to admit the cogency of arguments that cast doubt on the reality of anything that could justly be called 'the self' while continuing to insist on the defensibility of a notion of free will that presupposes the existence of such a self.

It may again be objected that to require a single mental thing in the way described above is unacceptable, because to do so is necessarily to require endorsement of the metaphysically illegitimate picture of the contentful or character-possessing self as something that is in some way ontically separate from all its thoughts or mental contents generally considered. But the present suggestion about why self-consciousness is necessary for freedom can be stated in a qualified form—in such a way that it does not commit one to endorsing this picture (which corresponds to (5) in 9.3). In qualified form, all it claims is that there must in the case of a free agent be some being that *sees* or *experiences* itself as mentally single, in a way that corresponds to (3) above, at least, if not to (5).

The question to what extent a being's sense of itself as mentally single can possibly be supposed to confer some sort of *real* singleness upon it specifically *qua* mental can be left open. One suggestion might be this: that a being's conceiving of or experiencing itself as mentally single, whether simply in a (3)-like way, or in a (5)-like way, is sufficient for its actually being mentally single, at least *in the way that we require for potential free agenthood.* Perhaps one could simply lay it down that possession of a sense of self as single just *qua* mental is constitutive of, or is a necessary part of something, which we have chosen to *call* 'mental singleness', that we require of any free agent. If we cannot have a mental self, as ordinarily and uncritically conceived, we can at least have this.[30]

It seems, then, that the primary intuition about self-consciousness is that only in the self-conscious case is there 'someone there'. There is

[30] A 'Reductionist' view of the specifically mental aspect of the life of a person, which reduces it to the existence of a series of mentations, can accept this suggestion, suitably modified into the suggestion that free agenthood requires the possibility of the occurrence, within the series of mentations, of mentations with a certain *content*—'I'-thoughts or 'I'-mentations. Equally, it can accept the suggestion that (3) is a condition of free agenthood, similarly modified. (For a—somewhat puzzling—attempt to develop the view that self-conscious thoughts might by their occurrence suffice to constitute a genuine entity called 'the self', see R. Nozick, *Philosophical Explanations*, pp. 87–94.)

certainly something it is like, experientially, to be a cat, or Fido, or Nemo; there is a subject of experience, or, as one might say, an *experiential position*, in such cases. But there isn't a 'someone' in the way for which full self-consciousness is necessary.

The corresponding primary intuition about freedom is that an agent can be truly responsible and free only if its mental life is of such a kind that there is 'someone there' in (at least) the present sense. This is necessary, at least. For only then can there be a 'someone' one can address, a someone that is is answerable, accountable, a someone that can act 'in full consciousness', as we naturally say, of what it is doing, and can know, grasping or conceiving of itself as itself, that it is itself that is doing what is being done when it acts, in such a way that it can properly and unequivocally be said to be truly responsible for its actions. Most simply, we need an agent that can see itself grasped as itself as the planner and chooser of, and as responsible for, its actions (this line of thought is developed in Part III); something, therefore, that can see itself as a single thing mentally considered, the chooser, planner, and initiating producer of action. (Once again present concern is with that natural conception or experience of oneself (grasped as oneself) as somehow mentally single that human beings, for example, certainly do have; not with whether this conception is in the final analysis factually or ontically correct or possible.)

Perhaps we have a very bad picture of what we are like, in so far as we are mentally aspected beings—a picture that is built into our experience of self. But the picture is a real picture, even if bad. And, like a portrait, there is certainly something it is a picture (relationally) of— even if it is a bad portrait. It is our representation of ourselves to ourselves in so far as we have a mental aspect—as we most certainly do. And even if the failure of resemblance is too great for one to talk of its being a picture of these mental matters at all, despite the fact that they have a vital causal role in its production,[31] yet it is about them in some sense: my experience of myself as a single mental thing is experience that can reasonably be said to be experience, on my part, of the single psychophysical thing that I am specifically in so far as that thing is mentally propertied, and that thing has, as mentally propertied, a certain considerable unity, continuity, coherence, connectedness of a general thematic kind. Such experience is not pure illusion.[32]

[31] And as the object of the picture, not just as the means of its production.

[32] For some further views on the connection between free agenthood and the sense of self, see Appendix E, which continues the present discussion in the light of the claim, examined in Part III, that believing one is free is a necessary condition of being free.

9.5 WHO IS TO BLAME?

One might add the following as support for the claim that, whether or not full self-consciousness necessarily involves possession of a possibly illusory sense of oneself as something that is single just *qua* mental (even if also physically and psychophysically single), we require such a sense of self for true responsibility.

What is responsible? Our natural thought, again, is that what is responsible is not a body with a gaggle of thoughts, beliefs, desires, and so on that are seen as making up a single collection because attached to a single body. We think that it is a self or subject that is somehow single just *qua mental* that is the true locus of responsibility; its being embodied (and, if embodied, singly embodied) is irrelevant to its being an entity of the kind that is truly responsible. (If one can imagine true responsibility at all, and unembodied minds, then one can imagine an unembodied mind that is, contrary to what it believes, completely incapable of having any effect on others or on the world, making what we would consider to be morally good or bad choices about what to do, and being held to be truly responsible for, and praiseworthy or blameworthy on account of, those choices.) And it seems that possession of a sense of oneself as somehow mentally single is nothing less than essentially constitutive of the presumed single mental self without which there cannot be true responsibility; this being so however dim the prospects are for making decent metaphysical sense of the mental self.

Consider guilt, and the idea of moral badness. You feel guilty. What is guilty? You are—and here it is you in some purely mental aspect, and as a thing that is a definite single thing considered purely in a mental aspect, who is seen as having done wrong. Again, what does retributive punishment aim at? In a clear sense, it is the person simply as mental thing that is aimed at. That alone is the thing that is morally good or bad. Whatever one's view of retributivism as a source of justification for practices of punishment, this conception of people as being in a crucial respect mental things and, as such, most definitely single things, permeates all aspects of our life.[33]

9.6 SELF-CONSCIOUSNESS AND CHOICE

So far as our ordinary view of what a potential free agent must be like is concerned, the account given in 9.4 of why we suppose self-

[33] This is not, of course, Cartesianism of any sort at all; it is just phenomenology.

consciousness to be necessary for freedom has, I think, quite a lot to recommend it. It expresses some of our reasons for thinking that no unselfconscious agent could ever be a free agent, and some of them are good reasons. It connects, too, with the idea that we can be and are truly responsible agents simply because we can and do act 'in full consciousness of' (i.e. in fully self-conscious consciousness of) what we are doing, in a way that the unselfconscious can never do. Exactly what this idea amounts to is unclear, perhaps; but it expresses something fundamental to the sense of freedom.

Another line of thought shifts the emphasis. In 8.3 it was suggested that a dog can be able to choose in the same sense in which we can be, but that it is never able to choose freely, in the way in which we think we are. The suggestion may now be made that what is lacking in the dog's case is simply the possibility of explicitly self-referring self-conscious belief on its part *that it* (*itself*) is able to choose—knowledge which we can and commonly do have. According to this suggestion, full self-consciousness is perhaps all that is missing, in Fido or Nemo's case.[34]

On this second view, it is simply the possibility of fully self-conscious awareness that one is able to choose that is crucial for being able to choose freely.[35] And this connects with the topic of 3.6: it connects with the point that one thing that makes the belief in freedom so difficult to renounce is the simple fact that even if one believes that determinism (or non-self-determinability) is true, still, if one is now confronted with a choice, then although one may believe that one will after acting be able to say truly that what one chose to do and did do was determined, still one cannot now not face the fact (it seems like a fact) that it really is *entirely* up to one what one does choose, in such a way that one will be truly responsible for what one eventually does—even though one knows that all one's desires, values, and so on are, ultimately, not self-determined. As an ordinary adult human being one has a more or less explicit, more or less irrepressible sense that one can take re-sponsibility for oneself and one's actions *whatever* the facts are about determinism, just in so far as one is a reflective, fully self-conscious being fully apprised of one's general situation. It is full self-

---

[34] Great complexity or diversity of desires, beliefs, and so on is certainly not a con-dition of free agenthood; and one does not have to be a moral agent, or have a conception of moral right or wrong, in order to be a free agent (3.3).

[35] 'How could this alone possibly be thought to make the vital difference?', ask the incompatibilist determinists. Their question is a powerful one, but they are being ignored at present. The suggestion is discussed at length in ch. 14.

consciousness that gives one this view of one's situation, and allows one to grasp it as one's own; and the availability of this view, and this grasp, seems itself to be a necessary condition of free agenthood— whether or not it must ultimately be conceded to involve some sort of illusion.

9.7 CONCLUSION AND ANTICIPATION

We now have two main suggestions about why self-consciousness is necessary for free agenthood. According to the first (9.4), self-consciousness is necessary because it is necessary for 'someonehood'. According to the second (9.6), it is necessary simply because a free agent must in certain situations be able to think of itself conceived as itself (i.e. fully self-consciously) as able to choose.

What of the further claim that full self-consciousness is an addition to purposive agenthood that is not only necessary but also sufficient to turn canine or Nemonic purposive agenthood into free agenthood— given (*a*) that we ourselves are free, and also (*b*) that the problem that determinism (or non-self-determinability) poses for freedom, waived by an explicit ruling in 7.1, is still waived.

If this claim looks correct, on these conditions, then this may be partly because certain common assumptions about the nature of full self-consciousness are being tacitly carried along, assumptions that need to be made explicit and examined—assumptions, in particular, about what a being's experience of or *attitude* to itself and its agency must be like if it is both a purposive agent and a fully self-conscious being.

In Chapters 12 to 14 it will be argued that this is indeed so. In particular, it will be argued that full self-consciousness involves less than we may ordinarily suppose; that even if we ourselves are free, self-consciousness is not sufficient to turn canine or Nemonic agenthood into free agenthood; that the experience and attitudes of a fully self-conscious purposive agent needn't be at all like ours ordinarily are; and that trying to establish what they might minimally be like leads to the proposal of further Attitudinal conditions on free agenthood.

So much for trying to make direct connections between freedom and self-consciousness. In Part III, other necessary conditions of freedom which presuppose self-consciousness are proposed. In this way further indirect connections are established.

With this background, we may now turn to the question 'In what way, if any, do the 'Structural' *S* conditions (1)–(5) first stated in 7.3 need supplementation, as an account of free agenthood?' The libertarians think it obvious that they need supplementing, for they do not include a condition requiring the falsity of determinism. But those who wish can add such a condition; it has no bearing on anything that follows. The present aim is a relatively limited one. It consists, as remarked in 7.1, in the attempt to show that even if one puts all questions regarding determinism and non-self-determinability on one side, the S conditions are still inadequate, and are so even if one accepts a wholly compatibilist view of freedom according to which there may be free agents even if determinism is true. The argument that follows employs the standard analytic technique of putting the ordinary, strong notion of freedom under various kinds of strain.

III

THE SUBJECTIVIST CHALLENGE

10

Evidence and Independence

10.1 THE PRINCIPAL CLAIM

It seems plausible to say that any satisfactory definition of free agenthood has to take account of the fact that believing one is a free agent is a necessary condition of being a free agent. In what follows, I propose to examine this suggestion—which I shall call 'the principal claim'—at some length.

The principal claim seems very problematic in certain respects, and one natural objection needs to be noted immediately, if only to be deferred. It is this: as it stands, this claim entails that incompatibilist determinists (for example), who do not believe that they are free, are indeed not free, simply because they do not believe they are. And to this it will be objected that, to the extent that we ordinarily hold ordinary people to be free and truly responsible for what they do, we will also hold those who are out of the ordinary only in being incompatibilist determinists to be free and truly responsible for what they do.

This objection will be considered later. Here I will simply assert that, whatever *theoretical* beliefs people purport to espouse, they must continue to think of themselves as free in some fundamental sense, in order for us to be right in holding them to be free and truly responsible agents.

10.2 EXPLICIT* BELIEF

The condition of being a free agent, as presently conceived, is a persisting or standing condition, not one that comes and goes. But if having the belief that one is a free agent really is necessary for being a free agent, it does not of course have to be a permanently occurrent rather than an ordinarily dispositional belief—though it may well be occurrent at particular times.[1] I shall say that it has to be an *explicit* belief: it has to be explicit in at least this sense: one has to be aware*

---

[1] For 'occurrent belief', see ch. 8 n. 5.

that one is a free agent.[2] Or, in other terms: to believe explicitly* that one is a free agent is to believe that one is a free agent in at least the sense in which it is true to say that one believes this if it is true to say that one *conceives* of oneself as, or thinks of oneself as, a free agent.[3]

It is hard to imagine how it could be true of anything that it conceived of itself as a free agent—conceived of itself conceived of *as itself* as a free agent, that is, in the way characteristic of full self-consciousness (9.1)—and not also be true of it that it was capable of some linguistic or quasi-linguistic mode of thought. But the question of the necessity of language for this belief or conception can be left open here. When concerned with the claim that no being can be a free agent and not believe (explicitly*) that it is one, we are in any case concerned with fully self-conscious belief—whatever the minimal form of fully self-conscious belief may be.

The following discussion is conducted mainly in terms of freedom and belief in freedom. But one could equally well frame the principal claim in terms of responsibility: no being can be (properly held to be) truly responsible for its action, at a particular time, unless it believes (explicitly*) that it is a truly responsible agent, or possesses a conception of itself as an agent truly responsible for its actions.

10.3 THE PRINCIPLE OF INDEPENDENCE

If it is true that no being that does not believe itself to be a free agent can be one, it would seem to follow that a being's belief in its freedom is a necessary condition of its freedom. But this, taken in one very natural way, seems most implausible. It appears to offend against the *principle of independence*: the principle that if one has a belief, B, then the obtaining of the state of affairs that makes B true cannot (ever) depend upon or necessarily involve one's having B; the principle that one's having B cannot be among the truth-conditions of B. According to this principle, a true belief must be supposed to be a representation of some state of affairs essentially other than itself; to be something

[2] For 'aware*', see 8.2. There is no connection between the '*' superscript as attached to 'explicit' and as attached to 'aware'; in the latter case the 'factive' or 'success' implications of the word are cancelled, and this corresponds to nothing in the case of 'explicit'.

[3] This sense of 'explicit' is less exclusive than the one defined in 8.2, according to which *a* explicitly+ believes that *p* just in case *a* is *presently* aware* that *p*. The explicit* belief that one is a free agent does not have to be so 'near at hand in the mind', as it were, as the explicit+ belief that one is now able to perform actions of kinds X and Y has to be when one is now able to choose between performing an action of one of those two kinds. This may seem unhelpfully imprecise—see ch. 8 n. 7.

which can always in principle be subtracted from the world in a way that leaves its object—the state of affairs it is a belief about—untouched.

Present concern is only with what may, without further explanation, be called ordinary, factual beliefs—although the principle of independence is of quite general application; and with beliefs conceived as real things, people's mental states, which I am supposing to be such that they can be called true or false, as when we say 'He has many true (or false) beliefs.' It may be objected that properly speaking it is the belief *qua* abstract object, the proposition, that is true or false. But this can be granted—although it is natural to talk of beliefs conceived as mental states as true or false *qua* representational objects of a certain kind. For the principle of independence remains plausible in asserting that the obtaining of the state of affairs in virtue of which a proposition, *p*, is true, cannot depend essentially upon the obtaining of the state of affairs of anyone's believing the proposition *p* to be true.

The principle of independence can also be stated as follows. If a man, *a*, has an ordinary factual belief, then, if the belief is true, it is true in virtue of the obtaining of some state of affairs. Obviously. The principle of independence states that the state of affairs of *a*'s having the belief cannot be *part of* the state of affairs in virtue of the obtaining of which his belief is true.

Prima facie, then, the claim that believing you are free is a necessary condition of being free offends against the principle of independence. The problem remains if one replaces 'believes it is' by 'conceives of itself as', in the statement 'a being is a free agent only if it believes it is a free agent'. For if it is indeed true that we are free agents, then we are correct in our conception of ourselves. But according to the principle of independence it must be the case that what makes us correct in our conception is a how-things-are that does not include our having the conception in question. The conception must pick up on, represent, or reflect the independent how-things-are. Surely the conception's being correct consists (as does a belief's being true) in its being a genuine representation of a how-things-are that is independent of it and that it can therefore take as its object as a whole, in a way that it could not do if it were itself in some paradoxical way a part of its own object? That, I take it, is the basic intuition.[4]

---

[4] It might be taken to be similar to the intuition behind Bishop Butler's remark, made when discussing Locke's theory of personal identity, that "one should really think it self-evident, that consciousness of personal identity presupposes, and cannot therefore constitute, personal identity; any more than knowledge, in any other case, can constitute truth, which it presupposes" ('Of Personal Identity', p. 258). Thus one might cor-

The Objectivists' position about freedom is defined by reference to the principle of independence. They hold that the principle cannot be contravened in the case of freedom and belief in freedom. In the next two chapters I will consider the principle at some length, going beyond what is strictly necessary to discussion of the problem of freedom. I will consider a number of apparent contraventions of the principle, both in the hope that they may throw light on the case of freedom, and because they seem independently interesting.

10.4 EVIDENT PROPOSITIONS

What is it for the having of a belief, B, to be a necessary condition of B's being true? Several preliminary distinctions seem useful.

Bernard Williams has defined the notion of a proposition p's being *evident* for someone as follows: a proposition p is evident for a man a if, if p, then a believes that p.[5] Representing 'a believes that p' symbolically as '$B(a,p)$', one may rewrite this as the claim that if p is evident for a, then $p \rightarrow B(a,p)$.[6]

Since the following is concerned mainly with beings' beliefs about themselves—for if any propositions are evident for a in the sense defined, they are more than likely to be propositions about a himself—the version of this formula that will be of particular interest is '$\phi a \rightarrow B(a,\phi a)$', where '$\phi$' is some property; that is, if a is ϕ, then a believes that he is ϕ. The principal claim is of this general form: applied to a, it states that if a is free, then a believes he is free. It seems that if one is free, then the proposition that one is free is 'evident' for one. The question is, why is this so?

10.5 FULLY SELF-CONSCIOUS BELIEF

Before trying to answer this question, the emphasis on beliefs about oneself—*fully self-conscious* beliefs about oneself, in particular—necessitates a digression. H.-N. Castañeda has pointed out that special

respondingly suggest that consciousness of, awareness of, or true belief in freedom equally presupposes, and cannot therefore either constitute or even help to constitute freedom. The present case is not exactly parallel, however. For what is being claimed is merely that one's *belief* in (consciousness* of, awareness* of) one's freedom might help to constitute one's freedom. And clearly one's belief in one's freedom does not presuppose one's freedom, even if it cannot constitute it, or even help to constitute it.

[5] In *Descartes: The Project of Pure Enquiry*, pp. 77 and 306.

[6] '$\rightarrow$' is thus taken to symbolize the ordinary, strong, central sense of 'if . . . then . . .'. Sometimes it will be used where causal conditionship relations are in question, sometimes where strict entailment is in question—just as 'if . . . then . . .' is used.

formal provisions are required for the symbolic representation of such belief.[7] For it is not enough that a simply believe, relationally of himself, a, that a is ϕ. For a may believe this, believing that c is ϕ, and not know that he, a, is c—in which case he does not have a fully self-conscious belief about himself. This makes it necessary to require that so far as all formulae of the form '$\phi a \to B(a,\phi a)$' are concerned, a's belief about himself is to be understood to be not only relationally but also *notionally* about himself. That is, the notional content of the belief as entertained by a[8] is *that he himself is* ϕ (i.e., the content of his belief is 'I (myself) am ϕ'). Or, if the content of his belief is *that d is* ϕ, for some designator d, then it must be true that he also believes, notionally of himself, that he himself is d (is called 'd').[9]

He must then believe both relationally and notionally of himself that he is ϕ.[10] For the sake of simplicity I will in what follows take 'a' as it occurs coupled to a predicate in contexts like '$B(a, \ldots)$' to be a special name of a which is such that '$B(a,\phi a)$' is to be read 'a believes (of himself conceived of *as* himself, in the way characteristic of full self-consciousness) that he himself is ϕ'. One could write something like '$B(a,\phi$ he-conceived-of-as-himself)' each time. But the present device— which in effect notices the difficulty only to ignore it—is preferable because simpler. Universally quantified versions of the formula that is of principal concern, which have the form '$(x)(\phi x \to B(x,\phi x))$', will be understood in a similar way, as saying that if any being x is ϕ then it believes, relationally and notionally of itself, that it is ϕ.

By way of a reminder 'B' will at certain points in what follows be replaced by 'B_{NR}', this being understood to stand for 'believes, both

---

[7] In, e.g., 'On the Logic of Self-Knowledge'.

[8] Such talk of the 'content of the belief as entertained by a' is understood to be compatible with the belief's being non-occurrent, although explicit*. (For the relational/notional distinction, see 9.1.)

[9] Strictly speaking, it is not even enough that he both believe that ϕd, and that he himself is d. He must also connect up the beliefs—in such a way that, at the very least, whenever he is disposed to assent to 'ϕd' he is also, and *ipso facto*, disposed to assent to 'I am ϕ', if he has the use of a first-person pronoun. If he does not, what must be true is that his belief that ϕd is correctly described as a belief on his part that he grasped as himself is ϕ.

[10] In fact one cannot believe, notionally, that one is ϕ, in the way characteristic of full self-consciousness such as we have, and not also believe, relationally of oneself, that one is ϕ. Roughly because designations used by oneself to designate oneself in thought cannot miss their mark. (One can be wrong, stuck in a muddle of mirrors, in saying, on the basis of observation, 'I have a funny mark on the back of my neck'. But one does necessarily refer to oneself; that's *why* one's wrong, if the neck one sees does indeed have a funny mark on it.) The point is a familiar one. As Williams says, "with regard to 'I', unlike other pronouns, the mere fact that it is used in genuine thought is enough to guarantee that it does not miss its mark" (op. cit., p. 93).

notionally and relationally': thus '$B_{NR}(a,\phi a)$' states that a has a belief (relationally) about himself, and the (notional) content of the belief is: that he himself is ϕ. He believes that he is ϕ in the way characteristic (and arguably constitutive) of full self-consciousness such as we ordinarily have.

10.6 EVIDENTNESS — A NATURAL PICTURE

If a proposition about a state of affairs is evident for a, then its truth is sufficient for his believing it;[11] and in that sense the obtaining of the state of affairs of a's having the belief is a necessary condition of the obtaining of the state of affairs believed to obtain (given the standard philosophical understanding of the terms 'necessary' and 'sufficient' according to which something is necessary for whatever is sufficient for it and vice versa). But, as above defined, evidentness is in itself no bar to the possible independence of a belief from—roughly—the fact that it is a belief about. The state of affairs of a's having the belief is necessary for the obtaining of the state of affairs believed to obtain in the sense that the latter cannot occur without the former. But it is not as if the obtaining of the former state of affairs need be necessary for the obtaining of the latter because it is part of what the latter *consists* in.

Thus it may be that '$\phi a \rightarrow B(a,\phi a)$' is true because '$\phi a$' is evident for a. But if this is so, then it is natural to suppose that this is because the obtaining of the state of affairs of a's being ϕ inevitably gives rise *causally* to a's belief that ϕa. And it is natural to suppose that the converse is not the case—that a's having the belief that ϕa is not one of the causal conditions of its coming to be the case that ϕa. Equally, it is natural to suppose that a's belief that ϕa is not one of the *constitutive* conditions of its being the case that ϕa, i.e. one of the non-causal (but also non-logical) conditions of its being the case that ϕa.[12]

Where these suppositions are correct, (a), the obtaining of the state of affairs believed to obtain, is in a clear sense independent of (b), the obtaining of the state of affairs of the first state of affair's being believed to obtain. Causally related, (a) and (b) are, presumably, 'distinct existences', in Hume's phrase.

In the case of freedom, however, it is not at all clear that there is such independence.

[11] Evidentness is, as Williams points out, the converse of incorrigibility.

[12] By 'non-logical' I mean 'non-formal-logical'. 'Logical' has a wider and a narrower use; here I intend the narrower use.

10.7 'CAUSALLY EVIDENT'

Let 'causally evident' be defined as follows: the proposition 'ϕa' is causally evident for a just if a cannot be ϕ without his being ϕ giving rise causally to a belief on his part that he is ϕ.

Whether or not there are any propositions that are causally evident in this sense may seem dubious. More generally, it may seem dubious that there are any properties which are such that it is causally impossible that a being should possess them and not believe that it does. But it is certainly natural enough to understand the apparently epistemological notion of evidentness in terms of causal evidentness. For the natural picture of evidentness is simply that there are, or may be, some states that are so present to one's consciousness (as it were) that one cannot be in them and not know it (or not believe it truly, at least), although one's believing one is in them isn't actually partly constitutive of one's being in them in any way.[13]

But when it is suggested that it is a necessary condition of actually being a free agent that one believe one is a free agent, the relation between (*a*), having the property of being a free agent, and (*b*), having the property of believing one has the property of being a free agent, appears to be such that (*a*) depends on (*b*) in some non-causal way. It does not appear to be such that the former merely invariably gives rise causally to the latter. It seems that one's believing one is a free agent is part of what *goes to make up* one's being a free agent. It seems that it is a necessary constitutive condition of one's being a free agent, in precisely the way that looks problematic.

Anticipating, one might say that there is an *awareness condition* on free agenthood. Whatever its capacities and abilities, nothing can count as a free agent that is not aware* that it is one. This suggests a parallel that will be examined below: it seems plausible that no being can be said to be entering into a contract on its own account, whatever physical actions it performs, that does not believe (that is not aware*) that it is doing so. There seems to be an awareness condition on entering into a

---

[13] Consider the arguably Cartesian claim that 'I think' is not only an incorrigible proposition for me (i.e. such that 'I believe I think $\rightarrow$ I think' is true), but also an evident proposition for me (i.e. such that 'I think $\rightarrow$ I believe I think' is true). Such a claim (cf. Williams, op. cit., p. 77) would seem to rest upon the problematic supposition that thought, or consciousness(*), or belief, or awareness(*) that one is thinking is somehow essentially constitutive of one's thinking. Given that Descartes had fully self-conscious thinking in mind, a more plausible claim might be this: that if I *can* think in a fully self-conscious manner, then, necessarily, I am aware that (I believe explicitly* that) I can think in a fully self-conscious manner. (Cf. 9.3.)

contract. At the very least, a special ruling to the effect that the being did enter into a contract will be required if it did not, at the time of doing whatever it did do (and we may suppose that it did whatever is conventionally taken to be sufficient by way of overt physical action or outward form for entering into a contract), believe that it was entering into a contract.[14]

10.8 GENERALIZATION; EVIDENT PROPERTIES

So far the discussion has been in terms of a single arbitrarily selected individual *a*. But the principal question is whether there are properties which are such that *no* being can (possibly) possess them without believing it does, and with the question whether the property of freedom is one such. Let '*F*' symbolize 'is a (potential) free agent'. The question is not just whether '*Fa* → *B*(*a,Fa*)' might be true, and why, though it is often convenient to talk in terms of a single individual *a*. The question is whether the universally quantified statement '(*x*)(*Fx* → *B*(*x,Fx*))' might be true, and why.

This being so, it will be convenient to talk of a being's possession of a property being evident for it, instead of talking merely of the proposition that it has the property being evident for it. Indeed it will be best to talk simply of a *property* being an evident property (for its possessor) if no being can possess it and not believe it does.

10.9 THE PROBLEM RESTATED—NON-CAUSALLY EVIDENT PROPERTIES

One may put the problem another way. Suppose that one is ϕ. If all that is the case is that ϕ is a causally evident property, then one's believing one is ϕ isn't part of what actually constitutes one's being ϕ. And I shall take it that if this is so, then that in virtue of which one is ϕ

[14] Various prima facie counter examples can be constructed, in which the agent (1) intends to enter into a contract (and wants to), but, in the event, (2), believes that it does not in fact do so, on account of some failure of overt performance, but (3), does in fact do all that is necessary by way of overt performance. In such cases it may be granted that it did enter into a contract; that is, what happened may be allowed to count as its having entered into a contract. But this 'allowing it to count' suggests, precisely, that the agent cannot be said to have contracted without a special ruling, although the only thing that was missing was its belief that it was contracting.

A number of other odd cases can be constructed. I will use the example of contracting although it is not in fact strictly correct given current legal terms, according to which one not only acquires certain legal rights when buying something from a shop, but also enters into a contract.

(that in which one's being ϕ consists), is in principle fully specifiable independently of mention of the fact that one believes one is ϕ.[15] If on the other hand believing one is ϕ is, somehow, a non-causal or constitutive condition of one's being ϕ, then, presumably, that in virtue of which one is ϕ is not fully specifiable independently of mention of one's believing one is.[16]

The principle of independence can be restated in these terms: in the case of any ordinary factual true belief that p, that in virtue of which the belief is true must be fully specifiable independently of mention of the fact that any being believes that p. Or, more restrictedly, for any object, x, and for any property ϕ possessed by x, that in which x's possession of ϕ consists must be fully specifiable independently of mention of the fact that x believes that it is or possesses ϕ, if indeed x does believe this.[17]

This leads to a different statement of the basic problem: there are, as remarked, apparently cases in which propositions of the form

'$\phi a \to B(a,\phi a)$',

or rather,

'$(x)(\phi x \to B(x,\phi x))$',

are true: nothing can be a free agent and not believe it is one; a being is

---

[15] This will be so not only where, as in the present case, it is supposed that one's believing one is ϕ is an effect of one's being ϕ, but also in the dubious case (see Appendix D) in which it is supposed that one's believing one is ϕ is a cause of one's being or coming to be ϕ.

[16] Here it is assumed that, briefly, independent specifiability (independent specifiability in principle) follows from distinct existence. It is arguable that there are situations in which we give causal explanations (of actions, say) that throw doubt on this assumption; but I take it that all they do is (at most) to increase the emphasis on the phrase 'in principle'. Certain views about how best to specify the content of beliefs about the world may also be thought to provide grounds for an objection to this assumption. (For a discussion of this issue, see C. McGinn, *The Character of Mind*, ch. 3.) But they are controversial, and do not in any case cast doubt on the acceptability of the assumption in the present context.

[17] If there are self-referring beliefs, beliefs that are about themselves, then the principle of independence may be false in their case. Are there? Consider the following occurrent belief or thought: I think (believe) that *this* thought (belief)—the one I am now entertaining and writing down—is puzzling. In this case my present thought (belief), call it 'Q', is the thought (belief) *that Q is puzzling*; that is its content. So Q is a true thought (belief) (if and) only if Q is puzzling. So that in virtue of which Q is true is not fully specifiable independently of mention of Q itself. This does seem perfectly possible, and not in any deep way paradoxical. (The paradoxes that arise in connection with such thoughts as the thought that *this* thought—the one now being entertained—is incorrect or false do not arise simply from the self-referentiality of the thought, but from the combination of such self-referentiality with the notions of incorrectness and falsity.) But it is not the fact that I believe that Q that has to be mentioned in specifying that in virtue of which Q is true. What has to be mentioned is simply my belief itself, Q.

a truly responsible agent only if it believes it is; a being promise
(asserts) that *p* only if it believes that it is promising (asserting) that *p*
one enters into a contract (obeys an order to do X, follows a rul
enjoining Y)[18] only if one believes one does so. It seems clear tha
these propositions are not true because they concern causally eviden
properties. So there must be evident properties that are not causall
evident in the sense defined.

How might this be? Well, so far, a property is said to be causall
evident when its possession is causally sufficient for, sufficient to giv
rise causally to, a belief on the part of its possessor that it has th
property. Could the propositions just mentioned concern propertie
that are not causally evident in the sense defined, but are evident be
cause possession of the belief that they are possessed is causally *neces
sary* for their being possessed? If so, the relation between (*a*) possessio
of one of the putatively evident properties, say ϕ, and (*b*) possession o
the property of believing that one possesses ϕ would still be causal, an
to that extent unproblematic, (*a*) and (*b*) still being 'distinct existences'

But the answer to the last question is surely 'No'. One point is this
the possession of the belief that one possesses ϕ cannot be a merel
temporally precedent cause. For the belief has to be possessed for a
long as ϕ is possessed. Independently of this, it simply seems completel
implausible to suppose that causal connections are in question at al
in the case of the propositions presently being considered; rather as i
would be implausible to suppose that causal connections are in questio
when equiangularity and equilaterality are said to be conditions o
squareness.[19]

Let it be granted that the cases of apparently evident propertie
considered above are not cases of causally evident properties. If sc
then if the claims considered there are none the less true, there must b
non-causally evident properties. This question then arises: given tha
there are non-causally evident properties, are there non-causally eviden
properties that do not contravene the principle of independence, as nov
defined? That is, can any property ϕ be such that its possession
conditions are fully specifiable independently of mention of the fac
that its possessors believe they possess it, even though (1) one canno
possess ϕ and not believe one does, and (2) one's possessing ϕ is no
the cause of (or partly caused by) one's believing one possesses it? I

[18] These won't be cases if one can be said to obey an order to do X, or follow a rul
enjoining Y, without being conscious that one is doing so. Consider, also: *a* castles (i
chess), or huffs (in draughts), etc. only if he believes he does.

[19] For a red herring, see Appendix D.

there can be such properties—it is not clear how there could be—is the property of being a potential free agent, or being truly responsible, one of them? If there are not—if all non-causally evident properties do contravene the principle of independence—is this necessarily problematic?

If all non-causally evident properties do contravene the principle of independence, then it is false as it stands. For it seems clear that there are non-causally evident properties. It seems clear that one cannot truly be said to promise that *p* if one does not believe one is doing so at the time. There is an awareness condition on promising, if for no other reason than that the intention to promise that *p* (though not necessarily to do what is promised) must be present. And it seems that the belief that you are promising that *p* cannot be a merely explicit* belief, and, as such, possibly non-occurrent; it seems it must be an occurrent belief. [20] Furthermore, one's having the belief is certainly in *some* sense a constitutive condition of one's being such that one actually is promising that *p*; it is a condition of one's *counting* as promising that *p*.

At the same time, there is something right about the principle of independence. We have a natural picture of what it is for ϕ to be a straightforwardly objective property according to which an object *x*'s possession or non-possession of ϕ is a matter entirely independent of whether anyone does or does not believe *x* to possess ϕ. Whether or not a person's belief that *x* possesses ϕ is true is a matter of how things are in a part of the world that is separate from the belief itself. It seems that this how-things-are must be separate from the belief in order for the belief to be able to take it as its object in such a way that it (the belief) has a fully and determinately specifiable content (though see note 17 above).

If, then, the principle of independence is false as it stands, but true for all 'straightforwardly objective' properties, this must be because there are properties that are not straightforwardly objective in the sense, rough as it is, of the last paragraph.

What of this? Well, it is certainly noteworthy that promising and asserting[21] that *p*, and entering into a contract, and so on, are all

[20] Or thought. There are complications in the case of promising similar to those considered in n. 14 above when discussing entering into a contract. (For a familiar objection to this sort of claim, see ch. 11 n. 5.)

[21] The claim is that one asserts that *p* only if one believes one is doing so; but I take it that one does not have to know the word 'assert' (or any word with the same meaning in the language one speaks) for it to be the case that one believes that one is asserting that *p*. It may be questioned whether the claim is true. For it may be said that 'assert' is

conventional activities, in some sense, things that one cannot do without having a grasp of certain conventions, linguistic or otherwise; and in Chapter 11 I shall suggest that it is this fact that renders the contraventions of the principle of independence to which they give rise unproblematic. But they seem none the less to be straightforwardly objective properties, real properties that people really have. The vague notion of 'straightforwardly objective' is not going to provide a workable principle of division on its own.

What is more, even if promising and asserting that *p*, and so on, can be shown to be conventional properties of such a kind that the contraventions of the principle of independence to which they give rise are not problematic, this does not obviously help in any way with the problem raised by freedom and belief in freedom. For freedom, true-responsibility-entailing freedom as ordinarily conceived, is in *no* obvious sense a property possession of which involves a grasp of certain conventions. If it is true that one can't be a free agent without possessing linguistic or quasi-linguistic abilities, then it can of course be said that being a free agent does indirectly involve having a grasp of certain conventions—linguistic ones. But it is only indirectly that it does so. And the case of freedom still seems completely different from that of entering into a contract (or promising that *p*), where the point is that one has to know (believe) that something—some physical thing, an action—that has no *intrinsic* connection with entering into a contract (or promising that *p*) *counts*, *conventionally*, as entering into a contract (or promising that *p*). For it is surely not as if, to be fully free, one has to believe that some condition that has *no* intrinsic connection with the condition of being free counts, conventionally, as being free.

10.10 CAUSATION AND CONSTITUTION; C-STATEMENTS

'Causally evident' was defined in 10.7. Let 'non-causally evident' be positively defined as follows: a property ϕ is a non-causally evident property just in case

(i) no being can be ϕ and not believe it is (i.e. $(x)(\phi x \rightarrow B(x, \phi x))$)

like 'say', and that it is not true that one says that *p* only if one believes one is saying that *p*: given that one is indeed speaking in a certain language, what one says is arguably just a function of what the words one utters mean, independently of any belief or intention that one may have about what they mean (see, e.g., G. Evans, *The Varieties of Reference*, § 3.2, esp. pp. 68–9; and consider slips of the tongue, or Epiphany). Whether such an argument could defeat the claim that one asserts that *p* only if one believes one does is questionable, for 'asserts' is not the same as 'says'. But nothing presently depends on the viability of this particular claim.

and

(ii) x's believing it is ϕ is partly constitutive of x's being ϕ (part of what its being ϕ consists in).

Now '$(x)(\phi x \rightarrow B(x,\phi x))$' is true both when ϕ is a non-causally evident property and when ϕ is a causally evident property. The formula doesn't display this difference. For this reason I propose to offer part of a more general account of the different possible reasons for which statements of the form '$(x)(\phi x \rightarrow B(x,\phi x))$'—or, more generally, '$(x)$ $(\phi x \rightarrow \psi x)$'—can be true, and to develop a simple symbolism to express the difference in question.

In this account, it will be assumed that where '$(x)(\phi x \rightarrow \psi x)$' does not simply state (*a*) an 'accidental uniformity' (like 'All the coins in my pocket are copper'), and is not true (*b*) for merely formal-logical reasons or (*c*) for reasons of identity, then it will be true either because of (*d*) the holding of *causation* relations or because of (*e*) the holding of *constitution* relations. That is, these are the only two options that lie between merely logical and merely accidental reasons why generalizations of the form '$(x)(\phi x \rightarrow \psi x)$' are true.[22] Causation relations and constitution relations can get closely tangled together in our account of why something is the case; many problems of philosophy derive ultimately from this fact. But the assumption that they can always in principle be sorted out—or, less absolutely, that they can always be sorted out relative to a given descriptive framework—is a plausible one nevertheless.

Causation and constitution relations are in any case what will concern us in what follows. (The question whether the principal claim is true on account of the holding of causation relations or constitution relations will be debated at some length below.)

1. Consider, first, causal relations (never mind exactly what they are supposed to hold between—events, or states of affairs).

Where causation is concerned, '$(x)(\phi x \rightarrow \psi x)$' can be true—roughly—either,

---

[22] What about 'Everything divisible by 4 is divisible by 2', and 'Nothing can be red and green all over'? There are, of course, other controversial cases—but they are of no importance given the present use of the distinction between causation and constitution relations. (In order to defend the claim that causal cases and constitution cases exhaust all cases between merely logical and merely accidental cases, one would have to classify both mathematical and colour-incompatibility cases as true in virtue of the holding of constitution relations: they are not causal truths, they are a priori truths that flow from the essential nature or constitution of numbers, and of colours.)

   (i) because being (coming to be) ϕ is a causally sufficient condition of being (coming to be) ψ,

or,

   (ii) because being (coming to be) ψ is a causally necessary condition of being (coming to be) ϕ.

Let (i) be represented as follows:

$$Cs/(x)(\underline{\phi x} \rightarrow \psi x)/; \tag{1}$$

to be read 'For all x, x's being ϕ (or x's coming to be ϕ, or x's ϕ-ing) is a sufficient causal condition of x's being ψ (or x's coming to be ψ, or x's ψ-ing)'.

And let (ii) be represented as follows:

$$Cs/(x)(\phi x \rightarrow \underline{\psi x})/; \tag{2}$$

to be read 'For all x, x's being ψ (or x's coming to be ψ, or x's ψ-ing) is a necessary causal condition of x's being ϕ (or . . . etc.)'.

(1) and (2) are not equivalent. The underlining represents the difference.

Some philosophers would hold (1) and (2) to be equivalent. But it is profoundly unnatural to do so. Let A and B be types of events. Then (I) to say that A is a necessary causal condition of B is to say that an event of type A is involved *causally or as a cause* in the production of, in the coming to pass of, any event of type B; and (II) to say that A is a sufficient causal condition of B is to say that whenever an event of type A occurs, it *causes* an event of type B to occur.

Now consider (I): if A is a necessary causal condition of B, it clearly does not follow that B is a sufficient causal condition of A—it clearly does not follow that whenever an event of type B occurs, it *causes* an event of type A to occur. And in any particular case of causation, if a particular event of type A, A_1, is causally necessary for the occurrence of a particular event of type B, B_1, then it is of course simply impossible that B_1 should also be causally sufficient for A_1, i.e. should be that which causes A_1 to come about.

Similarly for (II): if A is a sufficient causal condition of B, then it certainly does not follow that B is a necessary causal condition of A— it certainly does not follow that an event of type B is involved causally or as a cause in the production of, or coming to pass of, any event of type A (either of any single one, or of all events of type A). In any particular case of causation, if a particular event A_1 is causally sufficient for the occurrence of a particular event B_1, then it is of course simply impossible that B_1 is also *causally* necessary for A_1, and, hence, part of what causes A_1 to come about.[23]

Consider an example. Suppose for the purposes of argument that the presence of oxygen (PO) is a necessary causal condition of the lighting of any match (LM); the lighting of a match is not (thereby) a sufficient *causal condition* of the presence of oxygen. To say this is absurd. It is to ignore the meaning of the words 'cause' and 'condition', and to speak in an entirely unnatural manner. In this case, (*a*) 'If LM then PO' is true, *and* (*b*) it is a causal truth. But it is not true (of course) that (*c*) LM is a sufficient causal condition of PO. Philosophers have perhaps confused (*a*) and (*b*) with (*c*). They have wrongly taken (*a*) and (*b*) to entail (*c*).

There is, then, an asymmetry in causal relations—the asymmetry of causal priority, if you will—which is such that, given simply a statement of the form '$Cs/X \rightarrow Y/$', one needs some further symbol in order to express the difference between the two distinct possible reasons why such a statement might be true: either because X is a sufficient causal condition of Y, or because Y is a necessary causal condition of X. Hence the underlining.

2. Consider next constitution relations (which might be negatively defined as non-accidental, non-causal, and non-formal-logical relations).

Where constitution relations are concerned, '$(x)(\phi x \rightarrow \psi x)$' can be true either

(iii) because being ϕ is a sufficient constitutive condition of being ψ,

or

(iv) because being ψ is a necessary constitutive condition of being ϕ.

Let (iii) be represented as follows:

$$Cn/(x)(\underline{\phi x} \rightarrow \psi x)/; \tag{3}$$

to be read 'For all x, x's being ϕ is a sufficient constitutive condition of x's being ψ'.

And let (iv) be represented as follows:

$$Cn/(x)(\phi x \rightarrow \underline{\psi x})/; \tag{4}$$

to be read 'For all x, x's being ψ is a necessary constitutive condition of x's being ϕ'.

What (3) and (4) really represent are relations between properties;

---

[23] Although it does seem at least conceivable that As should cause Bs which in turn caused As, *ad indefinitum.*

whether these are intrinsic conceptual connections, such as the connection between being equiangular and being square—it is connections of this sort that are in question in discussion of freedom; or whether they are conventionally instituted connections, like the connection there might be between being entitled to receive money from some government and being disabled.

An example of (4) would be this: being equiangular (or rectilinear or quadrilateral or equilateral) is a necessary constitutive condition of being square. An example of (3) would be this: being equiangular and rectilinear and quadrilateral and equilateral is a sufficient constitutive condition of being square.

In fact the example just given is of a set of necessary and sufficient constitutive conditions, which might be represented, given appropriate interpretations of ϕ and ψ, as

$$\text{Cn}/(x)(\phi\underline{x} \longleftrightarrow \psi x)/; \tag{5}$$

to be read 'For all x, x's being ϕ is the necessary and sufficient constitutive condition of x's being ψ'.[24]

The list is completed with

$$\text{Cs}/(x)(\phi\underline{x} \longleftrightarrow \psi x)/; \tag{6}$$

to be read 'For all x, x's being ϕ (or x's coming to be ϕ, or x's ϕ-ing) is the necessary and sufficient causal condition of x's being ψ (or . . . etc.)'. (Nothing can have more than one set of necessary and sufficient conditions.)

3. It is obvious, I think, that (3) and (4) are no more equivalent than (1) and (2) are. Equilaterality is a necessary constitutive condition of squareness, but squareness is not therefore a sufficient *constitutive* condition of equilaterality, although it is of course a sufficient condition of equilaterality. Equilaterality is just a matter of having sides of equal length, and has nothing in particular to do with squareness. Being square is no part of what *goes to make up* being equilateral (it is no part of what goes to make up being an equilateral triangle, for example).

---

[24] In this case there is only one set of sufficient conditions—which is therefore the set of necessary and sufficient conditions. This will very often be so—it is natural to expect it to be so in the case of freedom, and in the case of many properties of philosophical interest. Some properties, however, such as the property of being entitled to French government benefit, are such that there may be different sufficient constitutive conditions of them—being French, and resident in France, and either pregnant or disabled, for example. The statement of necessary and sufficient conditions will in such cases contain a disjunctive clause of the following kind: for all x, x is entitled to receive benefits from the French government if and only if x is A and B and (C or D or E or . . .).

The notion of constitution relations is perhaps not determinate in all directions, but it seems clear enough in its principal features. There is an obvious connection between the notion of constitution relations and that of conceptual analysis, although science also discovers constitution relations. To analyse some concept or property is to give an account of what constitutes, or is essentially involved in, instantiating or possessing that property. In many cases there is such a thing as the correct order or direction of analysis; these things are not arbitrary. In these cases analysis will mirror constitution relations. Thus equilaterality has to be referred to in any correct and completed analysis of squareness; and the converse of this is not true. Thus although equilaterality is a necessary constitutive condition of squareness, squareness is not any sort of constitutive condition of equilaterality, since it need not be referred to in any correct and completed analysis of equilaterality. A somewhat less obvious case is this: it seems that self-consciousness has to be referred to in any putatively correct and completed analysis of free agenthood. Again the converse is not true.

4. What of (1)-(6)? All of them entail '$(x)(\phi x \rightarrow \psi x)$', just as (5) and (6) entail '$(x)(\phi x \leftrightarrow \psi x)$'. They may be called 'C-statements'; they provide *analytic frames* for statements of the form '$(X \rightarrow Y)$' or '$(X \leftrightarrow Y)$'. In addition to representing the fact that $(X \rightarrow Y)$ or that $(X \leftrightarrow Y)$, C-statements give information as to why '$(X \rightarrow Y)$' or '$(X \leftrightarrow Y)$' is true.

The difference between causal and constitutive conditions is, intuitively, obvious enough. It emerges clearly in one difference between (5) and (6): '$Cn/(x)(\phi x \leftrightarrow \psi x)/$' may be rendered 'being ϕ is constitutively necessary and sufficient for being ψ'. But this amounts to saying that being ϕ and being ψ are in fact identical; being a square just is being an equilateral equiangular rectilinear quadrilateral.[25] Nothing similar is true with '$Cs/(x)(\phi x \leftrightarrow \psi x)/$', which says that, for any x, whenever x is ψ, x's being ψ comes about just in case, and because, x's being ϕ has come about, and that this is so for purely causal reasons, x's being ψ being an effect of x's being ϕ.[26] It seems perfectly acceptable

---

[25] Statements of the form '$Cn/(x)(Ax \leftrightarrow Bx)/$' are what conceptual analyses of things like knowledge, freedom, perception, personal identity, memory, and so on often seek to culminate in. Such statements may represent an ideal of analysis, at least; showing why the ideal is unattainable may be an important part of the analysis.

[26] 'Purely causal reasons' because what is logically impossible is *a fortiori* causally impossible and, by the same reasoning, it might just be said that what is logically necessary is also causally necessary, so that there are causal reasons why it is so. But if something that is the case is causally necessary because logically necessary, it is not the case for *purely* causal reasons in the present sense.

to speak of one *type* of event being causally necessary and sufficient for another type of event (or to say that x's having entered into a state of type ϕ is causally necessary and sufficient for x to enter into some other state of type ψ), but to say this is certainly not to say that they are identical.

More could be said about these differences and distinctions, but the preceding is sufficient for present purposes.[27]

I 0. I I OPTIONS AND QUESTIONS

To return to the question of evident properties. If ϕ is an evident property, then $(x)(\phi x \rightarrow B(x,\phi x))$. But if this statement is true, why is it true? Given the present framework, there are four options.

   (i) $Cs/(x)(\underline{\phi x} \rightarrow B(x,\phi x))/,$
  (ii) $Cs/(x)(\phi x \rightarrow \underline{B(x,\phi x)})/,$
 (iii) $Cn/(x)(\underline{\phi x} \rightarrow B(x,\phi x))/,$
 (iv) $Cn/(x)(\phi x \rightarrow \underline{B(x,\phi x)})/.$

(i) was defined (in 10.7) as the case in which ϕ is a causally evident property. Cases of kind (ii) are of no interest here, even if they are not actually impossible (see Appendix D); for the case of freedom is clearly not of this kind. 'Non-causally evident' was defined in such a way that ϕ is non-causally evident just in case (iv) is true.

That leaves (iii); which states, bizarrely, that being ϕ is a sufficient constitutive condition of believing you are—so that your believing you are ϕ simply consists in your being ϕ; and it is not clear how this could ever be true (though see the discussion of pain in Chapter 11 for an imperfect parallel).[28] For it to be true in the case of freedom, it would have to be the case that one's believing one was free simply *consisted* in one's being free—that one's being free just *was* one's believing one was

[27] The notation adopted here for the representation of constitution relations and causal relations preserves an asymmetry which is already there in the word 'condition', but which is sometimes obscured in the minds of philosophers familiar with logic, in which anything is a necessary (sufficient) condition of anything which is a sufficient (necessary) condition of it. Against this, it is (as remarked) natural to say that if something X is a condition—a *condition*—of something else, Y, then Y is not in turn *ipso facto* a condition of X. (If getting As in your exams is a (necessary) condition of getting into university X, getting into university X is not in turn a *condition* of your getting As; similarly for equilaterality and squareness.) It is this natural use that the notion of constitution relations corresponds to. For this reason, it seemed best to adopt a new notation, instead of using such symbols as '□' and '▣', say, or '□→' and '▣→'.

[28] Taking 'ϕ' to be 'is in pain', (iii) is not true even if '$(x)(\phi x \rightarrow B(x,\phi x))$' is. But it does seem that '$Cn/(x)(\underline{B(x,\phi x)} \rightarrow \phi x)/$' is true—to hypnotize a man to believe that he has been hit in the stomach really is to hurt him.

free.[29] I shall assume that this cannot be so, and so leave the definition of 'non-causally evident' unchanged, thereby excluding case (iii).

So two options remain. If ϕ is an evident property, either (i) or (iv) is true: ϕ is either causally or non-causally evident. And three questions arise. (1) Are there in fact any evident properties? It will be argued that there are. (2) If there are, is free agenthood one of them? Objectivist attempts to deny that it is will be examined. (3) If free agenthood is an evident property, is it a causally or non-causally evident property? A large part of the following will be concerned with Objectivists who accept that free agenthood is an evident property, and who therefore seek to show that it is a merely causally evident property, because they think that to claim that it is a non-causally evident property is to contravene the principle of independence in an unacceptable way.

The next section diverges from the main argument in order to consider the notion of constitution relations in more detail.

10.12 CONSTITUTION RELATIONS—COMPLICATIONS

What are principally at issue are questions about relations between properties. Perhaps it is slightly odd to talk about causation and constitution relations between properties, but I think it is clear enough what is meant. Properties ϕ and ψ may be said to be causally related just if there are purely causal reasons why a being cannot have (or come to have) ϕ and not also have (or come to have) ψ, or vice versa. It is less clear just what are to be included in constitution relations, but the notion is none the less reasonably definite: crucial to the idea that x's-being-ϕ is a necessary constitutive condition of x's-being-ψ is the idea of ϕ-ness *contributing* to ψ-ness; the idea that x's-being-ϕ is a *necessary part or aspect* of x's being, specifically, ψ; the idea of x's being ψ *partly in virtue of* being ϕ; the idea of ϕ-ness being part of what ψ-ness *consists in.*

Consider a problem case: everything green is extended ($(x)(x$ is green $\rightarrow x$ is extended)), but is this true because extension is causally necessary for greenness, or because it is constitutively necessary? These seem to be the available options; for what relations other than C-conditionship relations can hold between ϕ and ψ in such a way that statements of the form '$(x)(\phi x \rightarrow \psi x)$' are true? The remaining pos-

[29] Presumably either in the way that being an equilateral rectilinear equiangular quadrilateral is being a square (!), or in the way that being pregnant, etc., is being entitled to government benefits (!). The supposition is absurd.

sibilities seem to be these. Such statements might be true because of the occurrence of some merely accidental uniformity, as when every coin in my pocket is copper;[30] or they might be true because of merely formal-logical connection, as when being ϕ is being F and G and being ψ is being G; or they might be true for reasons of identity—because, say, being ϕ is being Venus and being ψ is being Aphrodite.[31]

These possibilities provide no materials for an account of why it is true that everything green is extended, however; it is not an accident or a formal-logical truth, nor are the two properties identical. Assuming that the claim that everything green is extended is advanced as a necessary truth, causal relations cannot be in question. That leaves constitution relations.

But is this plausible? It is principally constitution-relation claims like 'being self-conscious is a necessary constitutive condition of being a free agent' and 'being practical-rational is a necessary condition of being a free agent' that are of present concern. And it seems natural to say that self-consciousness and practical-rationality are constitutive conditions of free agenthood because they 'contribute directly' to, specifically, free agenthood. But extendedness does not contribute directly to, specifically, greenness in anything like the same way. So if there are constitution relations between extendedness and greenness they must be less 'direct'.

Is this notion of directness any use? It is not precise, but it is serviceable. Consider the following explanation of why 'Everything green is extended' is true.[32] (1) Clearly, 'is a constitutive condition of' is a transitive relation: if X is a constitutive condition of Y, and Y is a constitutive condition of Z, then X is a constitutive condition of Z (if $Cn/(Y \rightarrow \underline{X})/$, and $Cn/(Z \rightarrow \underline{Y})/$, then $Cn/(Z \rightarrow \underline{X})/$). (2) If it is true

---

[30] Such a uniformity is accidental, in the relevant sense, whether or not I intentionally put nothing but copper coins in my pocket. It is accidental in the sense that there are no formal-logical or constitutive connections between being a coin in my pocket and being copper, nor any true causal law to the effect that if anything is a coin in my pocket it is copper.

[31] Statements of the form '$(x)(\phi x \rightarrow \psi x)$' and '$(x)(\phi x \leftrightarrow \psi x)$' will also be true where x's being χ is a necessary and sufficient causal condition both of x's being ϕ and of x's being ψ. Suppose—to take the most interesting variant of such a situation—that *being ϕ* and *being ψ* are two *otherwise unconnected* effects of a common cause. In this case, no C-statement can express why '$(x)(\phi x \rightarrow \psi x)$' and '$(x)(\psi x \rightarrow \phi x)$' are true, but one can still say that they are true for purely causal reasons. It suffices, for present purposes, to classify them as special cases of the holding of causal relations. The case of belief in freedom is certainly not a case of this kind.

[32] The main aim of the following discussion is just to make a point about constitution relations. It does not matter much if it is inadequate as an account of the relation between greenness and extension.

that everything green is extended, then this is because everything that is coloured (and *a fortiori* everything green) either reflects or emits light (i.e. photons), and because everything that can either reflect or emit light must necessarily be extended in space. Thus reflecting or emitting light of a certain wavelength (or set of wavelengths) is a necessary (and perhaps necessary and sufficient) constitutive condition of being green (it is (part of) what being green *consists* in); and being extended is a necessary constitutive condition of being such that one can reflect or emit light (it is part of what being a thing of such a kind that it can reflect or emit photons *consists* in). So, (3), given the transitivity of 'is a constitutive condition of' noted in (1), it is true, after all, that $Cn/(x)$ (x is green $\rightarrow$ x is extended)/. Extension is, one might say, no part of the greenness of greenness, but it is, *in*directly at least, a necessary constitutive condition of greenness, just as being alive or being sentient is an indirectly necessary constitutive condition of being a free agent or a person. It seems clear that one must expand the class of constitutive conditions to include what one might call indirect as well as direct constitutive conditions.[33] But there is nothing problematic about this.

It may next be objected that the relation between being square and being equilateral should not count as a constitution relation. It may be said that it is unlike the relation between being a free agent and being self-conscious, because it is simply analytic that all squares are equilateral.

But the source of the desire to keep these two sorts of case apart seems to amount to no more than this: that in the one case the relation appears to obtain for purely definitional reasons, while in the other case it does not. But that there is this apparent difference may be merely a matter of the pattern of our current ignorances, certainties, and uncertainties. And if one is going to talk about analyticity at all, then it seems right to say that all *true* statements about conditionship relations between properties that are established by conceptual *analysis*—such as the statement that self-consciousness is a necessary constitutive condition of free agenthood—are analytic. For if conceptual *analysis* es-

---

[33] This argument refers to causal phenomena in its account of what constitutes being green; but this creates no difficulty for the present approach, or for the causal/constitutive dichotomy as applied to statements. It can be simply true that reflecting or emitting light is a constitutive condition of an object's being coloured, even though these are causal processes. There is no implication that these notions must form part of the ordinary person's notion of being coloured. (Those who find this whole approach dubious can substitute the following argument for the one in the text: everything that is coloured is, necessarily, visible-in-principle, and everything that is visible-in-principle is, necessarily, extended in space.)

tablishes truths at all, in showing that having one property necessarily involves having another, then they must be *analytic*, *if true*—however much argument was needed to establish them, and however unobvious they once were.

There seems, then, to be no deep difference between statements about the relation between squareness and equilaterality, on the one hand, and statements about the relation between freedom and self-consciousness, on the other hand, that justifies counting only the latter and not the former as statements that are true on account of the holding of constitution relations.

This section raises up old issues and old unclarities. But here there is no need to try to work out the details of the relations between all the types of relations whose obtaining can make statements of the form '$(x)\phi x \to \psi x$' true, and I will now return to the main question.

10.13 SUMMARY; A COMPATIBILIST WAY OUT

The problem is this. It seems (1) that one cannot be a free agent if one does not believe one is. That is, it seems that

$$(x)(Fx \to B(x,Fx))' \tag{1}$$

is true. Assuming that it is true, one is led to ask why. There seem to be two main possibilities.

The first is (2) that the property of being a free agent is causally evident for whoever possesses it. On this view, possession of the property of free agenthood invariably gives rise causally to belief that one possesses it. So that (1) is true because

$$Cs/(x)(\underline{Fx} \to B(x,Fx))/' \tag{2}$$

is. If this is right, then the necessary and sufficient conditions of an agent's being a free agent must be fully specifiable independently of mention of its belief that it is a free agent—as the Objectivists believe.

The prospects for any such specification do not look good (this will be discussed further below). But the main alternative seems even less plausible. For if it is indeed true that all free agents believe they are free agents, then (*a*) it is certainly not a merely accidental truth; nor, (*b*), is it a simple (formal-)logical truth that being a free agent entails believing one is; nor, presumably, is it true, (*c*), because being a free agent just is the same as believing one is a free agent, as being angry is the same as being irate.[34] It is not even true, (*d*), because believing one

[34] Despite 4.3. I assume that mathematical cases (e.g. 'Everything divisible by 91 is divisible by 13') are, like geometrical cases, examples of constitution relations.

is a free agent is necessary for being one in the same way as the way in which being extended is necessary for being green (10.12). But it seems that there is only one other possible reason why (1) could be true. And that is, that it is true because believing you are a free agent is a condition of being one in the same way as the way in which being practical-rational or being capable of self-change is; that is, because (3) believing you are a free agent is a directly necessary constitutive condition of being a free agent—because

$$Cn/(x)(Fx \rightarrow \underline{B(x,Fx)})/. \tag{3}$$

But if this is so, then free agenthood is a non-causally evident property, and the principle of independence is contravened.

One simple rephrasal, already given above, may help to fortify (or perhaps engender) the belief that (1) is true: the claim is simply that no being can be free in and truly responsible for its actions in the way that we take ourselves to be if it has no belief in or conception of itself as a free or truly responsible agent. Consider the case of a particular action. How could we hold that a being had acted freely, and in such a way that it was truly responsible for its action, if it had, at the time of action, no sort of conception of itself as a free or truly responsible agent? (As so often, the claim seems clearer when stated in terms of responsibility rather than in terms of freedom.)

Suppose one could distinguish two types or levels of free agenthood, 'true' freedom and 'basic' freedom, say. Call these F_2 and F_1 respectively. One might then argue that in order for an agent to be F_2, or 'truly' free, it must at least believe that it is F_1—it must believe that it is free in the 'basic' sense defined in 1.1, for example. This sort of move would immediately solve the problem posed by the principle of independence. For there need be nothing to contravene it in the claim that you can be F_2 ('truly' free) only if you believe you are F_1 (free in the 'basic' sense); nor, indeed, in the claim that believing you are F_1 is a necessary constitutive condition of being F_2.[35]

But this manoeuvre will not solve the present problem. It is very probably true that one can be F_2 ('truly' free) only if one believes one is F_1 (free in the 'basic' sense). But it is not enough. For we are trying (however vainly) to establish full true-responsibility-entailing freedom; and it seems that it is *precisely* such full true-responsibility-entailing freedom that an agent must believe itself to possess if it is to be such

---

[35] Where 'F_1' is not partly defined in terms of 'F_2', that is. The full analysis might claim that being F_1 and believing you are F_1 are jointly sufficient for being F_2.

that it does in fact possess it. So it looks as if there is no future in this sort of two-level suggestion, given the present aim.

Nevertheless, something like it may have considerable appeal for those—compatibilists, for example—who are *not* trying to establish true-responsibility-entailing freedom, but who can see the force of the present suggestion that belief in freedom is necessary for freedom. For they can reverse and modify the suggestion just made, and argue as follows: in order to be free-F_3—i.e., free in some enriched but not true-responsibility-entailing sense of the word 'free' that goes beyond the 'basic' sense but remains entirely acceptable to compatibilists—one must *believe* one is free-F_2, free in the strong, true-responsibility-entailing sense; thus $Cn/(x)(F_3x \rightarrow \underline{B(x,F_2x)})/.$[36]

Now this looks like a very plausible claim for compatibilists to make; and it does not clash with the principle of independence. But one can agree with this while remaining convinced both that compatibilism is fundamentally inadequate as a positive theory of freedom, and that no two-level suggestion of this kind can help with the main problem—that of trying to determine the conditions of true-responsibility-entailing freedom. (Note, though, that it may be precisely the availability of this kind of position that underlies our recurrent sense that despite the allegations of paradox there is really nothing problematic at all about the claim that believing one is free is a constitutive condition of being free.)[37]

10.14 TRANSITIONAL

Are the Objectivists right to insist that the principle of independence must be respected in the case of freedom? It will help to consider other cases in which the principle apparently fails. First, though, the present claim about belief in freedom must be re-expressed in terms of 'potential free agenthood'.

This yields the claim that no being is a potential free agent unless it

---

[36] Here the view may be that being F_1 and believing you are F_2 are constitutively necessary and sufficient for being F_3. Such suggestions can be developed in various ways—i.e., various other substitutions for F_3 can be made. For example: in order to be free-F_4, i.e., a genuine participant in the complex social reality of freedom—the social reality constituted, in our human case, by those beliefs and practices associated with the idea that we are free agents—one must believe one is free-F_2: one must 'act under the idea' that one is oneself a free agent in the ordinary, strong sense.

[37] I return to this question in 15.3. Compare the apparently equally unproblematic claim that in order to be a *person*, in some familiar, loaded sense of the term, one must see oneself as (believe oneself to be) a person.

believes it is. To this it may be objected that 'potential free agent' is a semi-technical term, and that none of those whom we ordinarily suppose to be potential free agents have any such belief. But the phrase 'potentially free' is (as remarked in 7.2) only intended to articulate that very ordinary sense of the word 'free' according to which we conceive of freedom as a persisting and permanent property of agents; that sense of 'free' that features in 'man is a free agent' or 'human beings are free agents'. It is only this property that people are being claimed to believe themselves to possess, although they will never have come across the ungainly phrase 'potential free agent': the permanent property of being one of a kind of thing that can act freely.

Since 'potentially free' is just this sense of 'free', '*Fa*' will be retained unaltered to symbolize '*a* is a potential free agent'—and as before the word 'potential' will sometimes be omitted. The central claim is thus still that $(x)(Fx \rightarrow B(x,Fx))$. No implausible belief, in the sense of a belief that it is implausible that an agent should have at all, is being attributed to or demanded of those whom we ordinarily think of as potential free agents.

Although the discussion will be mainly in terms of potential free agenthood, I take it that one is a potential free agent if and only if one is a potential free chooser, i.e. if and only if one is such that there are circumstances in which one can choose freely (truly responsibly). '*Fa*', then, can equally well be taken to symbolize '*a* is able to choose freely', and the central claim can equally well be taken to be that *a* is able to choose freely only if he believes that he is (cf. 8.1). Later on the discussion will focus specifically on the notion of choice. The present point is that it is only some rather general belief in or conception of itself as free that is being demanded of any potential free agent. There is no need to demand that the agent have some belief in or conception of itself as, specifically, a being that is able to *act* freely, or, specifically, a being that is able to *choose* freely, and the discussion will be conducted in terms of both.

As noted, the belief that a (potential) free agent must have in its (potential) free agenthood need not be a permanently occurrent belief, although it must be an explicit* belief in the sense characterized in 10.2. Avoiding use of the word 'believe', in ways already prefigured above, one might put the central claim as follows: if a being has no *sense*, or *awareness**, or *conception*, or, most generally, *experience* of itself as a free agent, then it cannot be a free agent. Using words like 'sense', 'conception, 'awareness(*)', and so on should help to convey a grasp of the broad base of the claim represented by $(x)(Fx \rightarrow B(x,Fx))$ and indeed by $Cn/(x)(Fx \rightarrow \underline{B(x,Fx)})/$.

It may also help with a first, brief answer to the objection raised in 10.1. Incompatibilist determinists and 'non-self-determinationists' (p. 60) do not believe that they are free agents. Yet we would not normally regard a man's holding either of these views as exempting him from responsibility for his actions. We would be inclined to treat him as a free and responsible agent, when condemning him for some misdeed, say, even if we knew that his denial that he believed that he was free was sincere. It seems, then, that we would ignore the suggestion that belief in freedom is necessary for freedom.

The brief reply to this objection is simply this. If he holds this *theoretical* view of things and yet naturally and perhaps unavoidably continues to treat himself and others as free in everyday, practical life (as is extremely likely), then he still believes he is free in the current, broad sense of 'believe'. For, despite his theoretical view, he naturally and unavoidably experiences or conceives of himself as free. And when we treat him like others this is what we are in fact supposing to be the case. He isn't a *genuine* incompatibilist determinist or non-self-determinationist, he is only a *theoretical* one (cf.6.2).

If, however, he has dwelt intensely on his theoretical view in such a way that he really has ceased altogether to conceive of himself as free and responsible even in his capacity as a practical being (it is questionable whether this is possible for a human being), and if we somehow know that this is so, then, I suggest, we will no longer be inclined to treat him as free and responsible; and we will be wrong to do so in any case.

So much for the first reply. The question is reconsidered below.

In 7.3 a provisional Objectivist definition of potential free agenthood was stated: a being is a potential free agent if and only if it is a (1) desiring, (2) believing, (3) practical-rational (5) self-conscious being that is (4) capable of self-change. (1)–(5) are the S conditions, the basic 'Structural' conditions that are likely to provide the starting point for any account of free agenthood, be it libertarian or compatibilist, Objectivist or Subjectivist. '*Sx*' is to be read '*x* fulfils the S conditions'.

We may suppose that $Cn/(x)(Fx \rightarrow \underline{Sx})/$—that the S conditions are at least necessary constitutive conditions of free agenthood. This will be assumed henceforth. But are they also sufficient, as the Objectivist, Structural theorists suppose? If not, what must be added?[38]

The present chapter poses a problem for these Structural theorists. For if the 'principal claim' is true—the claim that the *attitudinal* (1.5.3) condition of believing one is a free agent is a necessary condition of being a free agent—then the S conditions can be sufficient conditions of freedom only if no being can fulfil them and not also fulfil the attitudinal condition of believing it is a free agent. In other words (letting 'F' stand for 'being a free agent', and '$B(F)$' for 'belief that one is a free agent'): if (1) $S \to F$ (as the Structural theorists claim), and if (2) $F \to B(F)$ (the principal claim), then, clearly, (3), $S \to B(F)$.

Defenders of the S-conditions analysis of freedom will therefore seek to defend (3), the 'Kantian' claim that a self-conscious rational agent cannot but think of itself as free (or 'act under the idea of' its own freedom). That is, they will seek to show that fulfilling the belief-in-freedom condition is just some kind of (presumably causally guaranteed) by-product of fulfilling the basic S conditions, which are all that really matter to the definition of freedom. (And in this way they will try to uphold the principle of independence.) Their Subjectivist opponents will seek to deny (3), and to argue that the belief-in-freedom condition is a separate, *Attitudinal* condition of freedom that is not entailed by the S conditions (or indeed by any plausible set of Structural conditions).

This debate will be taken up in Chapter 12. In the next chapter I will consider some other apparent cases of properties which are such that believing one has them is a necessary condition of having them; this in order to try to establish whether it is always an objection to an account of what the possession of some property consists in to say that the account contravenes the principle of independence.

---

[38] An Objectivist attempt to describe the minimally sufficient conditions of potential free agenthood, which started by trying to describe the most restricted case in which the S conditions are fulfilled, might be of considerable interest. But it will not be attempted here. (It seems that a potential free agent could be unembodied—or, if embodied, incapable of any intentional bodily movement; virtually memoryless; and only ever capable of entering into two desire states—this sufficing to open up the possibility of facing a genuine choice. See Appendix C.)

11

Contravention and Convention

This chapter does not offer a general theory of non-causally evident properties. Instead, various categories of cases in which contravention of the principle of independence does not seem to be problematic are considered. It is pointed out that the case of freedom does not seem to be a member of any of those categories, and maintained, on that basis, that the unproblematic cases of contravention fail to provide adequate grounds for supposing that contravention is also unproblematic in the case of freedom.

Failure to reach a definite conclusion at this stage about whether or not contravention is problematic in the case of freedom (on the basis of a general theory of the nature of apparent cases of contravention) is not prejudicial to the more general aims of the present discussion, for these aims are in any case best pursued by staging a debate between Subjectivists and Objectivists about whether or not believing one is a free (or truly responsible) agent is a necessary condition of being one.

Cases other than the case of belief in freedom that appear to contravene the principle of independence have already been considered: a promises or asserts that p, or enters into a contract or obeys an order to do X, only if he believes he does (10.7, 10.9). Other cases suggest themselves — a is omniscient only if he believes he is, a is acting immorally only if he believes he is, a makes a knight move only if he believes he does; even, perhaps, a is fashionable or chic only if he believes he is.[1] If the case of making a knight move is admitted, it points to a large class of predicates that can give rise to principle-of-independence-contravening claims. The class includes not only predicates attributing game-playing properties, but also, more generally, any movement-or-action-attributing predicate, ϕ, say, which is such that it is natural (or simply correct) to say of it that (for any x) x ϕs only if x does what it does consciously and expressly intending what it does to be, and, hence, *a fortiori*

---

[1] An example suggested by C. Peacocke.

believing it to be—assuming that nothing, in its view, goes badly wrong with its performance—a ϕ-ing.[2]

The main lines of the intuitive objection have also been sketched: someone's having a belief cannot itself be part of what constitutes that in virtue of which that same belief is true (10.3). A vague phrase captures part of it: no 'straightforwardly objective' property could be such that the statement of the conditions of its possession contravened the principle of independence (10.9).

The following observation appears to diminish the conflict: many cases in which the principle of independence seems to be clearly contravened involve properties that are in some sense *conventional* properties, conventionally or socially instituted properties. Having property X (where X is specified without reference to any conventions, e.g. just in terms of sound emissions or bodily movements) is held, conventionally, to count as having property Y (e.g., being such that one is entering into a contract). This being so, a further complex condition of truly having Y emerges, given that one has X and is aware (believes) that one does: one must (*a*) be aware of the convention, aware that having X counts as having Y; and one must, further, (*b*) apply this awareness to one's own case in such a way as to believe that one has Y. Thus there is a belief condition or *awareness condition* on certain conventional properties: if one is to possess such a property, at a given time, one must not only have a grasp of the general concept of the conventional property in question, and, in addition, know the local conventions regarding what counts as possessing the property (and so be a 'party to' the convention); one must also be aware* (believe) that one actually does have the property, at that time.[3]

This awareness condition appears, prima facie at least, to contain a threat of regress. This is one of the things that worries us about the prospect of contravention of the principle of independence. So let us consider it with reference to the case of entering into a contract.

11.2 CONTRACTS

Entering into a contract, the unreflective man believes that what he is

---

[2] Many of the action-describing verbs discussed by J. L. Austin in *How to do Things with Words*, for example. And many others.

[3] The point is intentionally made without reference to intention. Made with reference to intention, it is simply this: conventional actions, of the type in question, are such that one does not count as performing them (without some special ruling—see 10.7) unless one expressly intends to perform them in doing what one does—in such a way that it is true *a fortiori* that one believes that one is performing them.

doing, by way of physical action, is sufficient (in the circumstances) for entering into a contract. He *thereby* fulfils the awareness condition—the condition of believing that he fulfils conditions which are sufficient *tout court* for entering into a contract. But what of the more reflective man who knows (or believes) that there is an awareness condition on contracting? Can we say what he believes to be sufficient *tout court* for his contracting, in a given situation? Is it this: (1) his doing what is sufficient (in the circumstances), by way of physical action, for contracting, and (2) his believing that he is doing what is sufficient (in the circumstances), by way of physical action, for contracting? No, because, reflecting, he realizes *that* there is an awareness condition on contracting; that is, he knows that part of what it is to fulfil sufficient conditions for contracting is to believe quite simply and without qualification that one is contracting; that is, (3), to believe that one fulfils sufficient conditions *tout court* for contracting; not simply, (2), to believe that one is doing what is sufficient by way of physical action for contracting. (1) and (2) are not enough.

But such reflectiveness seems to draw him into regress: aware (as a philosopher) that fulfilling the awareness condition, that is, (3), is a condition of contracting, he realizes that he must fulfil (3) in order actually to fulfil sufficient conditions *tout court* of contracting. And so he may add (4), fulfilling the awareness condition (3), to the list of conditions he must believe that he fulfils before he can form the belief that he is fulfilling sufficient conditions *tout court* for contracting. But then, reflecting further, he realizes that in order to believe that he fulfils sufficient conditions *tout court* for contracting, he must believe that he believes that he fulfils sufficient conditions *tout court* for contracting— since (as remarked) fulfilling the awareness condition has itself turned up in his reflective head as a necessary condition of contracting. But then, of course, he realizes that for him to be able to believe that he fulfils sufficient conditions *tout court* for contracting he must fulfil the new condition that his reflectiveness has just presented him with: he must believe that he believes that he believes that he fulfils sufficient conditions *tout court* for contracting. And so on.

Another, simpler way of putting his problem is this: he realizes that to form a justified belief that he is contracting (that he fulfils sufficient conditions *tout court* for contracting) he must already have, and be aware that he has, that very belief.

The over-reflective man, spiralling into his abyss, holds that the unreflective man manages to fulfil the awareness condition only by a kind of error; not so much a positive error as an error of omission: the unreflective man takes something that is not strictly speaking sufficient *tout court* for being such that one is contracting to be so sufficient, and so fulfils the condition of believing (believing *sans phrase*) that he is contracting. Exactly analogous problems arise, for the over-reflective, in the cases of promising and asserting that p.[4]

What can we say to the over-reflective man? If he concludes that he— or we—cannot promise, and assert, and contract, he must himself have been led into error by his (insufficiently strenuous) reflections. For it is most certain that we can contract, promise, and so on, believing we are doing so as we do so, and knowing, if we are reflective, that our believing we are doing so is a condition of our doing so. No amount of reflection can undermine these abilities; we exercise them effortlessly, somewhere between the unreflective error and the over-reflective abyss.[5]

[4] But not, it seems, in the case of the claim that you obey an order only if you believe you do. Say you obey X's order to do Y if (i) you understand that X (or someone, at least) has ordered you to do Y, and (ii) you do Y, and (iii) you do Y because X (someone) has ordered you to—where the 'because' clause states part of your reason for doing Y, not just a causal connection that could hold independently of your reasons. (i) and (iii) entail that you believe or are aware that you are obeying an order to do X; but no error, in the over-reflective man's case, seems required.

It is worth noting that any general statement of the conditions of contracting would have to include existentially quantified clauses, along these lines: for any x, if x is contracting, then there exists some social group G, and some situation S, and some type of action A, such that performance of an action of type A is sufficient by way of physical action in S 'in' G, and x is in G, and x is in S, and x performs an action of type A, and x believes that it (itself) performs an action that is sufficient by way of physical action in the situation and group that it is in . . . and so on. (The statement of conditions becomes very complicated—partly because it is arguable that an agent can succeed in contracting despite all sorts of false beliefs about its action, situation, etc.)

[5] One can form a true belief on the basis of a false one, but it would be very curious if there were truths which one could come to accept, so long as one were reasoning in a reasonable manner, *only* on the basis of some false belief. As Evans says, 'truth is seamless; there can be no truth which it requires acceptance of a falsehood to appreciate' (*The Varieties of Reference*, p. 331).

One suggestion that may be made here is that what is necessary for contracting, or asserting that p, and so on, is not, positively, (1) that one possess the belief that one is contracting (asserting that p), but, negatively, simply (2) that one lack any belief that one is *not* contracting (asserting that p). But it is not clear that this will do. A being that did everything necessary by way of outward form for contracting or asserting that p (in a given society, or language), while having no sort of conception of what it was to contract (assert something), and *a fortiori* lacking any belief that it was not contracting (asserting that p), could not be said to contract (assert that p). And even if one adds to (2) the requirement that one possess the *concept* of contracting (asserting something) this does not seem sufficient. *Some* sort of present awareness or belief that one is doing the thing in question (e.g. contracting or promising) does seem to be a positive necessary condition of one's being such that one is actually doing it.

Promising, contracting, and so on are non-causally evident properties, then, properties specification of the conditions of which does indeed contravene the principle of independence. Yet it simply does not trouble us that this is so. In their case we recognize that there are awareness conditions on their possession. And it seems clear enough that the explanation of the fact that these properties do not appear problematic begins from the observation that they are conventional properties: something, X, is held (conventionally) to count as something else, Y (a production of certain sounds is held to count as the making of a promise, say), with which it has no intrinsic or necessary connection.

As remarked in 10.9, such an account of how it might be that belief in freedom is a necessary condition of freedom does not seem at all plausible. Before turning to this problem, it is worth considering some other apparent contraventions of the principle of independence. But there is one general point that takes precedence, concerning the attribution-conditions of beliefs.

II.3 THE ATTRIBUTION OF BELIEF

The case of the over-reflective man is not our case. It may be true that we know, in some sense—that is, we may grant on reflection—that believing you are contracting is a condition of your being such that you are doing so. But we do not have to be thinking about this, or that this is so, when we believe we are contracting. Nor do we have to have thought about it consciously at any time.

But what is also true, much more generally, is that it is not the case that a being has to be able to specify fully the necessary and sufficient conditions of ϕ-ness in order for the belief that something (itself, for example) is ϕ to be correctly attributed to it. So far as its grasp of what ϕ-ness is is concerned (or its grasp of the meaning of 'ϕ'), it suffices that it be able to recognize that something that is ϕ is so (that it be able to apply the word 'ϕ' correctly).[6] It may even be partly wrong about what it is to be ϕ.[7] Nor is it the case that to think (or believe) that something

---

[6] To put it differently. The 'opacity' of certain belief contexts no more allows the substitution of predicates with the same extension (e.g. the substitution of the complex philosopher's statement of the necessary and sufficient conditions of ϕ-ness for 'ϕ') than it does the substitution of singular terms with the same referent. Less, perhaps: perhaps belief contexts may be predicate-substitution-opaque without being referentially opaque.

[7] It appears, furthermore, that one can correctly be said to believe that something i ϕ even if ϕ-ness is in fact logically impossible. Thus people may believe they are free i the strong sense although such freedom appears to be demonstrably impossible. (I

is ϕ is, always and necessarily, to represent it explicitly to oneself as fulfilling all those conditions which one takes to be necessary and sufficient conditions of being ϕ. So there is no immediately inevitable paradox in saying that a's believing he is contracting is a necessary constitutive condition of his doing so. For it is not as if the fact that a has the belief he has, when he believes he is contracting, has to be represented in full, in some way, in the content of that very same belief. He is not *in error* if he is not over-reflective. He simply believes in one way that he is contracting (under one description, if you like): by means of a representation of this state of affairs (his contracting) that does not include, as part of its explicit content, any representation of the fact that he presently believes he is contracting (or indeed any representation of the fact that his present possession of this belief is necessary for his being such that he is contracting).

If we assume that computers can be said to play games like chess only if they can also be said to have beliefs, games furnish a vast family of cases that help to make this clear. a is castling (or huffing) only if he believes he is: without special ruling to the contrary, what he does counts as castling only if he has this belief. To use a naturally suited idiom: to castle is to do *this* (or this—and in a given setting) *in the belief* that one is castling: subtract the belief from the total mental and physical situation and no castling is done (otherwise a cat can castle and checkmate a king). But there is nothing paradoxical about this. Having the belief, we don't ever have to realize the following fact: that we have to have it in order for it to be true.

If such cases are indeed examples of contravention of the principle of independence, then the principle is massively contravened. Indeed it seems it must be contravened in such cases. For they concern conventional activities, and hence conventional properties; and it seems that an agent cannot have the property of participating in a conventional activity unless (*a*) it knows what the convention is, considered in a general manner; (*b*) it is aware of what it is in particular that counts, so far as physical action is concerned, as the performing of the

should be noticed, though, that a line of argument parallel to G. Evans's argument in *The Varieties of Reference* for what he calls Russell's Principle might lead one to conclude that if one apparently has the thought that ϕa, and if there is necessarily no such thing as ϕ-ness (round squareness, free agenthood), then one does not really have a thought at all.)

conventional action it wishes to perform; and, crucially, (c) it believes that it is itself now participating in the conventional activity in question.[8]

What about freedom? As before, I take it that being a free agent, performing a particular free action at a particular time, is not as such participating in a conventional activity.[9] If this is so, we do not have anything like the same sort of reason to suppose that the principle of independence *must* be contravened in the case of freedom as we do in the cases mentioned above. But we can at least transfer to the case of freedom the general point about the conditions of attribution of a belief that something is ϕ. Suppose that a believes he is, and actually is, a free

---

[8] Computers raise familiar problems of a sort relegated to Appendix A. Consider an attempt to escape contravention in the case of making a knight move (exactly analogous arguments are possible for contracting, promising, etc.). Let 'Ka' be 'a makes a knight move' (the argument could be given in universally quantified form, but it is simpler to consider an individual). If a makes a knight move he must perform a physical action of a certain kind, ϕ, say. (Many things external to a, board, piece, etc., have to be mentioned in specification of ϕ.) And he must believe he is making a knight move—'$B(a,Ka)$' must be *true*. But perhaps one can give an adequate analysis of 'Ka' without mentioning '$B(a,Ka)$'. For, it may be said, all that must be true is (i) that ϕa and (ii) that $B(a,(x)(\phi x \rightarrow Kx))$ (or alternatively, (ii) that $B(a,\lambda x[\phi x]=\lambda x[Kx])$). But this isn't enough. For clearly (iii) a must also believe that he is ϕ—or else he has no reason to believe he is K.

(i)–(iii) give the following analysis: Ka if and only if ϕa & $B(a,\phi a)$ & $B(a,(x)(\phi x \rightarrow Kx))$. (Actually it may not matter if (ii) and (iii) are false—one could have (iii') $B(a,\psi a)$ and (ii') $B(a,(x)(\psi x \rightarrow Kx))$—so long as (i) is still true.) But one can pose the following dilemma for this account: either (A) it won't do, or (B) it will do, but the principle of independence is contravened after all. The argument for (A) is simple. (ii) and (iii) don't entail (iv) $B(a,Ka)$; a might simply fail to make the admittedly enormously natural inference to his own case. But if (iv) is not true, then it is not after all true that Ka: the analysis is inadequate. The argument for (B) is also simple. If it were true that (ii) and (iii) did somehow necessitate (iv), then the principle of independence would be contravened. For it wouldn't be enough if having belief (iv) were a merely causal consequence of having beliefs (ii) and (iii), because the connection between making a knight move and believing one is doing so is not a causal or contingent one. So it would have to be true that having beliefs (ii) and (iii) just *amounted to* having belief (iv)—necessarily. In which case '$B(a,Ka)$' would really appear in the statement of conditions of 'Ka' after all—under another name, as it were.

[9] There are, of course, theories of freedom that would be inclined to treat freedom as a kind of conventional property, though they would have to treat the 'convention' in question as a convention that is not explicitly acknowledged to be such by members of the society in which it is found. Such a view could be attributed to P. F. Strawson (cf. his paper 'Freedom and Resentment') and even to Hume (cf. ch. 2 n. 36). Furthermore, the principle-of-independence-contravening claim that belief in freedom must be granted to be a necessary condition of freedom could clearly feature strongly in an *argument* to the effect that freedom must in the end be held to be some kind of merely conventional ('conventional') property, since conventional properties provide clear cases in which contravention of the principle of independence is not problematic (cf. n. 23). Such an argument might be rather powerful. But at present the aim is still to try to show what freedom or true responsibility conceived in the ordinary way as a non-conventionally-instituted, fully objectively instantiable property might be.

agent. He does not have to have any sort of conscious, spelt-out grasp of the necessary and sufficient conditions of free agenthood, whatever they may be, nor, in particular, of the apparent fact that belief in one's free agenthood is among those conditions, for it to be said truly of him that he believes he is, and is, a free agent.

Here as elsewhere the over-reflective man can embark on his regress, or turn in his circle (believing that belief in freedom is a necessary condition of freedom, and needing to have the belief already in order to be able to form it justifiably). But no one need do so; and this possibility is not itself a reason for supposing that contravention of the principle of independence is fundamentally paradoxical, either in the case of freedom or in any other. One reason why it still appears paradoxical in the case of freedom is that being a free agent does not seem to be a conventional property in *any* sense (remember that non-moral agents can be free agents). But whether or not it is paradoxical, it is useful for present purposes to go on supposing that it is.

I turn now to other apparent cases of contravention of the principle of independence. Such cases are of interest in their own right, independently of their relevance to the question of freedom. But those who wish may now turn straight to 11.9.

11.4 THE MYSTERY DRAW

Imagine the following mystery draw. Numbered tickets are sold at a fête. Winners in the mystery draw—call it 'M'—are all and only those who (1) believe that they are winners in M (no doubt known to them as 'the mystery draw at the fête going on today'), and (2) have tickets with prime numbers on them. All ticketholders gather at the end of the day, and the organizers ask all those who believe they are winners to raise their hands. And they do so. (The problem of possible insincerity need not detain us; but one can imagine that the sincerity of those who claim to believe they are winners is checked under hypnosis, or by some other means.)[10]

Let 'W' symbolize 'is a winner in M'. Clearly $(x)(Wx \rightarrow B(x,Wx))$.

---

[10] Sincere misidentifications of which draw is in question are equally irrelevant (even if generated by something like the 'Twin Earth' story—see H. Putnam, 'The Meaning of Meaning'). If one is wrong about which draw is in question, then one is not a winner, even if everyone thinks one is, including the distributors of any prizes that there may be. (Similarly, a person can wrongly be thought to have won the pools, and be given a cheque without having won. Receiving a cheque is not the true criterion of having won, given the rules of the draw, it is simply the normal consequence of winning.)

Indeed believing you are a winner in M is a necessary constitutive condition of being one: $Cn/(x)(Wx \rightarrow \underline{B(x,Wx)})/$. Being a winner is simply defined in the rules laid down beforehand as having a prime number ticket (or—a variant—any ticket) and believing one is W. So there is no question but that believing you have a property can be a condition of having that very same property—whatever one wants to say about promising, contracts, freedom, and so on.

It is worth adding a few details to the case. Purchasers of tickets are told that the conditions of winning are already determined. Many presume that certain numbers have already been drawn. Others know that there is every year some trick condition of winning: last year it was having blue eyes and a ticket that bore the cube of a natural number. It is entirely open to all participants to try to find out what the conditions of winning are. Rumours abound. Some people have an irrational conviction that they will be winners.

Suppose it is put about, (i), that it is holders of prime number tickets under 50 who will win. Hearing this, some holders of such tickets come to believe they will win and so become winners in fact. (One believes, falsely, that 27 is a prime number; but he also holds 29, and so is a winner.) Or suppose it put about, (ii), that holders of even numbers between 50 and 70 will win. All holders of such numbers come to believe they will win. Just one of them also holds a prime number ticket, and is therefore actually a winner.

In case (i), how do those who believe they have won come to believe this? Many believe, truly, that they have a certain property, having a prime number ticket under 50—call it ϕ; and they also believe that if you have ϕ then you are a winner. Their second belief is false—having ϕ is neither necessary nor sufficient for being a winner (though if you have ϕ then you have a prime number ticket, which is a necessary condition); but, having this belief, they believe they are winners, and this last belief is true. They could clearly acquire this true belief in indefinitely many ways.

The example of the mystery draw is artificial, but it is clear that there could be such a draw; clear, too, that there is nothing unacceptable or paradoxical about one's believing one has a property being a necessary (non-causal, constitutive) condition of one's having it, in this case. And yet it is unlike the cases previously considered—promising, contracting, and so on—in that it is not as if there is an *awareness condition* on being W. For to say that there is an awareness condition on possession of some property is to suggest that the property is in *some* sense already all there, and that one must just be aware that it is for it to be correctly attributed. This suffices to distinguish contracting, asserting that *p*, etc., from being *W*. For in the case of *W* it seems natural to say that there is *no* sense in which the property is already all there; having the belief that one is *W* is a quite definite extra condition (specified as such in the sealed envelope) of being *W*.

Of course this is also true, in a clear sense, in the cases of contracting, asserting, promising, etc. For the whole point of saying that there is an awareness condition on promising is, after all, that one simply doesn't count as promising unless one believes one is doing so. (The thought that the property can despite this be already all there in some sense in the absence of that belief comes, as remarked, to this: one can be doing what is sufficient by way of physical action or outward form for promising, in a given society, without believing one is promising. Actually promising is both doing this and being aware that one is promising.) Still, there appears to be a clear difference between aware-ness condition cases and the mystery draw, in which believing you are *W* is an absolutely independent necessary constitutive condition of being *W*, and not an awareness condition of it in anything like the way believing you are promising is an awareness condition on promising. (Consider the similar case of an exclusive club: according to its secret statutes, one of the conditions of eligibility for membership is believing one is eligible.)

As so far presented, of course, awareness condition cases are cases where the putatively evident property is an *action* property; and in this they differ both from the mystery draw case and from the case of being a free agent. The search for parallels between awareness condition cases and the case of freedom might prompt the following suggestion: if it is true that one promises that *p* only if one believes (occurrently and at the time) that one is doing so, then it is perhaps also true that one is a 'potential promiser'—i.e., a being that can make promises—only if one believes (explicitly*) that one is; i.e. only if one not only has a grasp of the notion of what it is to promise, but also has a (standing) conception of oneself as a being that is able to promise.[11]

This, if true, does provide a parallel with the case of freedom, where the required belief is, similarly, a standing, explicit* belief that one is a (potential) free agent. But it is not nearly as convincing as the claim about free agenthood.

---

[11] As remarked in 10.3, to put the point in terms of conceiving does not enable one to avoid the problem of contravention of the principle of independence.

These issues will be considered further below. Here some further remarks about the mystery draw seem worth while. For it is not without
its oddity. Consider the position of *a*, who is ϕ, i.e. a possessor of a
prime number ticket (number 17), should he find out that the two
necessary conditions of winning are believing you've won and being ϕ.
Finding this out, what does he do? Or rather, what happens to him?
Does he as a result of finding this out immediately form the belief that
he's a winner? In a way, it would seem that he can justifiably form this
belief, *on the basis of* his discovery that believing one is a winner is a
condition of being one, only if, considering himself, he finds that he
already believes that he's a winner, and so finds that he satisfies the
conditions of winning that he's just discovered. But presumably he does
not already have this belief, having no reason to have it. Still, he
should form it now, you may say, because he's found out that all those
prime-number-ticket holders who believe they're winners are winners.
But what epistemic justification does that give him to form the belief
that he's a winner? The oddity of the case is clear.

One supposes that he will nevertheless form the belief: discovering
that being ϕ and believing you're a winner is necessary and sufficient
for winning, and wanting to win, he can, surely, come to believe he will
be a winner, knowing that his coming to believe this will make the
belief true (he knows it's not just a matter of raising a hand, and that
hand raisers will be tested for sincerity). But the wanting seems to be
somehow necessary for the formation of the belief. And even then there
seems to be something uncomfortably false and precarious about his
situation. It's almost as if he can't really, or at least honestly, form it.
It's as if he would be better off if he just believed falsely that 17 was
the winning number. For, as things are, it seems that he believes-(1)
that he's a winner because he believes-(2) that he's a winner, and
believes-(2) that he's a winner because he believes-(3) that he's a
winner. . . .

But his situation is not impossible. It could happen to someone. And
it seems perfectly imaginable that he should be sincere (whether or not
under hypnosis) in saying that he believes he's a winner, knowing what
he knows, and so be a winner indeed.[12]

But suppose he doesn't want to win—he's taken a bet at uncomfortably long odds, which it was none the less rational to take, that

[12] There is some force to the suggestion that if he were a sufficiently reflective man,
then he simply could not form the belief that he was *W*, knowing what he knew—that
we simply would not wish to call any candidate belief-state that he could reasonably
come to be in a state of believing he was *W*, given the causes of its formation.

he wouldn't be a winner. Has he now no choice, knowing the conditions of winning? When asked, under hypnosis, whether he believes he's a winner, what does he say? What forces him to believe he's a winner? It half looks as if he can choose whether or not to believe he's won; and whatever he chooses, his belief will be true. But that doesn't seem right. And yet it does seem imaginable that he could answer 'No', under sincerity-guaranteeing hypnosis, to the question whether he believes he's a winner.

The case is odd. But it remains a real possibility; and it remains clearly true that believing you are W is a necessary constitutive condition of actually being W.

I I.5 NATURAL AND CONVENTIONAL PROPERTIES

If the case of the mystery draw shows nothing else, it shows that the principle of independence is not without exceptions, even if the other apparent contraventions of it turn out to be no such thing. Before considering two other cases, and a third prima-facie case, it should be remarked that being W is clearly a conventional property in some sense (cf. 10.9): for something is held to count as or to constitute being a winner which has no intrinsic connection with winning considered quite generally. Some other condition of winning could just as easily have been laid down. The case of the mystery draw is, certainly, different from the other cases of conventional properties that have been considered, but they are all similar in that it is recognition of the element of conventionality that underlies our lack of disquiet about the fact that they appear to contravene the principle of independence.

It does not seem that this element is to be found in the case of freedom as presently conceived. If freedom exists—if true responsibility exists, that is—then, we suppose, it is a property that can like the properties of being fecund or bald be instantiated independently of the beliefs or decisions of human (or rational) beings about what conventionally counts as what. If free agenthood is possible, then, we suppose, it is not only a straightforwardly objective property (as promising and contracting can be), but also what one might call a natural property, where 'natural' is opposed specifically to 'conventional' (or 'socially instituted'). It is a non-conventionally-instituted property in a way in which promising, making a knight move, and so on are not—instantiable, objective properties though they be.

And so the problem remains. How is it possible that the principle of independence should be contravened in the case of a 'natural' property (a property that a solitary non-moral being can possess, if any being can)?

Next to be considered are omniscience, immorality, and—with a provision—pain. The upshot will be that there are other ways in which contravention of the principle of independence can be unproblematic, but they do not provide adequate models for understanding what might be the case in the case of freedom.

I I.6 OMNISCIENCE

Any being that is omniscient must know it, and *a fortiori*, believe it: (x)(Omniscient $x \to B(x,$Omniscient $x)$). What of this?

One way of thinking of omniscience is as a capacity property, one in virtue of the possession of which a being actually knows all there is to know—an omniscience-producing capacity. The necessary and sufficient conditions of this capacity property—infinite intellectual ability, universe-encompassing perceptual awareness, and so on—are then specifiable independently of reference to any one of the infinite number of particular things that its possessor believes as a result of possessing it. On this view the most natural way of representing that in virtue of which it is true that one is omniscient only if one believes one is might be 'Cs/(x)(Omniscient $x \to B(x,$Omniscient $x)$)/'. One's belief in one's omniscience turns up as just one of the infinite number of true beliefs that one has in virtue of one's possession of the omniscience-producing capacity—it turns up as a causal result of the (presumably involuntary) exercise of the capacity.

Turning from omniscience considered as a capacity property to omnisicence considered simply as the property of knowing (believing) all truths, the following is true: (x)(Omniscient $x \to (y)(y$ is a truth $\leftrightarrow B(x,y)$)).[13] Clearly, 'x is omniscient' is just one of the infinite number

---

[13] I am assuming that if an omniscient being knows that p, then it also believes that p. To take being all-knowing to be believing all and only truths is (i) to suppose that all truths can be known, (ii) to suppose that omniscience entails infallibility, (iii) to omit explicit recognition of the fact that knowledge appears to require not merely true belief but also (appropriately) justifiable belief; there are a number of complications here. (i) might be questioned. But as regards (ii), if the omniscient being had any false beliefs it would know it did, and so—briefly—it would not really have them. Similarly as regards (iii): if its grounds for believing some true belief B were unjustified it would know this, and it would know why. So it would not really believe B on those grounds after all. Furthermore it would *ex hypothesi* know that B was true, and so it would have to have a justified belief in the truth of B.

of truths that can be put in place of the last occurrence of 'y' in this formula when '$(y)(y$ is a truth $\leftrightarrow$ . . .)' is removed, to give (x)(Omniscient $x \rightarrow B(x,$Omniscient $x)$)). It has no special status, no special constitutive role whatever. That is, if believing you are omniscient is a necessary constitutive condition of being omniscient, then so also is believing that $2+2=4$, and by the same token: your being all-knowing is made up of your knowing each particular truth, and in that sense your knowing and hence believing each one is a constitutive condition of your being all-knowing.

This case of contravention of the principle of independence can, surely, be dismissed as a logical oddity of a familiar kind—if it is indeed a case. No one who advocates respect for the principle is going to be troubled by it. It would be foolish to think that it can cast any light on the case of freedom.

11.7 IMMORALITY

Is it not true (1) that one acts immorally only if one believes one does? It seems that an action may be a bad thing whatever its performer thinks, but is not properly speaking a morally bad action unless its performer thinks it is.

Let 'Γ' symbolize 'acts or is acting immorally or morally wrongly'. Then the claim is that '$(x)(Ix \rightarrow B(x,Ix))$' is true. And it seems to be true because $Cn/(x)(Ix \rightarrow \underline{B(x,Ix)})/$—because it is actually constitutive of a's acting wrongly that he believes he is doing so. It is not true simply because there is, first, the morally wrong act, independent of the agent's belief that it is so, and, second, the somehow inevitably concomitant but none the less entirely independent epistemic constatation of the fact of turpitude on the part of the agent. On the contrary: if a really does not, at the time of action, in any way believe that his action is morally wrong, then, when all is said and done, it is not.[14]

It is doubtless true that when a acts morally wrongly in some way, he himself thinks the action wrong simply because of the kind of action it is considered independently of his beliefs about it: he considers it to be wrong simply because it is an action of kind ψ, say, and not because it is a ψ-type action which has the further property of being performed

---

[14] Sensible consequentialists can accept this view as easily as deontologists. For, given that an agent accepts their general view of what the good is, consequentialists may hold not only that for it to act morally rightly is simply for it to *try* to do what it believes will have best possible consequences, but also that part at least of what it is for it to act wrongly is for it to believe that what it is doing is not the best (or equal best) thing.

by someone who believes it is wrong. But this does not change the fact that we, assessing *a* and his action, may hold that *a* acted wrongly only if he believed he was doing so.

There are familiar objections to this claim. It may be said that one can be culpably ignorant when one acts, and that culpable ignorance can co-exist with failure to have any belief that one's action is morally wrong, in such a way as to render the action wrong despite the absence of such belief. It is not at all clear that this is right, however. An agent may perhaps be morally culpable in such a case, but if so we should strictly speaking blame it for its ignorance, or for preserving its ignorance, not for its actual action. It seems that one cannot, after having performed some action, truly be said to have been culpably ignorant in such a way that one's *action* was morally wrong without its being true that one had some sort of suspicion that there was something one ought perhaps to have tried to find out, or check up on, before acting; and having such suspicion will, I take it, either amount to or invariably be accompanied by some sort of belief that one's action might possibly be a bad thing, and hence wrong. In such a case acting without checking up may involve acting morally wrongly because of the presence of a belief (*a*) that there is something that ought to be checked up on—if, that is, having belief (*a*) leads one to have the further belief (*b*) that one is acting wrongly in going ahead with performance of an action which may turn out to be bad. But if having (*a*) simply does not lead one to have (*b*), then, once again, one will not strictly speaking have acted wrongly. It may be that one can in such a case be held to be morally odd or even morally mad, given what one has done; but it seems that one cannot properly be held to have *acted* morally wrongly.[15] Any account of morally culpable ignorance must make some move of this sort, or it runs the risk of incorrect moral condemnation of simple stupidity, innocent thoughtlessness, or sincere, theory-induced moral error. (In the latter case, one can condemn the erroneous moral theory without condemning the person who honestly believes it to be correct.)[16]

In fact, dispute about the truth or falsity of the claim that one acts

[15] This holds even for those convinced Nazis who feature so regularly in philosophical examples, though in fact few if any of them can have fulfilled the condition of having no sort of suspicion that there was anything wrong with what they were doing. Cp. Sidgwick on Torquemada, *The Methods of Ethics*, p. 226 n.

[16] It is true that we can feel remorseful and guilty about thoughtless actions, *ex post facto*; and the many devices of self-deception confuse the issue. But they do not affect the central claim that if we really have no feeling that there is anything remaining to be checked up on, and really do not believe that what we are doing or are about to do is wrong in any way, then it is not, although we may later condemn ourselves.

morally wrongly only if one believes one does is less important, at present, than the fact that contravention of the principle of independence seems so entirely unproblematic in the case of acting wrongly.[17] It is not obvious that this can help to lessen the difficulty felt in the case of freedom; but it may be instructive to take the discussion of morality further.

A parallel though intuitively less convincing case can be constructed for the claim that believing you are acting morally rightly is a necessary constitutive condition of doing so. The claim is Kantian in spirit: if to act rightly is to do your duty because it is your duty (to do your duty for duty's sake), then no entirely spontaneous, unpremeditated action can be morally right. No action can be morally right unless it is, in being performed, thought to be (*a* does his duty at time *t* only if *a* believes he is doing his duty, at *t*).

Counterexamples to this claim can of course be adduced. They appeal to the notion of virtue—they involve reference to actions which are entirely spontaneous (unpremeditated) displays of virtuous dispositions, and which are commonly held to be morally right. But these cases are not decisive as counter-examples. It seems that all they really prove is, once more, that there are deep and perhaps irreconcilable tensions in our notions of morally right and wrong action. On the one hand we think that actions that are entirely spontaneous manifestations of virtuous dispositions are morally good. On the other hand we incline with Kant towards the view that an agent must have made some sort of conscious choice of its action, of a kind that is incompatible with such spontaneity, if it is to be genuinely morally responsible for it, and, hence, possibly praiseworthy on account of it. We do undoubtedly have a special admiration for spontaneously virtuous actions; but it also seems that our understanding of the word 'moral' has an aspect to which the Kantian claim is faithful.[18]

[17] Consider a weaker principle-of-independence-contravening claim: it may not be true that belief that one is acting immorally is a necessary constitutive condition of doing so, but there are none the less many cases in which *a*'s belief that he is acting wrongly is undoubtedly partly constitutive of the fact that he is.

[18] It is obvious that there are deep tensions and inconsistencies in our moral thinking. Some of these show up in the form of objections to certain of the claims considered here. But this can happen even though these claims are completely true to certain aspects of our thinking. It has been suggested that these tensions are the result of a historical process of accretion of different and incompatible views of morality. Aspects of this view have been presented by A. MacIntyre in *After Virtue*. Against this it is arguable that inconsistency resulting from such historical accretion is less important than, and indeed arises partly on account of, a permanent and in some clear sense non-historical possibility

Defenders of the Kantian view may argue against the claim that spontaneously virtuous actions are *sensu stricto* morally right by saying that if an action of kind A 'flows from the agent's character' without the agent consciously registering the view that an action of kind A is right at the time that it acts, then although the agent's character may be morally *admirable*, 'the agent itself' is, in a crucial sense, not properly morally *responsible* for the action.[19] For there is no morally assessable, conscious choice on the part of the agent to perform an action of kind A. It has produced an action of a type that is called morally right, but there seems nevertheless to be a clear sense in which it has not acted morally rightly at all in performing such an action, a sense in which its (entirely spontaneous) action is a morally neutral phenomenon—simply because there is a clear sense in which it cannot be held truly morally responsible for it.[20]

This argument raises familiar questions about what 'the agent itself' might be, and about what true moral responsibility is, questions considered in Chapter 2. Ignoring these questions I shall, simply for the purposes of discussion, add the Kantian claim that believing you are acting rightly is a necessary constitutive condition of acting rightly to the more plausible parallel claim about wrong action.[21]

of tension and inconsistency internal to the whole business of thought about morality; one which has a close parallel in, and which indeed has all its main roots in, the tensions and inconsistencies that are to be found in our attitudes to the crucial notion of *responsibility* for action. Very briefly: on the one hand we naturally subscribe to the strong desert-entailing notion of responsibility; and this ties in with our natural tendency towards ethical Kantianism. On the other hand we recognize, more or less unconsciously, that such true responsibility is impossible, as much in the case of premeditated actions as in the case of spontaneously virtuous actions. And this connects with our tendency to treat spontaneously virtuous actions as just as morally praiseworthy as premeditated actions. (However—and this is a *typical complication*—it also connects with our tendency to treat people as somehow truly responsible for their characters.)

[19] Unless of course it is responsible for its character. In ch. 2 it was argued that it cannot be responsible for its character in the required way. See also 6.5, and W. K. Frankena, 'Prichard and the Ethics of Virtue'.

[20] On the general topic, see Sidgwick, op. cit., Bk. III, ch. 2. As so often, Sidgwick is very accurate about our view of moral matters. Noting the possibility of spontaneous virtuous actions, he rejects the Kantian view. He agrees that there may be 'virtuous acts . . . done so entirely without deliberation that no moral judgement was passed on them by the agent' (p. 225), and remarks that 'it is not . . . commonly held to be indispensable, in order to constitute an act completely right, that a belief that it is right should be actually present in the agent's mind' (p. 207 n.). But he also notes, of the virtuous act, that it is 'clearly necessary that such an act should not even vaguely be thought to be bad' by the agent (p. 225).

[21] If we are not really free agents at all, as ch. 2 argues, then we are *never* truly morally responsible for our actions, and there is, therefore, a crucial sense in which all our actions are morally neutral phenomena, whether we think of them as spontaneously virtuous or

One kind of objectivist about ethics might see the present claim—that believing that one is acting morally wrongly or rightly is a necessary condition of one's actually doing so—as imposing a kind of *awareness condition* on moral action: on this view, the property of objective moral wrongness or rightness is in *some* sense already all there in the action even when it is considered independently of any moral beliefs the agent may have with regard to it (its non-moral beliefs may also be taken into account, of course).

But this does not seem plausible. Consider a particular case again. *a* performs a certain action A. It seems clear that whatever non-evaluative description of A is available to us or to him (and indeed whatever evaluative description of A seems correct to us, or to him), still, so long as he has no sort of belief that A is wrong or immoral, he cannot truly be said to act wrongly—to act in such a way that he is morally culpable specifically on account of having performed A. (This is not to say that *a* is not beyond the moral pale. He may be.)

This just restates the initial claim. But there it is. It may be said that a holy fool, spontaneous and ignorant, can act morally rightly. But it is equally plausible to maintain that if such a being has no conception of morality, hence no belief that it acts morally rightly, then it is, in an inescapable sense, a non-moral being, one of whom it is simply not correct to say *sans phrase* (if at all) that it acts morally, or morally rightly.

This last case leads naturally to consideration of a somewhat different principle-of-independence-contravening claim, one that closely parallels the central claim about freedom. This is the claim (2) that, for any *x*, *x* is a moral agent or being only if it believes (explicitly*) that it is. It must have the concept of morality, and, in addition, believe it is or conceive of itself as a moral agent or being, in order to be one. To be a moral agent, one must have a certain view of things and of oneself. This is what the holy fool lacks.

This claim looks rather plausible (though it will be questioned below); and its contravention of the principle of independence again seems unproblematic. It seems to be just obvious that if one is to be a moral agent one must see oneself as such; and the question arises as to whether examination of this claim can help to diminish the sense of difficulty

---

* as consciously dutiful. There may be consequentially good and bad actions in this case, but there aren't really any morally good and bad actions—simply because there aren't any moral agents.

encountered in the case of the claim that belief in freedom is a necessary condition of freedom.

Before considering this question, however, it is necessary to say something about objectivism and subjectivism.

We have two principle-of-independence-contravening claims: (1) one *acts* wrongly (or rightly) only if one believes one does; (2) one is a moral *agent* only if one so conceives of oneself. Do they force one to take sides in the debate between moral objectivists and moral subjectivists?

They do not. It is true that (1) and (2) have affinities with the subjectivist-sounding 'There's nothing either (morally) good or bad but thinking makes it so'. And they certainly involve a *Subjectivist* (1.5.4) view of what it is for actions to be morally good or bad. For to hold a Subjectivist view of some phenomenon is, precisely, to hold that that in which the existence of the phenomenon consists cannot be specified independently of mention of the fact that certain beings believe that it exists. But it does not follow that they involve a view of ethics which is subjectivist in the stronger, conventional sense of the word, according to which to have a subjectivist theory of some supposed phenomenon is to hold that there is a paramount sense in which the phenomenon is not itself part of the objective world. And in fact (1) and (2) do not commit one to subjectivism about ethics. For it is an unquestionable objective fact that there do exist beings who have beliefs to the effect that their actions are morally wrong (or right); and it is perfectly possible for someone to acknowledge this, and then to go on to claim (*a*) that it is an objective fact that such beings act morally wrongly (or rightly), (*b*) that they act morally wrongly (or rightly) only when—and partly because—they act with such belief, although (*c*) it is a consequence of (*b*) that what the wrongness (or rightness) of their actions consists in cannot be fully specified independently of mention of their beliefs. This is a possible position for an objectivist about ethics; it is a Subjectivist objectivist position.

(1) and (2) are also compatible with the objectivist view that there is a sense in which certain general *types* of acts can be held to be objectively speaking morally right (because just or fair or utility-maximizing, say even when considered independently of particular agents and their moral beliefs. That is, (1) and (2) are compatible with the objectivist view that one can sometimes say what the morally right thing to do would be in a given situation independently of any consideration o

any agent's beliefs. Given such objectivism, what follows from (1), the claim that an agent acts wrongly (rightly) only if it believes it does, is simply that no *actual* action, no action that is actually performed, is ever morally wrong (or right) unless the agent believes it is. Thus types of action can be classified as right or wrong when specified in general terms, but moral wrongness (rightness) is not a property that can be correctly attributed to any act that is an actual phenomenon in the world—nor indeed to any agent on the basis of an act that it has performed—unless the agent has the requisite belief about or attitude to the act.[22]

To say all this is certainly not to deny that there may be other grounds on which to deny that immorality (or moral goodness) is ever an objective property of agents, however; and (1) and (2) are eminently compatible with moral subjectivism.[23]

Are the two claims problematic? With regard to the first, the inclination to claim that *a*'s belief that what he is doing is morally wrong is an essential part of what makes it wrong (if anything does) is very strong. It is true, as remarked, that agents who believe that what they are doing is morally wrong will not usually believe that their believing that it's wrong is part of what makes it wrong. They will usually believe it's wrong simply because it is, considered independently of their beliefs, an action of a certain kind, ψ, say. But this fact does not in any way cast (1) into doubt.[24]

But nor does (1) seem in any way problematic. It is not problematic for moral subjectivists, who treat acting morally wrongly (or rightly) as just one more kind of conventional property with an awareness

[22] Note that moral objectivism (consequentialist or otherwise) is also compatible with the view that no being can ever be truly responsible for its actions. For an objectivist who accepted this view could claim the following. If free agents who were also moral agents *had* existed, then they would have been able to act objectively morally rightly in performing certain types of acts in certain circumstances. But there are in fact no free agents, so no one in fact acts morally rightly. On this view, there does remain a sense in which we can be said to do the objectively morally right thing just in performing certain types of acts in certain circumstances, even though we are not in fact free agents. But, in the end, it is only, and exactly, the sense in which a robot, or at least an ordinarily sentient being that has no sort of conception of moral right or wrong, can do the morally right thing.

[23] For the view that they provide an argument for moral subjectivism, see e.g. Hume, *Treatise*, III. i. 1, esp. pp. 467–8. See also Nietzsche, *Daybreak*, § 148.

[24] The over-reflective man of 11.2 can get into his characteristic difficulty here, by becoming aware that believing an action is wrong is part of what makes it wrong; but we need not follow him. (Some, wanting to perform the bad action they used to perform in innocence, may think 'If only I didn't know it was wrong.')

condition on its possession. And while it may perhaps be too simple, it is not in any way illegitimate for moral objectivists simply to *define* morally wrong action as action that is (i) of a certain kind (ϕ or ψ or whatever—a very large range of descriptions can feature here), and (ii) believed by its performer to be morally wrong (for whatever reason). They may similarly define a predicate of agents, 'is acting morally wrongly'.[25]

(2) may seem more important in the present context of discussion, for it parallels the claim about free agenthood much more nearly, formally speaking. And we do indeed have a strong inclination to say both that people really are moral agents, and to grant, on reflection, that each one's having the belief that he or she is a moral agent is an essential part of what makes the belief true.[26] But (2) can also be disputed. It may be said that in order to be a moral agent, and, hence, to be capable of performing actions correctly describable as morally right or wrong, one must of course possess the concepts of moral right and wrong, and be disposed to classify things in terms of them; but it is not necessarily the case that one has to think explicitly of oneself as a moral agent. Moral agents will no doubt do so, but, arguably, doing so is not actually a necessary constitutive condition of being a moral agent, in the way that thinking of oneself as a free and truly responsible agent is a necessary constitutive condition of being a free and truly responsible agent. In the case of thought about morality, as it affects oneself, one's thought is essentially directed outward on to features of actions and the world. In the case of thought about freedom and true responsibility, as it affects oneself, one's thought is essentially directed on to oneself.

If this line of thought is cogent, then the case of moral agenthood does not after all provide a close parallel to the case of free agenthood; it is not after all a parallel case of contravention of the principle of independence which, by seeming entirely unproblematic, might help to show the case of free agenthood to be similarly unproblematic. But even if being a moral agent does involve believing one is a moral agent

---

[25] In some cases we may be inclined to say that an agent acted wrongly just because (ii) it thought that its action was wrong, *qua* ϕ-ing, say, although ϕ-ing is not one of the descriptions listed in (i). In such a case we take bad intention to be not only necessary but also sufficient for wrong action. But our intuitions about this vary from case to case.

[26] Some may even be tempted to say that we really are moral agents, believing what we believe, even if we are not, in the end, free agents. This is not Sidgwick's view, but elements useful for the elaboration of a related, more plausible position can be found in *The Methods of Ethics* I. V (esp. § 3), where Sidgwick defends the view that there is a point to doing ethics even if free will is impossible. Cf. n. 22.

in such a way that the principle of independence is contravened, the parallel is of questionable value. And part of the reason for this is as follows.

(i) It seems natural to conceive of accession to moral agenthood as a kind of cottoning on to certain aspects of reality that are essentially independent of oneself and one's beliefs. It seems natural to conceive of it in this way whether (*a*) one is a certain sort of subjectivist about ethics, and sees the cottoning on as nothing more than the acquisition of a grasp of a certain kind of complex, socially instituted practice, or whether (*b*) one is a certain sort of objectivist about ethics, and sees the cottoning on as acquisition of some kind of (quasi-perceptual?) ability to become aware of certain sorts of non-socially-instituted objective facts.

(ii) It seems implausible to conceive of accession to free agenthood (or true responsibility) in a way parallel to (*b*)—as some sort of cottoning on to something that can be already all there quite independently of the agent's beliefs. But if one is trying to prove that we really are free agents, only something like the parallel with the objectivists' (*b*) is worth considering. For to conceive of accession to free agenthood in a way parallel to the subjectivists' (*a*) is to treat it as ultimately nothing more than entry into participation in a certain kind of socially instituted, conventional practice of *treating* people (including oneself) as free, a practice which exists although strictly speaking no one is really free at all.[27]

(iii) Why is the parallel with (*b*) implausible? Because in (*b*) objective moral facts of the matter are conceived as already there, independently of the agent's beliefs, ready to be latched on to. Their apprehension assists the passage into moral agenthood. And there is no clear parallel for this in the case of freedom. The closest one can get is to suppose that an agent's freedom or true responsibility can be already all there quite independently of its beliefs, already a full feature of its agency in such a way that it can already be acting truly responsibly in particular cases before having any idea that this is so. But this idea seems as implausible as ever (though it will in fact be pursued in 15.3).

It may be said that there is another and better way for objectivists to conceive of accession to moral agenthood. It is better because it allows, as (*b*) does not, for the possibility that a being may become a genuine moral agent and yet get the content of morality wrong. On this view

[27] Some may be happy to accept such a view. It may be the best option. See n. 9.

accession to moral agenthood is simply (*c*) acquisition of a tendency to be influenced by claims that are agreed on all sides to be distinctively moral in character (having the form 'You ought to do X', or 'It is right, or just, or kind, or noble, to do Y', for example), even though disagreement may persist about whether they are true or not.

This is plausible. But it does not seem to help in any further way with the case of freedom; it doesn't seem to furnish any more illuminating parallel. And in fact it may seem foolish to look to the case of morality for final illumination of the case of freedom. For the notion of morality is, in the end, a murkier notion than the notion of freedom. Furthermore, it seems clear enough that one cannot really be a moral agent without being a free agent; to that extent the problem of free agenthood lies deeper than the problem of moral agenthood.

It may—finally—be questioned whether we need any such parallel. As remarked, some fail to see any paradox in the claim that believing one is free is a necessary constitutive condition of being free. Others, however, think that the paradox is acute, and that specification of the attribution conditions of a property like true responsibility cannot possibly involve such contravention.

I think the claim is very paradoxical, in fact, but that this can be hard to see, because in order to do so one has to focus tightly on the point that true responsibility is (as ordinarily conceived) not only a straightforwardly objective property, but also a property that is entirely non-conventional in nature (and hence akin to obviously belief-independent properties like being pregnant or six feet tall). This focus easily slips, and when it does it can appear entirely unproblematic to say that belief in true responsibility is a condition of true responsibility. The issue is a puzzling one. Here as before I continue to assume that there is indeed a problem.

11.8 PAIN

Consider finally the case of pain, as a way of introducing some new elements to the discussion.

It seems plausible to say of adult human beings that they cannot possibly be in pain and not believe that they are, and that this is not simply a causal truth. However, it does not seem true to say that for any *x*, if *x* is in pain, then it believes it is; i.e.—taking '*P*' to symbolize 'is in pain'—that $(x)(Px \rightarrow B(x,Px))$. For beings that cannot plausibly be said to form beliefs at all, let alone fully self-conscious beliefs, experience pain. And although the present sense of 'believes' is a very wide one, including as one of its senses 'is aware* that', '*B*' was defined (in 10.4) in such a way that it covered only fully self-conscious belief or awareness.

It is worth temporarily relaxing the restriction of attention to fully self-conscious belief or awareness. Consider the term '*E**', to be read, inelegantly but intelligibly, 'experiences* that', and to be understood as standing to 'experiences that' just as 'believes that' stands to 'believes truly that'.[28] And suppose, for the moment, that to say that $E^*(x,\phi x)$ does *not* imply that x is self-conscious, nor that x is capable of thought that is articulated in the way that ours can be, given that we are linguistic beings. It then seems plausible to say that $(x)(Px \rightarrow E^*(x,Px))$, and indeed that $Cn/(x)(Px \rightarrow \underline{E^*(x,Px)})$—that experiencing* that one is in pain is a necessary condition, and indeed a necessary constitutive condition, of being in pain. Indeed it seems that it is constitutively necessary and sufficient—it seems that $Cn/(x)(\underline{E^*(x, Px)} \leftrightarrow Px)/$. And this appears to be so despite the fact that the same general problem of independence may be seen to arise for the current notion of experience* as for the notion of belief: in virtually all cases of experiencing* something, although apparently not in the case of pain, one's having the experience cannot be supposed to be a condition of the obtaining of the state of affairs whose obtaining makes one's experience veridical, if indeed it is veridical.

These claims about pain are familiar. As regards sufficiency, clearly, hallucinated pain, or pain consisting in no more than a hypnotically induced belief that one is in pain, is indeed pain. As regards necessity, unnoticed pain is no pain at all. All in all, pain is pain-experience; its *esse* is *percipi*.[29] Suppose that there were something, which one could

---

[28] The neologism is worth perpetrating although the distinction between experiencing* that p and experiencing that p (or between experience* of x and experience of x) can be made without it, as when one talks of the possible difference between someone's (necessarily veridical) experience of seeing a piano and someone's (possibly illusory) experience *as of* seeing a piano. (One presently unimportant difference between 'experiences' and 'believes truly' arises from the fact that there is a causal condition on the provenance of the experience, if it is to be veridical, whereas there is no such condition on the provenance of the belief, if it is to be true. In this respect 'experiences' is more like 'knows' than 'believes truly'.)

[29] This is no doubt why Locke, considering the extreme sceptical hypothesis about the existence of the external world, and seeing that it is not strictly speaking defeasible, always recurs to the fact of pleasure and pain (in the widest sense). For it is true that 'I seem to see a table' does not entail 'I see a table'; but 'I seem to feel a pain' does entail 'I feel a pain'. So scepticism loses its force—cannot open up its characteristic gap—with regard to that which ultimately most concerns us, pleasure and pain. See Locke's *Essay*, IV. ii. 14 and IV. xi. 8.

call 'X-fibre stimulation', which always occurred whenever bodily damage above a certain degree of seriousness occurred (or whenever anything occurred that could cause non-hallucinated or non-hypnotically-induced pain); if there were, it would be neither necessary nor sufficient for pain, not necessary because of hallucination and hypnosis, not sufficient because one's X-fibre stimulation could continue while one's pain did not—one could sleep, or again be hypnotized, this time into unawareness of pain, or be distracted in such a way that one did not feel pain although one would feel pain if one were not so distracted. Stubbing his toe while running for his life, a man may not notice pain that would otherwise have made him cry out loud.[30] A day later he may notice the bruise with surprise. There was, one may suppose, X-fibre stimulation, but no pain. This is so although it is admittedly natural to talk as above of his 'not noticing the pain'—as if it were really there, although unnoticed. There was no pain; no one suffered it. Pain is pain-experience, which can come and go, given an underlying continuous process of X-fibre stimulation, say—coming and going with attention and distraction, or with the presence or absence of a certain state of activation of the reticular activating system in the brain, which is held to be necessary for consciousness.

Some might accept that $Cn/(x)(\underline{E^*(x,Px)} \rightarrow Px)/$, but query $Cn/(x)$ $(Px \rightarrow \underline{E^*(x,Px)})/$; they might accept that hallucinating pain is being in pain, but not that one cannot be in pain without noticing it. They might cite people groaning in their sleep, woken by pain; or the phenomenon of once again *becoming aware* of pain one had ceased to notice— certainly our ordinary ways of talking about pain allow that it can continue unnoticed; or the general possibility of tracing in people's behaviour the effects of their awareness, in some sense of the word, of stimuli which they deny any knowledge of.

In reply one might ask whether the unnoticed pain was unpleasant— or painful, indeed. But a more conciliatory reply could defend the strong claim that one is not in pain if one is not aware that, or does not experience that, one is, while offering a broader account of an experiential state, including in it phenomena of peripheral consciousness, and so on. Without retracting the claim that the *esse* of pain is *percipi*, one could give a broader account of what it is to perceive, and, in particular, to perceive pain.

[30] Thomas Reid is one of many to have noted this: 'In the tumult of a battle, a man may be shot through the body without knowing anything of the matter, till he discover it by loss of blood or strength' (*Essays on the Active Powers of the Human Mind*, II. III, p. 77).

Is the case of pain an instance of contravention of the principle of independence? Not really. Even if one allows that claims of the form '$(x)(\phi x \rightarrow E^*(x,\phi x))$' do in general contravene the principle of independence, and can do so even though 'E^*' is so understood that to say that $E^*(a,\phi a)$ is *not* to imply that a has any sort of fully self-conscious apprehension of self, the present case is not really a case of contravention. For experience of being in pain just is being in pain, on the present view: '$(x)(Px \rightarrow E^*(x,Px))$' and its converse are true simply because the two properties in question are identical. Pain just *is* pain-experience. So of course it is true that experiencing pain is a necessary (and sufficient) condition of being in pain.[31]

Formally, then, being in pain is a (non-causally) evident property: awareness* that one is in pain appears, formally, as a necessary constitutive condition of being in pain. But this is not a genuine contravention of the principle of independence. It is little more than a trick of the language of pain, which makes two things that are really the same seem distinct in the way that experiencing* getting soaked and actually getting soaked are distinct. I shall consider no more cases of contravention, real or apparent.[32]

11.9 'E^*'

Given the present definition of 'E^*', or 'experience(s)* that', '$E^*(a,\phi a)$' carries no implication that a is self-conscious. From now on, however, concern is only with fully self-conscious experiences, i.e. experiences that are experiences of oneself apprehended as oneself (in the way characteristic and constitutive of self-consciousness, however exactly it is described) as having a certain property. And so 'E^*' will now be restricted by definition in the way in which 'B' was restricted in 10.5:

[31] Even if you can be in pain and not *mind* at all. D. Dennett makes some interesting observations about pain in 'Why You Can't Make a Computer that Feels Pain' (esp. the second half of section II).

[32] In the spirit of compendiousness it is worth observing that one way of characterizing the *intentionality* of much sensory experience—the way our concepts essentially inform our sensory experience—is to say that there is a sense of the word 'see' (for example) according to which you can be said to be seeing a piano (say) only if you have the concept of a piano, and, further, believe that you are seeing a piano. If so, then there are indefinitely many more non-causally evident properties. About such cases it suffices here to remark that this sense of the phrase 'seeing a piano' is a secondary sense, secondary to the sense in which a being can see a piano without having the concept of a piano; and that in so far as there are indefinitely many more evident properties of this sort, they pose no problem as such. See G. E. M. Anscombe, 'The Intentionality of Sensation'.

'$E^*(a,\phi a)$' is to be read 'a has experience (of himself) to the effect that he (grasped fully self-consciously as himself) is ϕ'.[33]

Why introduce 'E^*' at all into the present discussion of freedom? Simply because it may be useful in counteracting the potentially misleading influence that exclusive use of the strongly cognitivistic word 'believes' and its symbol 'B' may have on one's grasp of what mental activity that is properly describable as fully self-conscious mentation (and which is such that the question of the contravention of principle of independence can arise in its case) can possibly and minimally be like. (The phrases 'sense(*) of' and 'aware(*) of' will also be useful in this connection.) The term 'believes' used on its own lacks comprehensiveness—vague though it is. For this reason, the claim that belief that one is free is a necessary (constitutive) condition of one's being free will be re-expressed as the claim that *experience** of oneself as free is a necessary (constitutive) condition of one's being free.

But one thing that needs to be made very clear now is this: unless there is an explicit ruling to the contrary, 'E^*' and 'experience*' will be understood to attribute propositional-attitude-like mental states, states, that is, that purport to have a certain objective-state-of-affairs-representing and indeed property-to-object-attributing content, and to be, therefore, states of such a kind that the question of whether or not the principle of independence has been contravened can always arise with regard to them when they are attributed in statements of the form '$(x)(\phi x \rightarrow E^*(x,\phi x))$' or '$a$ experiences* that ϕa'. Generally, it will be supposed that the problem about independence that arose paradigmatically for beliefs can arise with equal acuteness for experiences, which may have veridicality conditions just as beliefs have truth conditions.[34]

It would, furthermore, be a complete misapprehension of the present way of understanding 'E^*' and 'experiences*' to think that their use commits one to providing any detailed *phenomenology* of freedom of the sort attempted in Chapter 6. All one need say is this: to experience oneself as a free agent, in the present sense, is just for one's experience to have that common character, whatever exactly it is, that the experience of all those of whom it is true to say that they believe them-

[33] One could make explicit the fact that it is experience that is both relationally and notionally of oneself by the device introduced in 10.5: what is in question is $E^*_{NR}(a,\phi a)$.

[34] Thus in the particular case of experience* of freedom, the problem is with the idea that a's having of the experience* that he is free ('$E^*(a,Fa)$') should itself be a necessary constitutive condition of the existence of the state of affairs whose obtaining it purports to represent or contain awareness of ('Fa').

selves to be, or conceive of themselves as, free and truly responsible agents has specifically on account of the fact that they have this belief or self-conception. Their daily experiences may have very little in common. They may inhabit different galaxies. But if they all believe that they are truly responsible agents in the ordinary strong sense, there will be at least one fundamental and experience-pervading respect in which they apprehend or experience things—themselves, their world, their agency—in the same way: for they will all experience themselves as free agents, in the present sense. Here my intention is simply to designate this experience, without going into any precise phenomenological description of what it is like (we know the kind of thing that is in question from our own experience).

Some philosophers mistrust pseudo-neologisms like 'experiences* that', holding not only that they tend to mislead, but also that anything of philosophical value can be said in ordinary language. But just as our first intuitions and ordinary patterns of thought about things can not only be in error, but can also obstruct the hard imaginative pursuit of real if strange possibilities, so too our ordinary language can reflect and protect these intuitions and patterns of thought, and the sources of resistance to speculation that they contain. No doubt the use of unfamiliar expressions carries certain risks. But it can also be valuable in its interruption of these customary patterns of thought. Using 'experiences* that' instead of 'believes that' may help to loosen preconceptions about what fully self-conscious thought can possibly and minimally be like—fully self-conscious self-attribution of properties, in particular. More will be said at the beginning of Chapter 14 about how exactly 'experiences* that' is to be understood.

One problem with the word 'believes' is this: one wants to say both that belief in freedom is a condition of freedom, and that theoretical incompatibilist determinists, who, as such, may sincerely not believe they are free, are nevertheless free—if we are. Appreciation of the force of the principal claim that one is free only if one believes one is may then lead one to say that there is another sense of 'believes', a sense in which they do after all believe they are free.[35] Such tensions of sense make it seem worth varying the vocabulary used to describe our sense of freedom.

11.10 CONCLUSION

This chapter has surveyed some of the cases in which the principle

[35] See 10.14, and 12.10 below.

of independence may be contravened. In none of them did it seem particularly problematic or contrary to intuition that it should be contravened. Nor, therefore, did it seem particularly problematic that the properties discussed should be classified as non-causally evident properties.

Do these cases give reason to suppose that it is also unproblematic to claim that potential free agenthood is a non-causally evident property? It is not clear that they do. The cases considered can be divided up—rather roughly—as follows.

1. Cases of 'conventional' properties. These can be subdivided.

   (i) There are cases like those of entering into a contract, promising that *p*. These two, and others like them, are 'awareness condition' cases.

   (ii) The property of being *W*—being a winner in the mystery draw— can also be counted as a conventional property, though it is not an awareness condition case.

   (iii) Moral subjectivists, and certain moral objectivists, will claim that in so far as we can truly be said to exemplify the properties of (*a*) acting morally wrongly or rightly, and of (*b*) being moral agents, these too are conventional properties.

2. Cases of natural (i.e. not conventional) properties that are purely experiential properties, like the property of being in pain. These don't really count, for reasons given.

3. Cases of natural properties that are not purely experiential properties, but whose non-causal evidentness is in some sense a matter of mere logic—such as omniscience: if you know everything, then necessarily and *a fortiori* you believe that you know everything. (Omnicredence, requiring infinite inconsistency of belief, would be another such property: you believe everything only if you believe you believe everything.)

We are left with the non-conventionalist moral objectivists' account of the properties of (*a*) acting morally wrongly or rightly, and of (*b*) being a moral agent. But doubt was cast on whether (*b*) really is a straightforward case of contravention (p. 220). As for (*a*), it is entirely unproblematic for these objectivists. There is no reason why they cannot say that an agent's moral beliefs about what it is doing when it performs an action A are quite simply *part* of A—that complex psychophysical thing—in so far as A is an object of moral appraisal.

In this case the classification of A as right or wrong can clearly depend essentially on the agent's belief-state, for it is actually part of A.

Perhaps this is not very satisfactory. The notion of morality is very puzzling. But whatever the case with respect to moral agenthood, the property of being a free or truly responsible agent does not appear to fall into any of the three somewhat ramshackle categories proposed above. As we ordinarily conceive of it, it is not in any sense a 'conventional' property. It is a property that a solitary rational being could in principle possess independently of any society (and of any grasp of the notion of morality), so long as it had been created self-conscious and, perhaps, endowed with the power of thinking as we do (presumably in a language-like fashion). Equally, it is a property that can be fully described, if indeed it can be fully described at all, independently of any reference to the society, institutions, or conventions of rational beings.[36] It is, we conceive, an objective, natural property; but it is certainly not a purely experiential property, merely a matter of how things feel. Nor is it a mere matter of logic (or of mere accident) that it is true that one can be a free or truly responsible agent only if one believes one is—if indeed it is true.

Later on (15.3) I will consider the suggestion that free agenthood may be a kind of awareness-condition case even though it is not a conventionally instituted property. For the moment, though, I will take it that the property of freedom fits into none of the categories of intuitively unproblematic cases of non-causally evident properties that have been proposed in this chapter.[37]

The main options are then these: either free agenthood is a non-causally evident property of a kind not yet encountered, that has yet to

[36] The fact that the solitary being may need to possess linguistic or quasi-linguistic abilities is no grounds for an objection to this. For, (1), reference to language comes in only indirectly, as a possible consequence of the fact that it has to be able to have thoughts of a certain complexity; and, (2), even if this indirect reference to language does bring with it doubly indirect reference to social institutions, this does not affect the sense in which freedom itself is a natural (i.e. non-conventional) property. In any case, (3), such a solitary being could in principle be created by divine fiat out of a few chemicals and some water, without any societal conventions or institutions also being created, thinking away entirely unreflectively in a language-like manner—in exactly the manner of a person on a desert island who has forgotten that other people exist, for example. It could be completely unreflective, as most people are, about what its use of language involved. (It would not of course have a private language in Wittgenstein's sense.) See also 6.5.

[37] Here it may be worth recalling the 'two-level' solution to the problem of contravention considered and rejected in 10.13.

be shown to be unproblematic; or it is irredeemably problematic; or it is not a non-causally evident property at all: being either causally evident; or not evident at all. All these suggestions will be considered.

11.11 ANTICIPATION

The basic structure of the discussion that is to come is as follows. The Objectivists admit the plausibility of the principal claim that belief in freedom is a condition of freedom—they admit the plausibility of

$$(x)(Fx \rightarrow B(x,Fx)).\tag{1}$$

But they deny that belief in freedom (experience of oneself as free) can be a necessary *constitutive* condition of freedom. That is, they deny that

$$Cn/(x)(Fx \rightarrow \underline{B(x,Fx)})/.\tag{1.1}$$

So they are committed to giving some other account of why (1) is true.

Their basic strategy will be as follows. First, to try to produce some set of Objectivist, Structural conditions like the S conditions (7.3) that are constitutively necessary and sufficient for freedom—that are such that

$$Cn/(x)\underline{Sx} \leftrightarrow Fx)/;\tag{2}$$

and then to claim, in Kantian fashion, that any being that fulfils the S conditions cannot but believe it is free—to claim that

$$(x)(Sx \rightarrow B(x,Fx)).\tag{3}$$

(1) is then derivable from (2) and (3). (1.1) is not.

But these Objectivists will then have to say what *sort* of truth (3) is. They will try two answers; but in fact neither will do. One is that (3) is, ultimately, a causal truth: it is true because

$$Cs/(x)(\underline{Sx} \rightarrow B(x,Fx))/\tag{3.1}$$

is true. This appears to allow them to preserve what they want. For from (2) and (3) or (3.1) one can deduce (1), which they accept, but not (1.1).[38] If they take this line they are of course committed to holding that (1) is also ultimately a causal truth, and this seems implausible. But this line has its attractions, and to have Objectivists pursue it will be a useful way of articulating discussion of the nature of our thought about freedom.

---

[38] One can deduce (1) because (2) entails (5) $(x)(Sx \leftrightarrow Fx)$ and in particular (6) (x) $(Fx \rightarrow Sx)$, and (6) and (3) entail (1). (1.1) could be derived from (3) and (2), and in particular from something entailed by (2), i.e. (6.1) $Cn/(x)(Fx \rightarrow \underline{Sx})/$, if (3) were a *constitutive* truth—if (3.2) $Cn/(x)(Sx \rightarrow \underline{B(x,Fx)})/$ were true. For (6.1) and (3.2) entail (1.1), given the transitivity of the relation 'is a necessary constitutive condition of' (10.12).

Because they run into trouble with the claim that (3), and so (1), are ultimately causal truths, Objectivists will also attempt to claim that (3) is true because there is some condition, Z, say, that is numbered among the S conditions, and that is constitutively sufficient for belief in freedom; so that

$$\text{Cn}/(x)(\underline{Zx} \rightarrow B(x,Fx))/ \qquad (4)$$

is true—where 'Zx' is not simply an abbreviation of '$B(x,Fx)$' itself. Having done this, Objectivists can then claim that (1) can be derived,[39] and derived as a *non-causal*, necessarily exceptionless truth, whereas (1.1) still cannot be derived.

All actual suggestions that have the form of (4) will be rejected. A more general reason why this line of argument cannot succeed will also be given.

If neither approach to the question of why (3), and (1), are true will do, Objectivists may have to reject (3) and (1) altogether, and argue that belief in freedom is not a necessary condition of freedom after all. This Objectivist option will also be considered. (The only alternative is to agree with the Subjectivists that (1.1) is true—that belief in freedom is indeed a separate, Attitudinal (1.5.3), constitutive condition of freedom.)

The Subjectivists, who accept (1.1), will naturally oppose the Objectivists here and at all points. They will seek to show that all the Objectivists' proposed conditions of free agenthood, 'Structural' or otherwise, are insufficient for freedom because insufficient to guarantee the presence of belief in (experience* of) freedom. They will seek, that is, to show that a separate, extra Attitudinal condition requiring belief in (experience* of) freedom needs to be added to any adequate account of the conditions of freedom.

Most of the discussion that follows deals with the nature of the subjective experience and attitudes of beings who are likely candidates for free agenthood, although it purports to be an attempt to work out what the objective conditions of free agenthood might actually be. This may seem odd, but it seems that it is impossible to get a proper perspective on the philosophical problem of free will until one is prepared to go beyond the attempt to state simple factual conditions of free agenthood in the traditional manner, and to enquire closely into the nature and conditions of our experience* of freedom.

[39] From (4) and (2) together with $(x)(Sx \rightarrow Zx)$, which is, given the present suggestion, *ex hypothesi* true.

In fact the debate between Subjectivists and Objectivists provides a context for a quite general enquiry into the question of whether there are experiential or Attitudinal conditions on free agenthood—the question, that is, of whether being a free agent necessarily involves possessing certain experiential or attitudinal properties whose possession cannot be supposed to be necessarily involved in possession of any of the Structural or capacity properties proposed by the Objectivists as necessary for freedom. In the next chapter, for example, belief in (experience* of) freedom is not of principal concern. The chapter presents an argument by description for a certain Attitudinal condition of freedom.

12

The Spectator Subject and Integration

Back in 7.1 the problems posed for freedom by determinism (and, equally, by the impossibility of self-determination) were simply shelved. It was explicitly (and compatibilistically) assumed that they could be solved or dissolved—the idea being that this assumption would permit a freer examination of those problems that arise for a theory of freedom *before* the issue of determinism (or self-determination) is considered. The assumption still holds, and will not be relinquished until later, although it is surely false.

The present question is this: is it plausible, given this assumption, to suppose that the Objectivist, Structural S conditions, first stated in 7.3, are sufficient as well as necessary conditions of potential free agenthood? (Compatibilists believe the assumption is true, so for them the question is simply this: are the S conditions sufficient as well as necessary conditions of potential free agenthood?)

It will now be argued that they are not—not even for compatibilists. It will be argued that the S conditions can be shown to be inadequate before the problems posed by determinism and non-self-determinability have been raised at all. It will be argued that there are *Attitudinal* conditions (1.5.3) on free agenthood that are essentially over and above the Structural theorists' S conditions: mere Structural conditions, which are by definition very general, cognitive-and-agentive-structure-specifying conditions, can never suffice as a characterization of what it is to be a free agent.

Three general points about procedure. First, some of the arguments in the next four chapters, particularly those dealing with such inherently vague things as forms of experience, lack any semblance of logically compelling demonstration. Many of them are simply controlled speculations, arguments by description, attempts (however unsuccessful) at "that arduous invention which is the very eye of research".[1]

[1] G. Eliot, *Middlemarch*, ch. 16.

Second, an equal and opposite dubiety. Attempts will be made to reach strong all-or-nothing conclusions in areas where it seems unlikely that such conclusions are to be had. One defence of this is as follows. Trying to build tight structures with vague conceptual materials is a good way of exercising thought about those materials. Necessary-and-sufficient-condition-style analyses of concepts like knowledge, perception, personal identity, and so on are always breaking down. But to try to complete them, even while knowing it can't be done, can be a good way of doing philosophy.

Third, the argument is from now on only imperfectly linear. Some ideas are returned to more than once, and developed in different ways.

12.2 *UNE ÉTRANGÈRE*

Imagine a woman who is a self-conscious, self-moving purposive agent. She fulfils all the Structural *S* conditions on potential free agenthood, but she does not appear to be a free agent on account of the peculiarity of her sense of self, and, in particular, on account of the peculiarity of her attitude to her desires and herself as an agent.

One might call her the 'Spectator subject'—or just 'the Spectator'. For she is experientially speaking detached from her desires—from her motivation generally—in some curious way. She acts, and for reasons that she can give, but it is as if it is not really she who desires, decides, and acts, but rather as if her desires and beliefs work it out among themselves beneath her detached, spectatorial, inward gaze. And the reason this is so is that this is how it seems to her—this is how she experiences desire and agency.

She is difficult to describe, but she is a bit like Camus's *étranger* at his most detached; she is somehow disengaged from life, including her own.[2] When *l'étranger* alludes to one of his own desires, it is half as if he were recounting a fact about a feature of the world which is extraneous to him; for he—what he most truly is—seems to be just the detached reporting self. The desire seems to be something that affects his life rather in the way that things external to one, details of one's surroundings, do. And yet it is still his desire—it is no one else's. It is, one might say, something he apprehends before it is something he feels; but that it is his is part of what he apprehends. The same is true of the Spectator.

The problem with the Spectator's attitude to herself can be described

[2] A. Camus, *L'Étranger*.

independently of saying that she fails to conceive of herself as a free agent, in the way that has been claimed to be necessary for freedom—although it will doubtless be true that she does also fail in this way.[3] And before considering the Objectivists' response to her specifically as one who appears to show that it is not true that fulfilling the S conditions is sufficient for belief in freedom (not true that $(x)(Sx \rightarrow B(x,Fx))$), it is worth considering her case in isolation from the claim that no being can be free that does not believe it is, and as providing a further, independent argument against the claim that the S conditions are sufficient for free agenthood (sufficient given the assumption that the problems posed by non-self-determinability can be solved, that is).

Although fully self-conscious, the Spectator has no strong particular sense of herself as a decision-making self-governing agent, as we usually (but not always) do. But this very fact appears to preclude her being a free agent. She doesn't really see herself as the decider and rational planner of action (and thus, *a fortiori*, doesn't conceive of herself as a free agent). Or, if she does so see herself, in some spectatorial manner, being, after all, aware of practical-rational calculations going on in her, still, vitally, she doesn't feel herself to be an agent in the definite participatory way in which we do; having no real sense of expressing herself in action, no sense such as we ordinarily have of having a will that issues in action in such a way that one is responsible for and in some way committed to what one does.

She may be aware that her actions are actions executed by a body that is hers, and motivated by reasons correctly identifiable as hers—they are certainly no one else's, and they do in fact motivate this her body. She will be able to give reasons why she did something, as we do—'I wanted X and believed doing Y was the best way to obtain X, given Z'; and it remains correct to say that she decides to do Y: no one else does, and she is a single psychophysical thing, not schizophrenic. But there is something missing in the way she wants X, and in her attitude to what are correctly identifiable as her projects and actions.

One might try to express this by saying that what is really true of her is best expressed impersonally: X was wanted, and it was reckoned that doing Y was the best way to get X, given Z. But this would be

[3] Support for the claim that such failure is independent of the particular problem posed by the Spectator's experience of self and agency will be provided by the case of the 'natural Epictetans' (to be discussed in ch. 13 below), who do not experience their agency or themselves in the way that the Spectator does, but who nevertheless fail to be free because they fail so to conceive of themselves.

inaccurate, for she is fully self-conscious. Her own desires may in a sense be things she perceives before they are things she feels. But she acknowledges them as her own, none the less, while remaining spectatorially detached from them. It is just that her sense of self remains unengaged in her actions in such a way that it does not seem that she—*she*—can be counted a free, responsible agent.

If complete lack of any such sense of engagement could be decisively established in a human being (here it is *ex hypothesi*) it might suffice even in a court of law to absolve from responsibility. Of course it would be very hard to establish in ordinary circumstances, especially in someone in all other respects apparently normal, like the Spectator (and *l'étranger*). But the question of what might plausibly be taken to have been established is not important here; and it is worth remarking that much of the effect of the later part of *L'Étranger* derives from the feeling that Meursault's sentence is inappropriate, indeed quite unjust, given his mental condition.

It may help to think of a woman who, although she remains outwardly normal and goes about her business, has entered into an acute state of 'existential' crisis, or a state of extreme accidie, or, more particularly, aboulia. Consider a woman for whom life has entirely lost its point, and who therefore acts merely mechanically in some sense, although outwardly normal, continuing to execute complicated and calculated actions, continuing with her job, for example. To us, ignorant of her inner condition, her actions seem to be ordinarily free and responsible actions—performed by one who is to all intents and purposes a free and fully responsible agent. But it is precisely the absence of the right kind of intents and purposes—or rather, perhaps, the right kind of relation on her part to the intents and purposes—that makes this appearance illusory. Given this lack it is as if *she* does not act or decide at all, in the required sense. But again that would be too strong. She acts, and decides, but she is not related to her actions and decisions in the right kind of way.

12.3 THE NORMAL AND THE SPECTATORIAL

The woman for whom life has lost its point is unhelpful in one way: for it is important that the Spectator's condition should not be seen as some kind of abnormality that constitutes a psychical constraint, and that is therefore irrelevant to the question of whether or not she is a potential free agent (7.2). If her condition were seen as a psychical constraint, it would be very plausible to hold that she was a *potential* free agent (at least to the same extent that we are, that is—she is after all a complicated, intelligent, self-conscious purposive agent), and, accordingly, to hold that she would be *actually* free if unconstrained, although she is in fact permanently constrained.

But this is not the right way to think of the Spectator. She is conceived to be of such a kind that she *naturally* experiences things in the way she does. She is not a human being, but an alien. Relative to the normal condition of aliens like herself she is not deranged in any way. She just has *one of the many possible* kinds of experience of self, agency, and life that self-conscious, purposive S-condition-fulfilling beings can have. We, I suggest, are inclined to hold the Spectator's kind of experience to be insufficient for, incompatible with, free agenthood. We place an attitudinal condition on freedom, a condition whose fulfilment involves something that is essentially over and above, and not an invariable concomitant of, being a self-conscious purposive agent. It is therefore an Attitudinal condition (relative to the present S-conditions account of freedom); and failure to fulfil it cannot be dismissed as merely subjection to a form of psychical constraint.

It is important to see that the Spectator's experience is just a different kind of experience from our own, then, in no way less good than, or somehow incorrect relative to, our own; and to see that it cannot be held to involve some form of psychical constraint just because it is different in this way. Even if one held that a human being who had experience like the Spectator's was a potential free agent, but a psychically constrained one, one would not thereby be warranted in holding that *any* being that had such experience was really a free agent, but a constrained one. It is not as if the Spectator has lost something she once had, or might have had; nor has she something extra which she might not have had—a psychologically characterizable disorder which has affected her adversely. It is simply that she naturally has experience of self and agency of such a kind that she fails to fulfil an Attitudinal condition on freedom which, thinking of the human case, one could call the condition of non-alienation, or, better, the condition of *Integration*. A positive characterization of Integration will be proposed in 12.8.

12.4 A RACE OF SPECTATORS

Imagine a whole race of Spectatorially detached beings, among whom the Spectator subject appears wholly normal. Suppose one agrees with the present claim that they cannot be said to act freely, in the full sense of the term. It is then most implausible to say that the reason this is so is that although they are potential free agents, they are, as a race, universally and permanently subject to a certain psychical constraint. For they are not *constrained* in any way. They are in full possession of their normal capacities. To say that they are constrained is unwarrantable anthropocentricity; it is to take the normal human condition as a universal standard of normal self-conscious rational agency. If the Spectators cannot be said to act freely it is not because they are unnaturally constrained in some way; it is because they as they naturally are are not potential free agents at all.

Placing the Spectator among her own kind may make it clearer that *if* she is never actually free, then this is not because she is, although a potential free agent, permanently subject to constraint. It is, rather, because she is not a potential free agent at all. But the case of the race of Spectators may also lead one to question whether it is right to say that they are not free agents on account of the nature of their experience. The charge of anthropocentricity threatens from another direction. Thus it is true that the Spectators fail to fulfil the condition of Integration, and in addition have no sense of themselves as free in the way we do. And for all their possible efficiency in action, they are somehow like sleepwalkers—to us. But if one imagines that they are supremely well-organized, technically advanced (space-travelling), highly rational-seeming (to us), then one may come to feel that our ordinary notion of freedom is mistakenly inflexible and anthropocentrically parochial in excluding them. The Spectators have all the appearances of self-determining beings, one may say; they pursue and achieve ends and know they do. Surely they are free agents, if we (or any beings) are? Intuition may waver.

Certainly conventional Structural-theoretic compatibilism has no reason, I think, to exclude the Spectators from the community of the free. Yet they still seem to lack something quite essential. They have no sense such as we have of what it is to be a free agent. They seem to us to pursue their goals in a strangely unengaged manner.[4] Both these

---

[4] Their children might be more like us, psychologically speaking, with a strong sense of self-governing freedom to act that faded with maturity. Their natural and powerful sense of themselves as truly responsible might contract to a mathematical point as they acceded to an adult understanding of the impossibility of ultimate self-determination as to character and desire, values, preferences, and so on.

things seem to count decisively against their being free agents—though our intuitions about freedom are inherently variable.[5]

12.5 RESTATEMENT

The essential point about the Spectator is simply this: that there can be fully self-conscious purposive agents as complex as we are who cannot be said to be potential free agents (even if we can be) *simply on account of the character of their experiential attitude to things*—on account of their attitude to themselves and their agency, in particular. And their having the experiential attitudes they do cannot be counted as their being subject to any form of psychical constraint.

Thus the Spectator never has the experience of participatory involvement in the mental stages of action-production that we can have— the experience underlying the sense that it is really I who decide and am responsible for my actions. This seems to matter a great deal. Unlike us, she doesn't naturally and involuntarily feel herself to be the decider and animator of action: and she thereby fails to be the decider and animator of action in the right kind of way for her to be a free agent. That she fails can be apparent although we lack a full, positive characterization of what the right kind of way is. She is not 'identified' with the process; she is merely someone who watches an action-producing process—her own—from an internal point of view. She is not a free agent but the—uniquely well placed—observer of a life. Yet at the same time she is correctly said to be an agent, a self-conscious rational agent.[6]

It seems, then, that the Spectator's case raises problems for the *S*-conditions Structural theorist even independently of consideration of the claim that no being can be a free agent that does not believe it is.

---

[5] Those who are generally inclined to reject the view that there are *Attitudinal* conditions on freedom, and generally inclined to sympathize with the view that being a free agent is just a matter of having a certain complexity of agentive and cognitive structure, are particularly vulnerable to the problem discussed in Appendix A—the problem of why exactly it should be thought to be necessary to have any sort of experience *at all*, in order to be a free agent.

[6] On Frankfurt's theory of freedom, it might be thought that the Spectator could be ruled out immediately on purely Structural grounds—on the grounds that she could not form 'second-order volitions', i.e. desires that other, first-order desires that she had should (be such as to) move her to action. But, from the purely Structural-theoretic point of view, she can have (can have the capacity to form) such second-order desires, in just the sense in which she can have first-order desires; it is just that she will be spectatorially detached from them as well. In fact even Nemo can form second-order volitions, in his own impersonal way; for he is possessed of 'mental reflexivity' (9.1), and can thus form desires (and beliefs etc.) about his own desires (and beliefs etc.).

For one does not have to note the Spectator's failure to believe this particular thing, or establish conclusively that she must so fail, in order to describe what it is about her that makes it seem incorrect to say that she is a free agent despite fulfilling the S conditions.

12.6 THE SPECTATOR AND BELIEF IN FREEDOM

Consider her now specifically as an example of someone who fulfils the S conditions but does not have the freedom-necessary belief in her freedom, and who thereby puts in doubt the Objectivists' claim that (x) $(Sx \rightarrow B(x,Fx))$.[7] One way in which the problem comes out is as follows. It seems that the Spectator might cease to be a problem if one could say 'She is really a free agent, but she simply doesn't realize this because of the way she is'. But her not realizing it—if this is how it can be described—appears to prejudice the very existence of the fact that is supposed to be there to be realized or not realized.

Suppose the Objectivists accept the case of the Spectator. They grant that one cannot dismiss her case by saying 'She is a *potential* free agent really, but she is never *actually* free in action simply because she is subject to the permanent constraint of spectatorial detachment'. Having done this, the Objectivists may backtrack, and decide to deny that (x) $(Fx \rightarrow B(x,Fx))$—to deny altogether that believing you are a free agent is a condition of being a free agent. In support of this they may propose the case of a deranged woman who resembles the Spectator in not having any sense of herself as a free agent, but who is none the less a potential free agent (they propose) because her lunacy counts as a

---

[7] Someone might suggest that she could have this belief in some formal or empty, convictionless way. Suppose one conceded this. Then one would have to point out that the relevant requirement is, precisely, that a free agent must believe in its freedom in a way that resembles the way in which we do—as the Spectator does not, even given this concession. It is not merely theoretical, lip-service belief that is in question, but rather a powerful and usually involuntary general experience of oneself as a free agent. It might be thought that such a concession, and such a vague requirement, weaken or at any rate confuse the case. But even if the concession is made, and even if the required degree of conviction is not sharply specifiable, it nevertheless seems clear that the Spectator would fall on the wrong side of the unclear line dividing the imagined convictionless belief in freedom from belief in freedom of the required kind; and, therefore, that someone as complexly capacitied as ourselves (someone who fulfils the S conditions) *can* fall on the wrong side; and this is the claim that matters. Less concessively, one could just as well claim that it does follow from the description of the Spectator's case that she cannot have such a belief in freedom. In fact, all that need be claimed is that someone like her in respect of spectatoriality could *possibly* not have this belief in or experience* of freedom. For here one is considering the Spectator simply as someone who puts in doubt the claim that $(x)(Sx \rightarrow B(x,Fx))$. And this does seem clearly possible.

sychical constraint. These Objectivists admit that in fact one would ot wish to call anyone free who did not believe that he, or she, was ee, but claim that the expression 'potential free agent' may be so nderstood that one may be a *potential* free agent and yet not believe ne is free.

But one can draw a sharp distinction between this lunatic and clear ases of potential free agents subject to constraint. People in prison, ven people suffering from major mental disorders such as obsessional eurosis, normally still believe they are free agents, in a basic sense. hey believe that they are still able to act freely in many respects, lthough subject to constraints, and that they would be able to act eely in many other ways if they were not subject to these constraints. hey are aware* of having the basic and persisting property of being ble to act freely when unconstrained—the property of potential free genthood. They have an immediate, massive, and rarely consciously nspected conviction as to their personal efficacy and complete self-eterminability in the smallest actions, getting up, sitting down, pacing he cell; a conviction as to their control of and responsibility for their ctions, a conviction too immediate and obvious for common ex-ression in private thought or public speech.

The lunatic presently before us lacks this belief altogether, and *ex ypothesi*. She is cast as a lunatic precisely in order to give colour to he idea that she lacks it. It is true that people classed as lunatics can elieve that they are free agents, and that they can do other than they do o, in the strong sense. They can agonize, as Caesar, beside imaginary Rubicons. But the lunatic presently in question is not like this. She has ost the belief altogether. And in so doing, she has moved right out of he class of potential free agents. (She is, if you like, a potential potential ree agent—that is, she is a fully self-conscious being, and in that sense as the mental wherewithal to acquire a conception of herself as capable f being truly responsible for her actions. But as things are she lacks his conception entirely. And so, as things are, she cannot be counted s a potential free agent.) This is simply to reassert the central claim hat believing you are a free agent is a necessary condition of being ne. But to deny it is to allow that a being could correctly be said to hoose and act freely and truly responsibly while having *no* sense or elief that this was so. And this is unacceptable.

Routed through our natural tendency to suppose that to be a fully ledged agent (i.e. an agent of more or less human capacity—for that is ow we sometimes tend to think) just *is* to be a free agent, the con-

nection that is presently being claimed to exist between freedom an
belief in freedom emerges in the following thought: that to lose th
belief in freedom is to cease to be a genuine agent—a true *agent-*
altogether. For if one asks oneself what it would be like to be onesel
and an agent, and yet to have *no* sense or belief that one was a fre
agent, one is likely to find that *one*, the agent, is—not there at all. It i
Christmas, you have ten pounds, and are hesitating between the of
licence and the Oxfam collecting box. But you have *no* sense that yo
are able to choose freely what to do, that it is up to you. But in wha
sense, then, are you, the agent, the rational planner and determiner c
action, really there at all, as an agent?

The claim that belief in freedom is a condition of freedom still seem
to be truly representative of our intuition, then, however indefensibl
it may appear from certain points of view. And so it seems that an
adequate theory of freedom—even a Humean or otherwise com
patibilist one—must take account of it.

12.7 AN INITIAL CONCLUSION

Faced with the Spectator's case, the Structural theorists have to es
tablish either that one can be a free agent while having no sense at a
that this is so, on account of having attitudes like the Spectator's (i.e
on account of failing to fulfil the Integration condition); or that
self-conscious agent's failure to fulfil the Integration condition (and t
have any sense of itself as a free and truly responsible agent) is alway
to be counted as a psychical constraint—a constraint on an agent tha
can be a potential free agent despite the constraint, just in so far as
fulfils the *S* conditions.

Both these alternatives have been rejected. The first involves a direc
contradiction of the principal claim, and no good arguments for givin
it up have been produced yet (the parochiality charge in 12.4 is nc
convincing). The Spectators are united in their rejection of the secon
as unwarrantably anthropocentric.

If these alternatives are indeed incorrect, we may conclude that Ob
jectivists must at least be Attitudinal theorists, even though they wi
never be Subjectivists. They must accept the Integration condition, a
least: one cannot capture what it is to be a free agent (as ordinaril
conceived)   just   by   reference   to   cognitive-and-agentive
structure-specifying conditions like the *S* conditions. The conclusio
is worth pondering: free agenthood cannot consist merely in th

possession of some perhaps as yet undiscovered maximally enabling set of cognitive and practical capacities. For we also require a certain attitude to self and agency, an experiential disposition which it is hard to specify precisely in a positive way, but which the Spectator at any rate does not have.[8] (This is one of those claims that tends to go on changing aspect. On the one hand it can seem rather obvious. On the other hand it can seem necessary to expound it with care, given the recurrent tendency to propose purely capacity-theory or Structural-theoretic definitions of free agenthood.)

One does not have to be convinced by the particular case of the Spectator in order to accept the fundamental point: that free agents must not only have certain general practical and cognitive capacities, but must also see themselves in a certain way; and that an agent's fulfilling the *S* conditions cannot guarantee that it will do this. The point will be debated again in Chapter 14 below. Here something more must be said about Integration.

12.8 THE INTEGRATION CONDITION

At present, Subjectivists and Objectivists agree that it appears to be true that one cannot be a potential free agent and not believe one is free. They disagree about why it appears to be true. Subjectivists assert what Objectivists must deny—that it is true because belief in freedom is a necessary constitutive condition of freedom.

Their dispute takes this form: the Subjectivists claim that the (Objectivist) *S* conditions are not such as to guarantee that anyone who satisfies them will also have the vital belief in freedom. But it does not seem that those who agree with the Subjectivists about this must therefore abandon Objectivism. It seems that they need only claim that the completed set of Objectivist conditions must contain some condition additional to the *S* conditions which is specifiable independently of any mention of belief in freedom but which does (either singly or in conjunction with the *S* conditions) guarantee possession of such belief. In fact there is something ropy about this whole strategy, as will appear; but adopting it is useful for purposes of exposition.

---

[8] It is most implausible to suppose that fulfilment of the Integration condition might be necessarily involved in fulfilment of some as yet unmentioned Structural or capacity condition which could be shown to be independently necessary for freedom. It will be assumed that this is not the case.

Will the Attitudinal condition of Integration do the trick? We need to know more about it. All that has been said so far is that the Spectator subject fails to fulfil it, given the character of her experience; that we as we ordinarily are fulfil it; and that the argument that Integration is necessary for freedom is independent of the argument that belief in one's freedom is necessary for freedom.

In the light of the discussion of the Spectator, one might propose a positive, if crude, characterization of the Integration condition as follows: as complex self-conscious agents, we have both a spectator *aspect* and a desirer *aspect*, although we do not have detached experience of the specifically Spectatorial kind. We have spectator and desirer aspects simply in the following sense: we are all spectator subjects simply in so far as we are fully self-conscious cognitive beings, and are thereby capable, among other things, of (introspective) self-observation, and of ascertaining and expressing to ourselves what we desire, value, believe, and so forth; and we are all desirer subjects simply in so far as we are (self-conscious) desiring beings. (In introducing these two terms, I do not intend to assert anything that is not obvious.)

Given this description, one may say that if *a* is to be free he must not experience or conceive himself, *qua* spectator subject, as separate from himself *qua* desirer subject, in the way that the Spectator does. True, in normal life we may sometimes attain an attitude of complete detachment from particular pro-attitudes and projects that we have— even, it seems, from what we suppose to be our values.[9] But we are most certainly not permanently in such a state with respect to all our desires, pro-attitudes, and so on. The Spectator is. She is permanently and naturally in a state of radical detachment, and is for that reason not a potential free agent, according to the present suggestion. She fails to fulfil the the Attitudinal condition of Integration.

Taking '*a*/*S*' to symbolize '*a* as spectator', and '*a*/*D*' to symbolize '*a* as desirer', one could give an (admittedly very unnatural) representation of the Integration condition as follows: '$E^*(a, a/S = a/D)$': for *a* to be Integrated is for *a* to experience himself, as spectator subject and as desirer subject, as one and the same. One could restate it negatively and more naturally, in English, by saying that *a* must not experience

---

[9] Consider the experience, when reading, of sympathetic identification with fictional or indeed non-fictional characters whose values, aspirations and style of life are very foreign to—and at odds with—one's own; and the experience of reading a book of aphorisms, and seeing a part of truth in points of view that one is ordinarily inclined to reject.

himself as split:[10] for in order to fulfil the Integration condition, he need not have any positive conscious experience of himself as single and double-aspected, as '$E^*(a,a/S = a/D)$' may suggest. He need not think of himself in such terms at all—we don't, and we count as Integrated. More naturally still, one could express a's fulfilment of the Integration condition simply by saying that he, a self-conscious purposive agent, has a sense of himself as a thinking 'mental someone' who has and acts upon pro-attitudes or desires he feels to be his in a way that one can characterize by saying that, for him, their being involved in the determination of the action (citable in true rational explanations of it) *just is* his being so involved.

Stepping back from the present context of argument, it seems clear enough that it is indeed a feature of our ordinary notion of a free agent that any free agent should have some such Integrated self-conception or sense of self. It is indeed a question how thin this Integrated sense of self can become in a being that we would be prepared to call a free agent. But in the Spectator it is too thin—or indeed entirely lacking.

The formula '$E^*(a,a/S = a/D)$' mirrors the least natural form of expression of the condition. It has the advantage of graphic over-articulation, and of answering directly to the problem in the form in which it was raised by the Spectator. I take it that when one is trying to characterize a form-of-experience condition or *attitudinal* condition, one does not have to restrict oneself, in one's representation of the content or nature of the form of experience or attitude, to expressions that can plausibly be supposed to represent directly some possibly explicit thought-content (or, more generally, mentation-content) of the being whose form of experience or attitude it is. One need not suppose that a would naturally come up with the expression 'spectator subject', any more than we would. '$a/S = a/D$' may be apt as a diagrammatic, theoretical representation of a's general experiential set even though a has never actually consciously conceived of himself as having two aspects in this way.[11]

---

[10] i.e. $\neg E^*(a,a/S \neq a/D)$. Even if one preferred to take the Integration condition as negative in this way, as requiring that one lack a certain experiential attitude to oneself, it would still be an Attitudinal condition of freedom, if the Spectator's case is cogent: being an attitudinal condition whose fulfilment is not guaranteed by fulfilment of the S conditions. But a positive characterization of it is not wrong; it is in virtue of actually having some particular sort of general experiential attitude to oneself that the Spectator does not have that one may be a free agent although she cannot be.

[11] Note that even if the experiential attitude attributed by the Integration condition is best not thought of as a propositional-attitude-like representational mental state, many other experiences or experiential attitudes can be said to have veridicality conditions (or apt or accurate representation conditions) just as beliefs have truth-conditions (cf. 11.9).

One could put the point simply as follows: if *a* is a normal human being then his experience of himself (considered as thinker and desirer) *is* Integrated, even if he never expressly thinks of himself *as* Integrated. Or as follows: although he never expressly thinks or conceives of himself as Integrated, he is Integrated, and the property of Integration is attributable to him purely on the basis of the character of his (probably extremely unreflective) general experience of and attitude to himself.

This, then, is one way—one way among others, no doubt—of putting the point about the Spectator.

12.9 AN ATTITUDINAL-THEORETIC POSITION

So much for a positive characterization of the Integration condition. Let '*Int x*' now abbreviate '*x* is Integrated', represented above as '$E^*(x,x/S = x/D)$'; and let '*S'*' be defined as 'fulfils the *S* conditions and the Integration condition'. That is, $(x)(S'x \longleftrightarrow Sx \ \& \ Int \ x)$.

Suppose next that the Objectivists have been converted by the Spectator from being *S*-conditions Structural theorists to being *S'*-conditions Attitudinal theorists (7.3). They now claim that being a free agent is fulfilling the *S* conditions and the Integration condition—that $Cn/(x)(\underline{S'x} \longleftrightarrow Fx)/$. They are still Objectivists, but they have given up the crucial Structural-theoretic claim that if free agenthood is definable at all, then it must ultimately be definable just in terms of possession of some set of cognitive and practical capacities.

If these conditions (*S'*) are indeed constitutively necessary and sufficient for freedom, then it is apparently not true after all that if one is free then one's belief that one is free is part of what makes one free. But it is the case that having a certain form of experience, or attitude to oneself (the having of which is *not* necessarily involved in fulfilling the original *S* conditions), is a necessary constitutive condition of free agenthood.

Have these 'Attitudinal-theoretic' Objectivists now arrived at the correct analysis of free agenthood—given that the compatibilist assumption made in 7.1 still holds (the assumption that the problems posed by non-self-determinability or determinism are not insoluble)? It does indeed seem plausible—though it will be questioned below—that one cannot be an actually acting, intelligent, complex agent, doing what one wants to do, experiencing oneself not only fully self-consciously as a thing that is somehow single just *qua* mental (9.3) but also as Integrated in the present special sense, and not be a fully free agent—if anything ever is, that is.

It may also seem plausible that one could not be all these things and not as a result acquire a belief in (a conviction as to, an invisibly all-pervasive sense* of) one's freedom and true-responsibility-creating self-governing efficacy in action (it may seem plausible that $(x)(S'x \rightarrow B(x,Fx))$). And the Objectivists may claim that this is indeed true, and for causal reasons—because '$Cs/(x)(\underline{S'x} \rightarrow B(x,Fx))/$' is true. They may go on to claim that we have simply mistaken a causal connection for a constitutive or conceptual connection, in asserting that belief in freedom is a necessary constitutive condition of freedom, rather than just an inevitable causal consequence of the real constitutive conditions.

The Subjectivists' response to this will be considered shortly. Here the suggestion that fulfilling the S' conditions may be sufficient for belief in freedom provides an occasion to reconsider the problem deferred in 10.1—the problem allegedly raised by those who are for theoretical reasons sceptical about freedom.

12.10 DETERMINISTS—LIFE AND THEORY

Take philosophers who are incompatibilist determinists and who fulfil the S' conditions. It may be said that they are surely free agents if any of us are. And yet they do not believe that they are free; so belief in freedom is not a condition of freedom.

To this one may first of all reply that it is not clearly true that fulfilling the S' conditions is sufficient for freedom (in fact it will shortly be argued that it is not true). Secondly, more importantly, even if it is true, the trouble with people who have become merely *theoretical* incompatibilist determinists is that they have not really given up their view of themselves as free at all. In practice, they still believe themselves to be free agents. They still naturally experience themselves as free agents.[12] If they were really to succeed in giving up this view of themselves, becoming *genuine* incompatibilist determinists, then their whole view of life, and in particular their whole experience of self and agency, would change quite fundamentally. They would perhaps cease to fulfil the Integration condition: either directly, coming to experience themselves as separate from their desires in the Spectatorial way, or indirectly, ceasing to have any recognizable sense of self at all—like spiritually advanced Buddhists, perhaps, whose personalities are some-

---

[12] For the distinction between 'theoretical' and 'genuine' see e.g. 6.2. All the points made in this section apply equally to genuine as opposed to theoretical 'non-self-determinationists' (defined on p. 60).

how annihilated in nirvana as they slough the 'false view of individuality' (6.6).

It may now be objected that if we grant that belief in freedom is a
condition of freedom we may have to say that a man who succeeds
in becoming a 'genuine' incompatibilist determinist thereby becomes
unfree, and yet was free (if indeed anyone is ever free) for so long as he
remained unable to give up his view of himself as a truly self-governing
agent; as if it were not the case that he had simply struggled successfully
to bring his natural and spontaneously arising attitudes to self and
agency into line with what he already saw to be the case theoretically
speaking, but, rather, had in so doing changed what was the case—and
had lost his soul, or rather his freedom, for an idea.

Two points suffice by way of reply to this. First, that this dramatic
change from possessing to lacking true responsibility can occur just as
a result of losing a belief only if we really are free and truly responsible
agents in the first place. If we are not, then no such dramatic change
takes place, and so the present problem does not arise.

Second, Subjectivists who claim that we are indeed free and truly
responsible agents may see the present objection—that what is the case
will change with change in (genuine) belief—as a positive advantage of
their position, and maintain as strongly as ever the claim that belief in
freedom is a constitutive condition of freedom. Those for example who
are sympathetic to Strawson's position in 'Freedom and Resentment',
and think that the phenomenon of non-rational commitment to the
personal-, moral-, and self-reactive attitudes he discusses is nothing less
than partly constitutive of the fact of freedom, in so far as it is a fact at
all, may be entirely willing to acknowledge that the incompatibilist
determinist may actually lose his freedom when his initially merely
theoretical belief in the impossibility of freedom gives way to a genuine
and total conviction as to its impossibility. For his formation of this
conviction may take him right out of the 'general framework' of ordinary interpersonal and intrapersonal attitudes. Further support for
this view will be provided by the discussion of the Genuine Incompatibilist Determinist in 14.8.

13

The Natural Epictetans

The Objectivists have been persuaded to accept the Attitudinal condition of Integration.[1] They may now face this worry: is it true that the S' conditions, i.e. the original S-conditions plus the Integration condition, are jointly sufficient for freedom? And, in particular, is it true that they guarantee possession of belief in freedom?

It would seem not. Imagine an enormously congenial world, and imagine—it is perhaps not easy to do so—a race of gifted, active creatures who fulfil the S' conditions but who are never undecided in any way; who never hesitate in any way about what to do; who never consciously deliberate about what ends to pursue, or about how to pursue them—having no need to; and who always succeed in doing what they want to do. It seems likely that the notion of freedom will have very little content for them, and that they may have no identifiable explicit* belief that they are free, such as we have, although they always do what they want to do, in a way that many take to be central to, if not sufficient for, actual freedom.[2]

One could call them pure natural Epictetans—never failing, never disappointed in their congenial world, always able to do what they

---

[1] Some of them recant in ch. 14, where the whole debate is recapitulated in different terms.

[2] They may have second-order desires, and what Frankfurt calls second-order volitions—desires that their first-order desires be such that they move or will or would move them to act, all of which are satisfied. It may be objected (1) that one could not possibly be fully self-conscious or capable of language-like thought unless one were a member of a socially interactive community, (2) that one simply could not have such effortless agency in such a community. But there is no very good reason to accept either (1) or (2). There are many ways of developing the story of the natural Epictetans that I will not consider. (One might for example suppose that the natural Epictetans are totally mentally 'transparent' to each other; or that they never need to co-operate—and are incapable of having conflicting interests; or that they are adults who live totally solitary lives, and evolve slowly into the state described.)

want to do because always wanting to do only what they are able to do.[3] Their experience is quite radically unlike ours. But they are not like the Spectator subject; the strangeness of their experience does not derive from a failure to fulfil the Integration condition.

They are fully able to choose in the sense defined in 8.2, but they never hesitate at all. They never ponder alternatives. One might say that they do not attach any sense to 'I could do otherwise'; or no freedom-connected sense. It has no place in their 'language-games'—or nothing like the place it has in ours. For it moves nothing connected with the notions of—or with a sense of—freedom and responsibility. It has no force for them as something vitally expressive of part of what is centrally involved in freedom.

Given their capacities, they are almost always capable of acting otherwise than they do in fact act; and they are, we may suppose, capable of the thought 'I could do otherwise'. But they never in fact think such a thought. And even if some of them, musing philosophically, were to think it, it would have no relations for them with the notion or experience of difficult pondered choice; for they do not know what it is to make such a choice. It would have no more import for them than either 'I have such and such capabilities' or 'I might have been, or wanted, otherwise'. In a way, they are like 'genuine' incompatibilist determinists.[4] And—this is the present point—they are like this simply because of the nature of their experience of agency. To presume that any being that fulfils the S' conditions must have experience of agency similar to ours is just unwarrantable anthropocentricity—or lack of imagination.

The pure natural Epictetans, then, are never in a situation in which they think 'I could have done A (could do A), if it had not been (were not) the case that C'—experiencing external constraint; nor, even more important, are they ever in a situation in which they might think 'I could do A, and I could do B, and I can't do both, so which shall I do?' —experiencing indecision. (They are no doubt cognitively speaking capable of thinking these things; but, given the automatic natural Epictetan nature of their volition, they never do so in fact.) In one way, as already noted, it seems that they enjoy all the freedom it is possible

---

[3] I have in mind Epictetus' injunction to adapt one's desires to one's circumstances, so that one is never frustrated by them. The name 'Epictetan' becomes more appropriate as certain features of the description are varied.

[4] Incompatibilist determinists who have fully comprehended the all-embracing nature of determinism without making the mistake of fatalism. See 6.2 and 12.10.

for a human—or any—being to have. But there seems to be a sense in which they do not enjoy freedom at all, because they do not properly know what freedom is.

For they are, with respect to the freedom they enjoy, like creatures that have ears, but live in a completely silent world. Although these creatures experience total silence (they hear it in the sense that we can be said to hear it), we may wish to say that they do not know what silence is. And if they do not know what it is, there is a sense in which they do not and cannot experience it as we who know noise can and do. Similarly, sighted sentients living in a lightless world may have no concept of darkness (or of light, or colour). Living in a uniformly blue world (with no differences of shade resulting from shadow or distance) they may have no concept of blue, or of other colours.

But what exactly is one to make of this? If one takes two things A and B (such as freedom and unfreedom) which contrast in such a way that there is either A or B but not both (A *aut* B), the complete lack of B should not have as consequence that there is no A. On the contrary; there is nothing but A. What may lack in such a case, however, is any experience of the contrast between A and B. And this may lead, as above, to lack of any explicit awareness or conception either of A or of B.

But why should lack of explicit awareness of A be supposed to have as a consequence lack of A itself, as lack of any sense or conception of freedom seems to have as a consequence lack of freedom itself? Well, that is the question. But it does seem to be so.[5] (Recall that 'free' is interchangeable with 'truly responsible', in its present use.) One cannot blithely say that the natural Epictetans just are free (or truly responsible), and that, should they come to know it, it would be a standard case of a belief being formed in such a way as to represent or reflect the already existing belief-independent fact. That is not true to our sense of how things are. There seems to be a sense in which the natural Epictetans are not free or truly responsible agents at all: precisely because—it is natural to put it in this paradoxical way—they don't have a proper grasp of the fact that they are.

The problem does not concern morality. The problem is not that they are non-moral beings, although it is presently supposed that they are. For, first, moral agenthood is not necessary for free agenthood, and, second, while experience of moral indecision may be very im-

---

[5] Compare the fact that Adam and Eve, when innocent, were not and could not be good.

portant to our sense of ourselves as free, the present point about the natural Epictetans is that they lack experience of indecision *tout court*, not just experience of specifically moral indecision. Connectedly, they lack any strong positive sense of themselves as negotiating a network of alternative possibilities.

13.2 ELABORATION

It certainly seems possible that the natural Epictetans should have no sense of freedom or true responsibility for their actions, given this description of their case. And, this being so, one may simply stipulate that they do not. For what matters is simply that the case be possible—that, logically possibly, $(\exists x)(S'x \,\&\, \neg B(x,Fx))$. But it is worth trying to describe it further.

One could say that in the case of the natural Epictetans the notion of freedom lacks essential contrastive grounding in at least two different forms of experience (these are in any case well worth distinguishing, so far as the human phenomenology of freedom is concerned):

(1) the experience of constraint, coercion and inability,

and

(2) the experience of indecision, of having to choose between alternatives.

It lacks grounding in experience of particular cases of (1a) not being able to do what one wants to do, because constrained in some way, and (1b) being unable to do other than one does do, for the same reason; and particular cases of (2) indecision, arising from some conflict of motives. The claim about (1) may be compared with the compatibilist view that the notion of freedom of action is to be expounded and understood principally by reference to the contrast in which it stands to the notion of checks and constraints on action. It seems plausible to say that since the natural Epictetans are *ex hypothesi* subject to none of these checks and constraints, they lack the basic experience of contrast in the light of which alone even the weak compatibilist notion of freedom can take on any appreciable experiential substance. Below, however, it will be suggested that (1) is insufficient for a fully fledged notion of oneself as a free (and truly responsible) agent, and that it is (2) that is vital if either is.[6]

This may yet be doubted. It may be objected that the Epictetans do

[6] Below in 14.2 the 'neo-Epictetans' suggest that (2) is not vital either.

in a clear sense know that they are free, just in so far as, unconstrained, they do what they want to do and know they do. But, clear or not, the sense in which they know they are free (truly responsible) agents seems just like the sense in which the inhabitants of the silent world know their world is a silent world. It is an insufficient sense.

It may next be suggested that as fully self-conscious agents they must at least be able to *conceive* of doing otherwise, of constraint, and even of experiencing indecision; whereas the inhabitants of the silent world cannot conceive of noise at all. It may be suggested that ability to conceive of the possibility of indecision, and indeed of choice-out-of-indecision, or at least grasp of the notion of options being open to one, is somehow constitutive of being such that one is truly capable of acting intentionally for self-ascribable reasons, as the Epictetans are by definition. But one may grant this (though one may also dispute some of it). For—to take one of the above suggestions—it is most implausible to claim that possession of the mere ability to conceive of difficult choice or indecision, without any actual experience of such choice or indecision, nor even any actual thought about the possibility of it, either intrinsically involves or necessarily yields anything that could suffice to provide the kind of belief in or experience* of freedom and true responsibility that we appear to require of potential free agents.

Notice, furthermore, that the present argument does not need to prove that such a conception of indecision cannot possibly be of any importance for the Epictetans. It need only show that it can possibly not be of any importance: it need only show either that, if they do entertain the conception, it may have no sense-of-freedom-founding importance for them, or that they may never have any actual thoughts about indecision at all.[7] And this is surely a clear possibility: such beings, having no natural occasion, may never formulate the possibility of indecision at all. They are not speculative creatures. They are without anxiety. Never having had conflicting desires, never having experienced indecision, an Epictetan will never actually *deploy* its general conception of itself as capable of doing many different things in the thought that it is now able to do other than what it is now about to do, in such a way as to encounter the strong, immediate sense of open choice that is so central to our lives.

[7] It is not necessary to establish a strong conclusion to the effect that the description implies 'not possibly *p*', but only to show that it implies 'possibly not *p*', and, perhaps, 'probably not *p*'.

One could say that the question of whether or not the Epictetans ever actually entertain any thought of the possibility of doing otherwise, or of indecision, is not particularly important. What is important is whether they ever *dwell* on these things, whether they ever matter to them in a certain way. And it is a consequence of the description of their case that these things do not matter to them, and that they have no reason to dwell on them. (I doubt whether we can fully imagine what such resistlessness would be like.) The natural Epictetans know— if they care to think about it—that they produce the actions they produce, that they are causally responsible for them in that sense. But, knowing this, they still lack any kind of strong, freedom-connected sense (such as we normally have) of themselves as truly responsible for the actions.[8]

Consider the following addition to the description of the natural Epictetans: if a natural Epictetan were subjected to constraint, so that it found itself unable to do what it had until that moment wanted to do, then it would by virtue of the *immediate Epictetan reflex* always immediately cease to want to do what it found itself unable to do. All natural Epictetans possess this reflex. So they can never be frustrated. (Here the epithet 'natural Epictetan' becomes more appropriate.)

If the natural Epictetans live out their lives in this way, then they cannot really be free agents. For there is something vital that we know about, given the way in which we experience things, which forms no part of their lives. They do not know what true responsibility is (it seems like a simple case of not knowing). But if they do not know what it is, then they cannot know it in the sense of possessing it. They cannot possess it because they do not know what it is.[9] They are not 'condemned' to freedom in Sartre's sense.[10]

---

[8] Indeed they may, by our emotional and conative lights, have no strong sense of self at all.

[9] Even if the freedom that a natural Epictetan is said not to know about is something impossible (as can seem obvious), it can still be true that there is something which is of enormous importance to us which it does not know about life: it does not know what it is to experience* freedom. And, this being so, it cannot possibly be a potential free agent. One could say that to be free in such a way that one doesn't even know that one is is the truest freedom of all. M. Frayn says this about liberty: "the *sense* of liberty is a message read between the lines of constraint. Real liberty is as transparent, as odourless and tasteless, as water" (*Constructions* § 85). In a way this is very plausible, but the other thought remains undiminished, given the present concern with freedom in the sense of true responsibility: not to have any sense* of freedom at all is not to be free at all.

[10] No doubt they would have great difficulty in imagining what it is like to be us; and, like the Spectators, they may be said to have, *in a sense*, a more correct view of things than we do, not being enthralled by the illusion of true responsibility. Unlike the

Here is one simple way in which we might try to imagine something of what it is like to be a natural Epictetan. What it is like for them all the time is something like what it is like for us when we are involved in doing something that we entirely unproblematically want to do, and that there is only one way of doing, and that we can do without any difficulty; something that involves performing a long sequence of simple intentional actions with regard to which we have no sort of thought that there might be alternative ways of doing them. Here there can be a strange resistlessness, no consciousness of choice or indecision. One should try to imagine everything being like that. But it may be that if one does then one's sense of self will start to thin out in a dramatic way.[11]

13.3 HINDRANCES AND INDECISION

The Objectivists are still trying to give a statement of the conditions of free agenthood that does not contravene the principle of independence, but which is none the less such that one's fulfilment of the conditions guarantees that one believes one is free. And their question is now this: given that the natural Epictetans do not count as free and truly responsible agents, although they fulfil the S' conditions, and given that one cannot simply add a separate belief-in-freedom condition, what can one add to the description of the natural Epictetans in order to make it overwhelmingly likely—or indeed inevitable—that they will believe they are (experience themselves as) free?

A condition relating to ($1a$) and ($1b$) in 13.2 above, and requiring

Spectators, however, they are not free from this illusion (if that is the word for it) on account of cold supersophistication, or intense, millennially prolonged dwelling on the impossibility of self-determination, but rather on account of the immediate circumstances of their agency.

[11] Unsurprisingly—it is essentially bound in with the sense of freedom. Some of Krishnamurti's remarks about the nature of advanced states of spiritual detachment are interesting in this connection: "You do not choose, you do not decide when you see things very clearly; then you act which [sic] is not the action of will. . . ." "Only the unintelligent mind exercises choice in life. . . . A truly intelligent [i.e. spiritually advanced] man can have no choice, because his mind can be aware of what is true, and can thus only choose the path of truth. It simply cannot have choice. Only the unintelligent mind has free will" (quoted in *Krishnamurti: the Years of Fulfilment*, by M. Lutyens, pp. 33, 204). S. Bellow has a related thought in his novel *Humboldt's Gift*, p. 140: "In the next realm, where things are clearer, clarity eats into freedom. We are free on earth because of cloudiness, because of error, because of marvellous limitation. . . ." See also nn. 9 and 10 above. Spinoza takes the opposite view. Cf. S. Hampshire in 'Spinoza and the Idea of Freedom', pp. 198 f.

that they have experience of constraint, or inability, would be inadequate. As regards (1*a*): on finding themselves unable to do what they wish to do on account of some constraint, the natural Epictetans will by virtue of the immediate Epictetan reflex always automatically cease to want to do what they find (or believe) they cannot do, and continue to fail actually to have or dwell on the thought 'I could have done A, if it had not been for C', in continuing always to do what they want to do, unregretting and unfrustrated. Similarly, as regards (1*b*), they will always automatically come to want to do what they cannot but do— true Epictetans in this.[12] And it is what actual thoughts and experiences they have, and their attitude to them, that matters, not what they are capable of thinking or conceiving given their cognitive make-up.

Suppose, contrary to hypothesis, that they do experience constraint, and that they do have thoughts of the form 'I could have done A, if it had not been for C'; and suppose further that the experience of such constraint does serve as a contrastive foil against which other, unconstrained actions are experienced by them aş free—as free = unhindered.[13] One could express this by saying that this gives them a certain kind of experience of being able to *act* freely (i.e. of being unhindered in action), as opposed to being able to *choose* freely. But it doesn't seem that this advances them much. For then what they still vitally lack is any kind of experience of being able to choose freely—of being free in and hence truly responsible for, choice.

This is a fundamental distinction. Having the presently imagined sort of freedom = unhinderedness in action, they need never be undecided in any way. They can still lack a source in their experience for any vivid free = can-choose-otherwise experience. And this seems essential to belief in freedom of the kind we require of a free agent. One could say that the natural Epictetans point up a contrast between freedom of choice and, not the no-choice of (1) coercion and constraint, but the no-choice of (2) simply never being in any way undecided as to what to do. It seems that it is not at all (1), the experience of lack of hindrance in action, but rather (2), the experience of pre-action indecision, that is

---

[12] This may make them sound unprincipled; but Epictetus was not unprincipled. Furthermore, they live in an extremely congenial world in which they are never in fact so constrained that they cannot but do what they do—let alone constrained in such a way that they cannot but do something they might consider unpleasant. What might happen to them in a less congenial world is not of present concern.

[13] This is a further supposition. They could have thoughts of the form mentioned without ever so experiencing their actions, as free = unhindered.

important. (1) alone, attributed to them here, is not sufficient for the sense of freedom we require of free agents; nor is it necessary.[14]

It is a further question whether (2) is necessary, or sufficient; in the next chapter it will be considered and rejected as the missing Attitudinal condition of freedom (the condition that needs to be added to the S' conditions so far proposed).

Although the natural Epictetans are never undecided, there is of course a clear sense in which they do take decisions, since they are rational agents, responding variously to circumstances in complex ways, beings who actually act and who are, precisely, never undecided. But decision is not something they ever apply themselves to in any way. It is not something they live through or dwell on or notice as such. Decision does not issue from previous indecision. It is not a resolution or conclusion of anything. For they are, precisely, never undecided. Perhaps their world is much less complicated than ours. But it need not be.[15] It remains true that their deciding is effortlessly smooth. Crucially, they never wonder or worry 'Which (action) shall I perform?'

Perhaps the concept of freedom presently under consideration is in some way parochial in excluding the natural Epictetans from the community of the free. But although the intuition behind the concept may waver under the various pressures of varying speculation, it does not go away. The central point is simply this: that not all fully self-conscious, Integrated, rational agents have to experience agency in the way that we do (just as not all of them have to have the sort of experience of self

[14] A creature that was never undecided as to what to do might experience freedom = unhinderedness of action in unconstrained circumstances solely as a result of the contrast afforded to such free = unhindered action by experience of hindering constraints in other circumstances. And, lacking the immediate Epictetan reflex, it might experience hindrance in doing what it wanted to do and think 'I could do (have done) A if it were not (had not been) for C'. It might even reason as follows: 'Since I cannot do A, I will do B'; or again, thinking ahead, 'If I cannot do A, I will do B'. But, thinking these things and these things only, it need never have any strong experience* of freedom of *choice* between two alternatives, nor any sense of true responsibility for choice. For it is still never undecided, and always knows immediately what it will do if it cannot do what it provisionally most wants to do. Trying and failing to do A need never provoke any problem about *what to do*. Thus it may experience the freedom of doing what it wants to do, given the contrast with hindrances, and yet never have any sense or experience* of freedom in choosing what it wants to do—any experience* of freedom in choosing *out of indecision*. This being so, it can simply fail to conceive of itself as a free agent in the required way.

[15] They may be extraordinarily intelligent, and find the complexity simple. If God existed, and were an agent, perhaps his experience of agency would be rather like a natural Epictetan's.

that we do). There is simply no such thing as *the* experience of agency of self-conscious rational agents. There can be great variety in such experience, and it is extremely important to take account of this variety when free agenthood is in question, for there are apparently limits on what a free agent's experience can be like.

Even those who are not sure what to make of the Spectator subject and the natural Epictetans may be prepared to accept that a being could be a fully self-conscious, Integrated, rational agent and yet not experience its agency in such a way that we would be inclined to say that it was, or could be, a free, truly responsible agent. And this is the crucial claim. (Further support for this claim is offered in 14.3, and again in 14.8, by reference to the 'Genuine Incompatibilist Determinist'.)

To conclude. A potential free agent is defined as an agent of such a kind that it is correctly said to act freely and truly responsibly just so long as it acts free from constraint. (The problem posed for freedom by determinism and non-self-determinability is still shelved.) The natural Epictetans are not potential free agents. For although they do regularly act free from constraint (as originally described, they always do so), they cannot be said to act freely simply because they are not aware*, in the right kind of way, of being free agents. They fulfil the S' conditions, but they still lack a necessary *attitude* to themselves.[16]

---

[16] Some may still be struck by the fact (remarked in 13.1) that the natural Epictetans are in a way as free as any agent could ever possibly be; and they may still be unsure about the appropriateness of placing any attitudinal (or Attitudinal) conditions on free agenthood at all. But it should be remembered that 'free' is in its present use interchangeable with 'truly responsible'; and the threat to theories that dismiss experiential or attitudinal conditions as unimportant that was described in Appendix A should also be borne in mind.

14

The Experience of Ability to Choose

During the discussion of the natural Epictetans it was suggested that it was (*a*), experience of oneself as able to *choose* freely, which was specifically connected to the experience of indecision, rather than (*b*), experience of oneself as able to *act* freely, in the sense of experience of being unhindered in action, that was vital to (*c*), experience* of freedom *tout court*. And although the principal claim of Part III, that experience* of freedom is necessary for freedom, remains quite general, it will be useful during this chapter to concentrate on experience of oneself as able to choose freely. That is, experience of oneself as able to choose in such a way that one is truly responsible for one's actions: the word 'free' is still being understood in its ordinary, strong, true-responsibility-entailing sense.

In fact, one could take (*a*), experience of ability to choose freely, as simply equivalent to (*c*), experience* of freedom *tout court*. For

(1) (*c*) is either (*a*) or (*b*): experience* of freedom *tout court* just is experience of oneself either as able to *act* freely and truly responsibly or as able to *choose* freely and truly responsibly.

But

(2) (*b*) necessarily involves (*a*): one cannot in fact experience oneself as (*b*) able to act freely, *in the present strong sense* (i.e. as able to act truly responsibly, and not merely as able to act unhindered and unconstrained in one's action), unless one also experiences oneself as (*a*) able to choose freely.

For

(3) to experience oneself as able to act freely, in the present strong sense, is to experience oneself as something from which actions flow in such a way that one is truly responsible for them. It is, in other words, to have experience that must involve possession of *some* sort of apprehension of oneself as a being engaged in, or capable of engaging in, the mental business of determining on

one action or another, i.e., of *choosing* one action or another. It is true that self-conscious rational agents are capable of the strangest ideas—just look at us all. But what else could we intelligibly suppose to underlie true responsibility for actions, other than some such mental business of choosing, or deciding or determining on, particular actions?

So

(4) (*c*) is effectively equivalent to (*a*): experience* of freedom and experience of oneself as able to choose freely may be taken to be interchangeable terms for the purposes of this argument.

The conclusion of this chapter will be that the Subjectivist claim that experience* of freedom is a necessary constitutive condition of free agenthood must be accepted. To this extent, it is the crucial chapter. The discussion is involved in places, and needs a certain amount of preparation. I begin with some points of terminology.

A. '*Fa*' will stand indiscriminately for '*a* is a (potential) free agent' and '*a* is a (potential) free chooser'. Experience* of ability to choose freely may be the particular topic of discussion, but it is merely one (crucial) aspect of the experience* of freedom considered quite generally.

B. The discussion will henceforth be conducted almost entirely in terms of experience* (and awareness*) of freedom, not in terms of belief in freedom. This seems useful because constraints on what are acceptable as specifications of the content of certain sorts of experiences[1] seem to be essentially and usefully looser than constraints on specifications of the content of beliefs: to require that one be aware* of or experience oneself as free is perhaps to require only that one's experience have a certain general form, not that one have some explicit* particular belief that one is free.[2]

Such experience or awareness is nevertheless still conceived as involving a putatively objective-state-of-affairs-representing mental state, and, in particular, as involving a representational state given which problems concerning the principle of independence can still arise: one is still concerned with the question 'What are the conditions of pos-

---

[1] Or—to look at it the other way round—constraints on the attribution-conditions of experiences with a given content-specification.

[2] The notion of explicit* belief is still not entirely clear. Some—such as those who think that attribution of beliefs or experiences is simply a matter of making sense of behaviour—may well consider the substitution of 'experiences(*)' for 'believes' to be a move without much substance.

session of a certain property (freedom)?', and with the thought that a necessary condition of possessing the property is somehow or other representing to oneself (or being aware* or experiencing*) that one possesses it. Somehow or other: one is *not* concerned with detailed phenomenology of freedom of the sort to be found in Chapters 3 and 6, for example (on this point see 11.9).

C. I speak sometimes simply of 'experience* of freedom (or indecision, or . . .)'. But it will always be fully self-conscious experience that is in question, unless the contrary is explicitly stated—fully self-conscious experience that is (notionally and relationally, or *NR*) *of oneself* as free (or undecided, or . . .).

This can matter; for when 'experience* of indecision' means 'experience* (*NR*) of oneself as undecided' it may be thought to be plausible to say that experience* of indecision at a particular time is sufficient for the fundamental experience of self as able to choose freely that we seem to require of free agents. Whereas if 'experience* of indecision' is taken as it stands, as not implying self-consciousness, it seems very plausible to say that Fido and Nemo can, although unselfconscious, have vivid experience* of indecision (cf. 8.3) and yet have no such experience* of freedom as we require of free agents. Throughout, then, it is specifically self-conscious experience (*NR*) of oneself as this or that which is of concern. The same goes for all the other words that will be used more or less interchangeably with 'experience*'—'awareness*', 'apprehension*', 'consciousness*', 'grasp*', 'sense*', and so on. (As remarked in 8.2, the '*' superscript is used only when it is necessary to cancel the 'success verb' implications of these words.)

D. It will be supposed that an experience, or rather a *form* of experience, can be understood to be a stable and continuous feature of one's mental make-up, in at least the way in which a belief can be, and that it can like a belief be said to be not necessarily occurrent. This is partly contrary to natural usage, according to which all experience, unlike all belief, is necessarily occurrent. But this way of speaking will be adopted none the less. As remarked, one's experience can be said to have a certain, persisting general form; and it is principally this that is presently in question. What must be permanent in a being that is a potential free agent is a standing, practico-intellectual (not merely cognitive) experience, conception, sense, or apprehension* of itself as a being that is free. It is experience* of freedom in this sense that is represented by '$E^*(a,Fa)$'; it is a *form* of experience, a fixed *conception* of or attitude to self that underlies particular experiences, that is in question.

Taking '*Con*' to symbolize 'conceives (that)', one could substitute '*Con*(*x,Fx*)' for '*B*(*x,Fx*)', rather than '*E**(*x,Fx*)', as here; and this might seem better, in so far as one can naturally attribute a permanent or dispositional conception of something to someone, but not such an experience of something. I shall however continue to use the term—the term of art—'*E**', or 'experience(*)'; firstly because 'conception', like 'belief', has narrowly cognitivistic implications that are worth playing down (11.9); secondly because the discussion will at various points be principally about *occurrent* experience* of freedom (and its relation to experience of indecision, say), and using a single term will help to mark clearly the connection between such occurrent experience* of freedom and the correlative non-occurrent, general experience-or-conception of oneself as free.[3]

I am not sure how far one can move away from the strongly cognitivistic notion of a belief state while remaining within the bounds of the notion of a representational state which is of such a kind that it makes sense to talk of its contravening the principle of independence. (Such talk requires the applicability of the notion either of truth-conditions, or of veridicality-conditions, or at least of correct-(or apt-) representation conditions. But it seems useful to try to work with vaguer notions than the notion of belief as ordinarily understood.)[4]

In what follows there is continual movement from talk about experience* or awareness* of being *actually* able to choose (or choose freely) *at a particular place and time* to talk about experience* or awareness* or conception or grasp* of oneself as being *generally considered* a thing of a sort that is able to choose (or choose freely)—as *potentially* able to choose (freely). The former sort of experience—experience* of being, now, able to choose (or choose freely)—will be occurrent.[5] The latter sort can be occurrent or non-occurrent. For one can be credited with a general experience/conception of oneself as potentially able to choose (or choose freely) even when one is not consciously so experiencing* or conceiving of oneself; and one can also consciously and

---

[3] '*Con*(*x,Fx*)' could be said to express in its dispositional aspect something that '*E**(*x, Fx*)' expresses in its occurrent aspect. But the single term '*E**' will be used nevertheless. The compound word 'experience/conception' will also be used: a being's experience can have a certain general form, and one can capture part of what is involved in a being's having experience of the kind required of a potential free agent by saying that its actual (necessarily occurrent) *experience* must be informed by its possession of some sort of *conception* (or idea, or sense) of itself (grasped self-consciously as itself) as a free agent.

[4] Nothing much hangs on this, ultimately. Later on the original formulation in terms of belief will be returned to. Those who are uncertain about this formulation in terms of experience may read '*B*' for '*E**'. Cf. ch.1, n.18.

[5] Or at least explicit+—see 8.2.

occurrently so experience* or conceive of oneself. The two sorts of experience, of oneself as actually and as potentially able to choose (or choose freely), are quite bound up in one another. For what is it to conceive of oneself as potentially able to choose (choose freely)? It is, precisely, to conceive of oneself as being such that one can be actually able to choose (or choose freely) at particular times and places. None the less they are distinct, and although they will not always be distinguished in the following, there will be a point to talking sometimes specifically of the one, sometimes specifically of the other.

E. It should perhaps be stated once again that the experience* of freedom that will be in question is of freedom conceived in the ordinary strong sense. It is experience* of oneself as a truly responsible being. It is experience which rests on one's possessing a conception or sense of oneself that is probably best illustrated by reference to those who believe they are *moral* agents, although it seems that one does not in fact have to be a moral agent to possess it (3.3): in moral agents, possession of the self-conception in question is inextricably bound up with possession of a conception of self as capable of being truly deserving of moral praise and blame for one's actions. Most people have a very clear sense indeed of what it is to have such a conception of self. Indeed most people actually have such a conception.

F. Finally by way of preparation, recall briefly a point about determinism. In Chapter 7 the search was begun for something that distinguishes us from dogs (and Nemo) in respect of freedom. It was observed that even if determinism does have something essential to do with freedom, it cannot have anything essential to do with the question of what if anything distinguishes us from dogs in respect of freedom, since we are all equally determined if determinism is true. The problem of determinism was thus put on one side. It is still on one side; the discussion still proceeds upon the no doubt false but useful compatibilist assumption that determinism (or non-self-determinability) may pose no problem for freedom. This allows one to attempt to give necessary and sufficient conditions of ability to choose freely, or potential free agenthood, on the understanding that if determinism (non-self-determinability) does pose a problem for these things then the proposed conditions are at best only necessary conditions.

I hope that the symbolic formulae employed below to express the various possible positions will both prove useful to those who are familiar with such things and be ignorable without loss by those who dislike them.

14.2 EXPERIENCE OF INDECISION

To return now to the question raised at the end of the last chapter. What is the further condition of potential free agenthood? The case of the natural Epictetans was intended to show that the S' conditions (12.9) need supplementation: i.e., that it is not true that to be a fully self-conscious, Integrated rational agent just is to be a potential free agent (not true that $Cn/(x)(\underline{S'x} \leftrightarrow Fx)/$). The enquiry is still guided by the Objectivist wish to specify necessary and sufficient (constitutive) conditions of freedom which, while they do not include experience* of (or belief in) freedom, nevertheless in some way guarantee its presence. For there still seems to be reason both to deny that experience* of freedom is a constitutive condition of freedom—in order to respect the principle of independence—and to suppose that it is *some* sort of necessary condition of freedom.

The current suggestion is that the missing necessary condition is that the agent have a further kind of experience: experience* of indecision in deliberation. The suggestion is that such experience* of indecision is crucial because it is crucial to experience* of freedom. It seems that it is precisely because they lack any sort of experience* of indecision that the natural Epictetans lack experience* of freedom.

Well, what of this suggestion? One may first of all note that there is a clear sense in which experience* of indecision is always experience of indecision. What seems, is, in this case. One may be so hypnotized that (1) one cannot but decide to do X, and yet (2) not know this, and experience indecision. Although in one sense one would in this case already be decided (being unable to decide otherwise), yet one would oneself genuinely be undecided, and genuinely be experiencing indecision—there is a paramount sense of 'undecided' according to which it suffices, for one to be in the objective state of being undecided, that one experience* indecision.

The same is not true of experience* of freedom: what seems, need not be. One might be so hypnotized that (1) one could not but do X, and yet (2) not know this, being so hypnotized that one still experienced oneself as able to choose freely between X and Y. Here one would not be able to choose freely, although one so experienced* oneself.

The asterisk is therefore superfluous in the phrase 'experience* of indecision'. But appealing to experience of indecision as a condition of freedom raises several problems. It seems too restrictive; and there are problems about occurrence—about the occurrentness of experience:

must the putative free agent merely have experienced indecision at some time, or must it experience it whenever it acts freely (if it ever does), or what?

It is not obvious that either of these things is necessary. For it seems that while creatures exactly like the natural Epictetans in not experiencing indecision *might* not have any sense of being free in and truly responsible for their choices, it is not the case that they *could* not do so; nor that they could not because they had never actually experienced indecision. It seems that there might be creatures—the 'neo-Epictetans'—who were exactly like the natural Epictetans except precisely for the fact that they did experience themselves as free and truly responsible agents and choosers, even though they had never actually experienced indecision.[6] In which case actual experience of indecision is not necessary for experience* of freedom, even if it is sufficient. It is difficult to see how one could rule out the neo-Epictetans a priori, as one would have to.

It may be suggested that (1) consciousness* of freedom to choose, essentially involves (2), consciousness* of the possibility of doing otherwise than one does. But even if (1) does entail (2), as it seems to, one cannot by appeal to this show that (3), experience of indecision, is after all necessary to (1). For it would seem that one may be (2) explicitly conscious* of the possibility of doing otherwise than one does, without (3) having or having had any sort of experience of indecision. Consider ourselves, in particular cases; and again, more decisively, the neo-Epictetans.[7]

Is experience of indecision, although not necessary, sufficient? Again there are problems about occurrence. A creature might have experienced indecision in the past, and might, indeed, have experienced itself as free at that time, but, after several millennia of natural Epictetan life, have completely forgotten about it, having become just like the natural Epictetans so far as its experience of self and agency was concerned. If so, experience of indecision at some time or other is not only not necessary, it is not sufficient either.

The present suggestion seems misguided. The natural Epictetans do

---

[6] The conclusion as to whether or not the natural Epictetans had experience* of freedom—call this *p*—was only of the form 'Possibly not *p*', not of the form 'Not possibly *p*'.

[7] Who suggest, in addition, that it is not even true that experience* of freedom involves the *possibility* of experience of indecision: given their possession of the 'immediate Epictetan reflex' (13.2), experience of indecision is impossible for them as they are.

not experience themselves as free, and their case prompts the attempt to isolate some further continuously instantiated property of agents, in order to be able to say that it is partly by virtue of possession of this property that an agent may be such that it presently experiences or continuously conceives of itself as free, and may therefore possibly be a free agent. But the experience of indecision is not what is wanted, although in the context of the natural Epictetans it seems very important. For it is occurrent or it is nothing, and it can't be permanent occurrent experience of indecision that is necessary for experience* of freedom.

Still, if one did permanently experience oneself as undecided about what to do, would this not be sufficient for correspondingly permanent experience of oneself as free? Well, it is surely true that experience of indecision at some time could give rise to a standing conception/experience* of freedom (given that one fulfilled the S' conditions). But is it also true that a being could not actually have experience of indecision about what to do at some time—fully self-conscious experience of itself as undecided, that is—and not also experience itself as free, occurrently, at that time?

14.3 BACKTRACKING

I will call the suggestion that an affirmative answer must be given to this question the Indecision Suggestion. It will be rejected. But examination of the Indecision Suggestion will be deferred until 14.10, for a different suggestion also demands consideration, and, as will appear, naturally takes priority.

This is the suggestion that it is simply fully self-conscious experience* or awareness* of oneself as able to choose that is sufficient for experience* of freedom. This suggestion will be called the 'Experience* of Ability to Choose Suggestion', or 'the Ability Suggestion' for short; and the account of freedom that it leads to, according to which (fully self-conscious) experience of oneself as able to choose is the missing necessary condition of freedom, the one that needs to be added to the S' conditions, will be called the 'Experience* of Ability to Choose Account', or 'the Ability Account' for short. Reasons for rejecting the Ability Suggestion and the Ability Account are already to be found, dispersed, in the preceding. But they merit discussion on their own terms.

The Ability Suggestion is a suggestion about the conditions of experience* of freedom; the Ability Account is an account of the conditions of freedom itself. Before arguing that both should be rejected, I will try to show that both are attractive, independently of any specifically Objectivist reasons that there may be for adopting them; and will show how the Ability Account of the conditions of freedom connects up with the account that has so far been developed in terms of the S (and S') conditions.

Before any of these things are done, however, it is worth pointing out that the natural Epictetans already constitute a refutation of the Ability Account, if they can really be as they have been held to be. The argument is this: given that they can act at all, the natural Epictetans must be supposed to have grasp of the notion of there being options open to them; for a grasp of this notion is necessary to any being to whom intentional actions and an ability to choose are correctly attributable. And, this being so, it may also be supposed (since they are fully self-conscious) that they have a conception of themselves as able to choose that is, purely intellectually speaking, fully adequate. Yet it remains plausible to say that the natural Epictetans need have no conception of themselves as able to choose *freely* (= truly responsibly), given their completely frictionless decision-making.

This is a direct consequence of the way the natural Epictetans are described. But a further point is this: assuming that the main argument of Chapter 2 is correct, freedom in the sense of true responsibility is demonstrably impossible. Now it seems to be true that nearly all human beings believe that they possess such freedom. And it is perhaps true that they cannot help believing this (though this suggestion has been questioned at various points). But it would be very surprising indeed if all possible self-conscious rational agents that were able to choose and knew it were compelled to believe they possessed such freedom—for it would be very surprising if all possible self-conscious rational agents, however intelligent and knowledgeable they were, were compelled to believe something demonstrably false.

Those who are convinced by the natural Epictetans can turn straight to Chapter 15—though they may like to consider the 'being of limited conception' and the Genuine Incompatibilist Determinist discussed in 14.8. The next four sections are somewhat involved, but most of the issues should become clear by 14.8.

14.4 THE ABILITY SUGGESTION AND THE ABILITY ACCOUNT

Let 'ACx' symbolize 'x is able to choose', and let 'FCx' symbolize 'x is able to choose freely', or 'is free to choose' ('free to choose' is an extremely tricky phrase, but I shall sometimes speak of x's being free to choose rather than of x's being able to choose freely, on the understanding that these phrases are to be taken as strictly equivalent in meaning).[8]

The Ability Suggestion is the suggestion that awareness* of being able to choose is sufficient for awareness* of being able to choose freely—i.e., that

$$(x)(E^*(x,ACx) \to E^*(x,FCx)). \tag{1}$$

The question arises, of course, as to why (1) is true, if it is: is it a causal or a non-causal truth, or what? But the first point to note is that whether or not (1) is true, its converse,

$$(x)(E^*(x,FCx) \to E^*(x,ACx)) \tag{2}$$

surely is: it is obvious that there has to be experience* of ability to choose for there to be experience* of ability to choose *freely*. Experience of ability to choose freely is just a certain kind or manner of experience* of ability to choose.

Experience* of ability to choose, then, is certainly necessary for experience* of ability to choose freely; (2) is certainly true. So the Ability Suggestion amounts in effect to the claim that the conjunction of (1) and (2), i.e.

$$(x)(E^*(x,ACx) \leftrightarrow E^*(x,FCx)), \tag{3}$$

is true: this is the claim that experience* of ability to choose is both necessary and sufficient for experience* of ability to choose freely.

It will be argued that (3) is not true, and that even if it were it would not help the Objectivists. Briefly: faced with the question of why (3) is true, if indeed it is, the options come down to two: it is true either in virtue of causal relations, or in virtue of non-causal (and indeed constitution) relations. But the causal option is implausible (and too weak in any case), while the non-causal option is too strong, because it makes the Ability Account collapse into Subjectivism.

But is the Ability Suggestion an attractive one independently of any supposedly good Objectivist reasons for adopting it? I think it is attractive, although false, given the Ability Account of freedom it leads to. One way of characterizing the Ability Account is this: if a fully self-conscious purposive agent that is able to choose in the sense defined in 8.2 is also fully self-consciously aware* *that* it is able to choose, then

---

[8] '*FC*' is introduced simply as an aid to clarity. It is not strictly necessary; '*F*' would do, for reasons given in 14.1 (A).

this is enough for it to be held to be accountable for its actions in the strong sense in which we take ourselves to be.[9]

This has a plausible sound. The idea is that it is merely full awareness* that one has the ability to choose that makes the difference in respect of freedom (between us on the one hand and Fido and Nemo on the other). Such full awareness is fully self-conscious awareness* *that I* am able to choose. It is essentially more than the bare, unselfconscious canine awareness of there being two options. For it is an awareness, on my part, in which I expressly grasp or represent *myself* as having the property of being able to choose, rather than a perception that is not explicitly self-concerned, and is merely an impersonal (or at least not expressly first-personal) apprehension of the world as option-containing. And, as such (so the argument for the Ability Suggestion goes), it essentially involves my having a grasp of myself as truly responsible for my choice and action.

The Ability Account of freedom, then, is simply this: to be a free agent, able to choose freely, is (i) to be able to choose (as Fido and Nemo are), and (ii) to be fully self-consciously aware* that one is able to choose: that is,

$$Cn/(x)(\underline{ACx \ \& \ E^*(x, ACx)} \leftrightarrow Fx)/.^{10} \qquad (4)$$

That is all there is to free agenthood, on this account. Its Objectivist proponents have a powerful-seeming question to ask: 'What more could one possibly want, as a condition of freedom? What other kinds of property could possibly be relevant?'

True, the spectre of determinism (or non-self-determinability) remains to haunt this account. But this is not our present concern; which is, as ever, to try to give an account of that which distinguishes us from Fido and Nemo in respect of freedom. As remarked, whatever distinguishes us, it cannot be a difference in respect of determinism.

But what about the principal claim of Part III—that nothing can be free and not so experience itself; the claim (to put it now in terms of '*FC*' rather than '*F*') that

$$(x)(FCx \rightarrow E^*(x, FCx))? \qquad (5)$$

Well, coupled with the Ability Suggestion, i.e. (3), the Ability Account entails (5).

---

[9] This suggestion was considered in 9.6. Problems raised by determinism and non-self-determinability are still waived.

[10] '*FC*' could be written for '*F*'. See n. 8.

Does this solve the Objectivists' problems with (5), the principal claim? No. For the question still remains as to whether Objectivists who want to accept (5) can, by adopting the Ability Account and the Ability Suggestion, block the Subjectivists' claim that (5) is true because experience* of freedom is a necessary *constitutive* condition of freedom—true, that is, because

$$\text{Cn}/(x)(FCx \rightarrow \underline{E^*(x, FCx)})/. \tag{5.1}$$

The answer to this question depends on what account these Objectivists can provide of why (3) is true. Given that (3) is not merely a formal-logical truth (if true at all), the choice seems to lie, in effect, between saying that experience* of ability to choose is *constitutively* necessary and sufficient for experience* of ability to choose freely, and saying that it is *causally* necessary and sufficient—i.e. between

$$\text{Cn}/(x)(\underline{E^*(x, ACx)} \leftrightarrow E^*(x, FCx))/ \tag{3.1}$$

and

$$\text{Cs}/(x)(\underline{E^*(x, ACx)} \leftrightarrow E^*(x, FCx))/. \tag{3.2}$$

It will be argued that neither (3.1) nor (3.2) is true, and that neither would do even if it were true.

An alternative open to Objectivists is, of course, to adopt the Ability Account and simply deny (5), the troublesome principal claim. So doing, they need not adopt the Ability Suggestion, nor, therefore, face the question of why it is true. But (5) still seems very hard to deny.

Some may find it odd that, ostensibly embarked on an analysis of freedom, one has to spend so much time discussing experience* of freedom, and such questions as whether experience* of ability to choose is sufficient for experience* of freedom. But as far as I can see the attempt to understand the bounds and demands and prospects of our ordinary notion of what a free agent is makes a careful consideration of such questions unavoidable; more generally, it is arguable that any discussion of freedom that does not treat questions about the character of our experience as central must in the end remain superficial.

It may take time to see this, both because it can seem obvious that the substantive issue of whether or not we are free must be largely independent of issues about the character of our experience, and because the traditional debate between compatibilists and libertarians is often rather enjoyable in its details. There is always plenty to say (although the main issues are in fact quite simple ones), and there is always room for a new and vivid way of putting things. For this reason I think that the discussion will keep returning to the traditional framework, and that much of it will remain superficial.

14.5 AN ALTERNATIVE APPROACH?

In the light of the Ability Account of freedom, some may now wish to object to the account of ability to choose given in Chapter 8, according to which dogs can be able to choose. They may now be inclined to say—in the by now familiar, apparently principle-of-independence-contravening way—that part of what it is to be *truly* able to choose is to know (believe) that you are able to choose, in a fully self-conscious manner; so that while we are truly able to choose, dogs are not. On this view, fully self-conscious awareness* that one is able to choose doesn't make the difference between (*a*) ability to choose and (*b*) ability to choose freely. Rather, it makes the difference between (*a*) being (truly) able to choose and (*c*) not being able to choose *at all*.

This can seem like a natural thing to say. But it is equally natural to say that a dog can be able to choose, in the situation described in 8.3, for example. (And remember the much more complex yet still unselfconscious Nemo.) Language slides around in this area; there is no simple right or wrong. Here the account of ability to choose according to which dogs can be able to choose will be retained, because, whether or not it is the best account, it is useful in the articulation of the conditions of freedom, it is at least as natural as any other, and no substantive questions are begged by it.[11]

(Someone who did want to adopt the account of ability to choose rejected here—the account according to which dogs are *not* able to choose—would have to deal with the apparent contravention of the principle of independence pointed out in the last paragraph but one. But it seems that this could be easily and plausibly done as follows: call 'true' ability to choose 'AC_2', and call basic or 'canine' ability to choose—as characterized in the description of Fido in 8.3—'AC_1'; then to be 'truly' able to choose is to have basic ability to choose and to be fully aware of this: $(x)(AC_2x \longleftrightarrow AC_1x \ \& \ E^*(x,AC_1x))$. Although this account of ability to choose will not be adopted here, all the main arguments in what follows can easily be adapted to accommodate it.)

14.6 THE ABILITY ACCOUNT, THE BASIC STRUCTURAL ACCOUNT, AND A QUASI-KANTIAN VIEW

How does the Ability Account of freedom, according to which to be

[11] As was pointed out at the beginning of 8.4.

free is simply to be able to choose and aware of this fact, connect with the account of freedom in terms of the Structural S (or S') conditions? In the following simple way. The S conditions consist of the necessary and sufficient conditions of purposive agenthood[12] plus self-consciousness; and the first condition proposed by the Ability Account, i.e., the ability to choose condition, is equivalent to the S conditions minus the self-consciousness condition. This is so by definition (8.4): the kind of purposive agenthood represented by the S conditions minus the self-consciousness condition just is the kind of purposive agenthood that includes ability to choose, as presently understood.[13]

What about the self-consciousness condition? Let 'S-C' symbolize 'is fully self-conscious'. Clearly, fulfilling the second condition proposed by the Ability Account, that is, the condition requiring fully self-conscious awareness* of self as able to choose, entails being self-conscious. But it will be argued in the next section that a being might be both (*a*) able to choose and (*b*) self-conscious and yet not have (*c*) fully self-conscious experience/awareness* of self as able to choose; such a being would not be a free agent, according to the Ability Account.

Because this is so, and because it is in any case a good idea to give a fully articulated statement of the elements of the present Ability Account, it is worth adding an explicit clause regarding self-consciousness to the account, to give

$$Cn/(x)(\underline{ACx} \ \& \ \underline{S\text{-}Cx} \ \& \ E^*(x,ACx) \longleftrightarrow Fx)/.$$

Since AC and S-C have already been held to be the same as S, the Ability Account, re-expressed in terms of the S conditions, amounts to this:

$$Cn/(x)(\underline{Sx} \ \& \ E^*(x,ACx) \longleftrightarrow Fx)/.$$

That is, to be a free agent is simply to fulfil the S conditions and, in addition, to be (fully self-consciously) aware* that one is able to choose. Even if this Ability Account is not right, it seems to have considerable appeal; and, coupled with the Ability Suggestion, it entails the 'principal claim' that if one is free then one believes one is. (The Spectator-inspired Integration condition is being left out of account for the moment. But one can suppose it added to the Ability Account, and change 'S' to 'S''' in the preceding formula.)

---

[12] Whatever exactly they are. The attempt to specify them, in 7.3, was not intended to be definitive.

[13] See 8.4. Unselfconscious Nemo and Fido fulfil the ability-to-choose condition.

In the last paragraph but one it was suggested that (*a*), being able to choose, and (*b*), being self-conscious, do not entail (*c*), being self-consciously aware* of oneself as able to choose.[14] If (*a*) and (*b*) *did* entail (*c*), then proponents of the present Ability Account could reduce the conditions of freedom to *S*, finishing up where the original Structual theorists started: for then possessing a fully self-conscious experience/conception of oneself as able to choose would not only be that which sufficed to distinguish us in respect of freedom from Fido, Nemo, and so on; it would also be a necessary concomitant of fulfilling *S* (i.e., of being a fully self-conscious purposive agent). And the Ability Account would thus boil down to the theory that

$$Cn/(x)(\underline{Sx} \leftrightarrow Fx)/$$

—to what one could call the 'Basic Structural Account'. (The Spectator subject would remain a problem, but one may for the moment suppose that problem solved.)

The Basic Structural Account's claim that being a self-conscious, purposive or rational agent just is, or is in itself sufficient for, being a free agent, is a view that many have found attractive. It too can couple with the Ability Suggestion to entail the principal claim that if one is free then one believes one is. Indeed it can be seen as lying at the heart of the Kantian or quasi-Kantian view that a rational being, simply as such, cannot act except 'under the idea' of freedom, and is truly a free agent (in some sense) precisely for this reason.[15]

Consider how the quasi-Kantian view can be built up out of the elements distinguished above: it is not because one is as a self-conscious rational and practical being necessarily conscious of the Moral Law that one cannot act except under the idea of freedom. Rather, it is simply because one cannot but be self-consciously aware* of oneself as *able to choose*; and because (this is the Ability Suggestion) to be thus aware* of oneself as *able to choose* just is to experience oneself as able to choose *freely*, or is at least sufficient for this. The intuitive argument is as follows. I am

(*a*) able to choose

[14] This has yet to be argued, in 14.7. But if it is right, it follows that the Ability Account is an Attitudinal Theory, though still an Objectivist theory, because the Structural conditions (*a*) and (*b*) do not entail the attitudinal—and hence Attitudinal—condition (*c*).

[15] In calling this view 'Kantian', one has to take 'rational', as it qualifies 'being' or 'agent', in our sense rather than Kant's (his sense includes and extends our sense), ignoring, in particular, the role he gives to the 'Moral Law' in his account of rationality and freedom.

and

(b) fully self-conscious.

And I am (therefore)

(c) fully self-consciously aware* of myself as able to choose.

But my being (c), fully self-consciously aware* of myself as able to choose, *just is* my being

(d) aware* of its being *truly up to me* what I choose—

for (c) and (d) just describe the same thing in different ways. Furthermore, (d), my being aware* of its being truly up to me what I choose, *just is* my being

(e) such that I experience myself as free or have experience* of freedom.

That is (to put it another way), my being (d) just is my being

(e) fully self-consciously aware* of myself as able to choose freely and as truly responsible for what I choose—

for (d) and (e) also describe the same things.[16]

Is this true? Even granting that (d) and (e) are the same (it seems reasonable to accept this as a matter of definition), are (c) and (d) also the same? It will be argued that they are not (and that (a) and (b) do not in any case entail (c)). But it does seem to be true that possession of (c), a fully self-conscious sense or awareness* of ability to choose, is commonly (implicitly) taken to be the vital *differentia* that justifies the distinction of ourselves from Nemo and Fido in respect of freedom. 'It is simply because we (unlike Nemo and Fido) are fully self-consciously aware of the possibility of choice that we are truly free and responsible.' This is the kind of thing that may be said or supposed. And somewhere behind this natural thought there lurks the idea that (c) does somehow or other simply amount to (d) and (e), and that it is partly or mainly *for that reason* that it suffices to make the crucial difference in respect of freedom.[17]

----

[16] Perhaps because he was primarily interested in grounding morality, and interested in freedom principally as necessary for morality, Kant supposed that a sense of oneself as a self-giver of the moral law was necessary for the experience* of freedom, or autonomy, or true responsibility. In fact, though, it seems that an entirely non-moral sense that what I do (or choose) is truly up to me could give rise to an experience* of true responsibility. See 3.3.

[17] This sort of suggestion is no good for Kant's purposes, of course. The mere sense of its being truly up to me cannot make me free so long as my motives—those, at least, which actually move me to action—are not truly self-determined in the way that

'How could (c) possibly matter, or make such an enormous difference', one may well ask, 'if determinism is true?' But most are likely to continue undisturbed in the belief that it really does matter, and indeed suffices to make the difference in respect of freedom: 'I am a free and truly responsible agent, unlike Fido or Nemo, when I choose a course of action, simply because there is a crucial sense in which, fully self-conscious as I am, *I know what I am doing*—a sense in which they do not know what they are doing.'

This view will be rejected in what follows—and for reasons that have nothing to do with determinism. It may be noted, though, that even if (c) cannot make the decisive difference it is called upon to make by the Ability Account it does seem to be at least necessary for freedom. For (c) is clearly necessary for (e) experience* of ability to choose freely, or experience* of freedom, for short; and (e) in turn still seems to be necessary for freedom. This, after all, is the principal claim of Part III. So we have established another of the necessary conditions of freedom: (c) must be added to S′.

14.7 COUNTER-ATTACK

We still need to know whether or not two claims about three things are true. The three things, already mentioned, are (b), full self-consciousness; (c), fully self-conscious awareness* of ability to choose; and (e), experience* of ability to choose freely (experience* of freedom). And the two claims are

(I) (c) is not only necessary but also sufficient for (e);
(II) the possession of (b), by a rational (or purposive) agent, is sufficient for that agent's possession of (c).

(I) is the Ability Suggestion. (II) is the proposal that led, with (I), to the 'quasi-Kantian view' or 'Basic Structural Account'. I wish to deny both—or (I), at least, even if not (II).

As for (II), many compatibilists have perhaps implicitly supposed that it is true. But surely a being could be (a) able to choose, and (b) fully self-conscious, and yet fail to have or form (c) any fully self-conscious conception of itself as able to choose? All necessary conditions of the possibility of its having such a thought are no doubt fulfilled; that is, the necessary and sufficient conditions of the possibility of its having such a thought are fulfilled. But it is not therefore the case that sufficient

conscious conformity with the moral law is supposed to make possible. Still, Kant's theory is at least partly an explanation of how we come to get the sense of autonomy we all actually do normally have, and as such it is open to challenge and revision.

conditions of the actuality of its having such a thought or conception are necessarily also fulfilled. Surely it can not only fail to have or to form a fully self-conscious conception of itself as able to choose in any particular case in which it is actually able to choose, but can also fail to form any general, standing conception of itself as a thing that is able to choose? If this is possible—it would seem so—then (II) above is not true. (It follows that (*c*) is not just an attitudinal but an Attitudinal condition of freedom, relative to the *S* conditions.)

There is no need to press this claim, however. It would not be fatal to the present view if (II) were shown to be true. For if it were, this would simply make it clearer that (I) is not true. And the main question, to which we may now turn, concerns (I), the Ability Suggestion: is it true that the experience/conception of oneself as able to choose is sufficient as well as necessary for the experience/conception of oneself as able to choose *freely*? Secondly, if it is true, why is it true—for causal reasons, or for non-causal reasons? It will be argued that it is not true.

14.8 THE REJECTION OF THE ABILITY SUGGESTION

14.8.1. *Up-to-me-ness and the being of limited conception.* It will help to consider the nature of experience* of ability to choose and of ability to choose freely in particular cases—cases of choice between X and Y, say. 'Able to choose between X and Y' and 'able to choose freely between X and Y' will be symbolized by '$AC(XY)$' and '$FC(XY)$' respectively.[18]

Is experience* of ability to choose sufficient for experience* of ability to choose freely, as the Ability Suggestion suggests? The answer, I think, is that that it is not. Consider a 'being of limited conception'. It is a very blinkered personage, a purposive agent that comes to be fully self-conscious, while remaining very limited in its general conception of things, including in particular its conception of its own agency. It is emotionally very dull, mentally very sluggish. (It may help to imagine that its actions are ordinarily of small importance, and that its thought is mostly concerned with the more or less immediate present—it moves through time inside a shell of self-concerned, short-term aims. But these things do not seem to be necessary features of its case, given the claim that it is designed to support.)

The being of limited conception may be aware* of being $AC(XY)$, in

---

[18] Simply for the sake of simplicity, it will be assumed that no other possibilities than X and Y are being considered by the beings in question.

a particular case, in the way that Fido can be; and it adds self-consciousness to this awareness, and may thus come to be fully self-consciously aware* of itself as $AC(XY)$.[19] But it seems that simply in being so aware* of itself it need neither have any occurrent thought of itself as at that moment able to choose freely, or as truly responsible, nor have any explicit* *general* conception of itself as so free and responsible.

Suppose that the being of limited conception is, in a particular situation of choice, occurrently and fully self-consciously aware* of itself as now $AC(XY)$. It is occurrently aware* of X and Y as the options it faces—as the options open to it, and this awareness* involves its apprehension of itself as now able to perform either X or Y. In addition, let us suppose that it is also aware* that it will very shortly opt for and actually perform either X or Y. (Fido and Nemo can have an unselfconscious version of all this.) Given all this, it still seems entirely possible that it simply does not advance to the thought that it is (or can be) *truly up to it* which it does. That is, aware of all that it is aware of, it still need not, and in this story does not, turn round upon itself and grasp* itself as free and truly responsible, as inescapably condemned (in Sartre's sense) to freedom by its situation. It simply lacks this view of things; this is surely possible. But I think it can be hard to see. As remarked, we are naturally inclined to think that fully self-conscious awareness* of ability to choose just is awareness* of self as free and truly responsible.

Suppose it is accepted as a matter of definition that (fully self-conscious) 'truly up to me' experience just is, or is sufficient for, experience* of ability to choose freely (as in 14.6). Clearly, we will not attribute any such experience to an unselfconscious dog—even when insisting that there is a clear and very important sense in which it (and Nemo) can truly be said to be able to choose. For, by definition, it cannot be fully self-consciously aware* of itself as so placed that it is up to it what to do. But although self-conscious awareness* of ability to choose is certainly necessary for the possibility of 'truly up to me' experience, it does not seem that it is in itself sufficient for the actuality of it—even in a rational agent. For, so far as the being of limited conception is concerned, the content or character of its awareness* that it is $AC(XY)$—its '$AC(XY)$ awareness', for short—may be in essentials just like a dog's (perhaps a rather uninspired dog) *in all respects in which*

[19] It *may* do so, and we may suppose that it does do so. But, as just noted in the last section, there is no reason why it must apply its self-consciousness to all aspects of itself and its experience, including this aspect.

it is awareness whose content is such that it is ability-to-choose-(XY) awareness*.

If this is so, the only difference between the being of limited conception's $AC(XY)$ awareness and Fido's $AC(XY)$ awareness is that the former is self-conscious and the latter is not. The two states of awareness differ only in respect of self-consciousness; and it is not the case that if they differ in this respect then they will also differ in that the being of limited conception's awareness is, just by virtue of being self-conscious, necessarily also a state of being aware* of being able to choose *freely* or *truly responsibly*. Fully self-conscious self-reference is also part of the explicit content of the awareness-state, in addition to $AC(XY)$ awareness, in the being of limited conception's case. But this may be so without the able-to-chooseness part of the character or content of the awareness-state being affected. It is not the case that the self-conscious self-reference must inevitably transmute the able-to-chooseness part of the content of the awareness-state into truly-up-to-me experience—experience* of freedom. For this last thing involves a further perspective, a further attitude to what is going on, a further way of thinking of self that the being of limited conception simply does not attain. (Here the point is made by reference to the possibility of an extremely limited conception of things. Below it will be made by reference to the possibility of an unusually wide-ranging conception of things—that of the Genuine Incompatibilist Determinist.)

So much for (occurrent) awareness* of self as now actually able to choose between X and Y in a particular situation. The same conclusions presumably hold for awareness* of oneself as a thing that is, generally considered, *potentially* able to choose. Suppose the being of limited conception does in fact have a general, standing conception of itself as a being that is able to choose (though it need not). Then there is no reason why this general conception should not have the same doggedly simple character as its occurrent $AC(XY)$ awareness did; it is not the case that this conception has to involve or amount to a conception of self as free or truly responsible just because the being of limited conception is self-conscious. The mere addition of self-consciousness need not make this difference.

The being of limited conception may have to have some sense of itself as a single thing that is single just *qua* mental, simply in so far as it is fully self-conscious (9.3). But it seems that it may still lack any strong sense of self such as we have. (Our sense of self standardly involves affective elements, and a certain commitment to self that doubtless derives at least partly from an instinct of self-preservation.) It may be, as it were, quite uninterested in itself—or so *we* might put it, at any rate.

It may be objected that possession of the *concept* of choice is necessary for freedom and for experience* of freedom, and questioned whether the being of limited conception can really be said to possess it, if it cannot be said to be aware* that it is truly *up to it* what to do. I think it certainly does possess the concept of choice—but will not consider this objection until 14.10.

Notice how this line of thought goes directly against the intuitions recorded on pp. 273-5 above. I suggest that our saturated familiarity with our own case, our unexamined supposition that any sense of self must be like our own, causes us to elide, and not to notice, a transition. The natural, mistaken thought is this: 'If I am truly fully aware*, now, that I am able to choose, surely I am *ipso facto* aware* that what I do is truly up to me, aware* that I am free and truly responsible for what I do? Surely there is no further basic content to my awareness* of myself as able to choose freely and truly responsibly than my awareness* of myself as truly, fully, able to choose?' The being of limited conception suggests that this is not so.

The simplest argument that this is not so appeals to the Genuine Incompatibilist Determinist, who has *ex hypothesi* acceded to a state of exhaustive comprehension of the consequences of determinism, and who may thus be genuinely aware* of facing a choice without any sense whatever of freedom or true responsibility. But consider, first, the Spectators and the natural Epictetans.

14.8.2. *The Spectators and the natural Epictetans.* There is a clear sense in which the Spectators and the natural Epictetans can be supposed to have an intellectually fully-fledged conception of themselves as beings that are, generally considered, such that they are able to choose—even the natural Epictetans. After all, each of them can fully understand a story in which it is faced with a button, and knows that pushing or not pushing it in the next twenty seconds will lead to very different results. There is nothing wrong with their basic intellectual conception of themselves as able to choose. But it falls short of a conception of self as able to choose freely. Neither the Spectators nor the Epictetans experience themselves as free choosers, free agents, in the way required.

They fail to do so in different ways. Concentrating on our own case, we are inclined to think that being fully self-consciously conscious* that one is able to choose just is (necessarily) being fully self-consciously conscious* that one is able to choose freely and truly responsibly. This being so, a natural way *for us* to express the different ways in which they fail to experience themselves as able to choose freely is as in-adequacies in the way in which they conceive of themselves simply as able to choose—even though there is in fact nothing wrong with their basic intellectual grasp of themselves as able to choose. Thus we may be inclined to say that, relative to the way in which we normally conceive of or experience ourselves as able to choose, the Spectator subject is inadequate in that she does not properly conceive of *herself* as able to choose; whereas a natural Epictetan is inadequate in that it does not properly conceive of itself as able to *choose*. That is, relative to ourselves, the Spectator's sense of self is too thin, while the Epictetan's resistless notion of choice is too thin.

But what this shows is not that they are not really able to conceive of themselves as able to choose after all. They, like *l'étranger*, Meursault, possess a perfectly good basic grasp* of themselves as able to choose. It is precisely because this does not in Meursault's case simply amount to a conception of self as able to choose freely that he is so very odd, as a human being. For we as we naturally are cannot in our ordinary thought about ourselves keep the two things apart.

In sum, it seems that we insensibly inflate the notion of experience of self as able to choose in such a way that it seems not only to be implicated in, but also to implicate, the notion of self as able to choose freely (as in the Ability Suggestion). For it is an 'experiential fact', for us, that we really do face choices and know that we do (3.6). And it can easily seem that this alone suffices to make us free agents, and, equally, to make us aware* that we are free agents (in line with the Ability Suggestion and the intuitions of 14.6 above). The fact that this is so is one of the principal sources of the free will debate. But here it has been argued that we must distinguish

(1) the property of being able to choose
(2) the property of being (fully self-consciously) aware* that one possesses the property of being able to choose,

and

(3) the property of experiencing or conceiving of oneself as able to choose *freely*—as free in and truly responsible for one's actions.

To possess (3) is to have a certain kind of attitude to oneself, as something that possesses (1), and is, (2), aware that it does, that goes fundamentally beyond whatever is involved in (2). We normally have all of (1), (2), and (3). Fido and Nemo have only (1). The present suggestion is that, contrary to the Ability Suggestion, there are or could be beings—such as the being of limited conception, the Spectator, the natural Epictetans—that have (1) and (2) but not (3).

14.8.3. *The Genuine Incompatibilist Determinist.*

The 'Genuine Incompatibilist Determinist', too, can have (1) and (2) and not (3). For it is fully self-conscious. It is Integrated.[20] And we can put it, too, in front of a button, in such a way that it cannot not be aware* that it faces a choice.[21] But it is so deeply intimate with the thought that everything that it is is determined that it has, in this situation, no sort of sense of itself as free to choose—as truly responsible for its choices—although it now knows that it is able to choose what to do. It neither has a sense of itself as free to choose in this particular case, nor of itself as a thing that is in general free to choose. It is a sophisticated fatalist.[22] It is indeed very hard for us to imagine what it is like to be a genuine incompatibilist determinist; it involves a radically non-human conception of things. But it seems that it must be allowed that there could be such beings. There is, after all, a clear sense in which true responsibility is demonstrably impossible. And it would as remarked in 14.3 be very curious if it were simply impossible for there to be an

[20] Engagement with one's desires of the kind that the Integration condition guarantees, and a strong interest in their fulfilment, are not incompatible with genuine espousal of the incompatibilist determinist position. That this is so is in turn not incompatible with the suggestion that human Buddhists seeking to achieve release from the suffering-creating bondage of desires, by achieving full comprehension of the doctrine of *an-ātman*, might do well to meditate upon determinism.

[21] Recall that its awareness* of ability to choose may be entirely veridical, given the current terms of discussion: for ability to choose, as defined in 8.2, is entirely compatible with determinism: facing a choice is a genuine everyday experience, one that we can have even if all our desires are determined in us. The current question of freedom is not a question about whether we really face choices at all—for even Fido and Nemo can do that—but about whether, facing choices in the particular way we do, we can really be said to be truly responsible for our choices.

[22] Naive fatalism holds that there is no point in doing anything because everything is predetermined (or is the will of God, for example), hence nothing you can do can change how things will be. It is false, because one's doings and deliberations can change things, being themselves real parts of the (possibly deterministic) causal process. Sophisticated fatalism doesn't make a mistake. It consists in the attempt (or is the result of a successful attempt) to comprehend fully the fact that one is wholly determined (and hence not self-determined or self-determining). If one is an ordinary human being, the trouble with it is simply that one cannot have recourse to it when faced, now, inescapably, with a difficult choice—or indeed any choice.

agent that was, like the Genuine Incompatibilist Determinist, both able to comprehend this fact and able to grasp that it was in a situation in which it was able to choose. (This is really the only *argument* that can be given for the possibility of the case. Here argument seems to be no substitute for imagination—imagination directed on to a given description.)

It may be objected that we just would hold the Genuine Incompatibilist Determinist to be a free agent like ourselves, given simply that it was indeed genuinely aware* that it was able to choose what to do. But if we did we would I think be guilty of insensitivity, of simply failing to appreciate what it is to be a genuine incompatibilist determinist. Suppose we accept the principal claim of Part III, that one cannot hold a being to be truly free in and responsible for its choice or action if it has no sort of conception of itself as so free or responsible, either at the time of choice or action, or in general. Then, in holding the Genuine Incompatibilist Determinist to be a free agent, we would again be assuming that

(A) to be genuinely aware* that one is able to choose

just is

(B) to experience oneself as able to choose freely and truly responsibly in the way that is necessary for freedom—

or assuming that (A) is at least sufficient for (B).

But this assumption is unwarranted. If in the present case we cannot see the gap between (A) and (B), it is perhaps because what we can't imagine is a human being who is a genuine incompatibilist determinist but is in other respects—including internal phenomenological respects—normal. But it is not surprising that we cannot imagine this, because it is impossible. If the Genuine Incompatibilist Determinist is human, then it (or he or she) is not normal at all. Either we must suppose that its sense of self is not recognizably human, or we must suppose that it has dissolved away entirely. The first supposition would seem to be a reasonable one, for the Genuine Incompatibilist Determinist is a self-conscious, embodied being, and can have an unexceptionable grasp of the simple truth that it is a single thing in the world, in addition to possessing that self-presence of mind, normal in the self-conscious, that involves a sense of oneself as something that is somehow single just *qua* mental. But, granted that it does have a sense of self, this cannot be supposed to fall within the range of the recognizably human: a conception of the characterful self as the truly responsibly self-determining subject of actions seems to be essentially constitutive of the ordinary human sense of self, whatever its many variations. And the Genuine Incompatibilist Determinist's sense of self is not like that. Given the nature of its experience of choice and agency it could not be like that. Its sense of self must be divested of any sense of true self-determination and true responsibility. (That the nature of an agent's sense of self is constitutively bound up with the nature of its experience of agency is a quite general truth, and both the Buddhists considered in 6.6 and the thought-experiment proposed in 6.2 are relevant to the present claim.)[23]

In sum, what is possible is the existence of a being which is intellectually speaking fully equipped and fully self-conscious, and which has goals (survival needs, perhaps), but which has absolutely no sort of conception of itself as a truly responsible agent, such as we normally have; this despite its being able to have fully self-consciously articulated (and possibly veridical) experience of itself as able to choose. Here it is supposed that this being is a genuine incompatibilist determinist. This is done precisely because the truth of determinism seems to render so clearly impossible the kind of self-determination and responsibility that we continue willy nilly, and despite the most strenuous theoretical excogitations, to attribute to ourselves: so that it seems that a truly comprehensive or in the present terms 'genuine' understanding of the truth of determinism must produce an experience of choice and action devoid of any sense of true responsibility.[24]

The line between awareness* of ability to choose and awareness* of freedom to choose may appear as a fine one in a book written for human beings, and by one; and a court of law might be impatient with such distinctions. For we are unable to see the distinction easily, and have difficulty in employing the device of sympathetic identification, the delicate investigative instrument of imagination, upon the case put forward for consideration. But in a book written for creatures of some

[23] Appendix E considers further the relation between the sense of self and the sense of freedom, returning to some of the questions considered in 9.4–9.6 in the light of the current discussion of experience* of freedom.

[24] One thing we find it very hard to accept is that human beings could opt out of ordinary moral or legal responsibility merely by becoming genuine incompatibilist determinists. But this is presumably because we do not think through how much they would have to have changed in other respects in ceasing to have any sense of themselves as free. Who knows what it might be like to be a spiritually advanced Buddhist (who has, perhaps, become a genuine non-self-determinationist), or how far Nietzsche got in his attempt to live with true *amor fati*, and what it was like for him? It is perhaps easier for us to think of genuine incompatibilist determinists who are not human, and who were never like us.

other planet, perfectly fatal creatures of a deeply deterministical persuasion, the difficulty might rather be to explain how any apparently intelligent race of beings could suppose the line to be a fine one between (i) being fully self-consciously conscious* of being able to choose when facing alternatives perceived as such, and (ii) being fully self-consciously conscious* of being able to choose freely, where this latter consciousness involves a sense of self as responsible for one's actions in some true-desert-implicating (and impossible) fashion.

Even this may be hard for us to accept, for there remains something very powerful about the idea, called quasi-Kantian above, that *any* rational being that is fully self-consciously conscious* of being able to choose cannot but suppose itself to be free in the strong, ordinary sense, by reason of that consciousness alone. But, having considered the being of limited conception, the Genuine Incompatibilist Determinist, the Spectator, Meursault and his variants, and the natural Epictetans, I submit that this idea is nevertheless wrong. Adding the Integration condition into the Ability Account can only deal with, by ruling out, the Spectator and *les étrangers*.

14.9 THE INDECISION SUGGESTION

Suppose it is now granted that experience* of ability to choose does not amount to (or necessarily involve, or have as an invariable concomitant) experience* of freedom—experience* of ability to choose freely of the sort that appears to be necessary for free agenthood. A previous suggestion now recurs. The natural Epictetans made it seem that some sort of experience of indecision was vital to experience* of freedom, vital in the sense that it would be sufficient for experience* of freedom (even if it was not necessary, given the neo-Epictetans).

Might the Ability Suggestion then be improved by adding a condition requiring experience of indecision, and claiming that it is experience* of ability to choose *plus* experience of indecision that entails experience* of freedom? Since (necessarily occurrent) experience of indecision entails experience* of ability to choose (at a particular time), this question reduces to the question whether experience of indecision entails experience* of freedom—exactly the question deferred in 14.3. To answer it in the affirmative is to adopt the Indecision Suggestion. It is to claim that experience of indecision, necessarily occurrent, is sufficient for (presumably equally occurrent) experience* of freedom.

Proponents of the Indecision Suggestion may ask a powerful-seeming

question: How can a being possibly be fully self-conscious, and Integrated, and aware* that it is able to choose, and be currently experiencing itself as undecided what to do, in a way that the natural
Epictetans never do, and not be (*ipso facto*) experiencing* itself as able
to choose freely? But the reply is that this is indeed possible. The
Genuine Incompatibilist Determinist may be undecided. Facing the
button it was presented with at the beginning of 14.8.3, it may find
itself calculating consequences. It is not compelled by this into any
sense of itself as free in a way that it knows to be impossible. The being
of limited conception may also be undecided—continuing, despite its
elevation to the ranks of the fully self-conscious, to experience its quan-
daries in a profoundly uninspired fashion, just as it continues so to
experience* its ability to choose. It does not have to be intellectually
limited in any way for this to be so. It is simply that there is nothing in
its perspective or circumstances, cognitive or affective, that leads it to
move on to the conception or experience of itself as a free or truly
responsible agent.[25]

In fine, it is simply not the case that fully self-conscious experience
of indecision or quandary in itself either amounts to or is sufficient for
(occurrent) experience of oneself as free or truly responsible. Here again
one should try to imagine something of what it might conceivably be
like to be like the Genuine Incompatibilist Determinist.

So much for the Indecision Suggestion.

14.10 OBJECTION: THE CONCEPT OF CHOICE

The following objection may yet be heard: *true* experience* of ability
to choose is not only necessary but also sufficient for experience* of
freedom to choose. The real trouble with the being of limited conception
and the natural Epictetans is that they don't really have the *concept* of
choice at all, and therefore do not have *true* experience* of ability to
choose. As for the Genuine Incompatibilist Determinist, either it
doesn't have it either, or it is not what it claims to be, for genuine

---

[25] Certainly it might not take very much for it to catch on. Suppose some other agent
tells it that it will be maltreated if it ever does again something that it is very given to
doing. Wanting to do it, and yet fearing maltreatment, the being of limited conception
may be assailed, suddenly, by the 'truly up to me' experience or attitude. (The nature of
its contingent circumstances matters as much to its experience* of freedom as the nature
of its given cognitive and volitional disposition.) But even in this case it does not have
to catch on. It is not unintelligible that it should not. (This case makes it worth noting
that dogs are in one way not a good model for beings of limited conception, for their
perspective on the world may not be (is not) *bland* in the way that the being of limited
conception's is.)

incompatibilist determinism is simply impossible for a being that possesses the concept of choice.

Take the being of limited conception. Can one really ascribe to it either

(1) (occurrent) awareness* with the content: I am now able to *choose* (*XY*);

or

(2) (possibly merely explicit*) awareness* with the content: I am a being of a kind that is able to *choose*—

stressing the word 'choose' in each case? Is not (1) essentially something more than the bare awareness*: I am facing two options *X* and *Y*? Is it not essentially something more than consciousness*-on-the-point-of-action of the fact of facing action-alternatives?[26] Is not to have the concept of choice—to be currently operating with or deploying that concept in such a way that the word 'choice' features in a correct specification in English of the content of one's experience of things—to add to minimal fully self-conscious option-facing awareness* the essentially-sense-of-freedom-involving idea that *I* can *pick* which one I want, that what happens lies in my hands, is truly up to me, and so on?

To this general line of argument the reply is this. First, the Genuine Incompatibilist Determinist is simply not to be dismissed as it has been. Second, it still seems quite wrong to say that anything at all is lacking, intellectually or cognitively speaking, in the being of limited conception's case, so far as possession of the concept of choice is concerned. The being of limited conception's awareness* that it faces options is its being aware* that it (*it*) has action-alternatives. It knows what it is to act, and that it can act. It knows, in sum, that it is able to choose between different courses of action. If we think that it lacks something, this is probably because the concept of choice is for us blended with strictly speaking extraneous affective or non-cognitive elements that make it hard for us to see that the being of limited conception has all that is necessary, so far as possession of the concept of choice just as such is concerned. Remember that one can put the natural Epictetans, the being of limited conception, and the Genuine Incompatibilist Determinist in front of the momentous button. They are intellectually fully aware of the situation. But they simply do not live it in anything like the way we do—because they have experience of being able to

---

[26] Cf. the description of the being of limited conception in 14.8.1.

choose, but not of being able to choose *freely* (in such a way as to be truly responsible for their choices and actions).

A large part of the point of the filigree work attempted in this chapter is simply to exercise thought about what we think a being's experience must be like if it is to be a potential free agent; and the rights and wrongs of the particular arguments matter less than that the various more or less covert determinants of intuition—and the different possible positions—should be identified.

Why does the preceding matter at all? It should matter to all those who believe free agenthood is possible, because they are presumably committed to the idea that a specification can in principle be given of what a being must be like if it is to be a free agent. Trying to give such a specification, one can simply say that (1), being a self-conscious rational agent, and (2), being, in respect of the general character of one's experience, as ordinary human beings ordinarily are, is sufficient for freedom if anything is. But to say only this is to ignore difficult and interesting questions about exactly which features of ordinary human experience are crucial. Some of these questions have been considered in the foregoing. It seems, for example, to be necessary to talk at length about experience* of ability to choose, about what exactly it does and does not amount to, presuppose, necessarily involve, or give rise to causally.

Those who do not think free agenthood is possible may be equally interested in trying to state necessary conditions of free agenthood. For them, doing so is simply part of the general project of examining those pervasive phenomena of human experience which are mistakenly taken to be phenomena in virtue of the existence of which we can truly be said to be free.

14.11 OBJECTIVIST OPTIONS

What are the Objectivists to make of all this? I shall now argue that those of them who are convinced by the arguments of this chapter must either give up (1) the principal claim that experience* of or belief in freedom is a necessary condition of freedom, i.e., the claim that

$$(x)(Fx \rightarrow E^*(x,Fx)), \tag{1}$$

or must give up their Objectivism. For the two things cannot be rendered compatible in any satisfactory manner.

The Ability Account states (2) that to be a free agent is to be an Integrated, fully self-conscious, rational agent that is able to choose and is self-consciously aware that it is. We may express this, fully spelt out, as follows:

$$\text{Cn}/(x)(\underline{ACx} \text{ \& } S\text{-}Cx \text{ \& } Int \text{ } x \text{ \& } E^*(x,ACx) \leftrightarrow Fx)/. \tag{2}$$

But the first two conditions, 'ACx' and '$S\text{-}Cx$', have been held to be equivalent to 'Sx' (p. 272); and 'Sx' and '$Int \text{ } x$' have been held to be equivalent to '$S'x$' (p. 246). So (2) may be re-expressed as

$$\text{Cn}/(x)(S'x \text{ \& } E^*(x,ACx) \leftrightarrow Fx)/. \tag{2}$$

If we now take 'S^+' to symbolize 'fulfils the S' conditions and is self-consciously aware that it is able to choose' we can shorten (2) to

$$\text{Cn}/(x)(\underline{S^+x} \leftrightarrow Fx)/. \tag{2}$$

Thus 'S^+' represents the Ability Account, the latest version of the Objectivists' account of the conditions of freedom. It consists of the original Structural conditions S plus two Attitudinal conditions.

Let us suppose that the Objectivists decide to accept the Ability Account. (It is, after all, unclear what else they could hope to include among the conditions of free agenthood.) In this case they immediately run into trouble with (1). For if the arguments of this chapter are correct, 'S^+x' does not entail '$E^*(x,Fx)$': the former is neither a causally nor a constitutively sufficient condition of the latter. So (1) is not deducible in any manner, given that one accepts the Ability Account. In which case it seems that it has to be rejected by the Objectivists.

Objectivists who wish to save (1) may try the following arguments (it is worth setting out the ways in which they fail). They may despite everything argue that (3) being S^+ is bound to give rise *causally* to the experience* of freedom that we seem to require of free agents. This is to argue that

$$\text{Cs}/(x)(\underline{S^+x} \rightarrow E^*(x,Fx))/ \tag{3}$$

is true, in order to deduce (1) from (3) and one half of (2), i.e.

$$\text{Cn}/(x)(Fx \rightarrow \underline{S^+x})/. \tag{4}$$

It is important to recognize that this causal suggestion is an attractive one.[27] But the example-based objection is simple—the preceding sections of this chapter were designed precisely to provide possible cases— the Genuine Incompatibilist Determinist, the being of limited conception, the natural Epictetans—in which (3) is shown to be false.

---

[27] Here as elsewhere there may be oscillation of intuition.

The more general objection is that even if (3) were true, it would not really give the Objectivists what they want. For it leads to an account according to which (1) too is a causal truth, true, that is, because

$$\text{Cs}/(x)(\underline{Fx} \to E^*(x,Fx))/ \qquad (1.1)$$

is; and that is not true to our sense of how things are; our sense—which the Objectivists are trying to accommodate—that it is not a logical possibility that a being could be a free and truly responsible agent while having absolutely no such sense of itself.

It seems, then, that the Objectivists have to try to show that (1), the principal claim, is an *absolutely exceptionless* truth, while at the same time maintaining that experience* of freedom is not a *constitutive* condition of freedom. What are they to do?

The only remaining option, apparently, is for them to claim (5) that the set of conditions S^+ does after all, and despite all the preceding argument to the contrary, contain conditions that are constitutively sufficient for experience* of freedom; to claim, that is, that

$$\text{Cn}/(x)(\underline{S^+x} \to E^*(x,Fx))/ \qquad (5)$$

is true. They can then try to derive (1) as a necessarily exceptionless and not merely causal truth while blocking the unwanted claim that (1) is true because experience* of freedom is a constitutive condition of freedom—the claim, that is, that (1) is true because

$$\text{Cn}/(x)(Fx \to \underline{E^*(x,Fx)})/. \qquad (1.2)$$

(For (1) but not (1.2) follows from (4) and (5).)

The example-based objection to this is the same as before: the natural Epictetans, the being of limited conception, and the Genuine Incompatibilist Determinist show immediately that (5) is not true. The more general objection is relatively complicated, and is presented in Appendix F.

14.12 CONCLUSION

It appears that the Objectivists must either (*a*) give up the principal claim that experience* of freedom is a necessary condition of freedom altogether, or (*b*) maintain that it is a merely causal truth. Unwilling to accept (*a*), they may persevere with (*b*). They may try to enrich their account further, alleging that fulfilling the S^+ conditions is not enough: they may claim that an Integrated, self-conscious, purposive agent must not only be fully self-consciously aware* that it is able to choose, if it is to be a free agent, but must also be aware that it is aware* that it is able to choose. The new condition that they are proposing can be expressed thus: $E^*(x,E^*(x,ACx))$; and if one calls the set of S^+ conditions plus this new condition 'the S^* conditions', their claim about freedom can be expressed as follows: $Cn/(x)(\underline{S^*x} \longleftrightarrow Fx)$.

If one thinks about what this involves, it can seem that, fulfilling S^*, the agent is caught inescapably in the light of its consciousness of its responsibility for its choices and actions . . .; it cannot but believe or experience* that it is truly up to it what it does, being turned reflexively upon itself as self-aware agent and chooser in this way; so that $Cs/(x)$ $(\underline{S^*x} \rightarrow E^*(x,Fx))/$ is indeed true—fulfilling the S^* conditions does inevitably give rise causally to experience* of freedom, and the principal claim can after all be held to be a merely causal truth.

It is, again, important that there is something plausible about this idea. But the general objection to any causal account of the relation between freedom and experience* of freedom remains unchanged. And, as for more particular objections, it is not hard to see how the detailed cases considered earlier in this chapter might be rejigged to reveal the possible gap between the experience of a being who fulfils these S^* conditions and that of a being who has experience* of freedom. The Genuine Incompatibilist Determinist, for one, will provide a counter-example to the above causal claim (and, *a fortiori*, any constitutive claim). So will the others.

If the Objectivists want to hold that fulfilling the S^* conditions is sufficient for free agenthood even though one can fulfil them without experiencing oneself as a free agent, then this is, for them, a perfectly acceptable position. But it involves abandoning the principal claim altogether; that is, it involves accepting that an agent could properly be held to be a free agent truly responsible for what it does even if it had no conception of itself as truly responsible in that way, either at the time of action or in general.

The conclusion of the present argument, then, is that Objectivists who still aim to show that we are free and truly responsible in the ordinary, strong sense must either abandon the principal claim or abandon Objectivism as presently defined; and that they must therefore abandon Objectivism. For experience* of (belief in) one's freedom is indeed a necessary constitutive condition of one's freedom.[28]

Perhaps the conclusion has seemed obvious from the start. To the extent that it has, the function of the argument for it has not been to persuade, but rather to provide a frame within which to consider some of the other issues that arise regarding the nature and conditions of free agenthood.

Those who wish to abandon the principal claim and stick with the Objectivists—claiming either, as unrepentant Structural theorists, that the conditions S, or, as Attitudinal theorists, that the conditions S', or S^+, or even S^*, are sufficient for free agenthood in the ordinary strong sense—may now proceed immediately to the problem posed by non-self-determinability (or determinism). They have their account of the *differentia* of the species *potential free agent* in the genus *purposive agent*. The question they must now ask is whether a potential free agent can ever be actually free, given either the truth or the falsity of determinism, and given the impossibility of ultimate self-determination. They are thus at the point where discussions of freedom usually start, and need not read the next chapter, which returns to the problems that confront those who continue to believe that the principal claim is true, and that it is not simply a causal truth.

In fact, even those who believe that experiencing oneself as free *is* causally guaranteed by fulfilling certain other independently characterizable conditions of freedom, despite all the claims to the contrary in this chapter, may still grant that the principal claim is not simply a causal truth. For even if it is true that no being can come to be a fully self-conscious, Integrated, rational or purposive agent and not also come to believe it is free in the present sense (this is the 'quasi-Kantian'

---

[28] It is important to note that Objectivists who are *not* trying to prove that we are free in the ordinary strong sense—Objectivists who are compatibilists, for example, and who think that the notion of freedom in the sense of true responsibility is incoherent—may be prepared to agree that having experience of oneself as truly responsible may be a constitutive condition of being a free agent, though they understand 'free agent' in some merely compatibilist sense. These theorists can therefore accept a modified version of the principal claim of the sort considered in 10.13 without having to abandon their Objectivism. This position may attract many who are inclined to compatibilism, but find the principal claim a plausible one.

claim of 14.6), the problem still seems to remain: it still seems to be a *non*-causal truth that experience* of oneself as a free agent is a necessary condition of being a free agent.[29]

[29] No appeal to the relation of 'supervenience' can help here. It may be suggested that the property of having experience* of freedom, or '$E^*(F)$', is supervenient on the property of being free, or 'F'. But what exactly does this amount to, over and above the claim that 'If F then $E^*(F)$' is (1) a non-causal truth, (2) a non-formal-logical truth, (3) a necessarily exceptionless truth—which is (4) none the less not true because $E^*(F)$ is a *constitutive* condition of F (for $E^*(F)$ is merely *supervenient* on F, merely a necessary *concomitant* of F, something that has to be there if F is)? There is as much reason as ever to reject (4). The notion of supervenience is problematic, and none of the apparent reasons for wanting to accept something appropriately similar to (4) in the case of the claim that mental (or moral) properties are supervenient on physical properties seem to obtain purchase in this case.

15

Subjectivism and Experience* of Freedom

It was the natural Epictetans who set off the enquiries of the last chapter. It was argued that they were not free agents, given the nature of their experience. But if we—or any beings—are free agents, then the natural Epictetans fail to be free agents by a very narrow margin. They are extremely well-endowed with practical and cognitive capacities, and are in addition maximally unconstrained. Indeed it does not seem that there is any difference that could possibly be relevant to free agenthood, among all the differences between a natural Epictetan and an ordinary adult human being (our paradigm candidate for free agenthood), other than the former's lack of indecision and, vitally, of any experience of itself as truly free in and responsible for its choices and actions.

I shall take it that this is so; and, therefore, that if one is, as an adult human being, a free agent, then this is essentially partly because behind one's possible occurrent experiences of oneself as free there runs a standing, persisting, explicit* experience or conception of oneself as free; a settled or continuing sense or conception of oneself as a kind of thing that can choose and act freely in particular cases. We are free (truly responsible), if we are, partly because we see ourselves and our action in a certain way—as free (or truly responsible). As the Subjectivists say, this is a *constitutive* condition of freedom. It is an Attitudinal condition. Free agenthood is not just a matter of certain practical capacities. A free agent must see itself in a certain specific way, and its seeing itself in this way is not a necessary consequence of its possession of any set of abilities or capacities or attitudes that does not include this way of seeing itself. This has not been proved by exhaustion of a determinately bounded field of possibilities. But no good reason has been found to doubt it. It still seems wrong to say of the natural Epictetans, or of the others considered in the last chapter, that they are free agents really, but simply don't realize it. Their not having any experience of themselves as free (to choose), or as potential free agents, appears to preclude their being potential free agents. (Somewhat similarly, the naturally impeccable saint who never chooses out of indecision, but automatically does the right thing, appears to be a non-moral being.)

Although the sense of oneself as free is not usually occurrent in thought, nevertheless its presence is a necessary condition of an enormous number of one's thoughts having the character they do—most of one's thoughts about action, for example. One might say that it is in this sense 'indirectly occurrent' in thought.[1] In something like the sense in which 'the "I think" ' *can* accompany all our representations, given that we are self-conscious, so, correspondingly, the 'I am able to choose freely' *does* accompany (virtually) all our practical reasonings, in some more or less explicit fashion.[2] Just as the natural Epictetans are never undecided, so we in deliberating prior to action are in a sense always undecided: even when we most ardently desire to do a particular thing: it is a formal or constitutive condition of our agency. Whether only virtually, or implicitly, or explicitly*, or explicitly+, or consciously, expressly, and occurrently, the 'I am able to choose freely' informs all our deliberations in some constitutive manner. And when one is faced with the apparent fact that no Objectivist account of freedom can be rendered adequate, given the apparently ineliminable experience*-of-freedom condition,[3]—the apparent fact that being free is essentially partly a matter of believing one is free—then it may sometimes seem obvious that one should conclude, not that there is no positive theory of freedom to be had at all, but rather that some Subjectivist or commitment account must not only be the best we can do, but must also be entirely adequate.[4] For many common situations inspire in us a

---

[1] It may be said that there could be a creature that did regularly have occurrent experience* of freedom to choose, but had *no* standing conception of itself as free. But there is really no issue here. One could say that it was actually a potential free agent whenever (and only when) it had such occurrent experience. Or one could say that the essence of the requirement that one have a standing conception of oneself as free is only that one be such that one tends to have occurrent experience* of freedom in certain circumstances.

[2] Cf. Kant, *Critique of Pure Reason*, B132. This is to take the Kantian 'I think' as a potential feature of empirical rather than transcendental self-consciousness.

[3] Not to mention—still—the impossibility of self-determination.

[4] Sometimes—one's view of the problem tends to go on changing.

sense of freedom of choice and action which has an unequivocally absolute character.[5]

15.2 SUBJECTIVISM: PROSPECTS FOR A POSITIVE THEORY OF FREEDOM

The basic claim of the Subjectivists is that experience of oneself as a free agent (as able to choose freely) is a constitutive condition of being a free agent. They claim that it is at least a necessary condition of free agenthood, whether or not there are any sufficient conditions.

Suppose that they now want to go further, and advance a *positive* theory of freedom—a theory that we are in fact free. Clearly they must first of all deny that (upper case) Subjectivism entails (lower case) subjectivism (the view that there is an ineliminable sense in which freedom does not exist). They must maintain that a Subjectivist account of freedom can, despite its Subjectivism, be a positive, fully objectivist theory of freedom. (A positive theory is by definition a theory that we really are free, and is therefore by definition an objectivist theory.)

Looking for a model, they may take the case of morality. One can be a Subjectivist about morals, holding that the phenomenon of things being morally good and bad is not something of which we can give an Objectivist account (an account which purports to show that the phenomenon exists without making reference to the fact of our belief or subjective conviction that it exists). But if one is a Subjectivist one need not be a subjectivist. One can be a *Subjectivist objectivist* about morals—holding that, given the objectively existing phenomenon of our subjective conviction as to the existence of moral values, agents (and, derivatively, acts) can be objectively morally good and bad; although they cannot be Objectivistically speaking good or bad, because the full account of that in which their being good or bad consists necessarily involves reference to their subjective conviction that they are morally good or bad (cf. 11.7).

If this is a coherent position (it can seem quite promising), then the question arises as to whether the same line can be taken about free agenthood.

[5] Notice that one could experience oneself as able to choose freely in the present sense even if one were throughout one's life so hypnotized that one was not really able to choose at all; one could in such circumstances be a potential free agent (if potential free agenthood is possible at all). As soon as one was not hypnotized in this way, then one would become actually free—on the account of being actually free according to which absence of constraint is (given a potential free agent) sufficient for actually being free.

The first thing to recall is that the problem raised for free agenthood by the impossibility of ultimate self-determination (as described in Chapter 2) has not gone away. Whatever form a positive Subjectivist theory of freedom eventually takes, it will have to take account of this. It will have to hold that the impossibility of such self-determination cannot be decisive to the question of whether we are free agents. No doubt it will lay great stress on the fact that we are not only self-conscious rational agents but are also ordinarily convinced that we are self-determining, and are, perhaps, inescapably committed to this view of ourselves.[6]

The view that this conviction and this commitment could somehow suffice to make us free looks as unpromising as ever. And yet when they rehearse the old arguments against all Objectivist theories, libertarian or compatibilist, some may conclude that a Subjectivist theory, however dubious a *tertium quid*, is quite simply one's best bet when one is trying to establish something one (thinks—or feels—one) just knows to be the case, unreflectively. For conventional, Objectivist libertarians are likely to end up either by making the demand that free agents be, impossibly, truly self-determining, or else by saying nothing that compatibilists would not agree with (apart from the fact that the libertarians will continue to insist that the falsity of determinism is necessary for freedom). While clear-headed conventional (Objectivist) compatibilists have in the end to ignore our profound commitment to the idea that the ordinary strong notions of responsibility and desert have application, and our requirement that any adequate account of freedom should show that they do. They have to hold out for a Procrustean, Schlickian revision of the notion of responsibility on an arguably dimensionless bed.

15.3 CONTRAVENTION: THE OPTIONS

So perhaps the Subjectivist option can look like the best one available.

---

[6] Sidgwick does not really put forward a *theory* of freedom at all, in *The Methods of Ethics*. But the way in which he dismisses the problem of freedom, as a problem for ethics, is instructive. We are faced with "the immediate affirmation of consciousness at the moment of deliberation" that we are free (p. 65); we "find it impossible not to think that [we] can now choose to do" what we conceive to be right, in situations of morally significant choice (p. 67). This being so, it is (he says) simply not "relevant to ethical deliberation to determine the metaphysical [i.e., in the present terms, objective] validity of [our] consciousness of freedom to choose" (p. 68). It is a short step to saying, in Kantian fashion, that for this reason we are as deliberators and agents really free—even if it is a short step across a bottomless chasm (and one that Sidgwick would not himself have taken).

(Perhaps it can also look unavoidable—if the argument that belief in freedom is a necessary constitutive condition of freedom is sound.) But it still does not seem particularly promising. And it still involves contravention of the principle of independence. So if such contravention is still unacceptable in the case of freedom, then Subjectivism is unacceptable for that reason alone—even if for no other.

Consider, therefore, one way of interpreting the condition that any free agent must believe it is free that avoids contravention. The idea is simple enough. It could be put this way: the principle is not contravened, because what is in question, in the case of a's belief or experience* that he is free, is not belief or experience relationally construed with respect to both object *and property*, as it were, but only with respect to the former.[7]

Consider a in his role as arbitrarily selected agent. It is experience* of freedom that is in question. But—so the present suggestion goes—it is not a question of a's experience*, with respect to (i), the property F, that is, freedom, and (ii), the object a, that is, himself,[8] of the latter's exemplifying the former. For to put things in this way is to make it obligatory to suppose that a could at least in principle be shown to exemplify F independently of any reference being made to his experience* of his exemplifying F. And it is precisely this that is ruled out by claiming that experience* of freedom is a constitutive condition of freedom. To put things in this way is simply to assume that F is a property that can exist independently of experience* of (or belief in) F, and can for that reason be an object of such experience (or belief). So the alleged paradox becomes inevitable.

Since this is no good (the suggestion goes), 'a's experience of himself as free', or 'a experiences* that Fa' ('$E^*(a,Fa)$'), must be relationally construed with respect to a but not with respect to F, which must be taken as attaching in some indetachably qualificatory way to 'experiences(*)'. What is in question, then, is a's *experience-as-F* of himself, a.

On this view, there is no objective or Objectivistically characterizable property of freedom, F, that exists independently of the objective property *experiences-as-F*. But this last property is indeed an objective (and Objectivistically characterizable)[9] property, and one which is un-

---

[7] It should be clear from what follows that this manner of speaking involves no commitment to any dubious ontology of properties.

[8] Castañedan problems about self-reference do not arise, given the ruling in 10.5.

[9] One does not have to experience* or believe one has *this* property, in order to have it.

doubtedly very widely exemplified. And although there is no Ob-jectivistically characterizable property of freedom that exists independently of the property *experiences-as-F*, to say that it cannot exist thus independently is not to say that it cannot exist at all, as an objective property. For it may be that *a*'s possession (unrenounceably) of the objective property of experiencing-himself-as-F is necessary for, and, given his possession of certain other properties (e.g. the conditions S^+, p. 288), sufficient for his possession of the thereby really existing objective property *F*.

The principle of independence is not contravened, on this account, for there is no longer a single property *F* which is such that *a*'s belief that he possesses it is a necessary constitutive condition of his actual possession of it. There are instead two distinct properties, *experiences-as-F* and *F*, and it is only *a*'s possession of the first that is a necessary condition of his possession of the second. Let 'E_F' stand for the two-place, unstructured, reflexive[10] predicate 'experiences-as-F'. Then the claim about freedom is not, as before, that

$$Cn/(x)(Fx \to \underline{E^*(x,Fx)}),$$

but rather that

$$Cn/(x)(Fx \to \underline{E_F(x,x)})/.^{11}$$

The predicate on the left hand-side does not appear on the right-hand side in an intentional or representational-state context; it does not appear there at all. And so the principle of independence is respected.

But does this manoeuvre help? It was mentioned in 4.3, and amounts to no more than this: 'experience-as-free' is just the name of a certain manner of experience (of self). To say that, to be free, *a* must experience himself as free is not to say that some belief, form of experience, or conception must be attributed to him which is such that having it is correctly characterized as involving being in, or being disposed to be in, a representational state with an property-to-object-attributing struc-ture of a sort which may be expressed thus: '$E^*(a,Fa)$' or thus '$B(a,Fa)$'. It is, rather, to attribute to him a certain state without such structure, a mere manner or style of apprehension or experience of self that does not involve any express self-attribution of a certain property, *F*.

On this view, creatures like ourselves, acceding to language, *may*

---

[10] Reflexive in the restricted sense that it attributes a manner of experience that one can only have of oneself: *x* experiences-as-free-from-the-inside *y*, as it were.

[11] One could alternatively treat 'E_F' as a one-place predicate, so that '$E_F x$' is read '*x* has experience of self as free'—to get $Cn/(x)(Fx \to \underline{E_F x})/$.

explicitly ascribe freedom to themselves in language or linguistically articulated thought. But the ability and tendency to do so is not in itself essential to freedom. What is essential is a certain *manner of being* that underlies this ability and tendency, one that is correctly described as experience* of freedom, and that does not essentially involve either being in or being disposed to be in some property-to-object-attributing, linguistically articulated representational state.

This line has a certain attraction. But I do not think it will do. For, given the present terms of debate, its proponents are committed to allowing that 'truly responsible' can be substituted for 'free' throughout. And it seems most implausible to suppose that a manner of experience, or of being, could correctly be said to be or to involve experience of self as truly responsible if it did not also involve the entertaining of, or disposition to entertain, some fully articulated conception or representation *of* oneself *as* possessed of a certain property that is of precisely the kind that appears problematic. That is, it would seem to be a consequence of the nature of the cognitively speaking fairly sophisticated notion of true responsibility that any experience of self which can properly count as experience of self as truly responsible must involve a representation *of* oneself *as* possessed of the property of true responsibility in an articulated form of thought which is of such a kind that the problem of contravention of the principle of independence can arise with respect to it. Indeed, although 'experience(*)' has been substituted for 'believe' in recent chapters, there seems to be little wrong, in the end, with the original claim that any free or truly responsible agent must believe it is one. When one enquires into the conditions of true responsibility, it is precisely the belief that one is truly responsible that seems to be necessary for true responsibility. This is why no two-level analysis of the sort suggested in 10.13 will help.

So what is to be done? Consider the problem one more time.

(1) It seems that any positive theory of freedom that enjoins respect for the principle of independence has to give an account of freedom according to which it is logically possible that an agent can be a free agent truly responsible for its actions without believing that it is one.

(2) Let the problem posed by the impossibility of true self-determination be put to one side again.

(3) Consider, for simplicity's sake, a non-moral agent: the question of morality can only complicate the issue, especially since it appears

that there is a sense in which an agent acts morally rightly, or at least morally wrongly, only if it believes it does.

(4) It has already been noted that there is an attractive Objectivist line of thought (the Ability Account) according to which an agent is a potential free agent when it is able to choose (in the sense defined in 8.2), self-conscious, and fully self-consciously aware that it is able to choose. If, further, it is physically and psychically unconstrained, at a particular time, what more could it possibly want or need in the way of freedom? What more could it possibly be thought to want or need, except—hopelessly—the property of being truly self-determining in the impossible way?

(5) The problem of self-determination has been put to one side. Nevertheless, suppose, now, that the agent in question is, *per impossibile*, truly self-determined; that it is, *per impossibile*, ultimately self-created and self-governing with respect to character and pro-attitudes. Now it has the only thing—so it seemed—that it could possibly be supposed to lack.

(6) But now suppose, finally, that the agent of whom all these things are true, the *ex hypothesi* truly self-determined (and to that extent truly self-determining) agent, has lost any sense or conception of itself as a free agent, as truly responsible, as truly self-determining in action. And ask whether it is a free agent.

The answer seems clear enough. No, it is not, simply because of the supposition in (6). That is not what it is to be free. In one sense it simply follows from the previous description that it is a truly responsible agent, given (5). But then it seems that we have only to suppose that it has no sense of itself as truly responsible, as in (6), to find that all the capacity-grounded and mysteriously metaphysically backed true responsibility attributed in (4) and (5) is simply not enough for the sort of true responsibility and freedom we require. Perhaps there is some sort of mirage here. Perhaps it is produced by some so far uneliminated anthropocentricity of outlook.[12] But if so, then this mirage appears to be an indispensable part of our ordinary, strong, clear-seeming notion of freedom, the present object of study.

How might the Objectivists reply to this? They might wish to reply, in a familiar way, that the agent in question simply cannot fulfil the conditions laid down in (4) and (5) and not also believe it is, or have a sense of itself as, a free agent. But Chapter 14 has given reasons for

---

[12] Cf. 12.4 and 13.3 *ad fin.*

doubting this; it seems that one might always fail to cotton on to the requisite way of thinking, whatever capacities one possessed. (Or one might lose it, having previously possessed it.) More importantly, it seems clear that the 'cannot' in the penultimate sentence cannot be a merely causal 'cannot', of a kind that might help to avoid contravention of the principle of independence. For it seems *inconceivable* that there should be true free agenthood without belief in freedom. It seems to be a non-causal impossibility: when one imaginatively subtracts any sense of freedom or true responsibility from the agent, its freedom or true responsibility immediately goes too.

Perhaps the only option left to the Objectivists is simply to deny that belief in or experience* of freedom is necessary for freedom. Although this position has been rejected here, it cannot be simply disproved. For at this point there are no demonstrative arguments. It is simply a question of what one wishes, or is prepared, to call 'freedom' or 'true responsibility'.

The Objectivists may say this: put yourself in the shoes of the agent described in (3)-(6): imagine yourself fitting the description with the smallest change in you as an agent that is compatible with your doing so. You may feel you've lost something vital. Certainly you've lost a grasp of the notion of morality; and you've also lost any sense of yourself as a free, truly responsible agent. But you haven't actually lost your freedom, however different things feel. That you have as much as you ever did. The only difference is that before you were aware that you were a free agent. You're still a free agent, you're just not aware of it.

To this the correct reply still seems to be that there is, as the Subjectivists insist, a paramount sense of 'free agent' given which you aren't really a free agent at all if you're not aware that you are: to be like the agent in question is not really to be a free agent at all. You haven't just lost awareness of something, you've (thereby) lost the thing itself.

The Objectivists may finish by saying this: that if it can be successfully maintained that the necessity of belief in freedom for freedom is part of the ordinary, strong notion of freedom, then they are simply offering a revised account of what freedom is: their account states what freedom really is—it states the most that it could be—whatever we ordinarily (and, they imply, confusedly) suppose. These Objectivists are then at liberty to go on to face the problem raised by the fact that true self-determination is also apparently necessary for freedom. Facing it, they may turn into outright compatibilists, in their attempt to produce a positive theory of freedom—re-iterating the claim that their (S^+ conditions) account, which makes no reference to determinism, already states the most that freedom could be, and so in effect rejoining Hume.[13] Or they may add some decorative but ultimately useless libertian embroideries.

What of the Subjectivists? They remain with their powerful question, the one that seems to commit them (and us) to contravention of the principle of independence: if, after an agent performs an action, we discover that it really has no sort of conception or experience of itself as able to choose or act truly responsibly, how can we possibly hold it to *be* truly responsible for its action? Put yourself in this agent's shoes: you act, when you do, with no sense of yourself as truly responsibly free in your choice or action. Can you call a life spent like that the life of a free agent? That is not what it is to be free.

So the principle of independence remains contravened. But surely this does not matter if freedom or true responsibility is impossible anyway, as, in an ineliminable, self-determination-requiring sense, it clearly is? For then there is no such thing as the property of freedom and, therefore, no true statement of the necessary and sufficient conditions of freedom that contravenes the principle of independence. And so we are, as it were, simply let off the problem. The property of freedom is not a real property after all.

This may not satisfy everyone; and it is worth pointing out that there is one way in which contravention does not create a problem even if freedom is possible. The point was made in 11.3: assume that *b* is a free agent; *b* does not have to have any sort of conscious, spelt-out grasp of the conditions of free agenthood, whatever they may be, nor, in particular, of the fact that belief in freedom is among those conditions, in order for it to be truly said of it that it is a free agent. We as theorists may require of a free agent that it believe it is one, but it need not itself know that this is a condition of freedom. Even if it does know this, it does not have to enter the over-reflective spiral (11.2), believing that in order to be free it must believe something (that it is free) that it cannot justifiably come to believe unless it finds that it already believes it. Nothing compels it to be so reflective. And this is one respect, at least, in which contravention is not problematic in the way in which it may first appear to be.

[13] Whose position—it would be foolish to deny it—has as much to recommend it as ever, unsatisfactory though it is.

The best way to capture the basis of the recurrent feeling that it is not problematic *at all* to suppose that belief in freedom is a condition of freedom is, perhaps, to consider the following idealized account of a process of realization*, on the part of a fully self-conscious agent, *b*, that it is a free agent.

(I) *b* is able to choose: (i) *ACb*.

(II) *b* is (fully self-consciously) aware that it is able to choose: reverting to '*B*' (in lieu of '*E**') one may express this by (ii) *B(b,ACb)*.

(III) At first *b* is only aware of this in a completely blinkered fashion, similar to that of the being of limited conception considered in 14.8. But then it realizes*[14] what being able to choose 'really involves' (this is how it would itself put the content of the realization): it realizes* that being able to choose *just is*, in effect, being a free, truly responsible agent. (Sartrean aware-ness* of freedom dawns upon it, and becomes inescapable for it from that moment on.) One may express this realization* by (iii) *B(b,(x)(ACx → Fx))*.[15]

(IV) Reflecting, it may then see that self-conscious awareness of ability to choose is also necessary for freedom, so that (iii) changes to (iv) *B(b,(x)(ACx & B(x,ACx) → Fx)*. But it may not; it doesn't matter.

(V) Believing what is expressed by (iii), or (iv), it doubtless also realizes* that it too is free; but this is none the less an additional step, additional to 'realizing* what being able to choose really involves', and amounting to the formation of a further belief, (v) *B(b,Fb)*, on the basis of (ii) and either (iii) or (iv).

Suppose we accept a positive Subjectivist account of freedom, and say that, all these things having happened, *b* is indeed a free agent. Belief in freedom emerges as before as a condition of freedom. But, given this story, it is perhaps easier to accept that there is nothing problematic about this. *b* reaches this belief, (v), partly on the basis of the strictly speaking false belief (iii), or (iv). But this doesn't matter, on the present view. *b* as it now is is none the less a free agent.

Here belief in freedom is seen as a kind of *awareness condition* on freedom (10.7, 11.1); and if this is acceptable, then it is not true that

---

[14] This describes how it seems to *b*—a realization.

[15] Or *B(b,λx[ACx]= λx[Fx])*—it believes that the two properties are identical.

only conventional properties can have awareness conditions. This does seem a reasonable view to adopt, for, in the sequence just described, it is not the case that *b* becomes aware that something—i.e. being able to choose, ± being self-consciously aware of this—counts, *conventionally*, as being free (the whole process of belief-formation can after all be imagined to take place in an entirely solitary being). *b* must rather be supposed to become aware* of what being able to choose (± being aware that this is so) intrinsically or *non*-conventionally amounts to. This is how it will seem to *b* itself, in any case.

On this view, freedom, like other properties with awareness conditions, is allowed to be already all there, in some weak sense, given ability to choose ± self-conscious awareness of ability to choose. But it is at the same time held to be not really all there because there is, precisely, an awareness condition on freedom. And so the catch remains: belief in freedom is not just full awareness of certain aspects of one's objective situation. For before the advent of this awareness* that one is a free agent, one's objective situation is, after all, not really that of being a free agent at all.

Perhaps this description helps to diminish the sense that contravention of the principle of independence is problematic in the case of freedom. And yet it may still seem that if belief in freedom is a condition of freedom, then freedom is somehow insubstantial, not a fully real, objective property, not like redness or baldness. If so, I have no further suggestions. But consider again the agent described in (3)-(6) above. It was *ex hypothesi* truly self-determined (and so truly self-determining) in the impossible way, but it had no sense of itself as free or truly responsible. Suppose that it now acquires such a sense of itself—for whatever reason. Then, surely, it is, indisputably, a free and truly responsible agent. Surely no possible obstacles or problems remain. But if so, then one of the things that is not problematic is its believing it is free, and, in particular, the fact that its believing it is free is a condition of its being free. . . .

Perhaps the feeling that this condition is still problematic derives from worry about the idea that it could form part of any truly sufficient set of conditions of free agenthood considered as a fully objective property. But when true, impossible self-determination is imported into the proposed set of conditions, it may seem that the belief-in-freedom condition is not itself problematic. And this may suggest that part of the worry, at least, was not about the idea that the belief-in-freedom condition could be part of any set of sufficient conditions, but only about the idea that there could really be any such set.

15.4 CONCLUSION

To conclude. If we are free agents, then being a (1) fully self-conscious (2) Integrated (3) rational or purposive agent that is (4) able to choose and is (5) fully self-consciously aware of this and (6) believes it is (or experiences itself as) free just is, or is at least sufficient for, being a free agent (i.e. $Cn/(x)(\underline{S^+x}$ & $E^*(x,Fx) \leftrightarrow Fx)/$, or at least $Cn/(x)(S^+x$ & $\underline{E^*(x,Fx)} \rightarrow Fx)/).$[16] But if, as can seem obvious, the impossibility of true self-determination means that we are not truly responsible, free agents after all, then these proposed (compatibilist) conditions of free agenthood are at best only necessary conditions. In which case we are left not very well off—unless, by some derived variety of paradigm-case argument, we simply stipulate that the phrase 'free agent' must have application, and that a free agent is any agent that fulfils those conditions that feature in whatever we take to be the closest we can get to a statement of the conditions of true, impossible free agenthood. On this view, we are free agents; and we have an account of what it is about us that makes this true.

Whatever is finally decided, we are left with the hard, experiential fact that we really do face choices, and know that we do. And one might say that although we are not and cannot be free, yet we really do have experience of what it is to be free. That is perhaps as good an expression as any of the 'antinomy' of freedom.

Fido and Nemo; Meursault and the Spectators; the natural Epictetans, the Genuine Incompatibilist Determinist, and the being of limited conception; the neo-Epictetans, the spiritually advanced Buddhists—they contribute to just one attempt at a detailed, constructive analysis of 'x is a free agent'.[17] No doubt there are other very different ways of approaching the question. As remarked at the beginning, however, the principal aim of the present discussion has not really been to try to state what free agenthood is. For on the apparently straightforward factual question of whether or not we are free agents

---

[16] 'S^+' is defined on p. 288; 'S'' would do, in fact, since (6) entails (5). Cf. (2) on p. 268.

[17] An analysis that does not simply assume that we, human beings, are free agents, if any beings are, and then ask what freedom is, but tries to build up a description of a free agent more or less from scratch.

it would be foolish to expect any fundamental advance from the dead lock of the existing, standard, opposed views:[18] according to the firs of which it is obvious what freedom is—true self-determination an true responsibility—and obvious, too, on reflection, that there is a clea sense in which it is impossible; and according to the second of whicl freedom is simply Humean freedom, ability to do what one want or chooses to do, something that can be enjoyed by a wide range o agents.[19] Here the attempt to give a conventional necessary and-sufficient-conditions analysis of free agenthood has been under taken for the sake of the general framework that it provides—a frame work within which to develop and complicate thought about thos complex phenomena of human experience that lead us to think an talk of ourselves as free, and to engage in the kind of philosophica debates about freedom that we do engage in.

[18] It would be foolish, for example, to think that advances in modal logic, quantum physics or neurophysiology could make any fundamental difference to the debate.

[19] Or Humean freedom $\pm$ various refinements of the sort discussed by H. Frankfur and G. Watson, for example.

16

Antinomy and Truth

But the question may still be asked—are we or are we not free agents? Are we ever truly responsible for our actions in the ordinary strong sense of 'truly responsible'? Are we ever truly responsible for our actions in such a way as to be—among other things—capable of being truly deserving of praise and blame for them? Or is the conclusion simply that we are not really truly responsible agents at all, although we cannot help believing we are?

Roughly, this is the conclusion. All the essential reasons for it were stated in Chapter 2, and they are worth summarizing here. First, though, consider an objection touched on in 1.1, and again at the end of 6.4. It comes in the form of a couple of questions: Why this concentration on the notion of true responsibility? Certainly we want to be free, but do we really want to be *truly responsible* for our actions? We are very often entirely free in the 'basic' (and wholly compatibilist) Humean sense mentioned in 1.1: that is, we are very often entirely free in the sense of being able to do what we want or choose or decide to do. Isn't this enough? Isn't this all that really matters, in the way of freedom? What more could anyone possibly reasonably want?

The principal answer to this objection is simple: from the theoretical point of view, the centrally important question about freedom is not what we want (or might on reflection want), but rather what we believe. And it is indubitable that we do ordinarily behave as if we believed that we (and others) have free will in the ordinary, strong sense—true responsibility. This belief plays a central role in our lives. That is why it is of fundamental importance for philosophy to examine this belief, its nature, origins, and consequences, and to try to determine its truth or falsity.

Suppose, though, that it is conceded that the belief is false: true responsibility is impossible. It may then again be asked: Why should anyone want it anyway? The question deserves consideration. For it can sometimes seem very plausible to say that 'basic' freedom to do what one wants or chooses to do is all that one could ever reasonably want in the way of freedom, as one pursues one's various concerns from day to day. Surely, to be able to do (or attempt) what one wants or chooses to do (or attempt) is to have complete freedom of action? So why should anyone want true responsibility? What does it really add? These are powerful questions for the compatibilist to ask.[1] Once again it is reasonable to make the question-pre-empting response that it is not so much what we want but what we believe that matters most. But it is worth facing the questions directly.

One can first of all concede that some (perhaps highly pragmatic and single-minded) individual human agents may have no reason at all to want any sort of freedom other than the 'basic' freedom described above. It depends entirely on what other things they want. In particular, it seems clear that someone who pursues goals, ideals, projects, opportunities, and satisfactions that have little to do with the entertaining of affective relations with other people may have no reason at all to want any sort of freedom other than 'basic' compatibilist freedom. This is undoubtedly an important point.

Things look different when one considers agents who give weight to the entertaining of certain sorts of moral and affective relations with other people. But these relations are not all of equal importance: the fact that we ordinarily behave as if we firmly believed people to be proper objects of blame, resentment, grudges, contempt, scorn, moral indignation, and so on, does not seem particularly important. For although we ordinarily behave as if we firmly believed that people can be proper objects of certain at least of these (predominantly negative) reactions, it is not obvious that this is something we particularly want to be the case.

Clearly, our more positive attitudes to other people are the best cases to consider. For when we consider these attitudes, the idea that people can be true originators of their actions in such a way as to be truly responsible for them emerges as integral to some of our strongest beliefs about what is valuable (and therefore worth wanting) in human life and interaction. It seems that we very much want people to be proper objects of gratitude, for example. And they cannot be proper objects of gratitude unless they can be truly responsible for what they do.[2] Our

---

[1] Cf. 6.4 *ad fin*. Dennett raises them directly in his book *Elbow Room*, which is subtitled 'The varieties of free will worth wanting'.

[2] It may be that they cannot be proper objects of gratitude without also being proper objects of resentment and blame; and it may be that one cannot maintain the positive attitudes without remaining susceptible to the negative ones; but we may put these points to one side.

ordinary conception of love also seems to require ascription of true responsibility to the one who is loved. True, one can love a person sexually, one can love their looks, their wit, their forgetfulness, their childishness; and none of these things presupposes any ascription of true responsibility to them. Infatuation, too, can happily treat the person who is its object as an entirely determined phenomenon, just as it can happily accept the idea that the infatuation is itself an entirely determined phenomenon. Nevertheless there is a leading notion of what it is to love someone in the fullest sense—to love someone as a person, so one might say, rather than as some collocation of desirable features—which makes ascription of true responsibility to the one who is loved an ineliminable part of love.

But why? What is it to consider and love a person 'as a person'? A familiar and off-putting sort of vagueness appears to be creeping in. Perhaps one could make the point this way. To take x seriously as a person, in the way that one must if one loves x not in a merely infatuated way, but in a way that involves the kind of emotional reciprocity that is commonly seen as that which is most valuable in love, is—at least—to conceive of x as a being that is independent and self-determining in such a way that one *could* properly feel gratitude to him or her for some action or gesture. Love implies a view of the one who is loved as a self-determining agent to whom gratitude can be an appropriate response. But the possible appropriateness of gratitude implies true responsibility. Hence love implies ascription of true responsibility. So to want love to be possible is to want people to be truly responsible.[3]

Again this may not be thought very satisfactory. Perhaps the best thing to do, in order to see the point, is to imagine someone one loves, or to imagine loving someone, and then, in thought, to strip away any idea of that person as a truly responsible agent—to think of him or her as just a determined phenomenon with a given character, an entirely determinately given range of responses. Most people who do this will find that something extremely valuable, real or imagined, seems to drain away from the relation—except perhaps lovers like Pygmalion, or those who are merely infatuated (or very self-centred or hard-headed—but then it may be said that they don't really know what love

[3] This is not to say that love necessarily involves feelings of gratitude. Some might even feel that feelings of gratitude imply a distance of relationship incompatible with true love. They might believe that the mutual certainties of true love are of such a kind that the true lover's natural response to an action that might in other circumstances have provoked gratitude will be to take it entirely for granted, any other response being a kind of betrayal of faith.

is). No doubt there is something vertiginously agreeable about the ineluctability of pure infatuation. But we find it hard to renounce the possibility of gratitude.

Some may find that generalising this thought-experiment leaves them feeling that they are all alone—alone in the world. If it does, this is because they have in pursuing the thought-experiment been unable to stop thinking of themselves as truly responsible (cf. 6.5); and so they have found that the thought-experiment leaves them surrounded by entirely determined entities with whom any interaction is ultimately only a mockery of 'true' communication—being essentially like inter-action with a programmed character in a computer game (there being only a difference of degree, not of kind). People who have this reaction will again have a reason for wanting true responsibility to exist (in other people).

No doubt the thing that seems to drain away in the thought-experiment is, in some ineliminable sense or other, an illusion—since true responsibility is demonstrably impossible. But that does not alter the fact that the thought-experiment may help to show that we *want* true responsibility, and want it because we want love (or want love to be possible, at least). Love is only the most dramatic case of what we want to be possible in human relations, moreover—and perhaps it is not even the best case. The possibility of gratitude seems even more important: we very much want it to be true that we can stand in relations to other people in which reactions like the reaction of feeling gratitude are appropriate, in that sense of 'appropriate', discussed in Chapter 5, which requires that people can be truly responsible for what they do in the ordinary, strong sense. This is profoundly important to us; many people's lives would lose their point without it. And those people whose lives would not lose their point are perhaps the worse for that.

It could be said that the collective and inescapable illusion of true responsibility is as good as the real thing, and that therefore we don't have reason to want the real and impossible thing itself.[4] But this is a point without much significance. If it is true, then it is true simply in the sense in which any inescapable illusion that something one desires is the case is as good as its actually being the case. The illusion fulfils

---

[4] For after all it seems that we really can have love, however fleeting and illusion-based it may be, although true responsibility is impossible. So actual true responsibility cannot be necessary for love.

the desire only because we desire the real thing. And if the illusion were impossible or unreliable, then we would want the real thing.

It is arguable, then, that we do have reason to want true responsibility. Most simply, perhaps, we want it to be true that people really can be truly *morally* responsible for what they do. But certain people—who may be highly egocentric, or devoted to researches that have little to do with other people, or just naturally solitary—may have very little reason to want true responsibility. And for this reason they may have difficulty in seeing (or feeling) the philosophical problem—even, perhaps, when facing some momentous choice between duty and desire. Some of us are far more naturally compatibilist than others.

Finally, it is arguable that long familiarity with the philosophical problem of free will may produce something of the same effect. It may work indirectly, like a practice of meditation, and slowly erode the basis of belief in true responsibility. And those to whom this happens may not feel that they have lost very much, when they reflect. For in losing the belief in true responsibility they may also lose the sorts of attitudes that made it seem important in the first place.[5] No doubt they will also lose the sense that the philosophical problem of free will is a deep problem. And perhaps this will be a sign that their understanding of reality has become more profound. But perhaps they should once again imagine facing the choice between their own torture and the torture of others described in 6.3.

16.2 WHAT SHOULD WE BELIEVE?

I now return to the main topic, and a summary of the reasons given for the conclusion that we are not really free and truly responsible agents at all, even if we cannot help believing we are.

(1) There is a clear and fundamental sense in which no being can be truly self-determining in respect of its character and motivation in such a way as to be truly responsible for how it is in respect of character and motivation.[6]

There can be no serious dispute about this. There can be serious dispute

[5] Perhaps philosophy can have the same sort of effect on one's belief in the persisting mental self or person—although D. Parfit suggests that the sceptical arguments that he considers in Part III of *Reasons and Persons* may stun one's natural belief in and concern for the persisting self only in a temporary fashion.

[6] It cannot be truly or ultimately responsible for how it is in any respect at all, for nothing can be *causa sui*. For brief replies to some of the more obvious objections to this claim, see, e.g., 2.1, and ch. 2 n. 32.

only about whether it follows from this that we cannot be truly responsible for our actions (i.e. about (3) below).

(2) When we act, at a given time, the way we act is, in some quite straightforward sense, a function of the way we then are, in respect of character and motivation. We act as we act *because of* how we then are, in respect of character and motivation.

However one understands the 'because' in this statement, there can be no serious dispute about its truth.

(3) It follows that there is a fundamental sense in which we cannot possibly be truly responsible for our actions. For we cannot be truly responsible for the way we are, and we act as we act because of the way we are.

There are all sorts of ways of objecting to this line of thought. But none of them, I suggest, can touch the fundamental sense in which it is correct.

Given that this is so, it seems that there is really only one way left in which to try to show that we are truly responsible for our actions: somehow or other, we have to show that fully self-conscious rational deliberation, of the sort creatures like ourselves are capable of, has some very special features indeed—features which can somehow or other make it true that when we act we can, on account of our general ability to engage in deliberation of this sort, correctly be said to be truly responsible for our actions even though we cannot be truly responsible for the way we are.

Is this at all plausible? Well, the nature of our experience of agency strongly suggests to us that fully self-conscious rational deliberation, of the sort of which we are capable, does indeed have the property of making us truly responsible for our actions in the strongest possible sense, despite the fact that we cannot be truly responsible for the way we are.[7] Somehow or other, we feel, our capacity for such deliberation suffices to *constitute* us as truly responsible agents in the strongest possible sense.

But one must not be swept away by the mere experience* of freedom or true responsibility. Here again the arguments of Chapter 2 are of

---

[7] One problem with this view is that we are strongly inclined to say that entirely spontaneous, entirely undeliberated actions are as free as actions preceded by some fully conscious process of rational deliberation. But we can suppose this problem solved for present purposes—by supposing, say, that it is our possession of the *capacity* for such deliberation that makes an ordinary action free, not necessarily any actual exercise of the capacity prior to the performance of that action.

crucial importance. The principal point is this: however much one deliberates, and whatever one does finally do when one actually acts, one does what one does for reasons R that one just finds one has (or finds occurring to one or seeming right or relevant to one) in the situation in which one then is. And whatever the precise nature of the processes by which one has come to have those reasons, R, for which one then acts in the way one does—heredity or environment, calculation or accident, rage or love, inference or impulse, 'existential choice' or successful fulfilment of some long-term plan of character de-velopment—there is a simple and fundamental sense in which one is demonstrably not truly or ultimately responsible for the fact that one has them. (Cf. (1) above.) And yet these reasons R are the reasons why one acts as one does; they are finally responsible for one's acting as one does. (Cf. (2) above.) And so it follows, from the fact that one is not finally responsible for the fact that one has them, that one is not finally responsible for acting as one does. (Cf. (3) above.)[8]

It may well be objected that this sense in which it is demonstrable that we cannot be truly or ultimately responsible for our *reasons* for action (such true responsibility being logically impossible) is not decis-ive, when it is our true responsibility for our *actions*, as ordinarily understood, that is in question.[9] To make such an objection is once again to challenge the derivation of (3) from (1) and (2). But it is in fact *precisely* this sort of logically impossible true responsibility that is required by our ordinary notion of true responsibility for action; and this is particularly easy to see when one considers the fact that we believe people can be truly responsible for their actions in such a way as to be truly deserving of moral praise and blame for them.

It is not only the supposedly romantic or metaphysically woozy incompatibilists or libertarians who are inclined to agree that this ex-

---

[8] It may be objected that this description falsifies matters by making it appear that one's reasons R are in one sense *external* to one, separate from one or from one's 'self', *qua* things that have an influence on how one acts, and so makes it seem that we are not free *because of* these inescapable 'external' influences on our action. This objection is mistaken, however. R may be explicitly characterized as things internal to the self, as aspects or features or even essential constitutive parts of the self ('I move in the desire; it does not move me'). The present point remains unchanged. For the fact that one cannot be truly responsible for having R remains unchanged. (Cf. e.g. 2.3.3, last paragraph, and 2.11, paragraph 2. (and n. 45).)

[9] It may be protested that one is truly responsible for one's actions just in case one performs them for reasons that are truly *one's own* reasons—where one does not have to be truly responsible for having some reason for doing something in order for it to be one's own in the required sense. And often, of course, this is a perfectly reasonable way in which to understand 'one's own'; but it does not touch the present point.

tremely strong notion of true responsibility is the one that matters, so far as our ordinary, strong notion of (desert-entailing) freedom is concerned. Nearly all supposedly tough-minded or clear-headed compatibilists agree. That, after all, is why they propose to abandon our ordinary strong notion of freedom altogether: they want to define the predicate 'free' in such a way that it can be fully satisfied, and they see that it cannot be fully satisfied, as ordinarily understood.[10]

I conclude that appeal to the special nature of fully self-conscious rational deliberation cannot—demonstrably cannot—overcome the initial objection to the idea that we are truly responsible for our actions (in such a way that we can be truly deserving of praise and blame for them). It goes on seeming that this is not so—for such is the nature of our experience of agency. But it is so—as most compatibilists would agree.

There is, it appears, one last alternative. It seems that one can, without being swept away by the experience* of freedom, argue that the fact that the experience* of freedom is as it is is a fact of crucial importance. It seems that one can argue that the way some things are may be partly a function of how they seem; and that if x has a belief B to the effect that it, x, is a truly responsible agent, then, if it is also a self-conscious, 'Integrated' rational agent, the presence of B can change the situation B is meant to be a belief about in such a way that B is made true partly by the fact of its own presence—so that it is true that x is a truly responsible agent, given that x believes it is true, although it is not true if x does not believe it is true. One can, it seems, argue that this is so *even though true responsibility (or freedom) is not in any sense a conventional property*,[11] but a straightforwardly non-conventional property like being bald or asleep.

To argue in this way is, it seems, to seek to revise our ordinary criteria of truth and falsity in some quite fundamental fashion—in the way envisaged by Sidgwick at the end of *The Methods of Ethics*, perhaps (cf. 4.4). At present I have no idea how such an argument can succeed; but, in conclusion, it is worth briefly considering one more attempt at such an argument.

---

[10] They may well go on to say: what more could we possibly want, if our reasons are truly 'our own' reasons, in the sense mentioned in n. 9? And in very many cases the answer is 'Nothing', as remarked in 16.1. But not always, it seems.

[11] If true responsibility were a conventional property, in some sense, then it might be entirely unsurprising that x had to believe that it was truly responsible in order to be truly responsible. Cf. ch. 11 n. 9.

Consider the suggestion that truth, for us, is 'our' truth; that 'our' truth is 'human' truth; that 'human' truth is just a matter of human 'forms of life'; and that, on these terms, the facts of science (for example) are, in the end, exactly on a par with the 'experiential fact' (4.2) that we are free agents truly responsible for our actions: thus there is, on the one hand, the 'doing science' form of life, in which certain things appear to be undeniably the case; and there is, on the other hand, the 'experiencing ourselves and others as free and truly responsible agents' form of life, in which certain things appear to be undeniably the case; and these forms of life are, as forms of life, and, therefore, as sources of truth ('truth', 'our' truth, 'human' truth), exactly on a par.[12]

On the whole, such arguments fail to convince.[13] But even if they do work in some cases, they lead at best to stand-off in the present case. For it is precisely within and on the terms of one of our most central forms of life—our theorizing, philosophizing, ratiocinative form of life—that the argument that true responsibility is impossible has such force (cf. 5.2 *ad fin.* and 5.3). And so the truth enshrined in (or generated by) one form of life is directly at odds with the truth enshrined in (or generated by) another form of life; and it looks as if the only clear solution to this difficulty is to abandon belief in the *unity of (theoretical) truth*, and to grant that one truth may be inconsistent with another.[14]

Now the philosophical conclusion that we are indeed truly responsible agents is a very desirable one. But abandonment of the belief in the unity of theoretical truth is a very high price to pay for it. It involves, to say the least, an earth-quaking revision of our ordinary criteria of truth and falsity. And it is a price that has to be paid in a currency that we value above all others, as theorists: the currency of consistency and completeness. It is a price we cannot pay except at great cost to (1) our belief in the basic consistency and coherence of our actual, admittedly incomplete overall view of the world, and (2) our commitment to belief in the existence of some one, single, *complete*,

[12] The phrase "forms of life" (*Lebensformen*) is Wittgenstein's, and arguments of the sort presently being considered sometimes take their inspiration from his later work.

[13] For a more promising approach to the suggestion that there may be no single available standard for what constitutes 'objective truth', see T. Nagel, 'The Limits of Objectivity', especially part I, §§ 1-5. Cf. also his book *The View from Nowhere*.

[14] One could perhaps, arrange forms of life in a hierarchy (if, that is, one could individuate them satisfactorily), and then say that in any conflict the truth delivered by the higher form of life takes precedence over the truth delivered by the lower form of life. But this is an intrinsically unattractive solution; and it ignores the fact that, on the terms of the 'form of life' approach, we live our lives within forms of life, and cannot plausibly see ourselves as standing outside them in such a way as to rank their modes of truth in the way suggested.

overall conception of the world that is internally consistent and coherent and is in principle attainable by human beings.[15]

To give up in this way the idea that there is, in some fundamental sense, one truth—and to do so specifically in order to derive the conclusion that we are indeed truly responsible agents partly from the fact that we do and cannot but so experience ourselves[16]—is, I think, to pay a higher price (in the currency of consistency and possible completeness of world-view) than the price one pays when one grants that true responsibility is impossible, and then patently continues to believe in it without question in one's daily thought and action (continuing to think and act as if one believed in it without question).[17] For to choose to pay the first price is simply to give up belief in the unity of truth. It is, to put it dramatically, to say that there is a sense in which truth itself is perhaps necessarily inconsistent. Whereas to choose to pay the second price is not to give up belief in the unity of truth. It is, rather, to say that *we* are perhaps necessarily inconsistent; it is simply to admit that we are not only finite and imperfect, considered as theorizing and speculative beings who are seeking to achieve a consistent and complete world-view, but are also severely hobbled in a certain quite specific respect, because our actual, overall, admittedly incomplete world-view is already demonstrably and perhaps irreparably inconsistent in a certain respect.[18]

This is too simple (there are no doubt some genuine arguments in

[15] Or attainable from the human perspective, at least: there is a distinction here, because we may imagine a creature that experiences the universe from within the human perspective, sensorily and cognitively speaking, but is an optimal human being in these respects, and has, in addition, unlimited memory capacity and, perhaps, unlimited time at its disposal. (In this case, it cannot of course occupy the human perspective in all ordinary emotional respects.)

[16] This qualification leaves open the possibility that there may be other, better reasons for abandoning the idea that there is, in some fundamental sense, one truth (from the human perspective). But even if there were such reasons, they would not *ipso facto* lend any support to the specific claim that we are indeed truly responsible agents. Something can be a reason for abandoning the view that there is one truth without providing any direct support for a claim whose truth is apparently incompatible with the view that there is one truth.

[17] See, however, Nagel's doubts about the idea of the unity of our criteria of objectivity, in 'The Limits of Objectivity' and *The View from Nowhere*. See also *Skepticism and Naturalism*, by P. F. Strawson, in which he argues for the irreducible "relativity of our 'reallys'" (pp. 44 ff. and *passim*)—for an irreducible relativity in our judgements regarding what is really or truly the case. (For his discussion of the case of freedom in particular, see pp. 36–8.)

[18] Another suggestion of this sort was considered in 9.3. It was suggested that we might as fully self-conscious beings be necessarily subject to an illusion, in being unable not to think of ourselves as single things single just *qua* mental.

favour of abandoning the unity of truth). Still, one thing that can be invoked to support the view that the second price is less high than the first is the claim that a being like the Genuine Incompatibilist Determinist could possibly exist,[19] or equally the claim that exceptional human beings may—as Buddhists, say—possibly be able to achieve a true view of the way things are that involves no sort of belief in true responsibility at all. For if such a claim is correct, then although we as we ordinarily are must admit our imperfection, as theorists, and abandon (1) above, we need not abandon (2).

Hume may be cited as someone who cheerfully chooses to pay something like the second price, and manages to make light of it in a convincing fashion. His position may be summarized roughly as follows: '(i) as a "first-order" philosopher I reach certain unattractive but seemingly inescapable conclusions; (ii) in common life I find that I can (and cannot but) simply ignore these conclusions; (iii) as a "second-order" philosopher, I can produce reasons for being unperturbed by the fact that both (i) and (ii) are true.' This response is not as strong here as it is in the sorts of cases Hume is usually concerned with, however. For Hume's characteristic sceptical conclusion is not that something we firmly believe to be true cannot be true; it is, rather, that we cannot know it to be true, and cannot provide any rational foundation for our firm belief that it is true. The present conclusion is different; it is that something we firmly believe is actually demonstrably false. So the Humean option is not obviously available.[20]

Which price should one pay? I cannot decide this dispute in a general way; many considerations bear on it, and they extend far beyond the particular problem of freedom. There is, in any case, a price to pay, if one takes the problem of freedom seriously. This is what many compatibilists have wrongly tried to deny. Pay one price, or pay the other. And if you pay the second, do not underestimate it.

[19] Cf. in particular the argument for the possibility of the Genuine Incompatibilist Determinist in 14.8.3 (pp. 281-2), and the reference there to 14.3.

[20] See D. Hume, *Treatise*, I. iv. 7. Hume's 'backgammon defence', as one might call it (cf. *Treatise*, p. 269), is not touched by this objection, however.

APPENDICES

A A PROBLEM ABOUT EXPERIENCE

Let 'experience' be defined as follows: X has experience, or is an experiencing being (either in general, or at time *t*) if and only if there is something it is like to be X (in general, at *t*). And consider a philosophical discussion of the nature of some property like free agenthood, or the ability to think, or intelligence, or the possession of a discriminatory capacity. A question that can always be asked is: is the having of experience (or the possession of a disposition to have experience) necessary for possession of this property? And a second question is this: if it is necessary—if you can't have the property and not be an experiencing being—what role, exactly, does experience (or the possession of a disposition to have experience) play in possession of the property? What contribution, exactly, does it make?

This is often a very puzzling question. In the case of free agenthood, the problem can be brought out by considering Hume's classic compatibilist capacity-theoretic definition of freedom. According to this definition one is free if and only if one is able to do what one chooses to do; even if one's choices are determined one is still free. Now imagine a machine that is experienceless in the present sense—there is nothing it is like to be it. It is a chess computer, say, with arms for moving its pieces and taking yours. It has goals and preferences in the sense in which machines can be said to have goals and preferences. It possesses a great deal of information and is able to absorb new information. It is able to perform movements (moving and taking pieces). It makes the movements it makes on the basis of its goals and information. It is always able to do what it chooses ('chooses') to do on that basis. It is not constrained.

So why, exactly, is it not a free agent? Well, for one thing, it is not self-conscious. But exactly the same problem arises for self-consciousness as arose for free agenthood: the problem of whether experience is necessary for self-consciousness, and of what exactly its role is in self-consciousness, if it is necessary. (It is arguable that to be self-conscious is just to be capable of having certain kinds of thoughts; and it is widely held that thoughts need have no experiential aspect at all.) In any case, we can equip the machine with a kind of experienceless analogue of self-consciousness—given which it can receive information about its own doings and can know (in the sense in which experienceless machines can be said to know things) that all these doings are doings of one single thing that it calls 'I', which is the same thing as the thing that knows that this is so. It can be 'behaviourally self-conscious', equipped with a word screen or artificial voice, and liable to say things like 'At first I thought I might move P-KB4, but then I thought that if I did that you would be able to take my queen's pawn. Finally I decided on P-Q5.' This is all perfectly feasible. But of course we feel that it is not enough. We feel that nothing can be self-conscious if there is nothing it is like to be that thing, experientially speaking. And nothing can be a free agent if there is nothing it is like to be that thing, experientially speaking.

Suppose we now imagine the chess machine to be endowed with experience or consciousness. It has exactly the same sophisticated practical and cognitive capacities and the same goals as before, but now there is something it is like to be it, experientially speaking. Surely it is now free, according to Hume's definition of freedom? But then what *exactly* is the difference that experience has made? Why, in particular, has it made the decisive difference with regard to free agenthood? What freedom-relevant capacity has experience added? This seems very unclear.

We may say that experience or consciousness is vital simply because there has to be 'someone there', a subject of experience, if there is to be a free agent: this is just a fundamental requirement, independent of all others. Of course this seems right. But what sort of requirement is it, exactly? Surely the experiencing and the experienceless machine are, in a sense, equally free in what they do? It's just that we don't call one of them free at all. (Consider the logical possibility that there should be an experienceless entity that is behaviourally speaking just like a human being.)

This example may be crude, but it suffices for the present point. Obviously one can simply insist that experience or consciousness is necessary for free agenthood without further explanation. But the question of the function or role of experience or consciousness must always remain as a background problem—especially for theorists attracted by the general idea of the capacity-theoretic approach. (See D. Dennett, *Elbow Room*, pp. 38–43, for an illustration of this point.) If it is not often seen as a problem in discussions of free will, this is principally because it is usually just assumed that it is human beings whose freedom is in question, and the fact that human beings have experience or consciousness is simply taken for granted.

B   FREE CHOICES AND OBJECTIVE BRANCHING POINTS

The general point can be put another way. Suppose that there are points in the history of the world where precisely what happens next is not fully determined by anything that has gone before. Suppose, for example, that when an event of type A occurs, either an event of type B or an event of type C (or type D, etc.) can occur next, and that absolutely nothing necessitates that it should be one of them rather than another. So the history of the world is continually reaching junction points—bifurcations, or trifurcations, or whatever. The history of the world has—to put it simply—the form of a single route up an ever spreading tree of branching possibilities. I shall say that on this view there are 'objective branching points'.

The natural thought is then this: that if there are free choices or actions at all, then they are located at, and indeed often constitute, these objective branching points. The human will is somehow such that it can give rise to these branching points.

But ask, now, how *a* can be free in such a way that he is truly responsible for what he does, if there are objective branching points. Well, *a* can only be thus free if he determines or can *control* what happens at them. So, skipping a multitude of objections, suppose that he can do this. Never mind how. The important question is then the 'why?' question. '*Why* did *a* opt to let or make B happen rather than C or D?'

In the vast majority of cases that are held to be cases of free action, there must be an answer to this 'why?' question that takes the form of a rational explanation, giving *a*'s reasons, R: 'He did it because . . .R . . .' But then familiar questions arise about his reasons R. Where do they come from? To be truly responsible on account of an ability to control or create objective branching points out of which one's actual actions emerge, one must be truly responsible for whatever features of oneself lead one to exit from the branching points along the particular branchlines that one does in fact exit along. But these features are, precisely, one's reasons. And it seems one cannot be ultimately responsible for having the reasons one does have, *whatever* the truth about objective branching points. Once again it is the necessity that free actions be, in general, rational actions that thwarts the attempt to substantiate true responsibility by appeal to some variety of indeterminism. (The idea that subatomic indeterminacy could help is as hopeless here as it is in any other context.)

C   THE BRAIN IN THE VAT AS FREE AGENT

It seems that a 'brain in a vat' can be a free agent, if any agent can be.

There are at least two versions of the brain in a vat story. According to one of them, one's brain is a brain in a vat with all its afferent and efferent nerve pathways linked up to a supercomputer, and *all* one's mental goings-on are computer-produced; not only all the *inputs* to one's brain, all one's sensory experiences, and so on, but also all one's thoughts, decisions, intention-formations, and attempted initiations of physical actions. (Something like this version of the story is employed at certain points in J. Glover's *What Sort Of People Should There Be?* Cf. e.g. pp. 96, 101, 108.)

According to a second version, which I shall consider here, the computer simply plays the experience-providing role that we ordinarily suppose the external world to play in providing our actual experiences. It provides all the sensory inputs, it sends all the afferent neural impulses, and so on, but it does not control all the workings of the brain, which responds to the afferent signals in just the way that your or my brain does in fact, both as regards its non-efferent internal operations, and as regards the efferent (and ostensibly physical-action-initiating) signals that it produces.

Suppose that determinism is true, and imagine that there exists a perfect tape of all the neural goings-on of a real, twentieth-century human brain—Louis's brain—from the very beginning of its active existence. A thirtieth-century computer processes this tape, extracts all the input signals, and sends these just as they originally occurred to a living and growing replica of the original twentieth-century brain. Determinism being what it is, the replica responds just in the way that the original brain did, both in its internal operations and in the output signals that it emits. And so, of course, a person—Louis*—develops, just as a person developed in the original twentieth-century case of ordinarily embodied human development. Louis* learns to think and hope and 'talk' and 'walk', and so on. He forms beliefs and desires. Output and input signals mesh in extremely complex ways, as, for example, when the computer-produced sensory (including 'kinaesthetic') input or 'feedback' jibes exactly with the brain's output signals during what Louis* takes to be a strenuous game of tennis, or philosophical conversation, in which he is participating.

In the second version of the brain in a vat story, it seems right to say that the brain is the brain of a person. In fact it may seem right to say this about the first version too, since there may in the first version be a subject of experience whose experience is in every way exactly like that of the person in the second version, and, indeed, exactly like your actual experience, here and now in the twentieth century. But the main present point is this: whatever one thinks about the person in the first case, it seems clear that the person in the second case is as much of a free agent as you or I. If you can be a free agent, then a person whose brain is a brain in a vat can be one too. If we are moral beings, capable of right and wrong, then so is the person whose brain is a brain in a vat. Louis* is as capable as we are of making genuine, praiseworthy-or-blameworthy, and (to him) momentous moral choices (cf 8.2, p. 140), even though he is in fact wrong in believing that he ever actually performs physical actions, or ever has any effect on other sentient beings.

Notice, finally, that it could be argued that if determinism is true then even the person who exists in the first version of the story is at least as free as we are. It could be argued that if determinism is true it cannot possibly make a deep difference to the question of freedom whether everything that happens in a brain is directly produced and controlled by an external computer, or whether it happens in the way it actually happens in our actual brains (assuming that we are indeed fully embodied physical things). This argument continues, via the lemma (argued for in Chapter 2) that assuming the falsity of determinism is of no help at all to any positive attempt to substantiate our freedom, to the conclusion that whether determinism is true or false, we are in any case no more free than a person who is a brain in a vat on the terms of the first version of the story. It is not clear that this conclusion should discountenance anyone who has taken in the argument of Chapter 2.

D   A STRANGE GOD

One could expand the definition of causal evidentness given in 10.7 as follows: a causally evident property is a property that is an evident property because of *some* causal connection between (*a*) *x*'s possession of the property and (*b*) *x*'s belief that it possesses the property; it being the case either (i) that (*a*) is a sufficient causal condition of (*b*), or alternatively (ii) that (*b*) is a necessary causal condition of (*a*). (The difference between (i) and (ii) is discussed in 10.10.1.) But there is no particular point in doing this. Cases of kind (ii) are of no interest: even if they are not obviously impossible, they are likely to be very outlandish.

One suggested case might be this. One benefits from the grace of some strange god only if one believes one does, one's believing one does being a necessary causal condition of one's doing so: if one comes to have the belief (and thereby shows one's faith), the god then bestows its grace upon one, for that reason, and continues to do so for as long as one continues to believe that it does.

For this to be an invariable connection it seems that the god must be both indestructible and quite unable to change its practice, and, hence, not fully omnipotent. In fact, though, it looks as if neither this nor anything else could suffice for it to be truly causally *impossible* that one should ever receive grace without believing one did. The universe would have to be governed by some very strange laws.

Consider also the possibility that there might be a psychosomatically based disease *D* of such a nature that no being could recover from it that did not believe it was recovering. Here it seems that believing one is recovering is a necessary causal condition of being such that one is in fact recovering. But this is not in fact a case of the required sort. For it is not the case that *no* being can be recovering from any illness and not believe it; nor is it true that no being can be recovering *from D* and not believe it. The necessary condition of recovering from *D* is just believing you are recovering from the illness you are afflicted with, not that you are recovering *from D*. (A doctor, knowing you had *D*, might tell you that you had some other familiar minor ailment that you knew not to be dangerous, so that you would more quickly form the necessary remedial belief that you were recovering.)

a may succeed in running a four-minute mile only because he believes he will succeed, confidence being for him a necessary condition of success. But it seems unlikely that there is any ϕ such that confidence in one's ability to ϕ is a universally necessary condition of success, for all possible beings. Generally, it looks as if it is not possible to describe properties that are causally evident properties because they satisfy condition (ii) of the expanded definition.

E   THE SENSE OF SELF

Nemo, who is as similar to us as it is possible to be without being self-conscious, seems to make clear the importance of self-consciousness for freedom as we ordinarily conceive it. It does not seem he can be a free agent. This view is supported by the claim that experience of oneself as free is necessary for freedom; for such experience presupposes self-consciousness. Here, however, I shall try to trace some independent connections between experience* of freedom and self-consciousness—returning to some of the questions about the nature of self-consciousness that were put aside in Chapter 9.

The unsystematic remarks that follow may seem nebulous in places—or perhaps falsely precise. But they are merely a record of some of the things one is led to say in the attempt to capture the nature of the kind of freedom we believe we have, and believe that Fido and Nemo cannot have.

I. *Singularity, Content, Transcendence, and Thinghood.* In 9.3 it was suggested that full self-consciousness of the sort we require of a potential free agent, initially defined by conditions (1) and (2) in 9.1, involves possession of

> (3) a sense of oneself as being in some way a single thing when considered merely in so far as one has a mental aspect.

(Note that this claim concerns only the *character* of experience.)

It is apparently a further question whether a self-conscious being must also

> (4) conceive of oneself as having a certain 'content' or character, *qua* the single mental being that it conceives itself to be given (3).

(The alternative is presumably that it somehow or other conceive of itself, mentally considered, as a 'bare thinking principle'—whatever exactly that may involve).

So too, it is a further question whether full self-consciousness necessarily involves

> (5) a sense of self as *transcendent*, *qua* single mental thing—

whether, that is, it necessarily involves possession of a sense of oneself, considered as something single just *qua* mental, as somehow irreducibly over and above (set over against, transcendent with respect to) any and indeed all of one's particular action-motivating desires, pro-attitudes, and mental contents in general (cf. 3.4, and 9.3 *ad fin.*).

The question of whether self-consciousness also involves

(6) conceiving of oneself as some sort of *thing* or entity, purely mentally considered,

is apparently not a further question, however. For (6) would appear to be entailed by (3).

(3)–(6) denote *conceptions* that a being can have of itself as something that possesses certain properties, or in other words fulfils certain *conditions*. One could number these conditions (iii)–(vi), corresponding to (3)–(6), and name them as follows.

(iii) is the single-just-*qua*-mental condition, or Singularity Condition for short.

(iv) is the mental 'content' or character condition, or Content Condition;

(v) is the condition that requires that the self be over and above, or transcendent with respect to, all its mentations—the Transcendence Condition.

(vi) is the condition requiring that one (one's self) be a mental thing or entity in some reasonably firm sense of these words—the Thinghood Condition.

Singularity, Content, Transcendence, and Thinghood—these are what most people ordinarily and vaguely think that a mental self possesses, in so far as they think about such things at all. And, just as questions arise about the relations between (3)–(6), so too questions arise about the relations between (iii)–(vi). The structure of our thought about the relations between these conditions and conceptions is of considerable interest, even if there is no such thing as a mental self that fulfils the conditions. Questions arise—for example—about whether self-consciousness, on the one hand, and free agenthood, on the other hand, entail possession of conceptions (3)–(6). It has already been argued that full self-consciousness entails (3). It may now be asked whether full self-consciousness entails (5).

II. *The Humean conception.* Some may wish to answer 'No' to this question. Thus they may for example suggest that a self-conscious being may have or attain some sort of austerely Humean sense or conception of itself, mentally considered, that involves no sense of mental self as transcendent, but involves, rather, a grasp of self, *qua* mental, as being nothing over and above one's particular thoughts (desires, perceptions, etc.).

But even if this is right—even if full self-consciousness does not entail (5)— it may still be true to say that any *free agent* must have (5). It depends, for one thing, on whether one can possibly have (*a*) experience of oneself as a free and truly responsible agent if one possesses (*b*) the putative purely 'Humean' conception of one's mental nature. If (*b*) rules out (*a*), then any free agent must have a 'non-Humean' sense of self as transcendent (given the argument of Part III that (*a*), experience* of freedom, is necessary for freedom itself). That is, any free agent must *experience* itself in this way—as transcendent. (The question of whether or not such experience could be actually veridical is a completely separate question.)

The question about whether the 'Humean' conception of self is compatible with experience* of freedom only arises, of course, on the assumption that it is possible at all for a fully self-conscious being to have a purely 'Humean' conception of itself (*qua* mentally aspected). I shall suggest that it is not possible, and that even if it were possible, it would be incompatible with experience* of freedom. It must be borne in mind that the question is not a question about whether the 'Humean' account might be correct as an account of what something called the self might actually *be* (in so far as it existed at all), but rather about whether a being, *b*, that was correctly called fully self-conscious could genuinely *conceive* of itself as nothing more than a series or stream or collection of thoughts.

In trying to answer this question I shall take it that *b* has 'I-thoughts' or 'I-mentations'. It is true that a fully self-conscious being need not have such thoughts or mentations; it may refer to itself, in thought or speech, only by proper name. But it must be capable of grasping the import of such I-thoughts or I-mentations. So it is legitimate to consider the consequences of attributing such thoughts or mentations to it.

The question is then this. Can *b* genuinely be said to conceive of itself in such a way that it believes things like 'I am (mentally) nothing more than the sum or series of my parts (thoughts or mentations); but I am indeed that—the sum or series of my parts, that is'? The question is not whether it can as a philosopher *believe* itself to hold this view. Clearly it can do this. Philosophers have done it. (Hume once did it.) Rather, the question is about whether it can *genuinely* conceive of or experience itself in this way, given that is is fully self-conscious. It is much less clear that it can do this. (Hume, for example, later admitted that he could not.)

For what is this mental 'I'? What does the being to whom we attribute this grasp of 'I' think this 'I' is, mentally considered? Itself, clearly: at the very least, the haver, the thinker, the subject of its thoughts. But now an old, decisive objection comes to bear: it cannot really experience the 'I', mentally considered, as just the sum or series of thoughts; for the 'I' is, for it, the thinker of its thoughts; and sums or series of thoughts cannot think at all. So even if it claims, as a philosopher, to think of the 'I' as a series of thoughts, this cannot be how it *really* conceives of itself. For the conception is quite simply incoherent.

Here we encounter again the thought argued for in 9.3: by its very nature, self-consciousness involves possessing some sense of oneself as somehow single just *qua* mental: one cannot genuinely think in the specifically self-conscious manner, thinking of one's thoughts or limbs *as one's own*, without at the time having some sense of oneself not merely as single, but also as somehow single just *qua* mental.

It appears to follow that self-consciousness does entail some sort of sense of oneself as transcendent in the present sense. For self-consciousness appears to entail (3), having a sense of self as single just *qua* mental; and (3), having a sense of self as single just *qua* mental, appears to rule out having a genuinely 'Humean' conception of oneself (mentally considered). (3) therefore appears to necessitate having *some* sort of view of oneself, mentally considered, as (5) something that is somehow over and above all one's particular thoughts, etc. For there do not seem to be any other options.

So much for the argument that a fully self-conscious being cannot genuinely conceive of itself in the 'Humean' way. (This is, in effect, the conclusion that Hume himself later arrived at.) There are many ways of arguing, further, that even if it could so conceive of itself, it could not then experience itself as free.

One of them proceeds by way of a thought-experiment: purely intellectually, it does not seem at all hard to accept *without reserve* the idea that ultimately one is, mentally considered, nothing more than a series of mentations including I-mentations. And one can, for a time, mimic something like the state of a being with a purely 'Humean' conception of self, by continually thinking of one's mental activity as nothing more than a series of mentations including I-mentations. But if one does this, it is, precisely, one's sense of self that quickly begins to fade away; for the sense that there is *just* this series of thoughts becomes overwhelming. And with one's sense of self, of course, one's ex-perience* of freedom also fades—one's sense of oneself as a truly responsible being and free agent, the originating thinker of one's thoughts and truly re-sponsible doer of one's deeds.

The end result of this thought-experiment is very similar to the end result of the thought-experiment proposed in 6.2, although the two thought-experiments are different in nature. In the thought-experiment of 6.2 it is the thought that one is in no way a free agent but totally determined that destroys the sense of the mental self. Here it is the thought that one is, mentally, nothing more than a series of mentations that destroys the sense of self and thereby destroys the sense of freedom. (For a related line of thought, see D. Parfit, *Reasons and Persons*, §§ 94, 95.)

III. *The Buddhist*. At the moment, then, it seems that full self-consciousness entails a sense of self both as (3) single just *qua* mental and as (5) transcendent. And this suggests that the Buddhist project of fully comprehending the doctrine of *an-ātman* or 'no-self', and thereby attaining nirvana, may be impossible for a self-conscious being—whether or not the project of attaining desirelessness is realizable.

One view of what might happen if a self-conscious being were to attain nirvana is that it might, in effect, achieve some sort of purely 'Humean' outlook on the mental. But it would in so doing have to cease to be fully self-conscious in the present sense, since a sense of self as single just *qua* mental still appears to be a necessary part of self-consciousness, and it seems impossible even to make sense of the notion of a genuinely 'Humean' self-conscious self-conception.

It might be said that if this is so, then attaining nirvana must involve some sort of stultification—loss of awareness of things of which one was previously aware. The Buddhist being can deny this, however. For, according to Buddhism, there just is no such single mental self; there are only mentations. And so to cease to have a sense of the self is not to cease to be aware of anything that is the case. It is just to lose an illusion.

This seems quite a plausible line for the Buddhist being to take. But I do not think that we can really imagine what it would be like to be this being, or to undergo this experiential revolution—despite the availability of the experience of dissolution produced by the thought-experiment described at the end of § II above. For the self—the experienced* self, that is—has *permanently* disappeared, for this being. Of course it can still talk in terms of 'I', if it wishes, referring to the thoughts and deeds of the single psychophysical entity that it appears to us to be. But it entirely lacks the characteristically fully self-conscious mode of thinking of things. And so it has in a sense disappeared, both for itself and for us. (It disappears for us because it disappears for itself: as remarked in Chapter 9, we are strongly inclined to judge whether or not a being has a self (or is a 'someone') on the basis of whether or not it *sees* itself as having (or being) a self.) It has disappeared into the series of thoughts, leaving nothing but a series of thoughts.

It might be suggested that the Buddhist being that attains nirvana in this way *is* still self-conscious, in so far as it is still possessed of mental reflexivity (9.1), and is, as it were, fully self-conscious behaviourally speaking, being able to use the word 'I' fully correctly; and that what this case shows is not that attaining nirvana entails losing self-consciousness, but rather that self-consciousness does not after all necessarily involve (3) a sense of oneself as single just *qua* mental, let alone (5), a sense of oneself as transcendent in the present sense.

I would reject this suggestion for reasons given in 9.3 and § II above. Notice that, as it stands, it allows that experienceless machines can be fully self-conscious; for experienceless machines can be possessed of mental reflexivity, as well as being fully self-conscious behaviourally speaking (cf. Appendix A). Some might welcome this conclusion. Others would regard it as a *reductio ad absurdum* of the suggestion that the imaginary Buddhist is still self-conscious. Here it suffices to signal the suggestion as a possible view. It is clearly a revisionary suggestion, relative to our ordinary notion of self-consciousness. (A gap between the Buddhist and the machine can easily be opened up, by observing that the Buddhist is still an experiencing being, unlike the machine. But a simple insistence that self-consciousness entails possession of a disposition to have experience, and that this is why the machine cannot be said to be self-conscious, while the Buddhist still can be, seems an inadequate response to the difficulty. Here one runs once again into the deep problem indicated in Appendix A—the problem of why exactly reference to the having of experience is necessary at all in giving an account of properties like self-consciousness.)

IV. *The Content condition*. The present claim is that self-consciousness not only necessarily involves (3) conceiving of oneself as somehow single just *qua* mental, but also necessarily involves (5) conceiving of oneself as somehow transcendent relative to all one's particular mentations. It is a further question whether (5) in turn involves (4), a sense of oneself as a character-possessing, contentful mental self: prima facie, it would seem that one might have a sense of oneself as transcendent that was a sense of oneself as the mere, bare, contentless thinker or 'thinking principle'. It is arguable, however, that (3), (4), and (5) are all necessary for free agenthood because they are necessary for experience* of freedom, and that this is so whether or not they are necessary for self-consciousness, and whatever the entailment relations that hold between them. This has already been argued for (3), in 9.4. What about (4) and (5)?

Even if (5) does not entail (4), it looks as if both of them are attitudinal conditions of free agenthood. (Whether or not they are also *Attitudinal* conditions depends on whether or not they are entailed by possession of the Structural capacity condition of self-consciousness.) For even if a being can have (5) without (4)—even if it can have a sense of itself as a single, mental thing that is transcendent with respect to particular mental contents and is at the same time a mere thinker or mentator devoid of any particular character-content—it does not look as if such a being can be a free agent. Indeed we naturally see a being's having some sort of sense of self as *contentfully* transcendent as essential to its very existence as an agent, in a special, strong, purely mind-concerned, freedom-necessary (and dog-excluding) sense of the word 'agent': we see it as essential to there being an 'agent-self', a (possibly truly free and responsible) planner of action.

This is, perhaps, already obvious. The general point is this. We require a free agent to have (3), a sense of self as single just *qua* mental, in order for it to be constituted as (or counted as) something more than just a collection of action-motivating beliefs, desires, and so on—in order for it to be a possibly responsible, answerable 'someone'. In exactly the same way (I merely report the structure of our thought), we appear to require a free agent to have a sense of self as a characterful or content-possessing single mental entity with plans, desires, intentions, and so on, in order for it to be a possibly responsible, answerable someone; in order for it to be more than a bare, contentless, non-personal thinker, a non-responsible thinking principle, a thing that is not a someone. (This argument that any free agent must have (4) and (5) runs closely parallel to the argument in 9.4 that any free agent must have (3), and there is no need to repeat it all.)

It is arguable, then, that (4) as well as (3) and (5) is necessary if an agent is to count as a 'mental someone' in the way we suppose to be necessary for free agenthood. However *wrong* we are about ourselves, ultimately or ontologically or metaphysically, in conceiving of ourselves as single, contentful, transcendent mental things, it seems that we think that anything that is to count as a free agent must resemble us in having some similar self-conception, whatever the minimal form of it may be. One way of putting this is to say that it seems that possession of such a self-conception is a constitutively necessary condition of the existence of some sort of mental 'someone' of the sort we require of any free agent, *even if it involves some deep illusion*. It follows that if (3), (4), and (5) are not entailed by self-consciousness, then they are Attitudinal conditions of free agenthood.

F THE OBJECTIVISTS' LAST DITCH

1. The more general objection mentioned in 14.11 consists of the following argument.

(I) Whatever is a constitutively sufficient condition of freedom—call it ϕ—must also be constitutively necessary.

(II) But to be constitutively necessary and sufficient for something is to be identical with it (10.10.4).

(III) So if ϕ appears as a condition in the set of S^+ conditions in such a way that

$$\text{Cn}/(x)(\underline{S^+x} \to E^*(x,Fx))/ \tag{5}$$

is true, then the experience* of freedom condition also occurs in S^+; in which case (1) is true because (1.2) is; which was precisely that which was to be avoided.

2. The argument—or rather, the defence of (I), its first premiss—will be put in two different ways, and needs some preparation. Perhaps it's obvious that one cannot when attempting to analyse concepts like freedom drive a wedge between types of absolutely exceptionless generalizations that are not formal-logical truths—between those that are and those that are not true because of the holding of constitution relations. I'm not sure. Setting out the Objectivists' attempt to drive such a wedge may help to show what is at stake—at the risk of engaging in some rather scholastic manoeuvres.

3. The experience* of freedom condition is an attitudinal condition. It attributes a form of experience. It follows that only an attitudinal condition (or set of attitudinal conditions) attributing a form of experience could be a *directly* constitutively sufficient condition of the experience* of freedom condition. For a statement of the directly constitutively sufficient conditions of a form of experience states what that form of experience actually consists in, as such (cf. 10.12). So, if there is any true statement of the form $\text{Cn}/(x)(\phi x \to E^*(x,Fx))/$, there must be a statement of that form in which what goes in place of 'ϕ' is a predicate, or set of predicates, attributing only attitudinal or experiential properties. To see whether (5) could be true, therefore, one should look at the

attitudinal conditions in S^+, in order to see whether they can be supposed to amount to constitutively sufficient conditions of experience* of freedom.

4. The attitudinal conditions explicitly included in S^+ are (i) the Integration condition, and (ii) the experience* of ability to choose condition. (These have both been held to be Attitudinal conditions—attitudinal conditions not entailed by the capacity or Structural conditions in S^+.) But we may now add, as a further, general explicit attitudinal (*not* Attitudinal) condition, (iii) the condition of being disposed to have those experiences or attitudes (if any), whatever exactly they are, which are such that a disposition to have them is necessarily involved in fulfilling S, the original Structural conditions. Let 'E/Sx' symbolize 'x fulfils condition (iii)'.

5. (i), (ii) and (iii) exhaust the attitudinal conditions in S^+. So if (5) is true we may take it that

$$\text{Cn}/(x)(\underline{E/Sx} \ \& \ \textit{Int } x \ \& \ E^*(x,ACx) \ \to \ E^*(x,Fx))/ \qquad (6)$$

is. (Here I assume that none of (i)—(iii) singly, nor any two of them jointly, are constitutively sufficient for experience* of freedom; the assumption is defended below in paragraph 7.) Now suppose we grant (*contra* the natural Epictetans, the being of limited conception, the Genuine Incompatibilist Determinist, etc.) that (6) is true, and that it states constitutively sufficient conditions of experience* of freedom. It is then most implausible to suppose that these sufficient conditions are not also necessary. (This is claim (I) in the argument as set out in paragraph 1.) For when one is dealing with the constitutive conditions of possession of properties like squareness, free agenthood, and experience* of freedom, rather than properties like being entitled to French government benefit (Chapter 10 n. 24), one does not expect to find different independent (non-interdefinable) sets of sufficient conditions. For one is, one supposes, dealing with real, non-conventionally-instituted properties, i.e. with things or phenomena that have a certain single essential nature or constitution; there being no two ways about it. (If two entities have qualitatively identical properties, their coming to have them may possibly have different sorts of *causes*, but those things in which their having those properties *consist* cannot have different constitutions or natures; there is only one way of being square, and equally, one supposes, only one way of having experience of self as free and truly responsible, where this is considered in itself, and not confused with those no doubt diverse things that may accompany it in different beings.)

6. If this is so, then, *if* (i)–(iii) are sufficient for experience* of freedom, then they are also necessary; so that

$$\text{Cn}/(x)(\underline{E/Sx} \ \& \ \textit{Int } x \ \& \ E^*(x,ACx) \ \leftrightarrow \ E^*(x,Fx))/ \qquad (7)$$

is true. But then (i)—(iii) are just identical with, or amount to, the experience* of freedom condition. (This is premiss (II); cf. 10.10.) In which case the Objectivists cannot argue that, from (7) and a consequence of (2), i.e.

$$\text{Cn}/(x)(Fx \rightarrow \underline{E/Sx \& Int \ x \& E^*(x,ACx)})/, \tag{8}$$

one can derive the desired (1) as a non-causal and non-constitutive but still absolutely exceptionless generalization, but not the unwanted (1.2). Because if (7) amounts to an identity statement, then the right-hand side of it can simply replace the left-hand side, as it occurs in (8)—which gives the unwanted (1.2) after all. (This is (III), the conclusion.) In this case one has a proposed analysis of experience* of freedom into its constituents (one which is false in fact, according to the argument of Chapter 14), but one has not after all avoided contravention of the principle of independence.

7. This is a general argument for (I). If satisfactory, it renders the following more specific argument superfluous. Condition (ii) is clearly a necessary constitutive condition of experience* of freedom: for being aware* of being able to choose is necessarily part of being aware* of being able to choose freely. (i), the Integration condition, has also been argued to be necessary: the Spectator subject could not as she was experience herself as a free agent. As for (iii), it is clear that having (or being disposed to have) whatever experience is minimally involved in being a fully self-conscious *agent* is a constitutively necessary condition of experience of self as a *free* agent. Given this argument for (I), the rest of the argument (I)-(III) goes through as before.

8. One may summarize all this in the following way. Let '*F*' be freedom, let '*E*(F)*' be experience* of freedom, and let '*C*' be some unspecified appropriate condition. It may look as if from

(i) $\text{Cn}/(\underline{C} \rightarrow E^*(F))/$

and

(ii) $\text{Cn}/(F \rightarrow \underline{C})/$

one can derive

(iii) $(F \rightarrow E^*(F))$

but not

(iv) $\text{Cn}/(F \rightarrow \underline{E^*(F)})/$

—since (iv) would follow (by the transitivity of 'is a constitutive condition of') only from (ii) and

(v) $\text{Cn}/(C \rightarrow \underline{E^*(F)})/.$

This seems attractive, because the wish is to give an account of freedom according to which *experiencing* oneself as a free agent is not actually part of what constitutes being a free agent, although it is a strictly necessary concomitant of it*. But if

(vi) $\text{Cn}/(\underline{C} \leftrightarrow E^*(F))/$

—and this appears inevitable, given (i), for reasons given above—then

(vii) $C = E^*(F),$

and so (ii) is the same as the unwanted (iv). In any case—an obvious further objection—even if there were a distinction between (1.2) and (1) as non-causal truths (or between (iii) and (iv)), (1) would be as much a contravention of the principle of independence as (1.2). The apparently unacceptable causal option is for that reason the only one open to the Objectivists.

Here end the logical follies of the Objectivists.

BIBLIOGRAPHY

ANSCOMBE, G. E. M., 'The Intentionality of Sensation', in *Metaphysics and the Philosophy of Mind*. Oxford, Blackwell, 1981.
—— 'Causality and Determination', also in *Metaphysics and the Philosophy of Mind*.
ARISTOTLE, *Nicomachean Ethics*, trans. J. A. K. Thompson. Harmondsworth, Penguin, 1953.
AUSTIN, J. L., *How To Do Things With Words*. Oxford University Press, 1975.
AYER, A. J., 'Freedom and Necessity', in *Philosophical Essays*. London, Macmillan, 1954.
BELLOW, S., *Humboldt's Gift*. Harmondsworth, Penguin, 1977.
BERLIN, I., *Four Essays on Liberty*. Oxford University Press, 1969.
BUTLER, J., 'Of Personal Identity', Dissertation I in *The Analogy of Religion*. London, Everyman, 1936.
CAMUS, A., *L'Étranger*. Paris, Gallimard, 1942.
CARR, E. H. , *What is History?* London, Macmillan, 1961.
CASTAÑEDA, H. -N., 'On the Logic of Self-Knowledge', *Nous*, 1, 1967.
COLLINS, S., *Selfless Persons*. Cambridge University Press, 1982.
DAVIDSON, D., 'Freedom to Act', in *Essays on Freedom on Action*, ed. T. Honderich. London, Routledge and Kegan Paul, 1973.
DENNETT, D. C., *Elbow Room: The Varieties of Free Will Worth Wanting*. Oxford, Clarendon Press, 1985.
—— 'Why You Can't Make a Computer that Feels Pain', in *Brainstorms: Philosophical Essays on Mind and Psychology*. Montgomery, Bradford Books, 1978.
DENYER, N., *Time, Action and Necessity; A Proof of Free Will*. London, Duckworth, 1981.
DESCARTES, R., *Meditations*, trans. J. Cottingham, R. Stoothoff, and D. Murdoch. Cambridge University Press, 1985.
ELIOT, G., *Middlemarch*. Harmondsworth, Penguin, 1965.
EVANS, G., *The Varieties of Reference*. Oxford, Clarendon Press, 1982.
FORD, F. MADOX, *Last Post*. London, Duckworth, 1928.
FRANKENA, W.,'Prichard and the Ethics of Virtue', *Monist*, 54, 1970.
FRANKFURT, H., 'Freedom of the Will and the Concept of a Person', in G. Watson, ed., *Free Will*.
—— 'Three Concepts of Free Action', *Proceedings of the Aristotelian Society*, 49, 1975.
FRAYN, M., *Constructions*. London, Wildwood, 1974.

GLOVER, J., *Responsibility*. London, Routledge and Kegan Paul, 1970.

—— *What Sort Of People Should There Be?* Harmondsworth, Penguin, 1984.

—— 'Self-Creation', *Proceedings of the British Academy*, 69, 1983.

HAMPSHIRE, S., 'Spinoza and the Idea of Freedom', in *Freedom of Mind*. Oxford, Clarendon Press, 1972.

HOBART, R., 'Free Will as Involving Determinism and Inconceivable without It', *Mind*, 43, 1934.

HOBBES, J., *Leviathan*. London, Collins, 1962.

HUME, D., *A Treatise of Human Nature*, ed. L. A. Selby-Bigge, second edition. Oxford, Clarendon Press, 1978.

—— *Enquiry into Human Nature*, ed. L. A. Selby-Bigge, second edition. Oxford, Clarendon Press, 1902.

HUMPHREY, N., *Consciousness Regained*, Oxford University Press, 1983.

JAMES, W.,'The Dilemma of Determinism', in *The Will to Believe*. New York, Dover, 1956.

KANT, I., *Critique of Pure Reason*, trans. N. Kemp Smith. London, Macmillan, 1933.

—— *Critique of Practical Reason*, trans. L. W. Beck. Indianopolis, Bobbs-Merrill, 1956 (trans. T. K. Abbott, London, Longmans, 1898).

—— *Groundwork of the Metaphysic of Morals*, trans. H. J. Paton. New York, Harper & Row, 1964. (*Fundamental Principles of the Metaphysic of Morals*, trans. T. K. Abbott. Indianapolis, Bobbs-Merrill, 1949.)

—— *Religion within the Limits of Reason Alone*, trans. T. M. Greene and H. H. Hudson. New York, Harper & Row, 1960.

LOCKE, J., *An Essay Concerning Human Understanding*, ed. P. H. Nidditch. Oxford, Clarendon Press, 1975.

LUCAS, J. R., *The Freedom of the Will*. Oxford, Clarendon Press, 1970.

LUTYENS, M., *Krishnamurti: the Years of Fulfilment*. London, John Murray, 1983.

McGINN, C., *The Character of Mind*. Oxford University Press, 1982.

MACINTYRE, A., *After Virtue*. London, Duckworth, 1981.

MACKAY, D. M., 'On the Logical Indeterminacy of a Free Choice', *Mind*, 69, 1960.

MACKIE, J. L. *Hume's Moral Theory*. London, Routledge and Kegan Paul, 1980.

NAGEL, T., 'Moral Luck', in *Mortal Questions*. Cambridge University Press, 1979.

—— 'The Limits of Objectivity', in *The Tanner Lectures on Human Values* I. Cambridge and Salt Lake City, Cambridge University Press and University of Utah Press, 1980.

—— *The View from Nowhere*. Oxford University Press, 1986.

NIETZSCHE, F., *Daybreak*, trans. R. J. Hollingdale. Cambridge University Press, 1983.

NOZICK, R., *Philosophical Explanations*. Oxford, Clarendon Press, 1981.

PARFIT, D., *Reasons and Persons*. Oxford University Press, 1984.

PEARS, D. F., 'The Appropriate Causation of Intentional Basic Action'. *Critica*, 7, 1975.

—— 'Predicting and Deciding', in *Questions in the Philosophy of Mind*. London, Duckworth, 1975.

—— 'Sketch for a Causal Theory of Wanting and Doing', also in *Questions in the Philosophy of Mind*.

PLATO, *Timaeus*, trans. H. D. P. Lee. London, 1977.

PUTNAM, H., 'The Meaning of Meaning', in *Language, Mind and Reality*. Cambridge University Press, 1975.

QUINE, W. V. 'Quantifiers and Propositional Attitudes', in *The Ways of Paradox*. New York, Random House, 1966.

REID, T., *Essays on the Active Powers of the Human Mind*. Cambridge, Mass., MIT Press, 1969.

RIMBAUD, A., *Oeuvres Complètes*. Paris, Gallimard, 1972.

RYLE, G., *The Concept of Mind*. Harmondsworth, Penguin, 1966.

SEARLE, J., *Minds, Brains, and Science*. London, BBC, 1984.

SHOEMAKER, S., and SWINBURNE, R., *Personal Identity*. Oxford, Blackwell, 1984.

SIDGWICK, H., *The Methods of Ethics*, seventh edition. London, Macmillan, 1930.

SPINOZA, B. de, *Ethics*, trans. E. Curley. Princeton University Press, 1985.

STRAWSON, G., 'On the Inevitability of Freedom (from a Compatibilist Point of View)', *American Philosophical Quarterly*, 23, 1986.

—— 'Realism and Causation', *The Philosophical Quarterly*, 37, 1987.

STRAWSON, P. F., 'Freedom and Resentment', in *Freedom and Resentment*. London, Methuen, 1974.

—— *Skepticism and Naturalism: Some Varieties*. New York, Columbia University Press, 1985.

THORP, J., *Free Will: A Defence Against Neurophysiological Determinism*. London, Routledge and Kegan Paul, 1980.

TRUSTED, J., *Free Will and Responsibility*. Oxford University Press, 1984.

van INWAGEN, P., *An Essay on Free Will*. Oxford, Clarendon Press, 1983.

WATSON, G., 'Free Agency', in *Free Will*, ed. G. Watson. Oxford University Press, 1982.

—— ed., *Free Will*. Oxford University Press, 1982.

WIGGINS, D., 'Freedom, Knowledge, Belief and Causality', in G. Vesey, ed., *Knowledge and Necessity*. London, Macmillan, 1970.

WILLIAMS, B., *Descartes: The Project of Pure Enquiry*. Harmondsworth, Penguin, 1978.

—— 'Moral Luck', in *Moral Luck*. Cambridge University Press, 1981.

INDEX

This index does not cite every occurrence of every listed term or topic. Page numbers in bold type indicate the place at which a term is introduced, defined, or redefined.